I hope to reach my goal
someday and then be able
to fill in the right eye on
this Daruma doll.

—*Yūki Tabata, 2015*

YŪKI TABATA

was born in Fukuoka Prefecture
and got his big break in the 2011
Shonen Jump Golden Future Cup
with his winning entry, *Hungry
Joker*. He started the magical fantasy
series *Black Clover* in 2015.

BLACK CLOVER
VOLUME 3
SHONEN JUMP Manga Edition

Story and Art by YŪKI TABATA

Translation ❈ TAYLOR ENGEL,
HC LANGUAGE SOLUTIONS, INC.

Touch-Up Art & Lettering ❈ ANNALIESE CHRISTMAN

Design ❈ FAWN LAU

Editor ❈ ALEXIS KIRSCH

Printed in the U.S.A.

Published by VIZ Media, LLC
P.O. Box 77010
San Francisco, CA 94107

10 9 8 7 6 5 4 3 2 1
First printing, October 2016

SHONEN JUMP MANGA

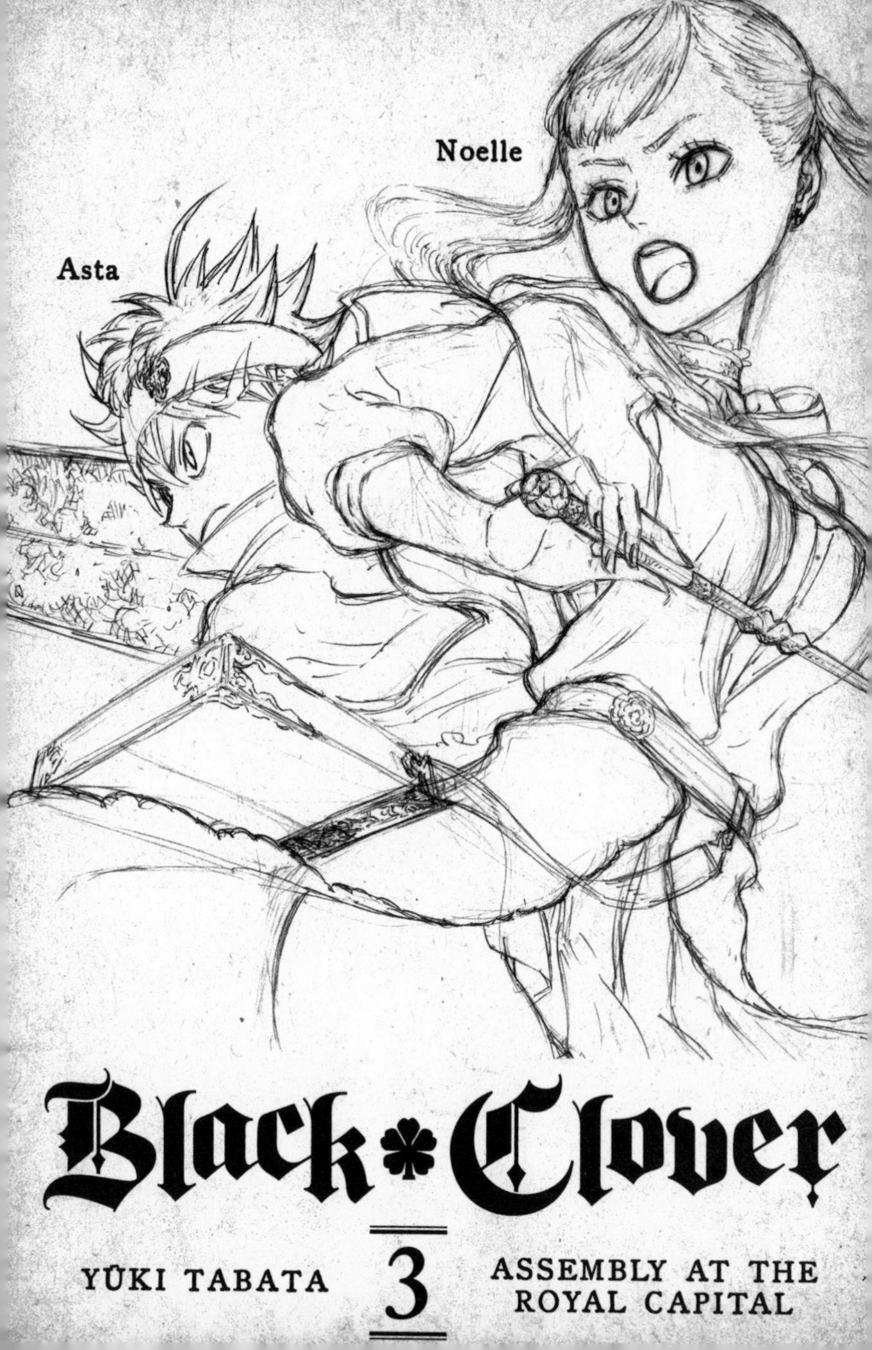
Noelle
Asta

Black Clover

YŪKI TABATA

3

ASSEMBLY AT THE ROYAL CAPITAL

Characters

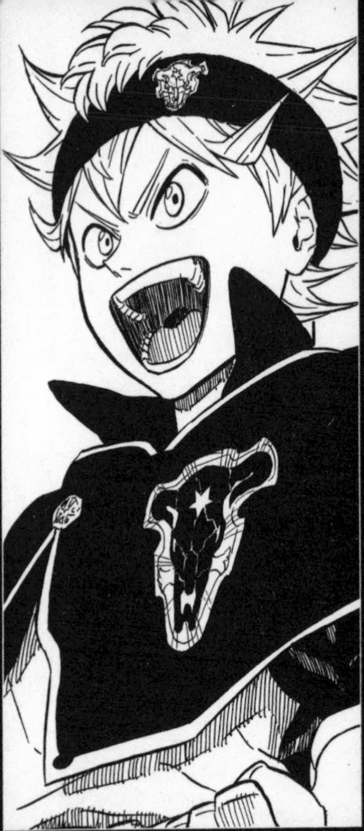

Asta

Squad: The Black Bulls
Magic: None (Anti-Magic)

He has no magic, but he's working to become the Wizard King through sheer guts and his well-trained body.

Yuno

Squad: The Golden Dawn
Magic: Wind

Asta's best friend, and a good rival who's been working to become the Wizard King right alongside him since they were little.

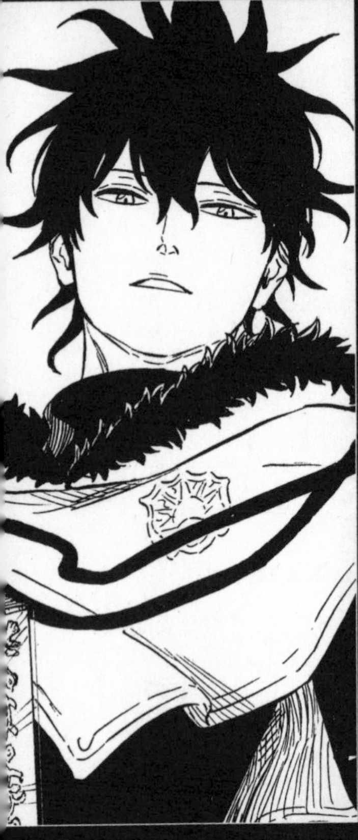

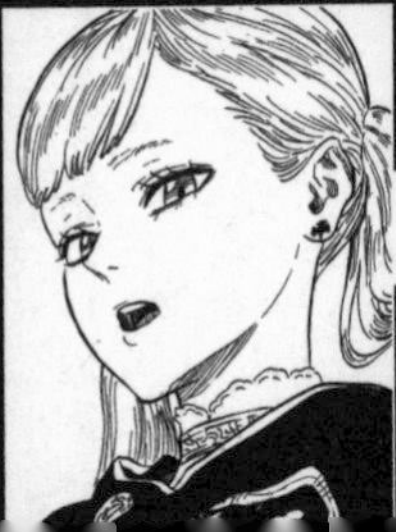

Noelle Silva

Squad: The Black Bulls
Magic: Water

A royal. She's really impudent, but can be kind too.

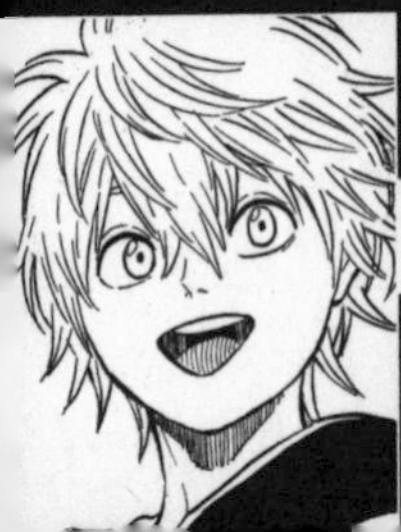

Luck Voltia

Squad: The Black Bulls
Magic: Lightning

A battle maniac who smiles constantly and has a problematic personality.

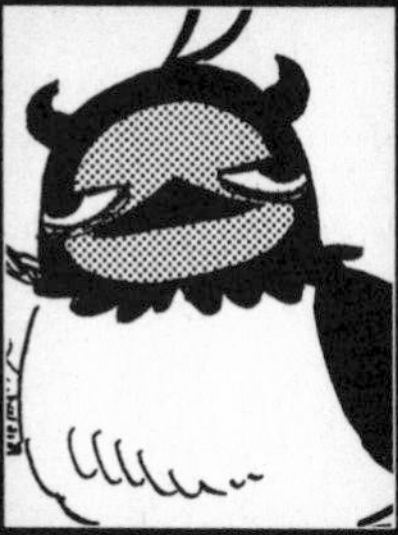

Nero

A mysterious bird that always follows Asta around, for some reason.

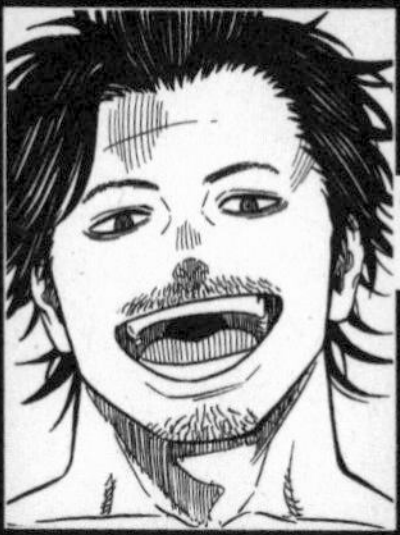

Yami Sukehiro

Squad: The Black Bulls
Magic: ?

Captain of the Black Bulls. He looks fierce and has a hot temper, but he's very popular with his squad.

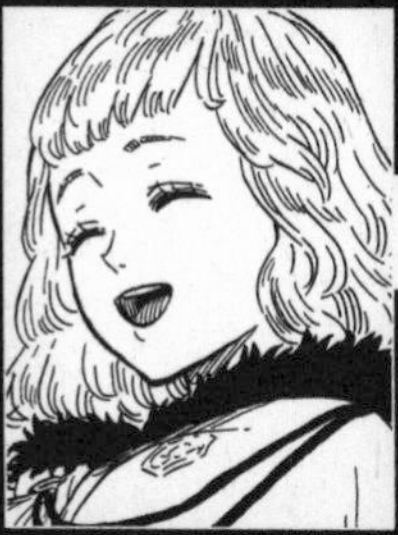

Mimosa Vermillion

Squad: The Golden Dawn
Magic: Plant

Noelle's cousin. She's calm, gentle and a bit of an airhead.

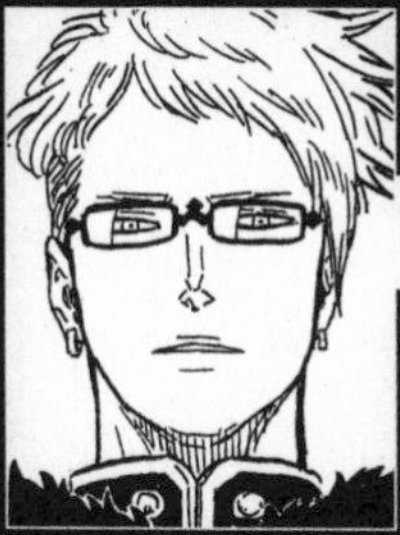

Klaus Lunettes

Squad: The Golden Dawn
Magic: Steel

A senior member of Yuno's group. Extremely proud.

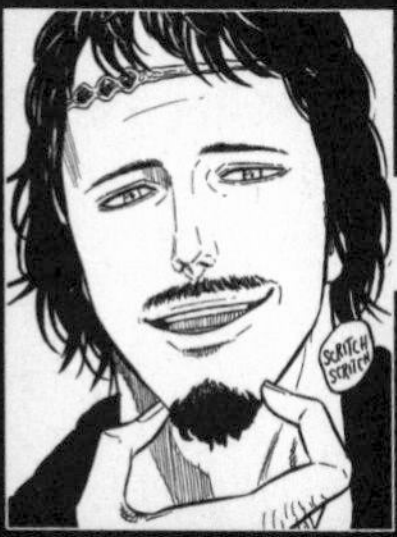
SCRITCH

Lotus Whomalt

Squad: The Diamond Kingdom
Magic: Smoke

An easygoing and very experienced mage. He's also a dad with three daughters.

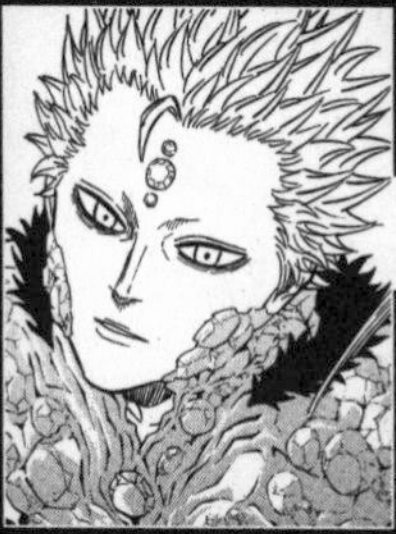

Mars

Squad: The Diamond Kingdom
Magic: Mineral

A mage warrior whose magic has been artificially boosted through a cruel training method.

STORY

In a world where magic is everything, Asta and Yuno are both found abandoned on the same day at a church in the remote village of Hage. Both dream of becoming the Wizard King, the highest of all mages, and they spend their days working toward that dream.

The year they turn 15, both receive grimoires, magic books that amplify their bearers' magic. They take the entrance exam for the Magic Knights, nine groups of mages under the direct control of the Wizard King. Yuno, whose magic is strong, joins an elite group known as the Golden Dawn. Asta, however, has no magic at all and thus joins the Black Bulls, a group of misfits. The two have finally taken their first steps toward becoming the Wizard King...

Asta and his teammates have been dispatched to a magical dungeon on orders from the Wizard King. They scramble to be the first to reach the treasure hall in the deepest part of the dungeon, but then find themselves in combat with mages from the invading Diamond Kingdom! Asta faces off against Mars, a tough enemy who's driven Yuno into a corner...

CONTENTS

BLACK ❀ CLOVER

3

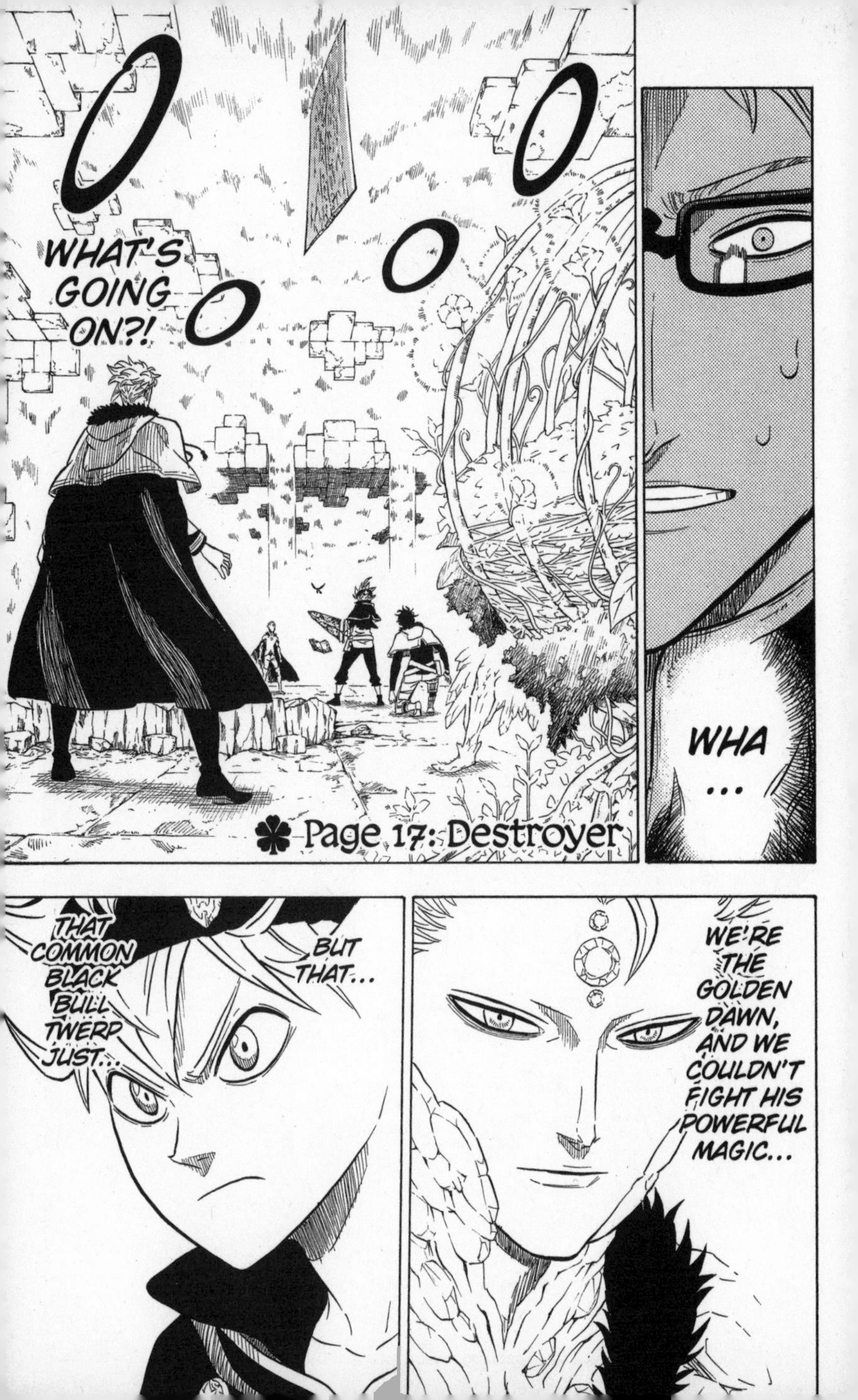
WHA...
WHAT'S GOING ON?!
Page 17: Destroyer
WE'RE THE GOLDEN DAWN, AND WE COULDN'T FIGHT HIS POWERFUL MAGIC...
BUT THAT...
THAT COMMON BLACK BULL TWERP JUST...

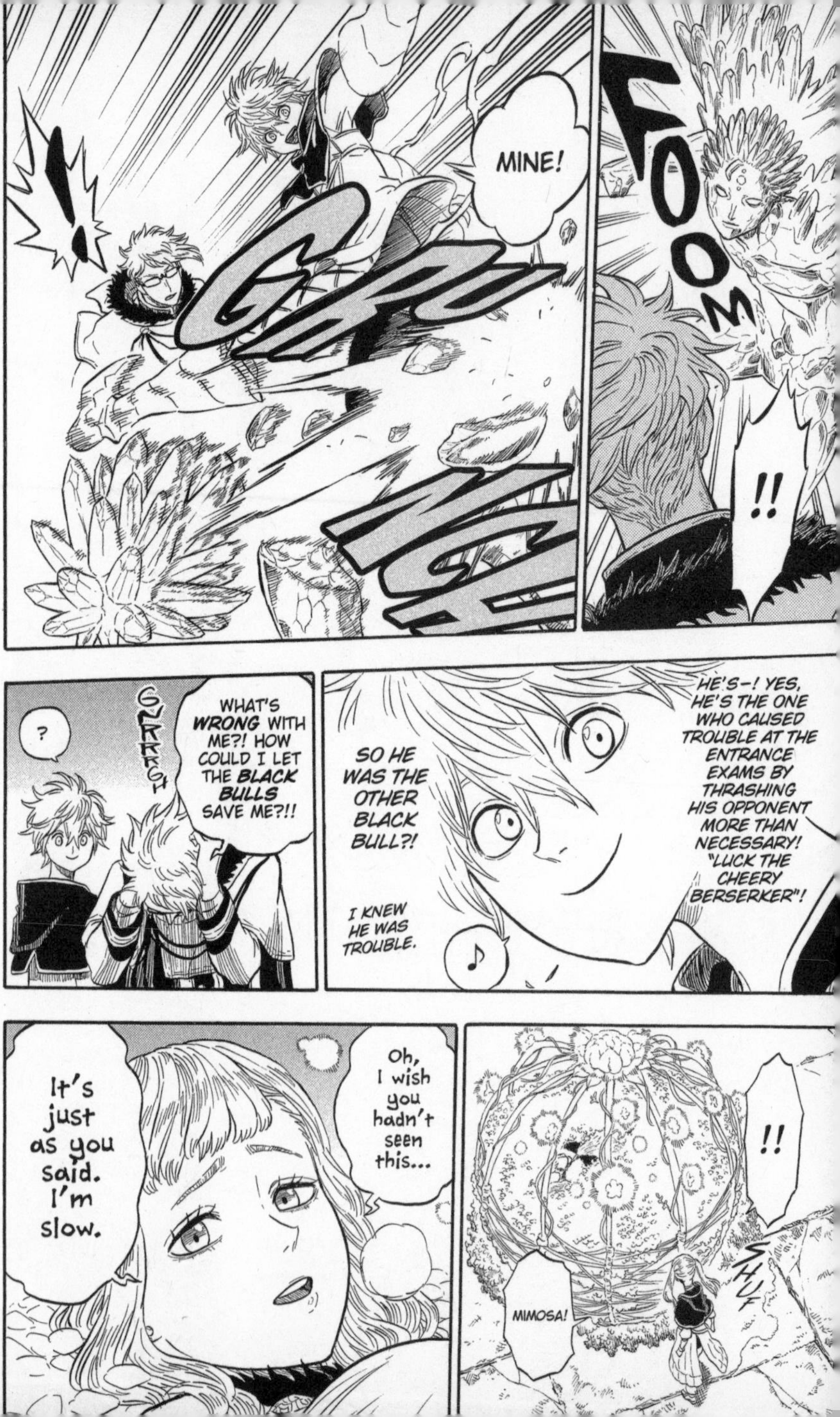
FOOM
!!
MINE!
CRUNCH
!
HE'S—! YES, HE'S THE ONE WHO CAUSED TROUBLE AT THE ENTRANCE EXAMS BY THRASHING HIS OPPONENT MORE THAN NECESSARY! "LUCK THE CHEERY BERSERKER"!
SO HE WAS THE OTHER BLACK BULL?!
I KNEW HE WAS TROUBLE.
♪
WHAT'S WRONG WITH ME?! HOW COULD I LET THE BLACK BULLS SAVE ME?!!
GNRRRGH
?
!!
MIMOSA!
SHUF
Oh, I wish you hadn't seen this...
It's just as you said. I'm slow.

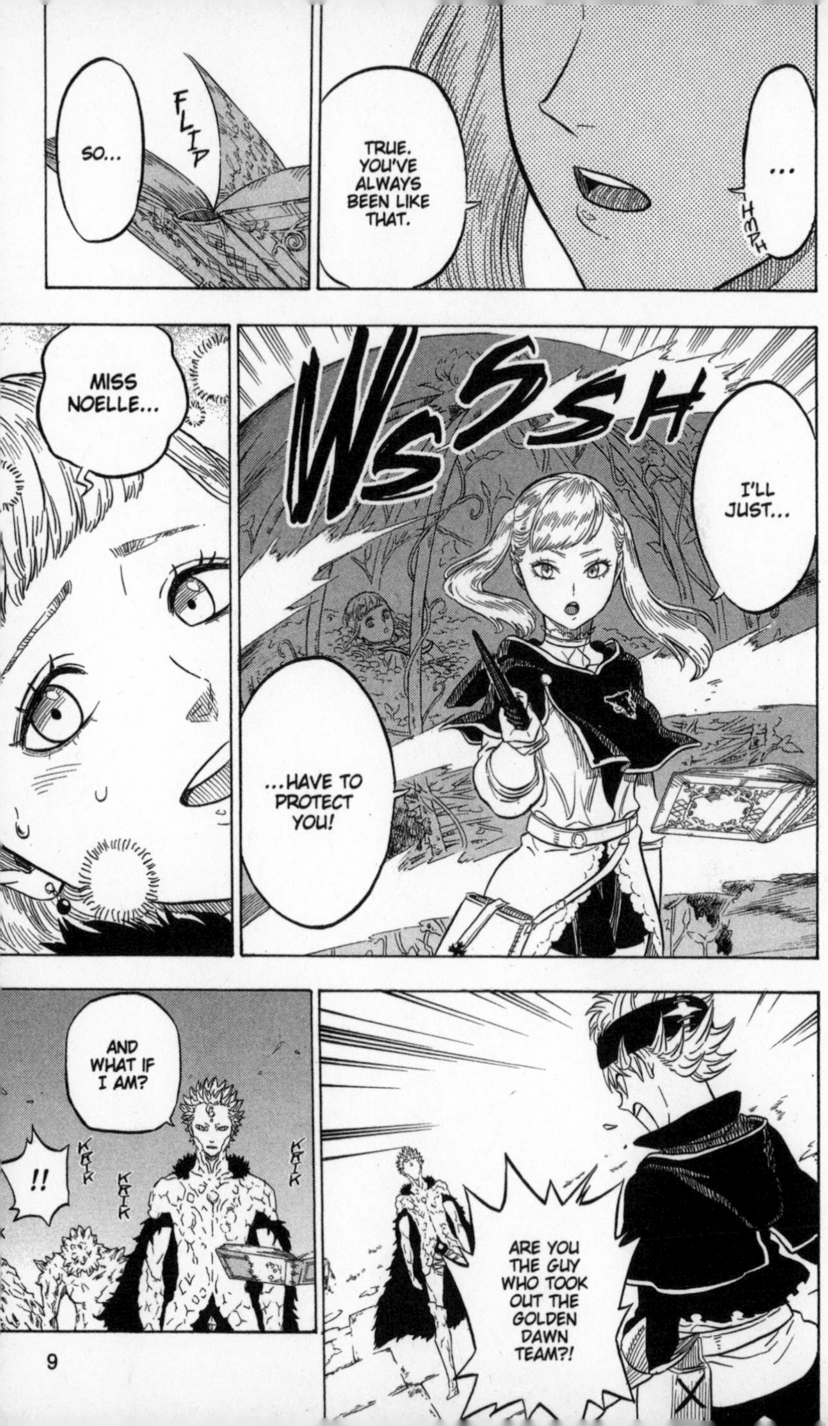
...
HMPH
TRUE. YOU'VE ALWAYS BEEN LIKE THAT.
SO...
FLIP
WSSSH
I'LL JUST...
...HAVE TO PROTECT YOU!
MISS NOELLE...
ARE YOU THE GUY WHO TOOK OUT THE GOLDEN DAWN TEAM?!
AND WHAT IF I AM?
KRIK
KRIK
KRIK
!!

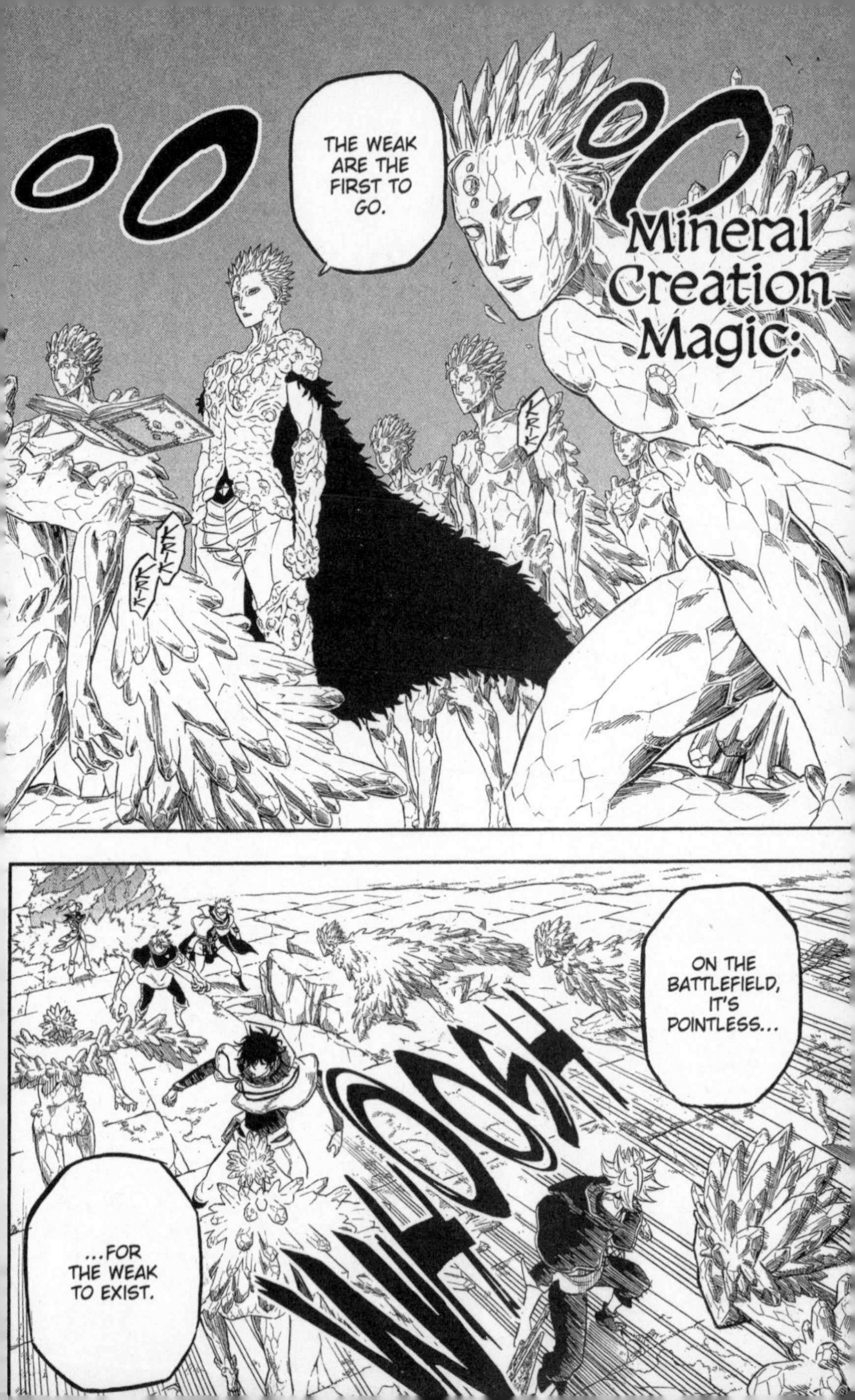
Mineral Creation Magic:
THE WEAK ARE THE FIRST TO GO.
KRIK
KRIK
KRIK
ON THE BATTLEFIELD, IT'S POINTLESS...
WHOOSH
...FOR THE WEAK TO EXIST.

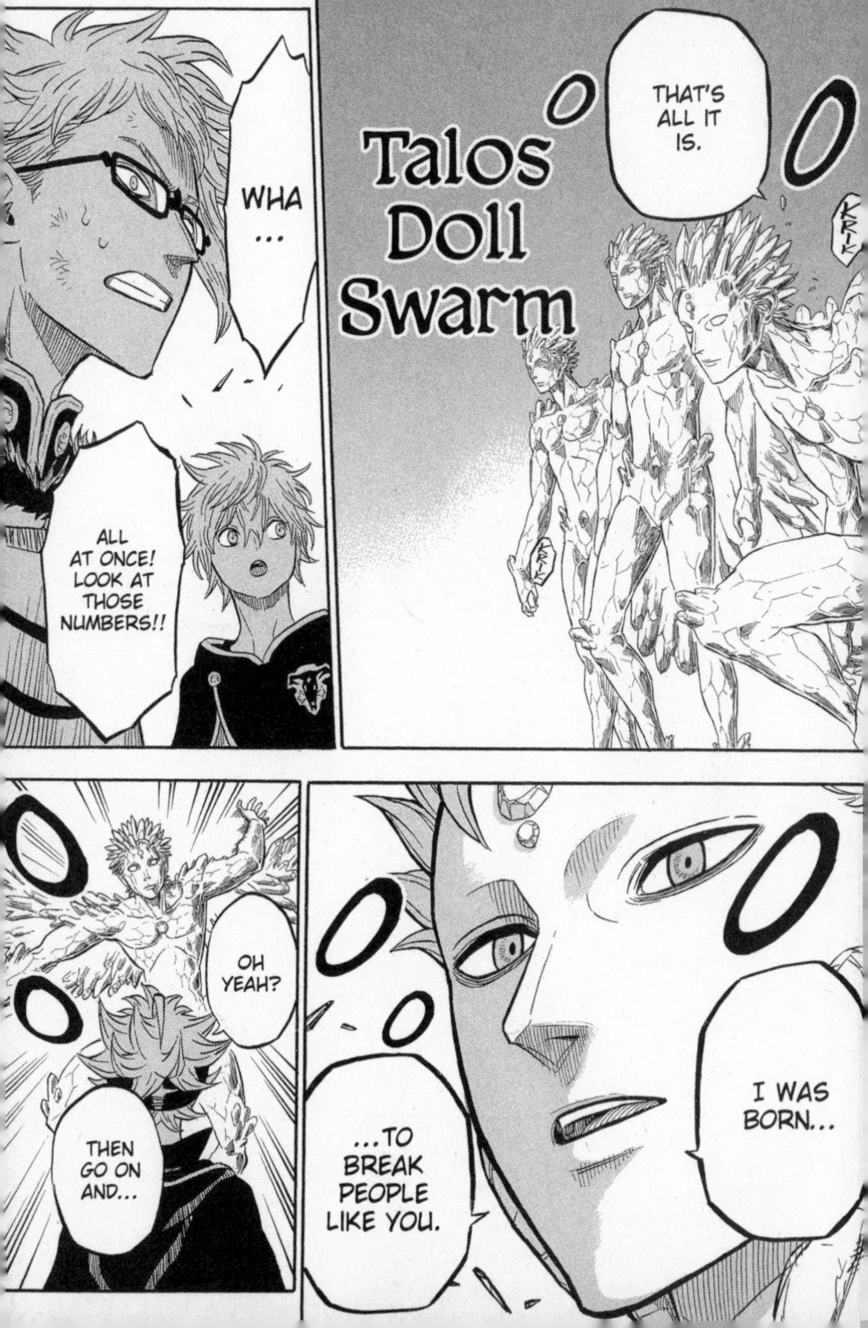
THAT'S ALL IT IS.
KRIK
Talos Doll Swarm
KRIK
WHA...
ALL AT ONCE! LOOK AT THOSE NUMBERS!!
I WAS BORN...
...TO BREAK PEOPLE LIKE YOU.
OH YEAH?
THEN GO ON AND...

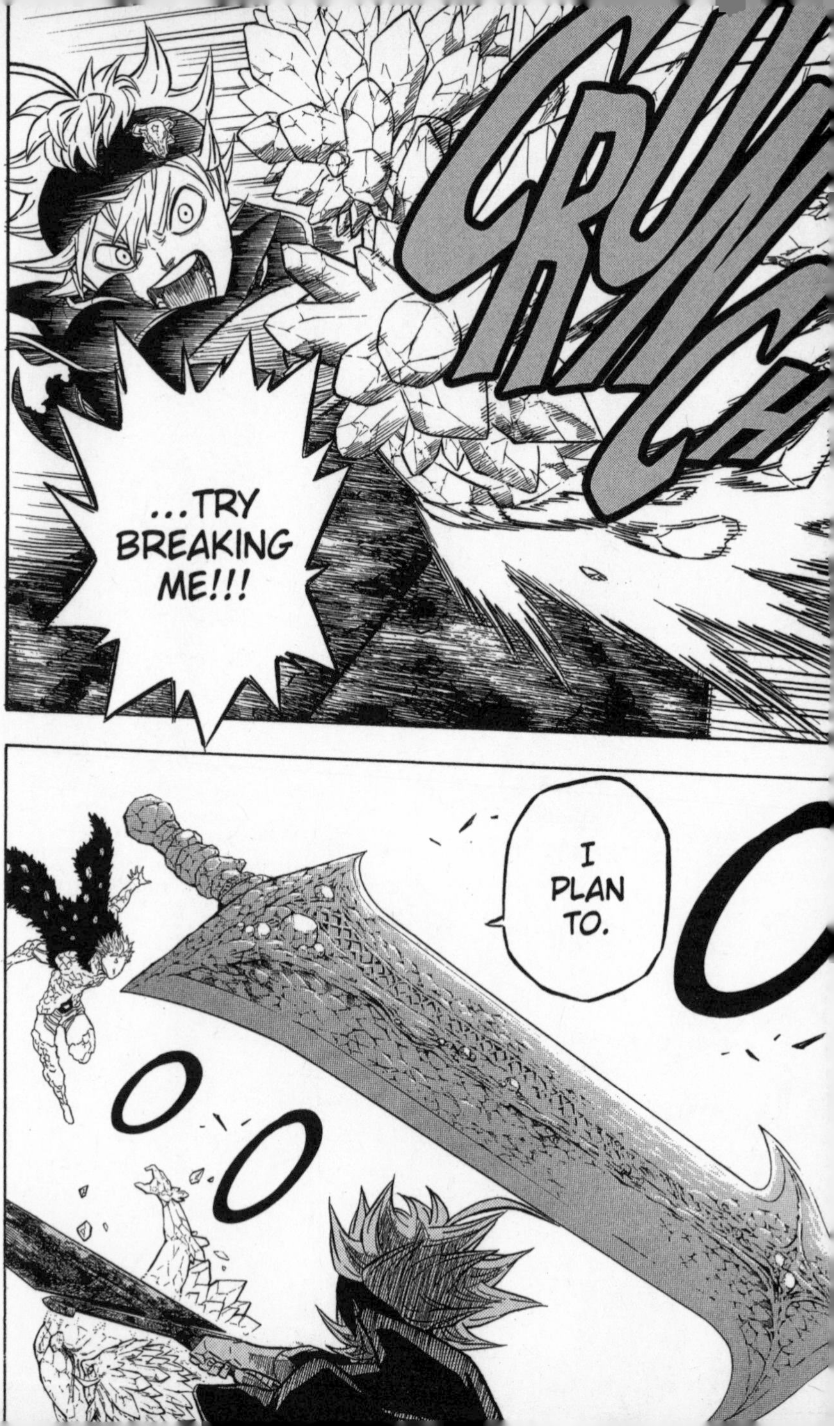
...TRY BREAKING ME!!!
I PLAN TO.

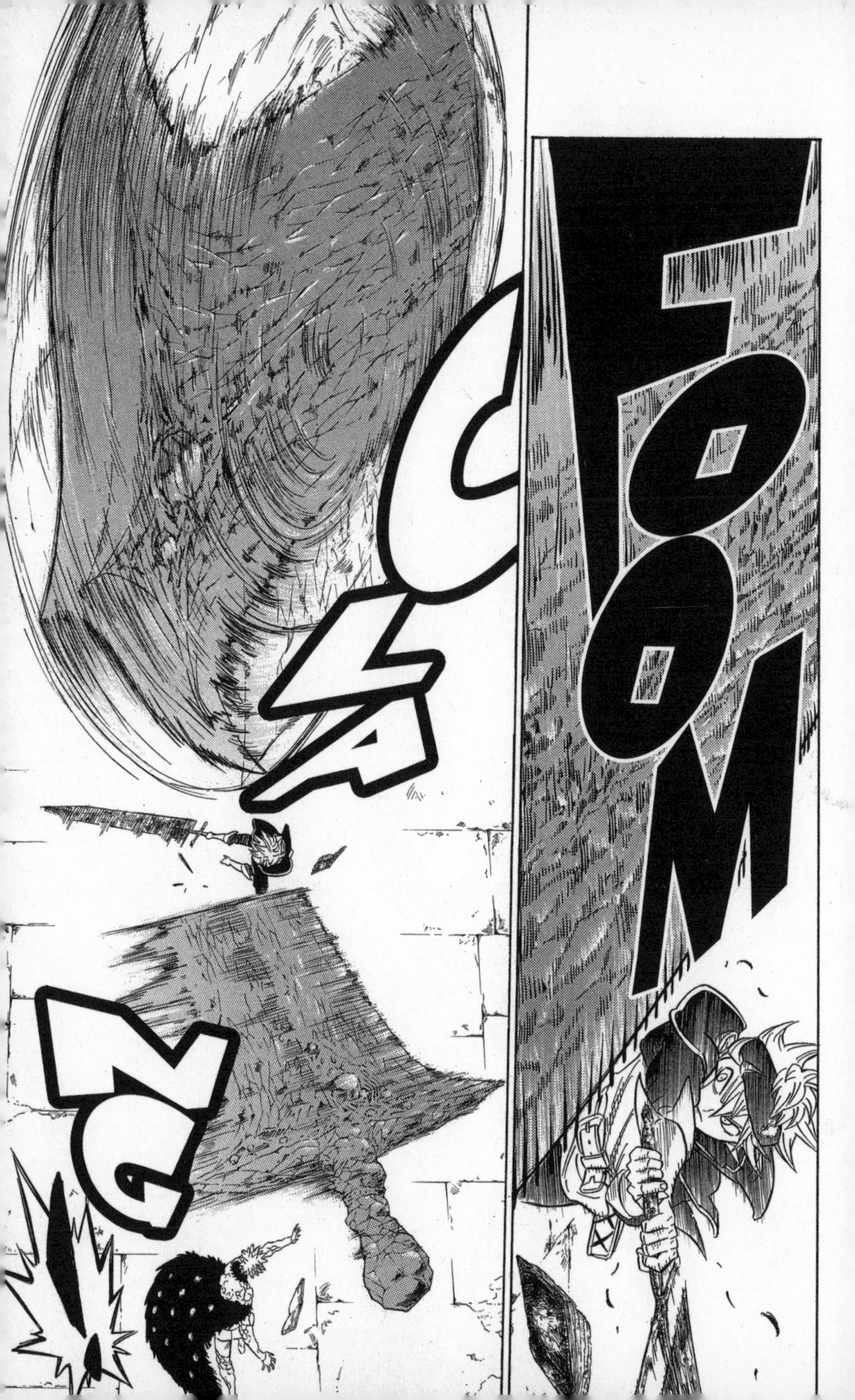
TOOM
CLANG

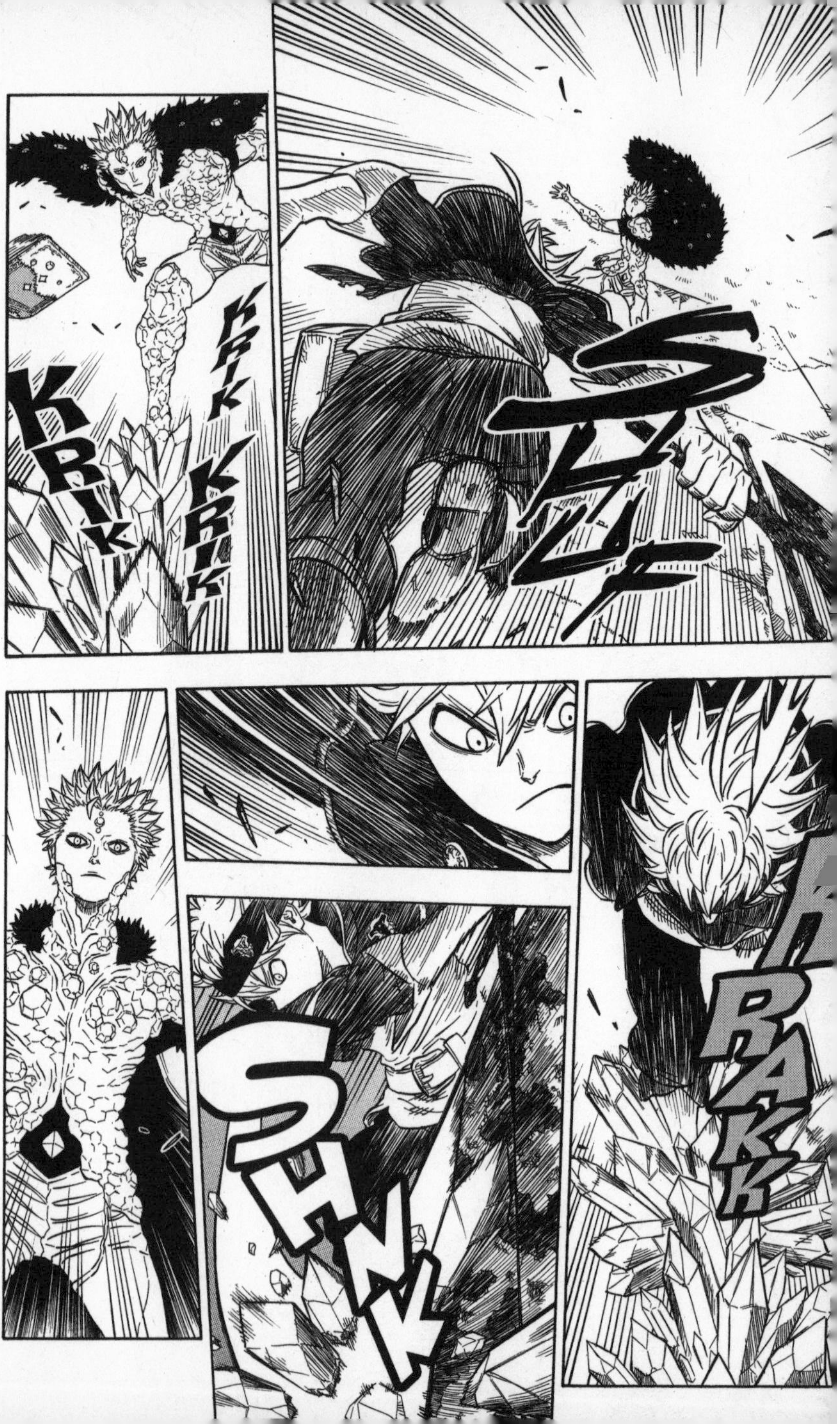
KRIK
KRIK
KRIK
SHNK

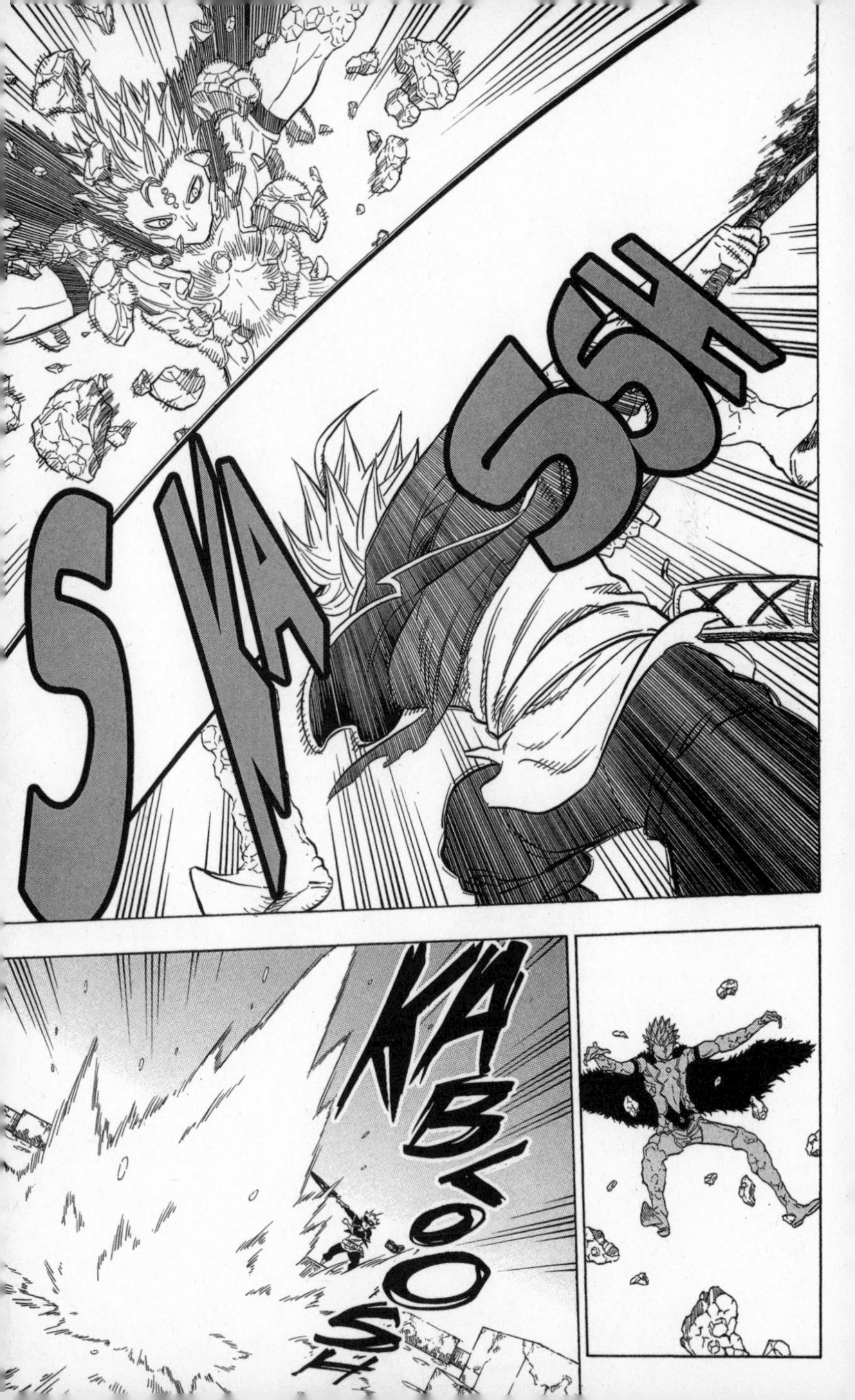
SKASSH
KABLOOSH

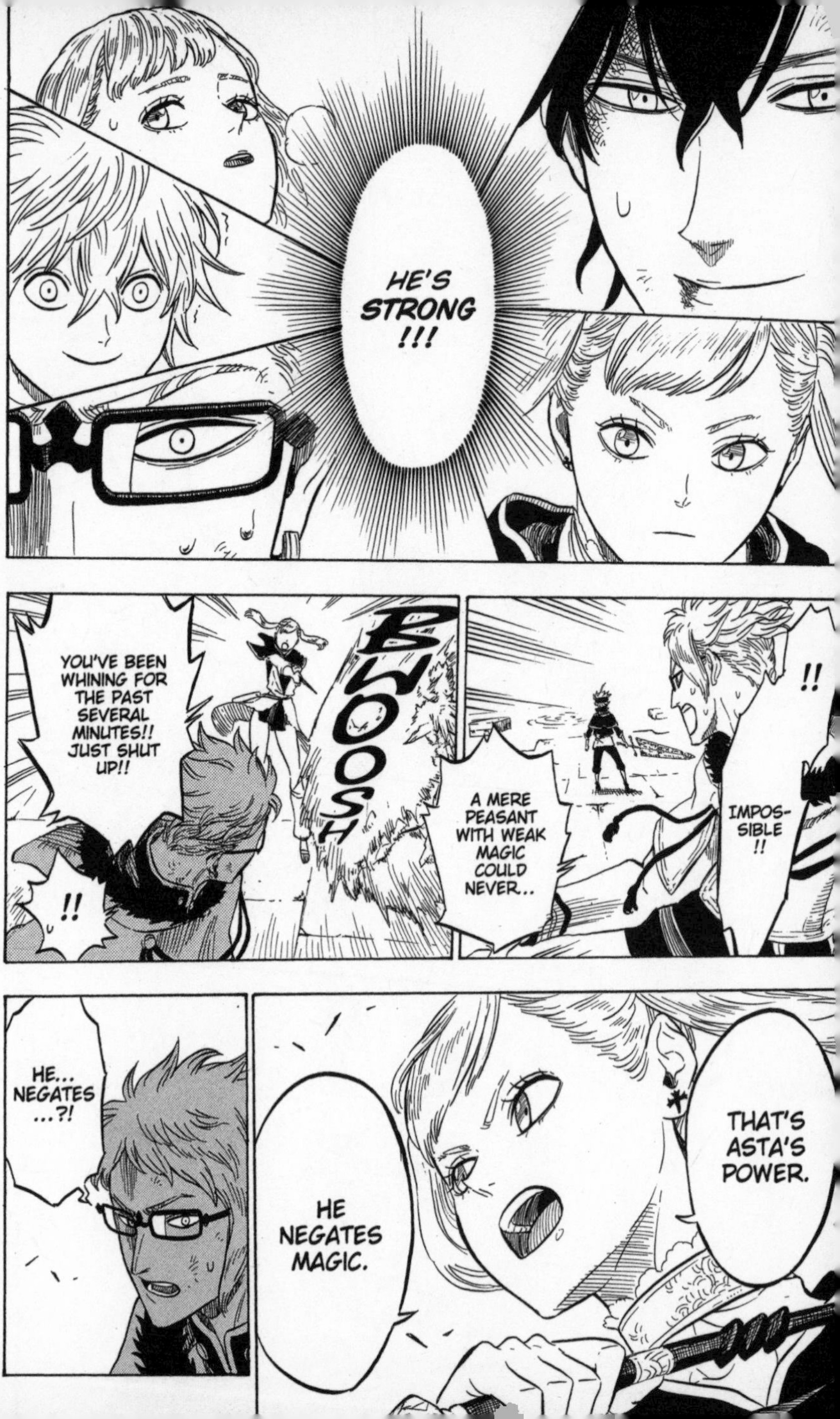
HE'S STRONG!!!
!!
IMPOS-SIBLE!!
A MERE PEASANT WITH WEAK MAGIC COULD NEVER...
BWOOOSH
YOU'VE BEEN WHINING FOR THE PAST SEVERAL MINUTES!! JUST SHUT UP!!
!!
THAT'S ASTA'S POWER.
HE NEGATES MAGIC.
HE... NEGATES ...?!

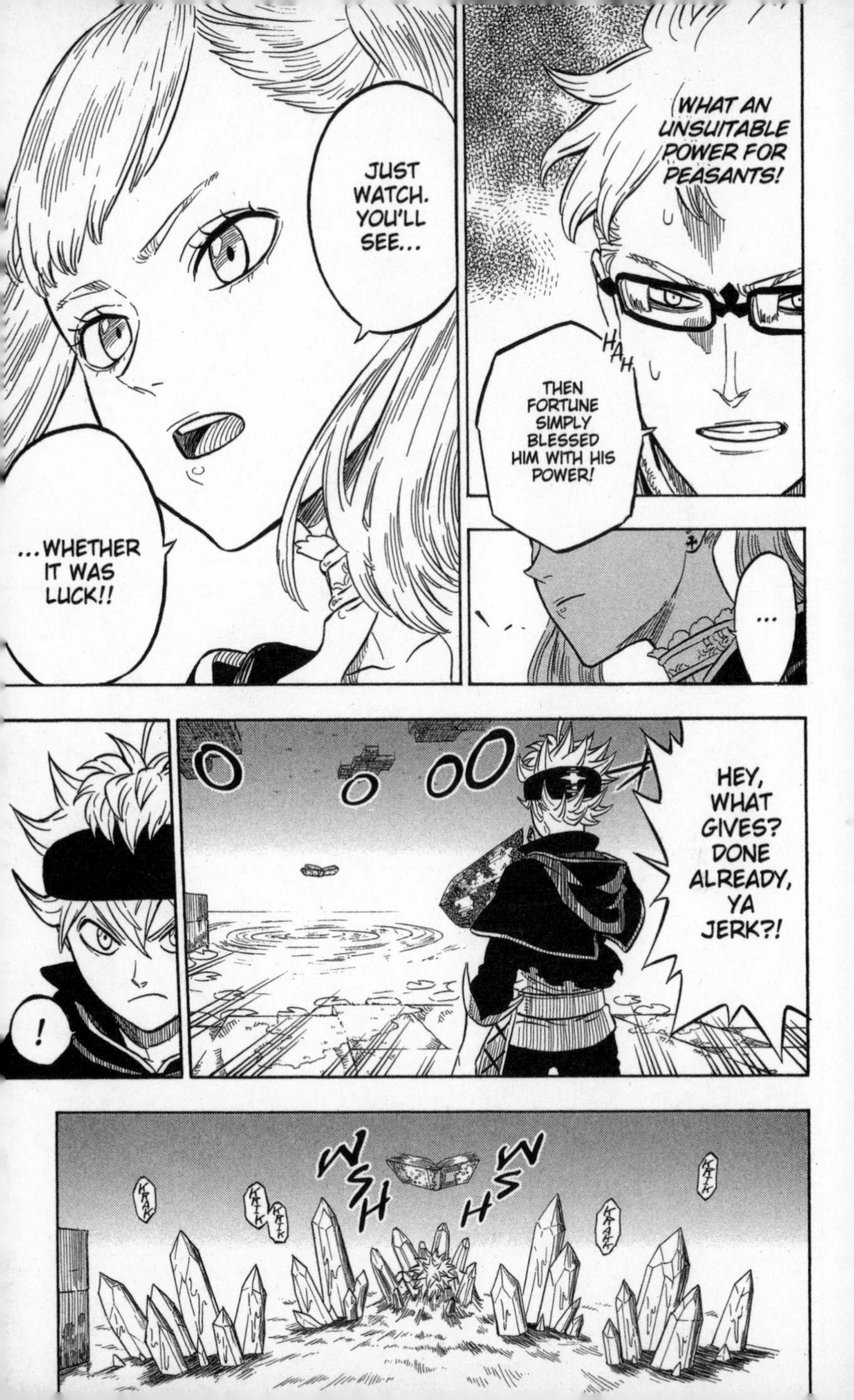
WHAT AN UNSUITABLE POWER FOR PEASANTS!
HAH
THEN FORTUNE SIMPLY BLESSED HIM WITH HIS POWER!
...
JUST WATCH. YOU'LL SEE...
...WHETHER IT WAS LUCK!!
HEY, WHAT GIVES? DONE ALREADY, YA JERK?!
!
WSH
WSH

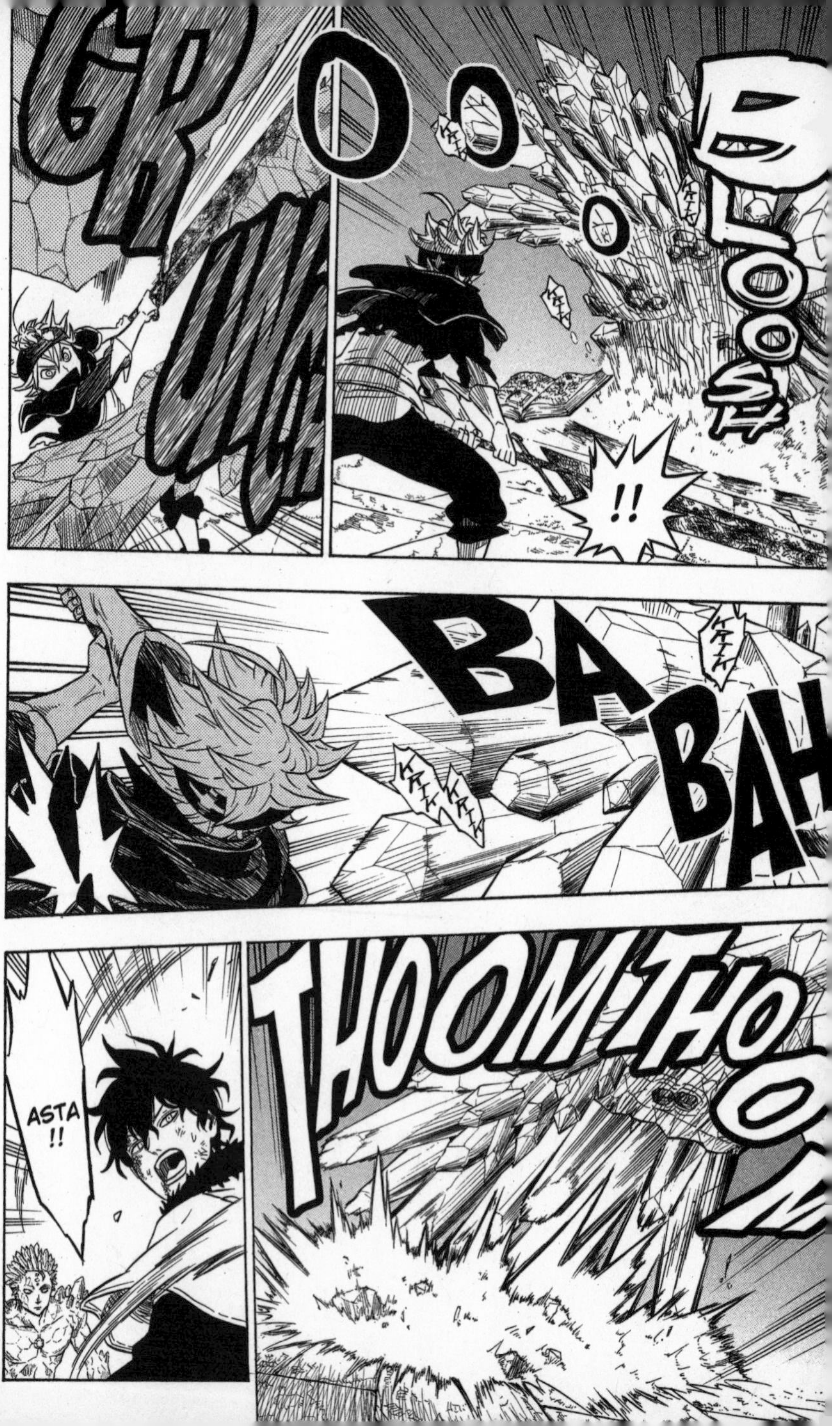

BLOOOSH
KRIK
KRIK
!!
BA BAH!
KRIK
KRIK KRIK
THOOM THOOM
ASTA !!

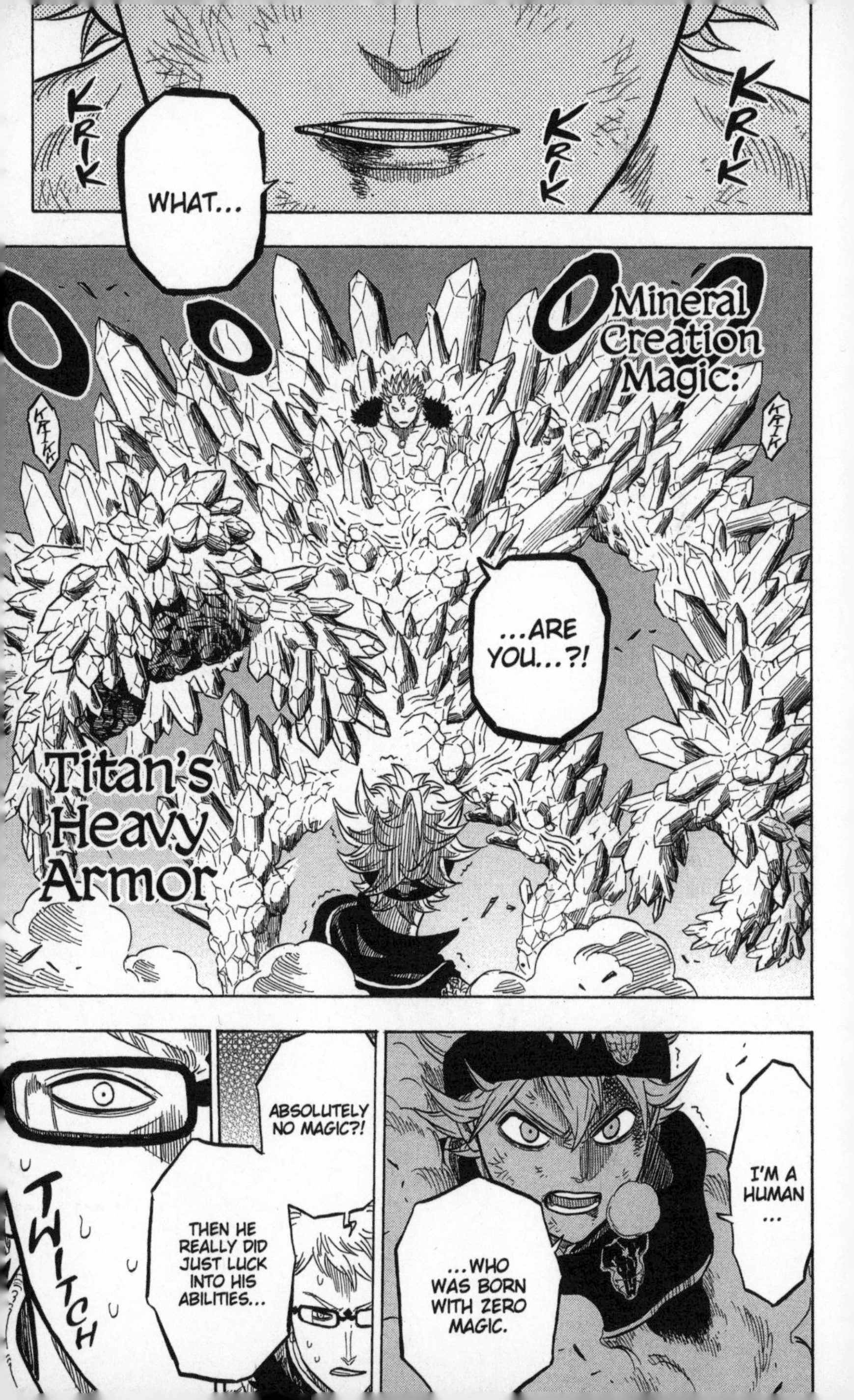
KRIK
KRIK
WHAT...
KRIK
Mineral Creation Magic:
Titan's Heavy Armor
...ARE YOU...?!
I'M A HUMAN ...
...WHO WAS BORN WITH ZERO MAGIC.
ABSOLUTELY NO MAGIC?!
THEN HE REALLY DID JUST LUCK INTO HIS ABILITIES...
TWITCH

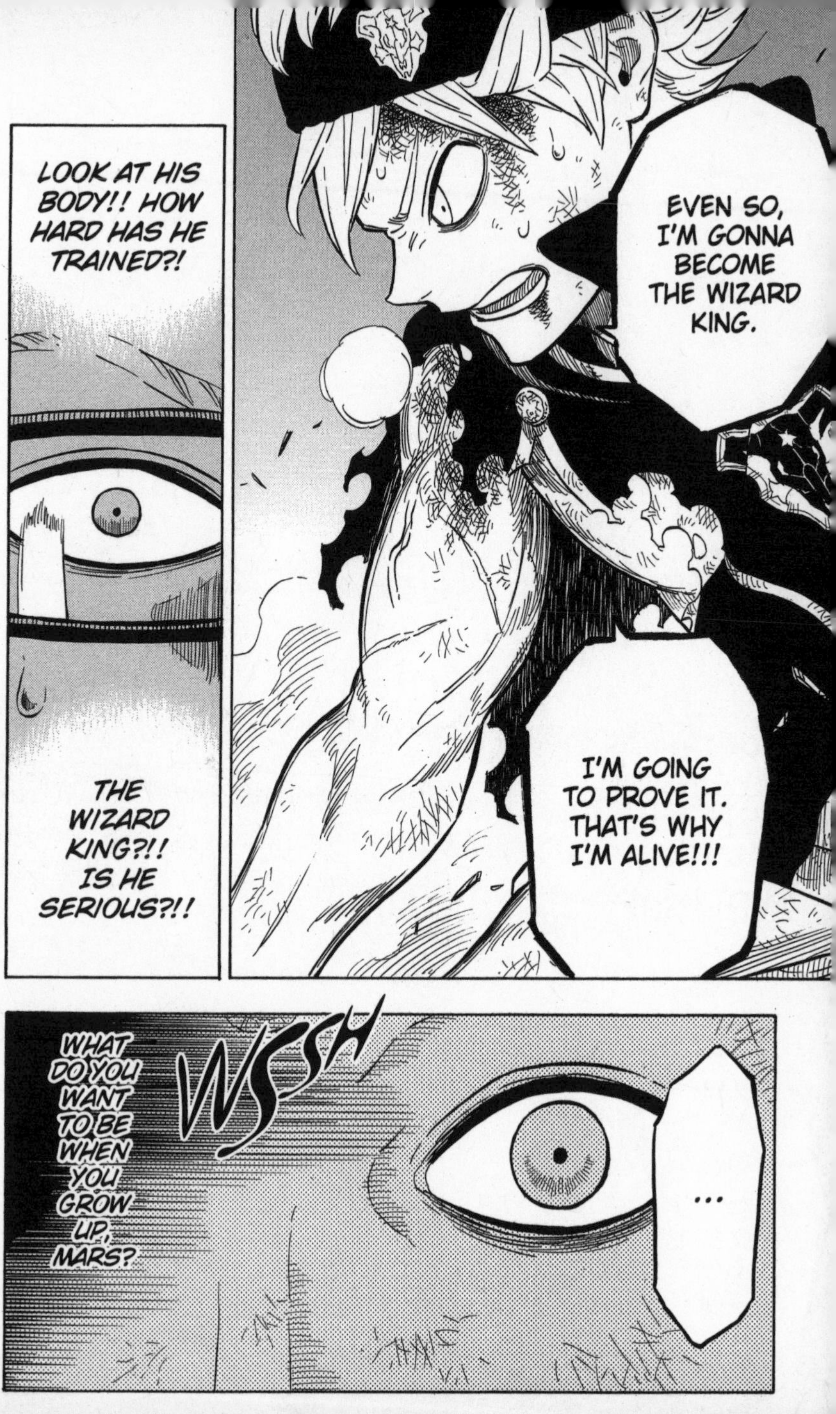
EVEN SO, I'M GONNA BECOME THE WIZARD KING.
I'M GOING TO PROVE IT. THAT'S WHY I'M ALIVE!!!
LOOK AT HIS BODY!! HOW HARD HAS HE TRAINED?!
THE WIZARD KING?!! IS HE SERIOUS?!!
...
WSSH
WHAT DO YOU WANT TO BE WHEN YOU GROW UP, MARS?

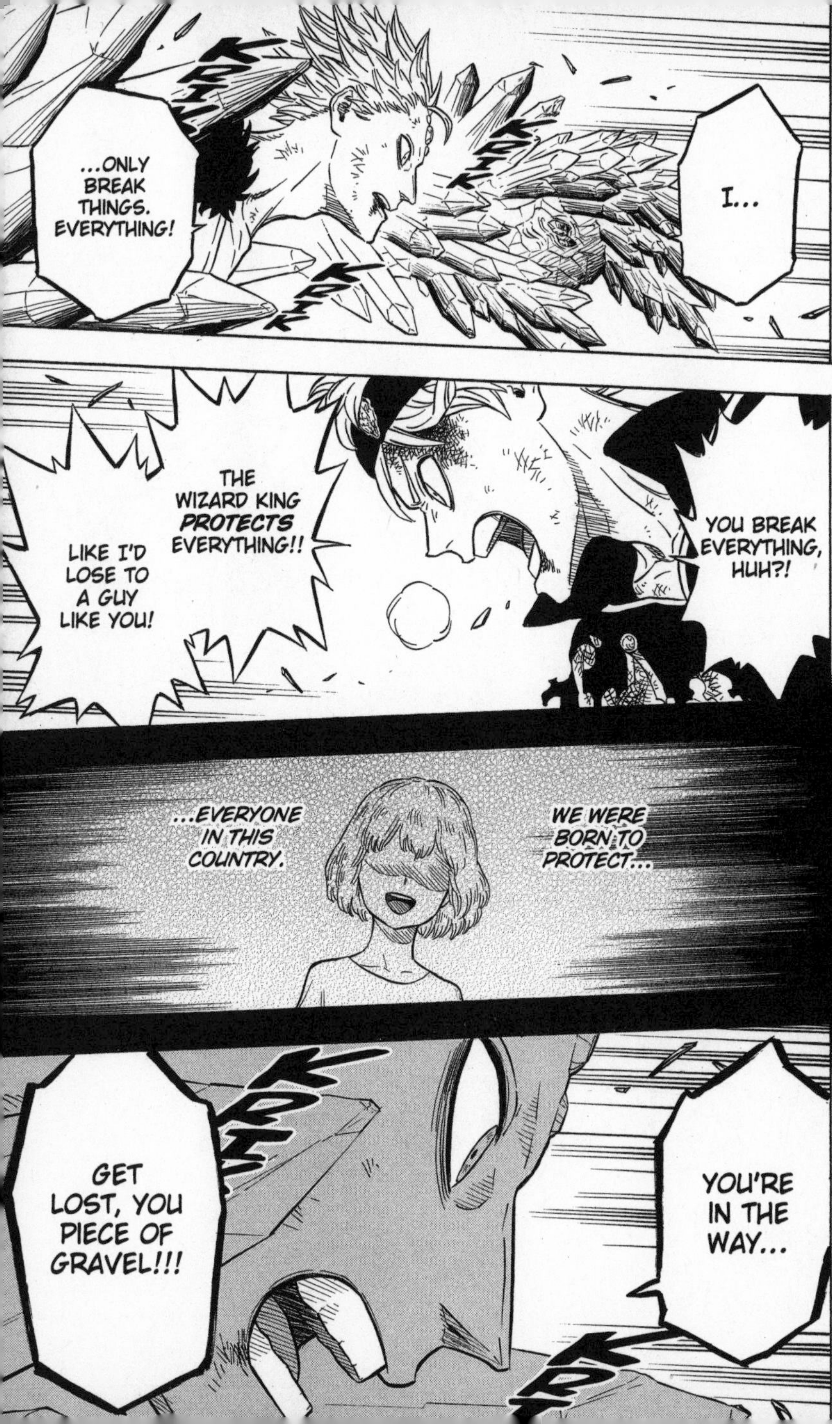
I...
...ONLY BREAK THINGS. EVERYTHING!
YOU BREAK EVERYTHING, HUH?!
THE WIZARD KING PROTECTS EVERYTHING!!
LIKE I'D LOSE TO A GUY LIKE YOU!
WE WERE BORN TO PROTECT...
...EVERYONE IN THIS COUNTRY.
YOU'RE IN THE WAY...
GET LOST, YOU PIECE OF GRAVEL!!!

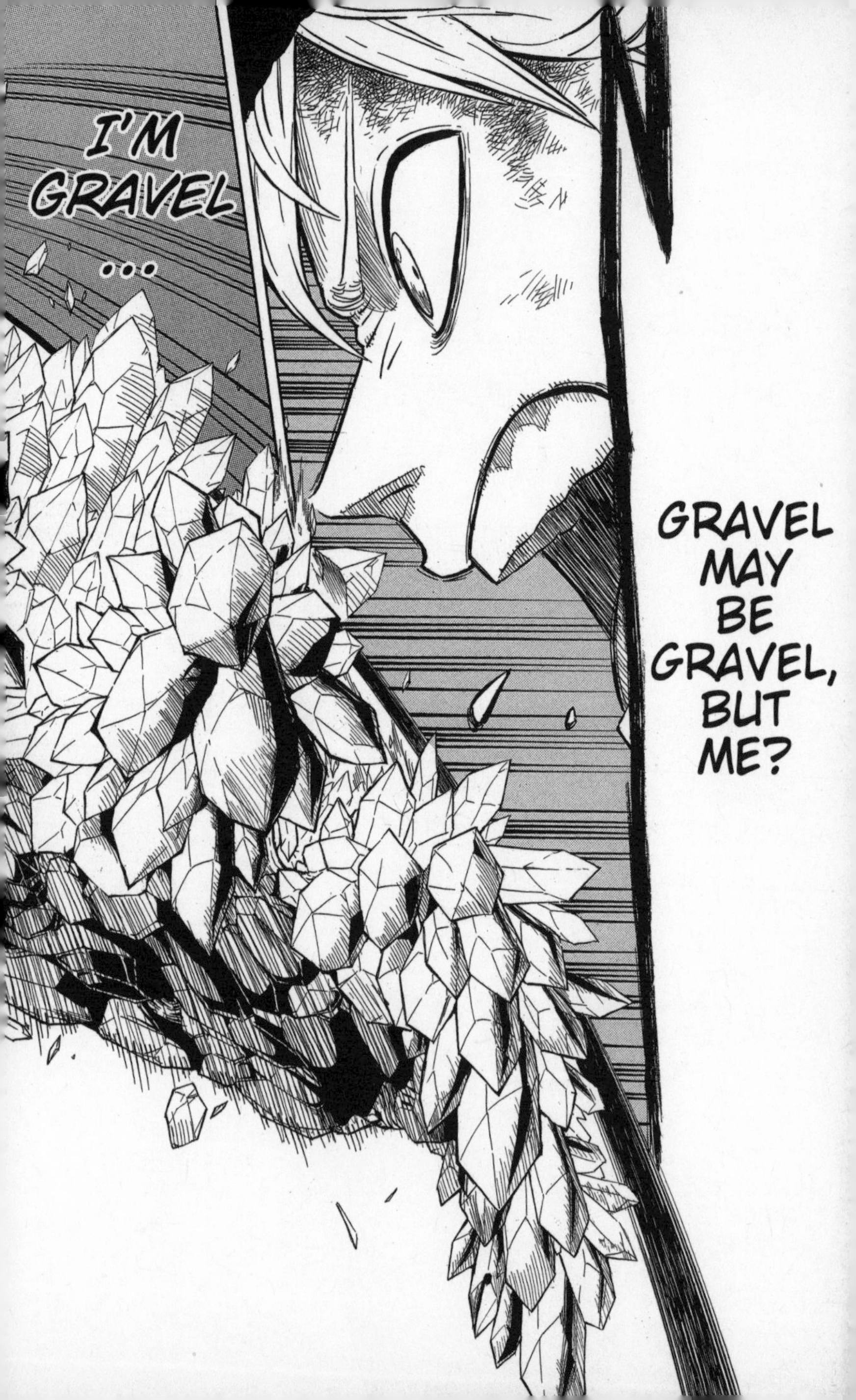
GRAVEL MAY BE GRAVEL, BUT ME?
I'M GRAVEL ...

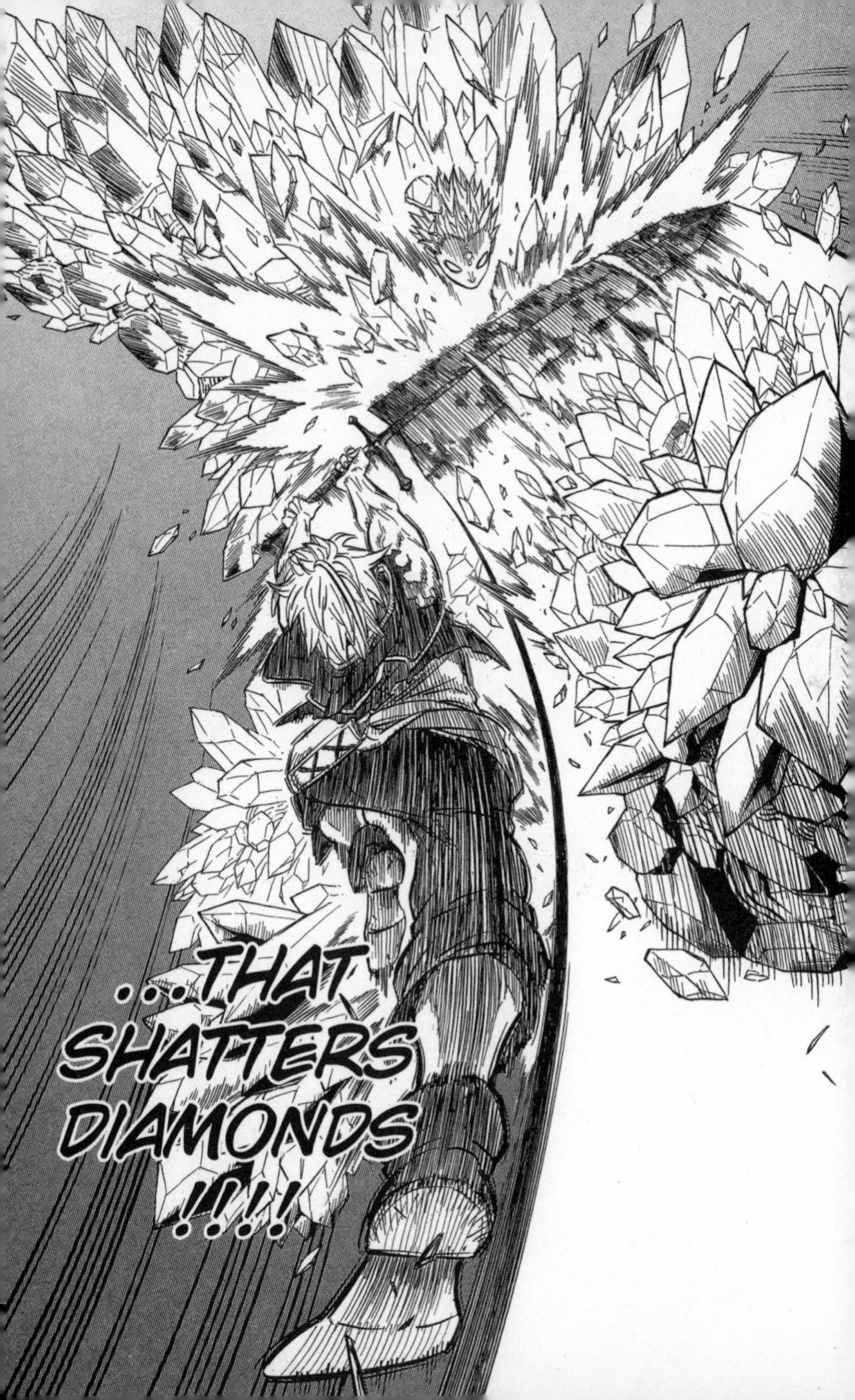
...THAT SHATTERS DIAMONDS !!!!

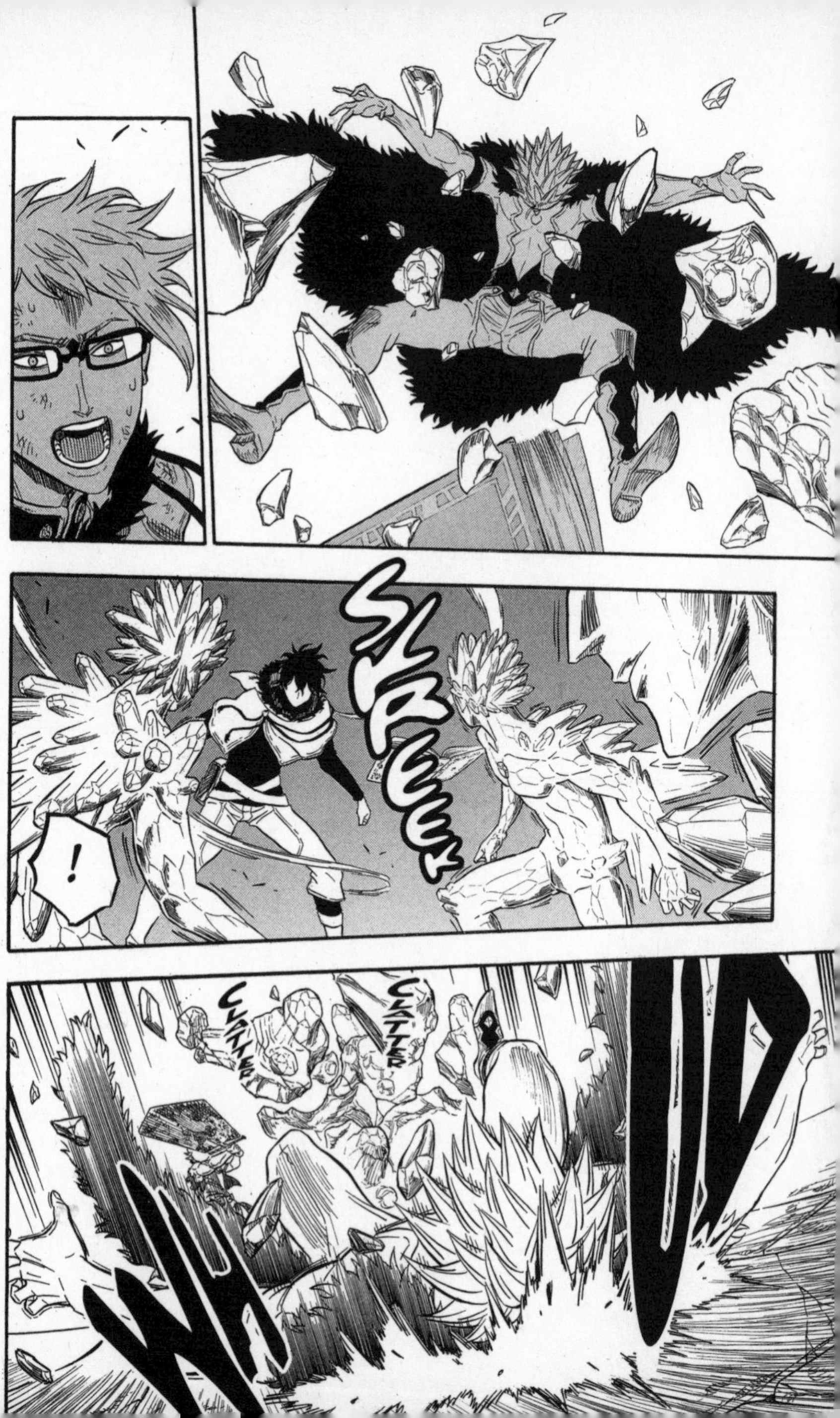
!
CLATTER
CLATTER

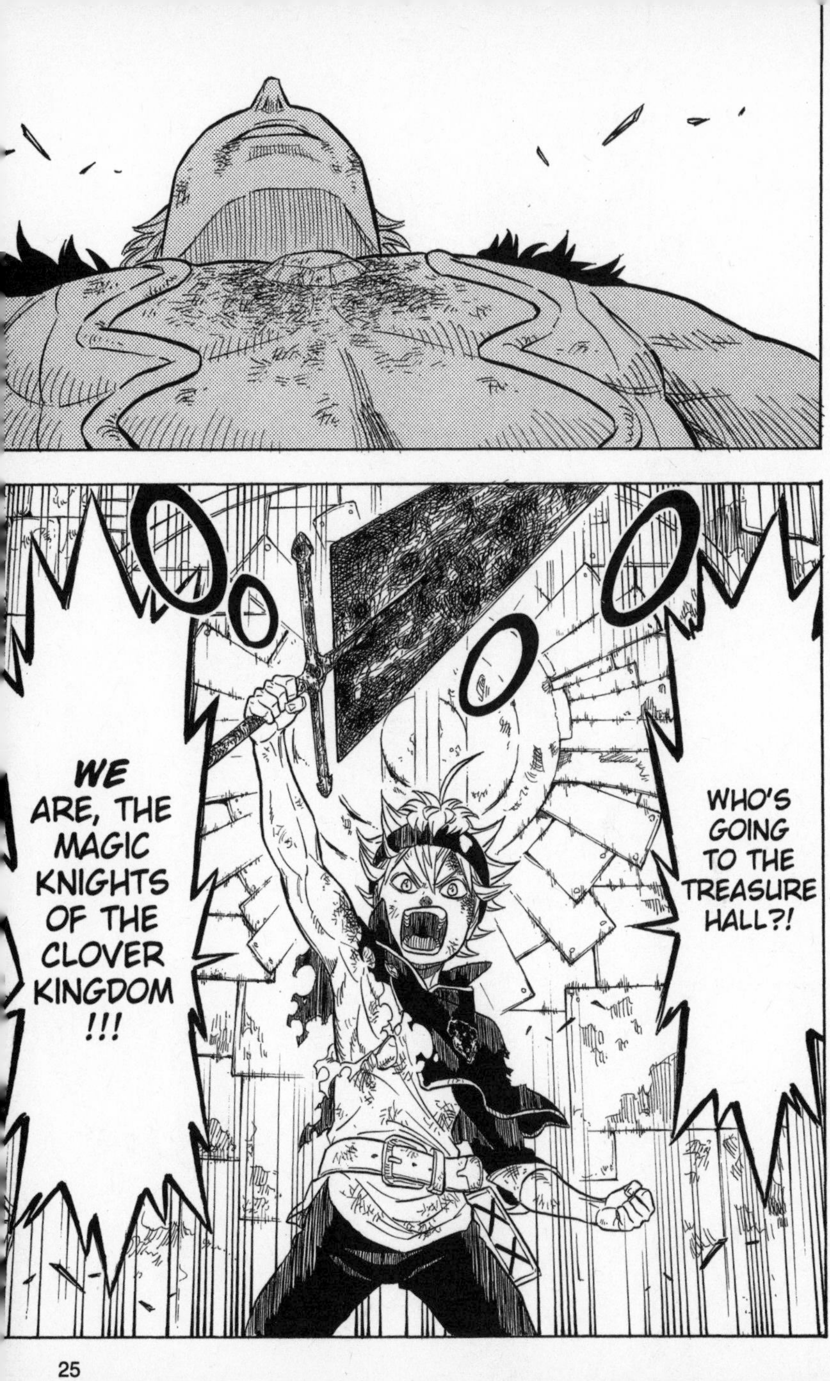
WHO'S GOING TO THE TREASURE HALL?!
WE ARE, THE MAGIC KNIGHTS OF THE CLOVER KINGDOM!!!

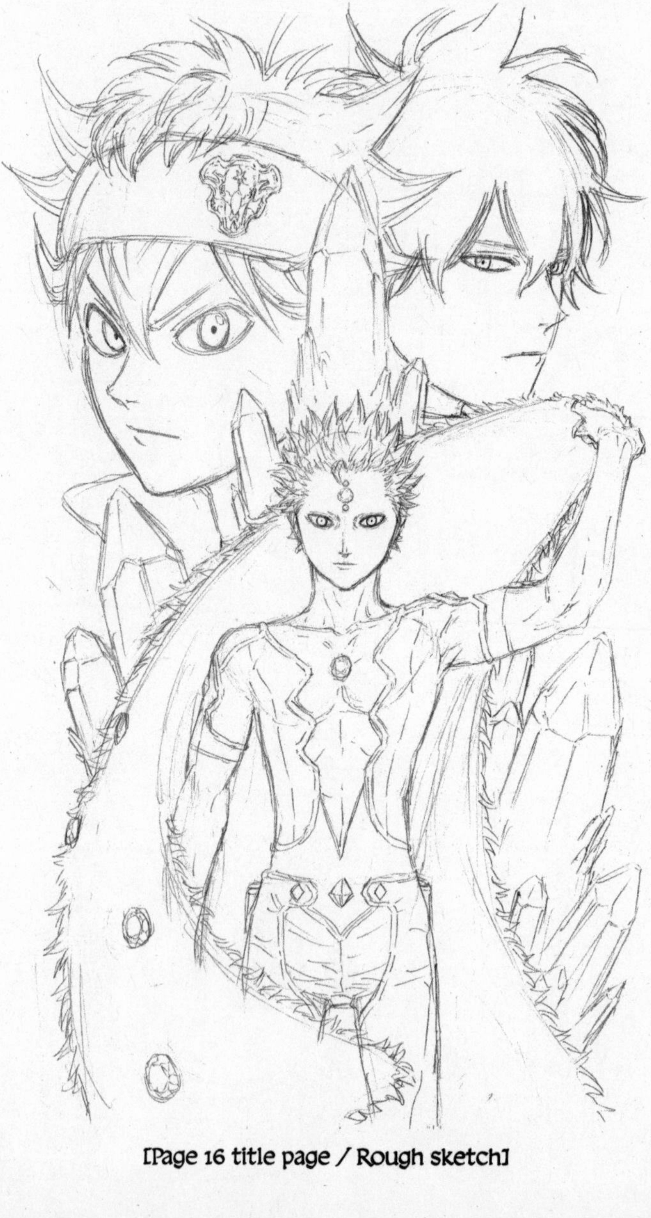

[Page 16 title page / Rough sketch]

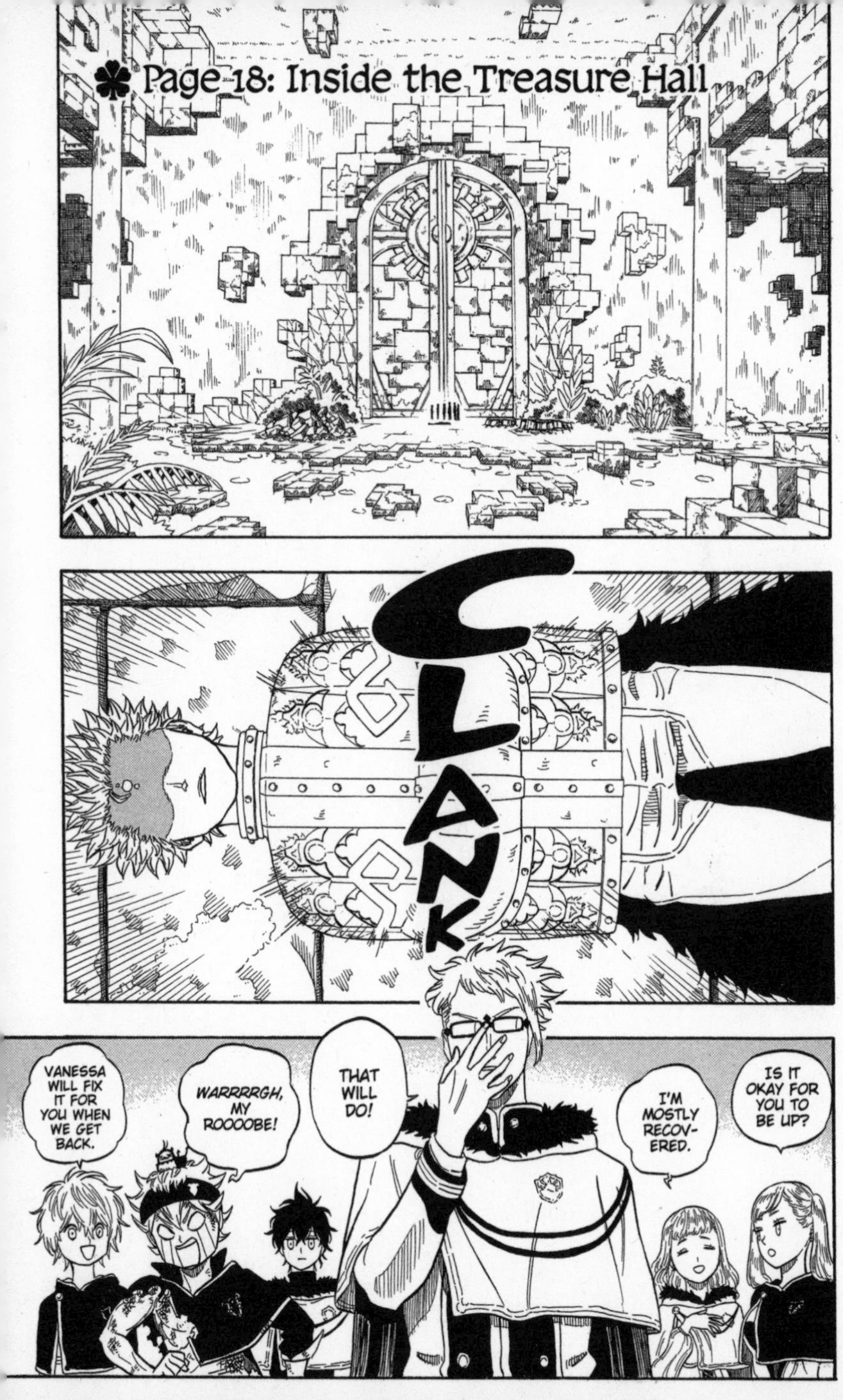
Page 18: Inside the Treasure Hall
CLANK
IS IT OKAY FOR YOU TO BE UP?
I'M MOSTLY RECOVERED.
THAT WILL DO!
WARRRRGH, MY ROOOOBE!
VANESSA WILL FIX IT FOR YOU WHEN WE GET BACK.

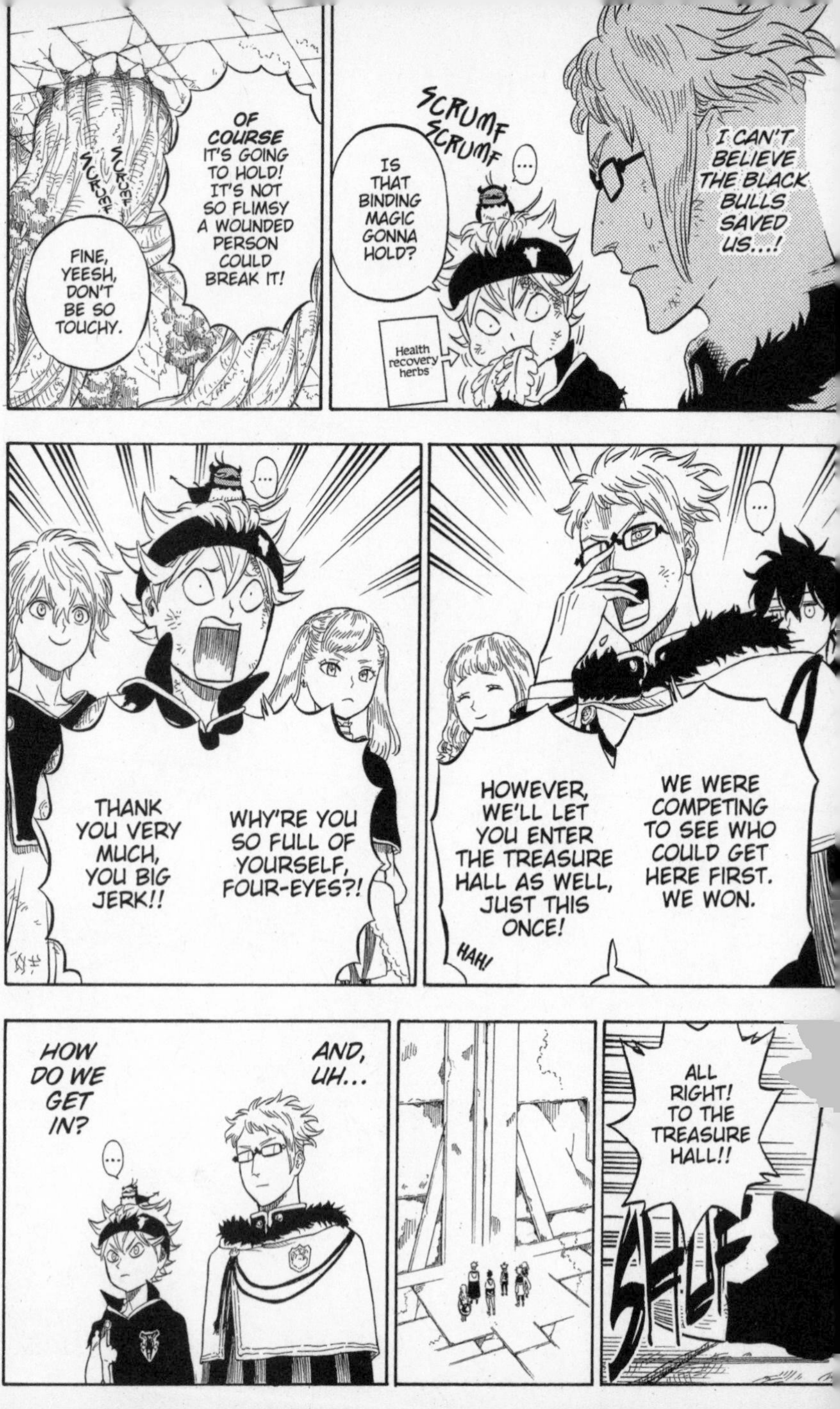
I CAN'T BELIEVE THE BLACK BULLS SAVED US...!
SCRUMF SCRUMF
...
IS THAT BINDING MAGIC GONNA HOLD?
Health recovery herbs
OF COURSE IT'S GOING TO HOLD! IT'S NOT SO FLIMSY A WOUNDED PERSON COULD BREAK IT!
SCRUMF SCRUMF
FINE, YEESH, DON'T BE SO TOUCHY.
...
WE WERE COMPETING TO SEE WHO COULD GET HERE FIRST. WE WON.
HOWEVER, WE'LL LET YOU ENTER THE TREASURE HALL AS WELL, JUST THIS ONCE!
HAH!
...
WHY'RE YOU SO FULL OF YOURSELF, FOUR-EYES?!
THANK YOU VERY MUCH, YOU BIG JERK!!
ALL RIGHT! TO THE TREASURE HALL!!
SHUF
AND, UH...
HOW DO WE GET IN?
...

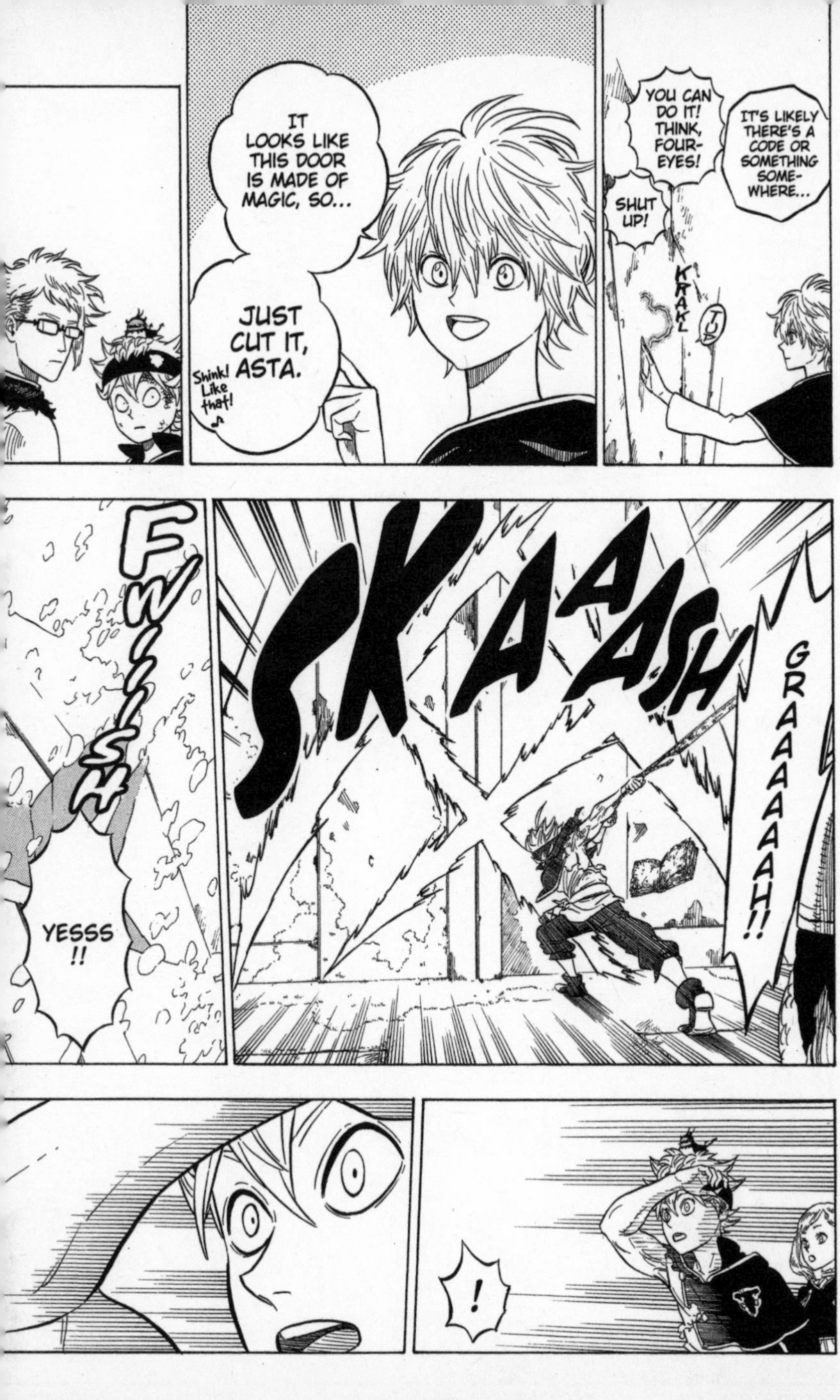

IT'S LIKELY THERE'S A CODE OR SOMETHING SOMEWHERE...
YOU CAN DO IT! THINK, FOUR-EYES!
SHUT UP!
KRAKL
IT LOOKS LIKE THIS DOOR IS MADE OF MAGIC, SO...
JUST CUT IT, ASTA.
Shink! Like that! ♪
GRAAAAAAAH!!
SKAAASH
FWIIISH
YESSS!!
!

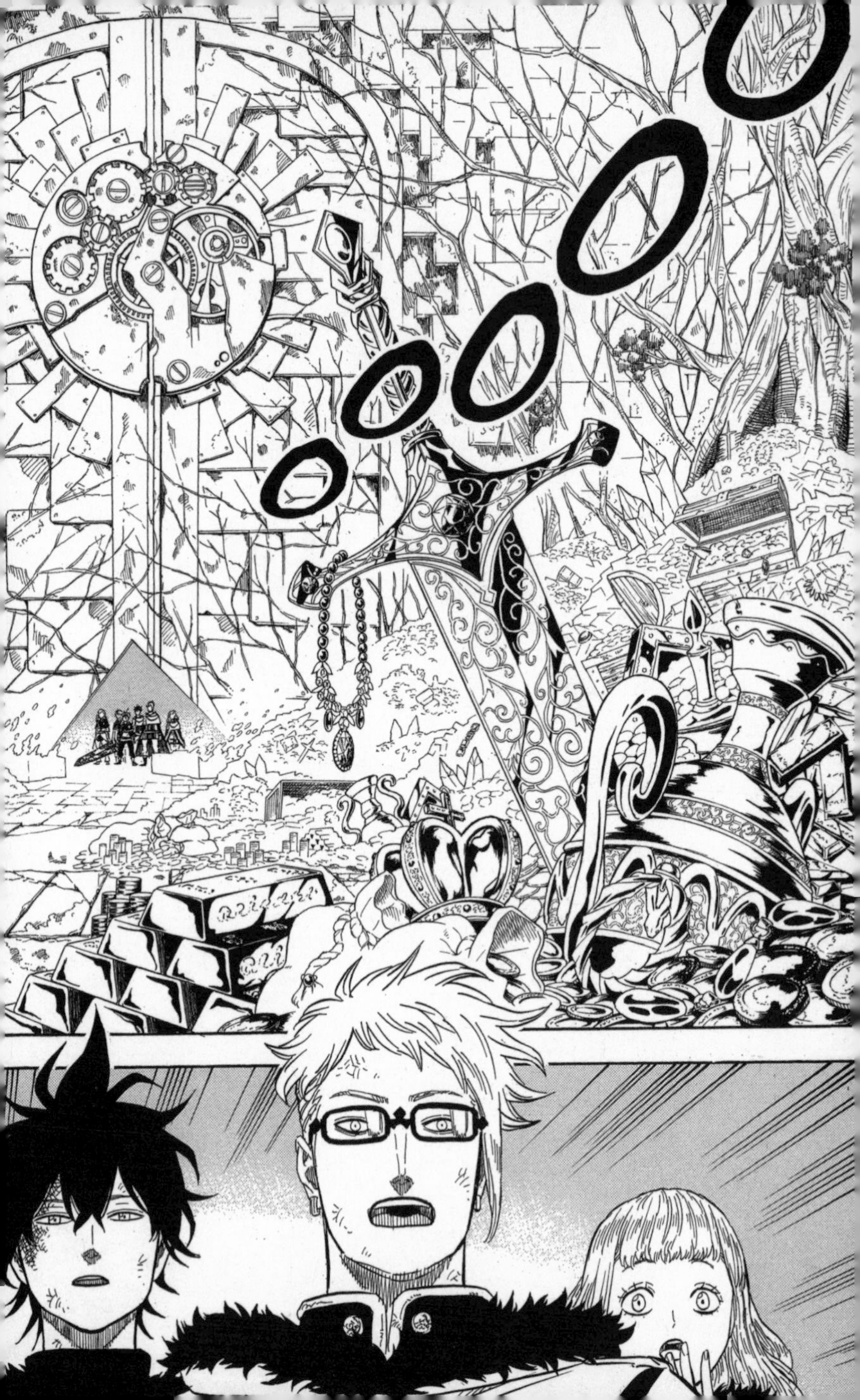

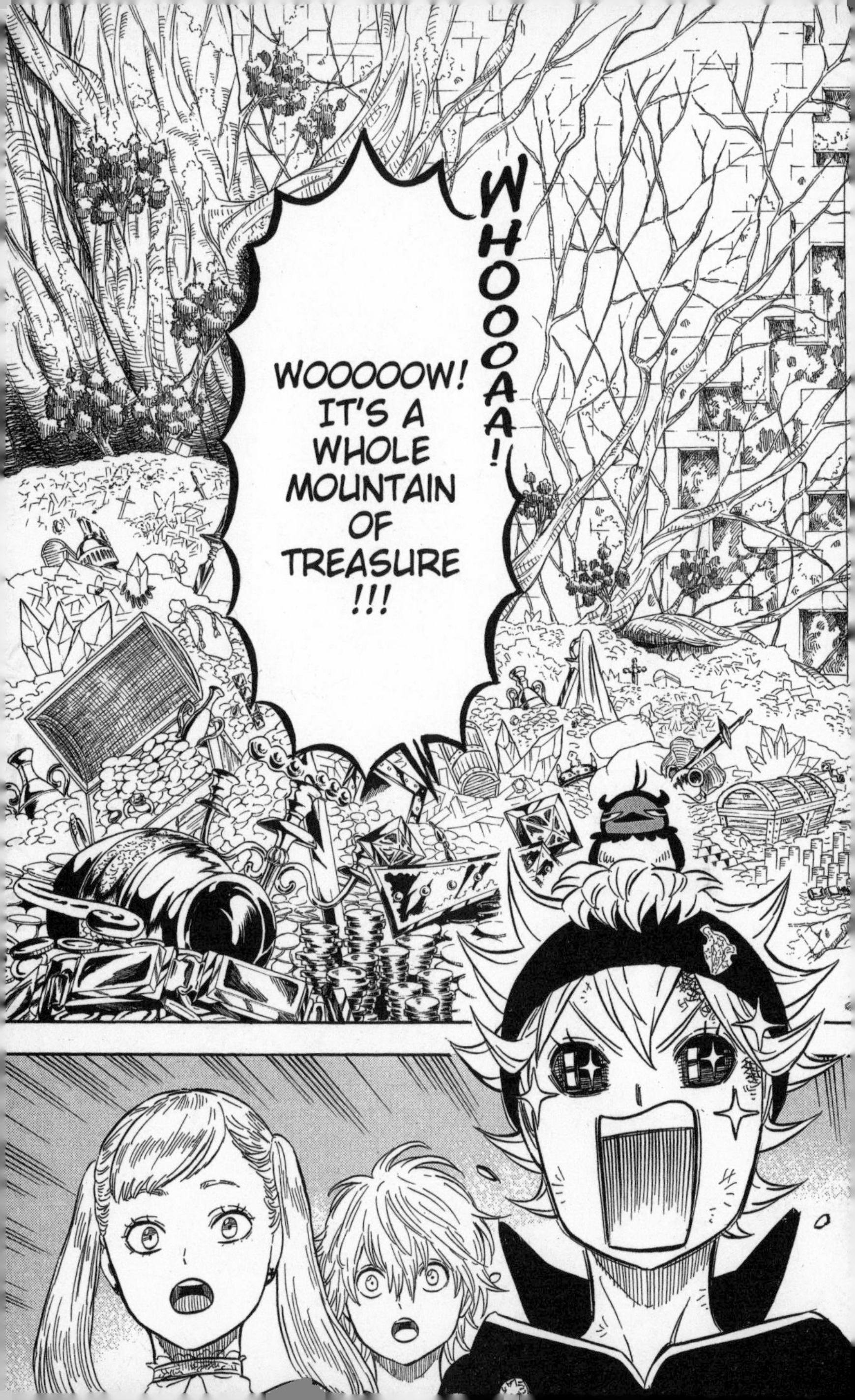
WHOOOOAA!
WOOOOOW! IT'S A WHOLE MOUNTAIN OF TREASURE !!!

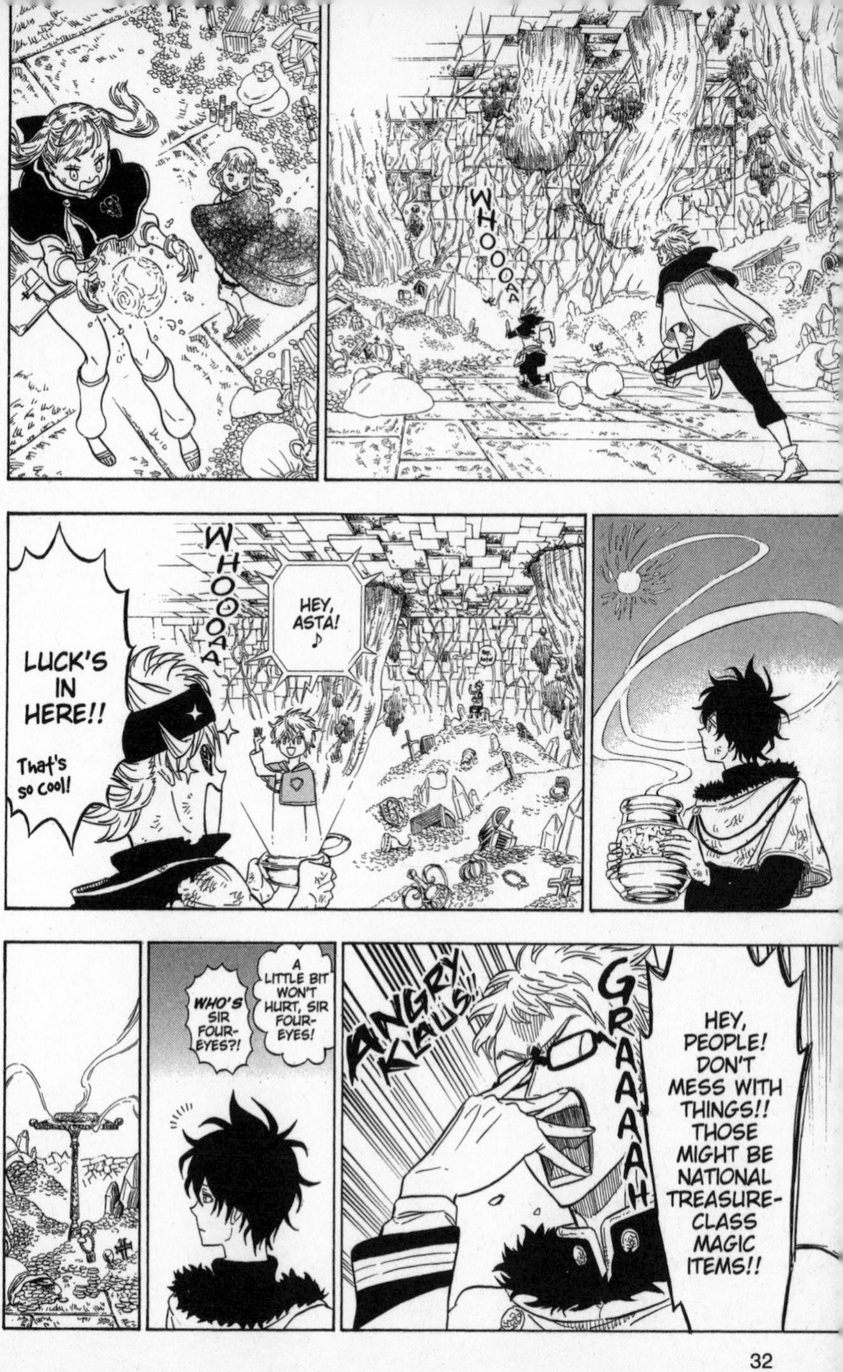
WHOOOAA
WHOOOAA
HEY, ASTA! ♪
LUCK'S IN HERE!!
That's so cool!
HEY, PEOPLE! DON'T MESS WITH THINGS!! THOSE MIGHT BE NATIONAL TREASURE-CLASS MAGIC ITEMS!!
GRAAAAH
ANGRY KLAUS!!
A LITTLE BIT WON'T HURT, SIR FOUR-EYES!
WHO'S SIR FOUR-EYES?!

...?

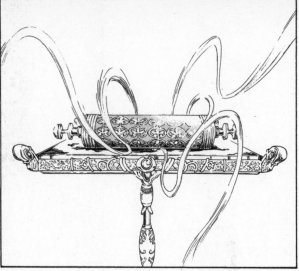

SHOOP

FOOOM

!

GWOOO

WHAT IS THIS WRITING...?

I'VE NEVER SEEN IT BEFORE.

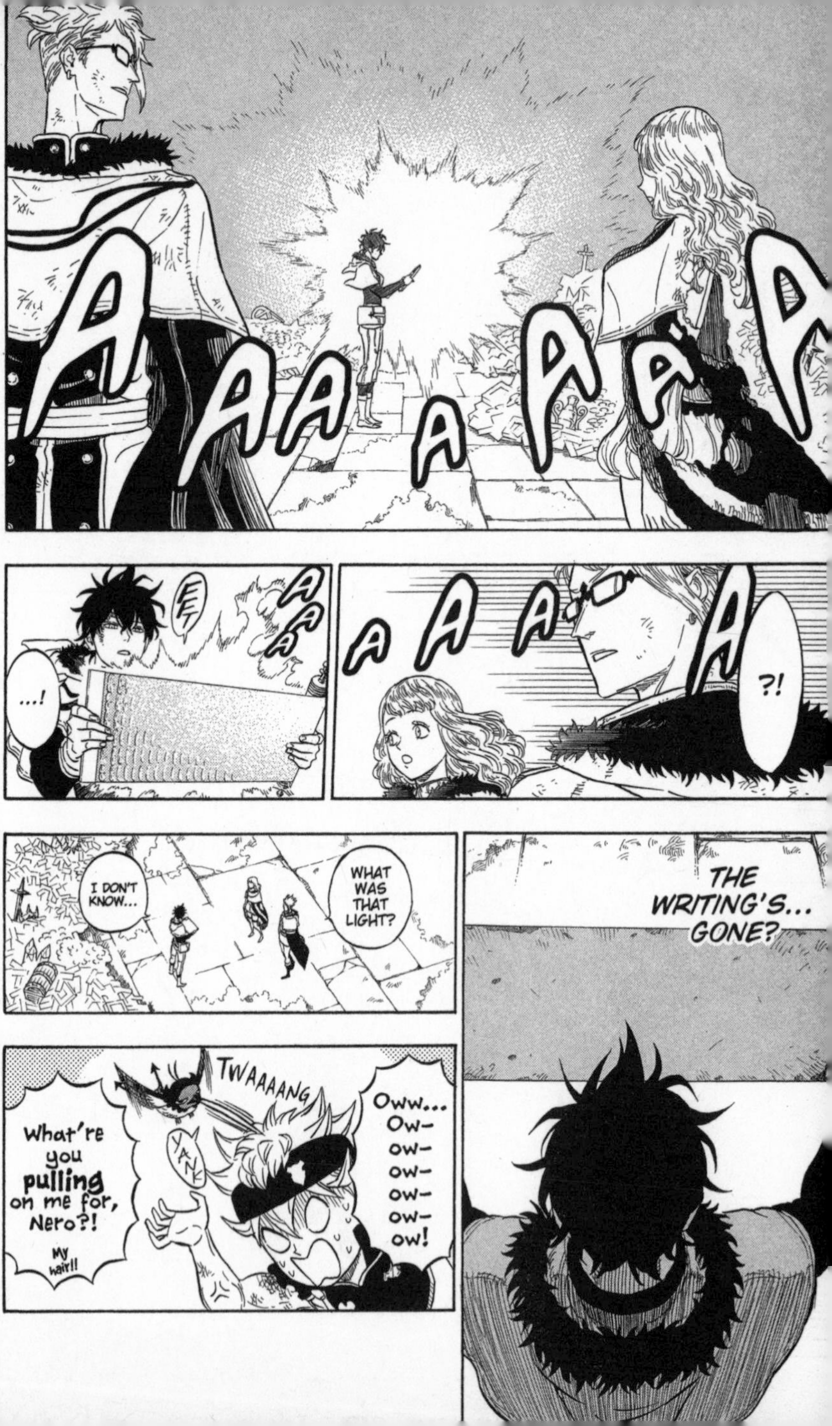
AAAAAAAAA
AAAAA
?!
AAA
...!
THE WRITING'S... GONE?
WHAT WAS THAT LIGHT?
I DON'T KNOW...
Oww... Ow-ow-ow-ow-ow!
TWAAAANG
YANK
What're you pulling on me for, Nero?!
My hair!!

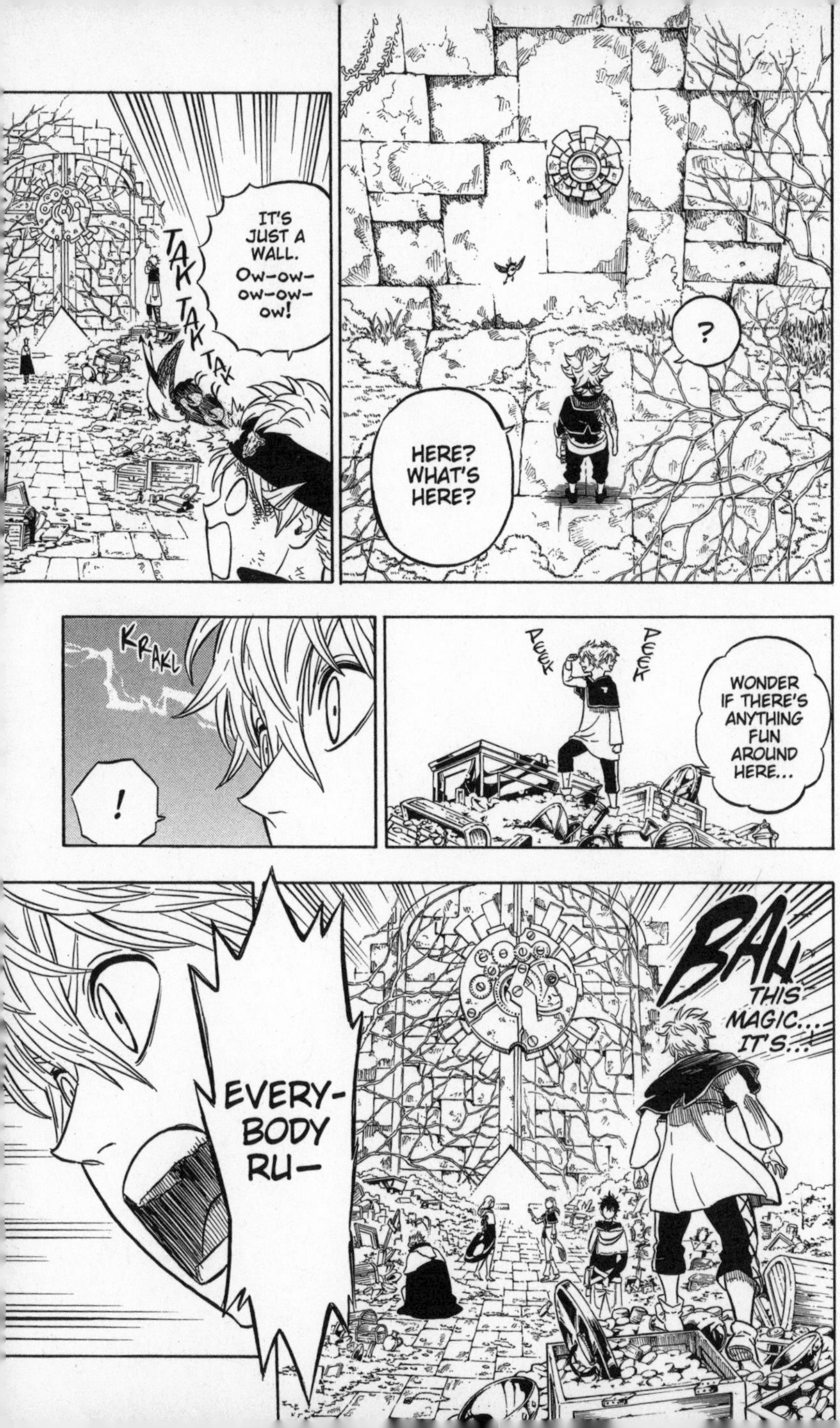
?
HERE? WHAT'S HERE?
IT'S JUST A WALL. Ow-ow-ow-ow-ow!
TAK TAK TAK TAK
PEEK PEEK
WONDER IF THERE'S ANYTHING FUN AROUND HERE...
KRAKL
!
BAM
THIS MAGIC... IT'S...!
EVERY-BODY RU—

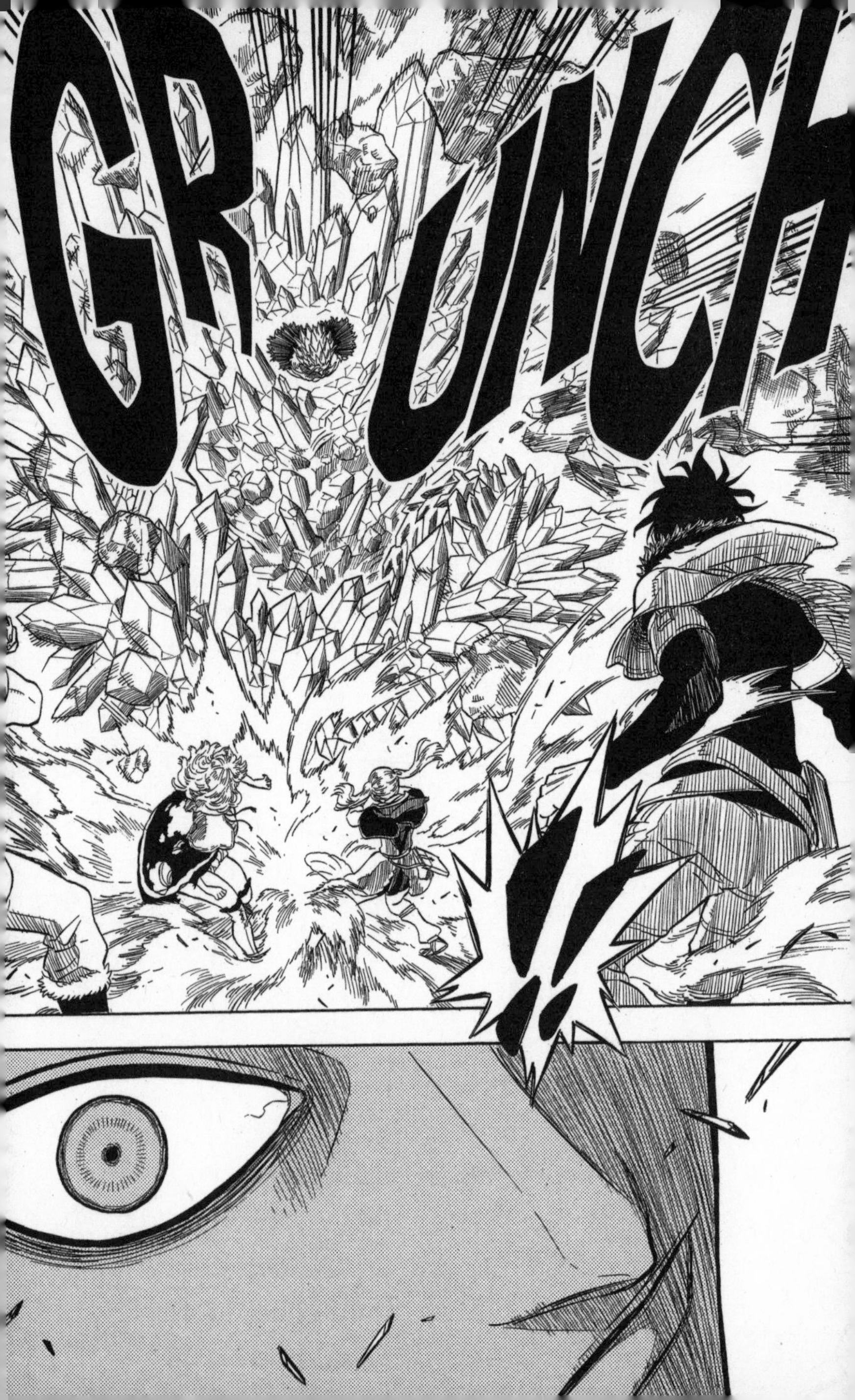
GRUNCH
!!

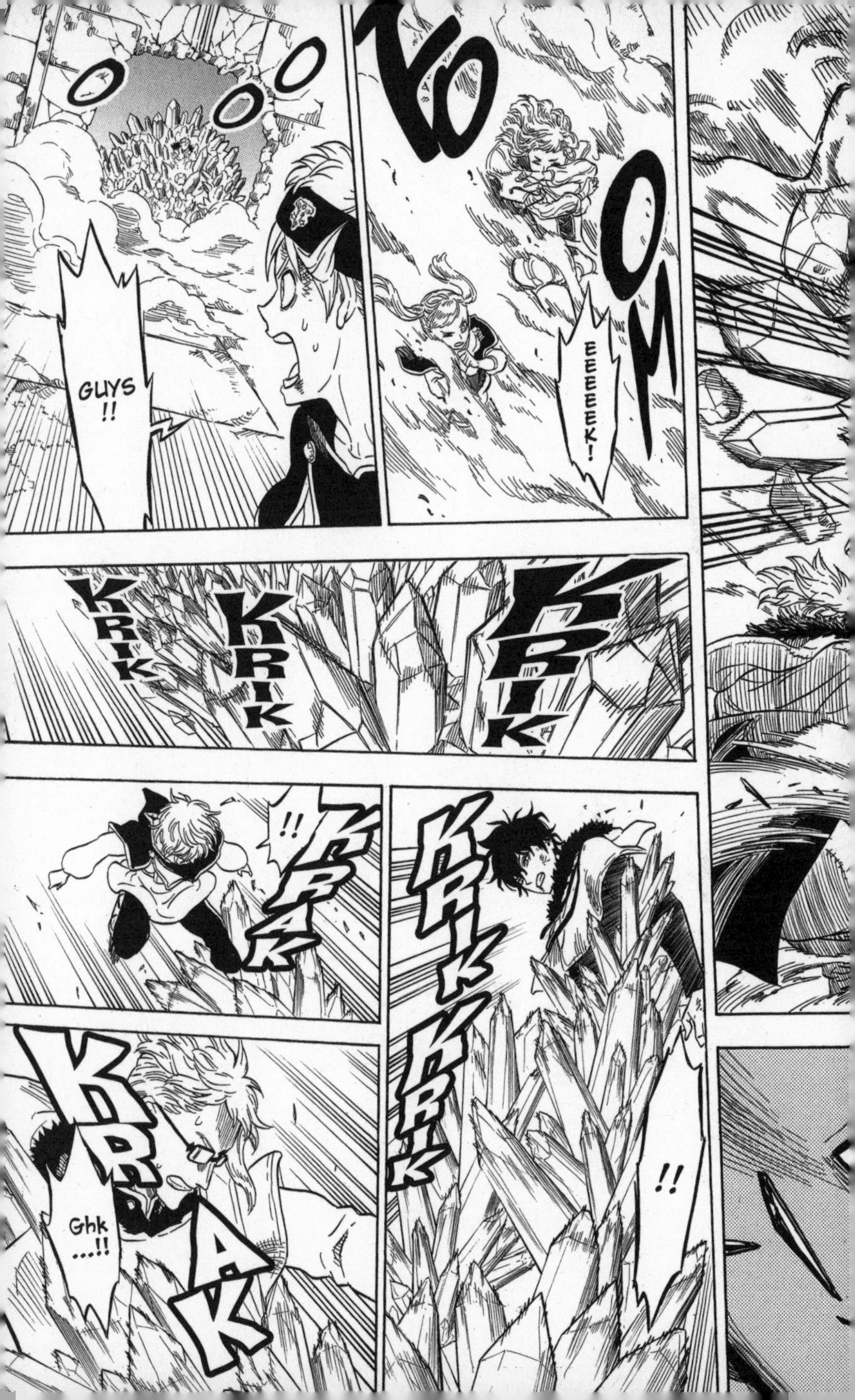

BO
OM
EEEEEK!
OOOO
GUYS!!
KRIK
KRIK
KRIK
KRIKRIKRIK
!!
!!
KRAK
KRAK
Ghk ...!!

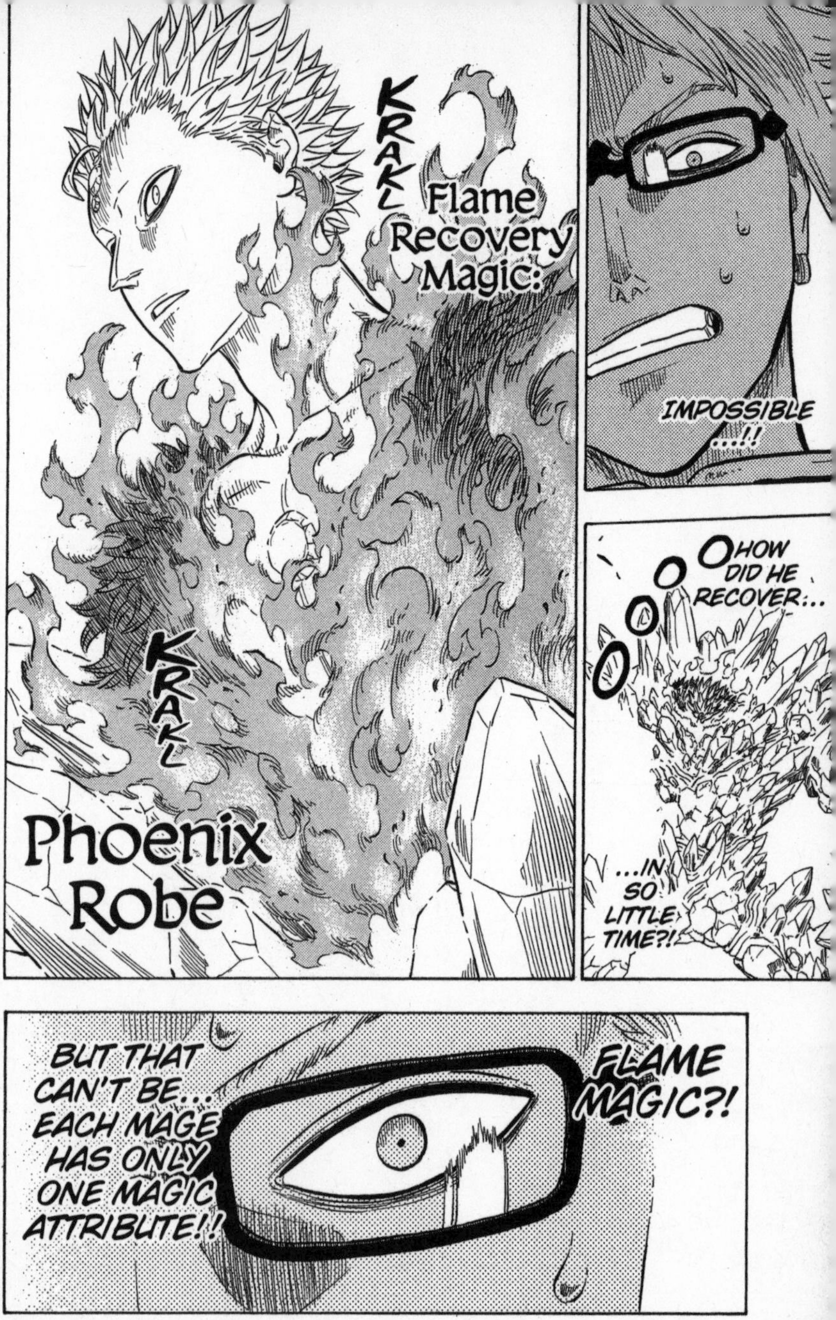
IMPOSSIBLE ...!!
HOW DID HE RECOVER...
...IN SO LITTLE TIME?!
KRAKL
Flame Recovery Magic:
KRAKL
Phoenix Robe
FLAME MAGIC?!
BUT THAT CAN'T BE... EACH MAGE HAS ONLY ONE MAGIC ATTRIBUTE!!

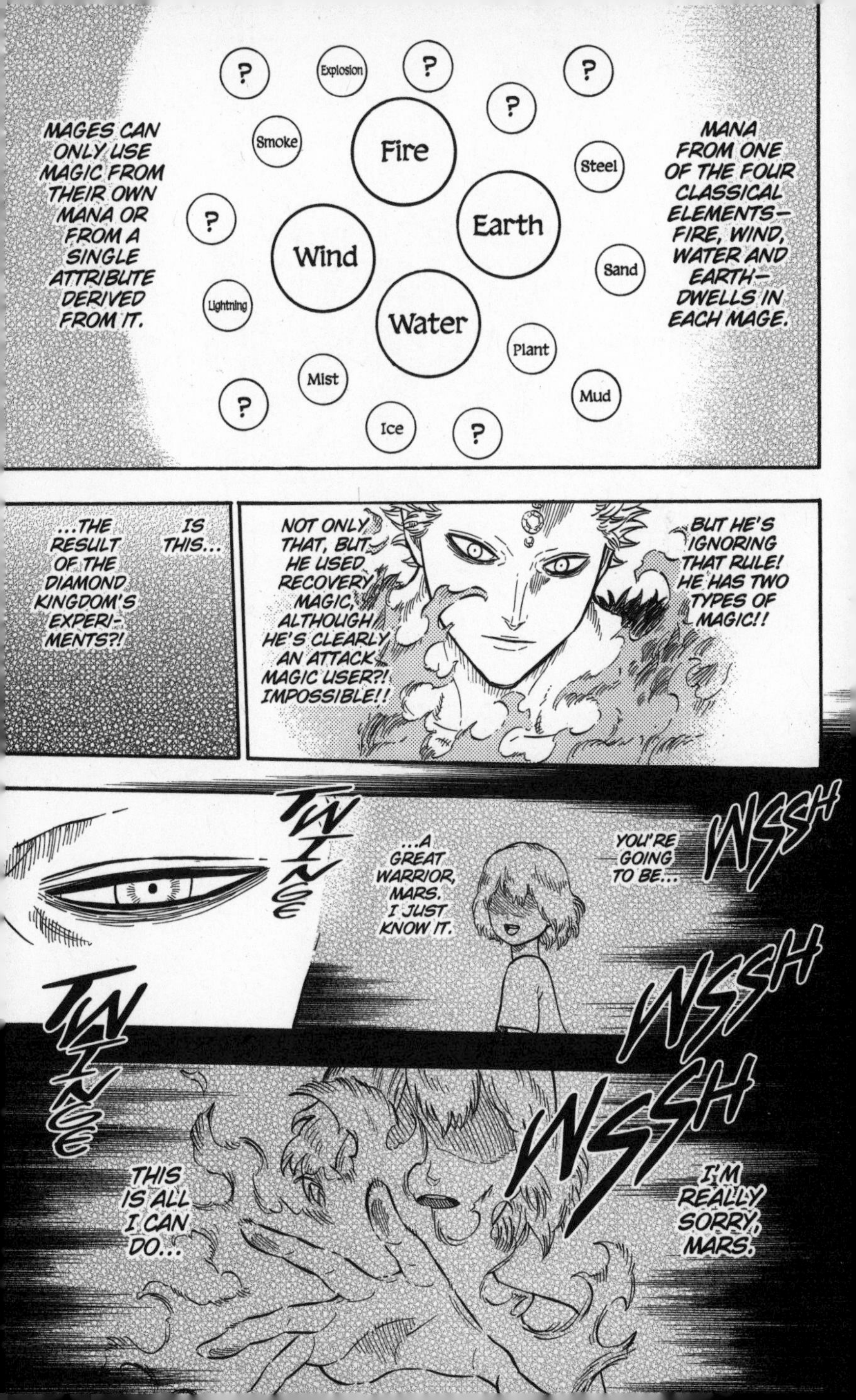
MANA FROM ONE OF THE FOUR CLASSICAL ELEMENTS— FIRE, WIND, WATER AND EARTH— DWELLS IN EACH MAGE.
?
Explosion
?
?
?
Steel
Fire
Smoke
Earth
Sand
Wind
?
Water
Lightning
Plant
Mud
Mist
?
Ice
?
MAGES CAN ONLY USE MAGIC FROM THEIR OWN MANA OR FROM A SINGLE ATTRIBUTE DERIVED FROM IT.
BUT HE'S IGNORING THAT RULE! HE HAS TWO TYPES OF MAGIC!!
NOT ONLY THAT, BUT HE USED RECOVERY MAGIC, ALTHOUGH HE'S CLEARLY AN ATTACK MAGIC USER?! IMPOSSIBLE!!
IS THIS...
...THE RESULT OF THE DIAMOND KINGDOM'S EXPERIMENTS?!
WSSH
YOU'RE GOING TO BE...
...A GREAT WARRIOR, MARS. I JUST KNOW IT.
TWINGE
WSSH
WSSH
I'M REALLY SORRY, MARS.
THIS IS ALL I CAN DO...
TWINGE

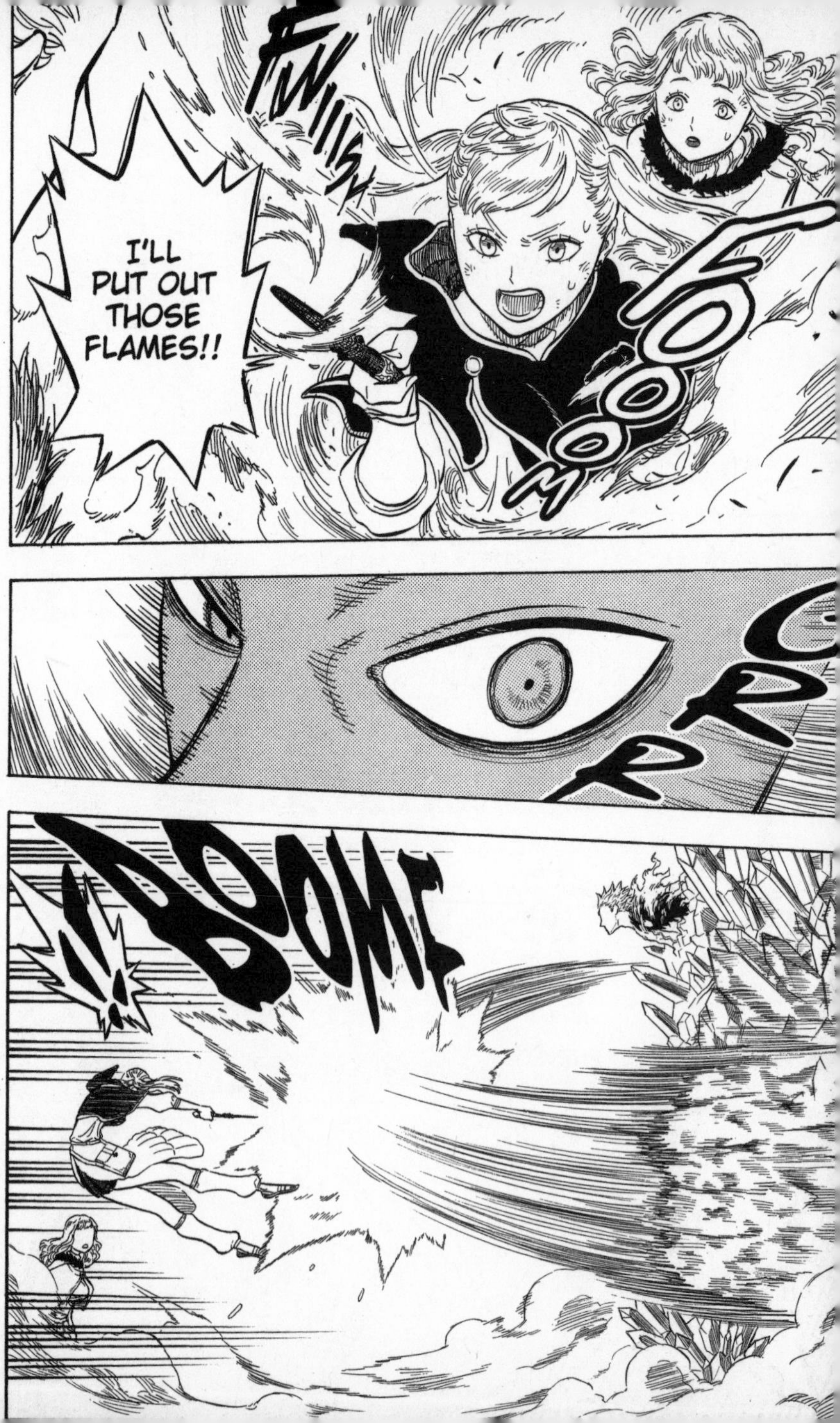
FWIIISH
FOOOOM
I'LL PUT OUT THOSE FLAMES!!
GRRR
BOOM!!

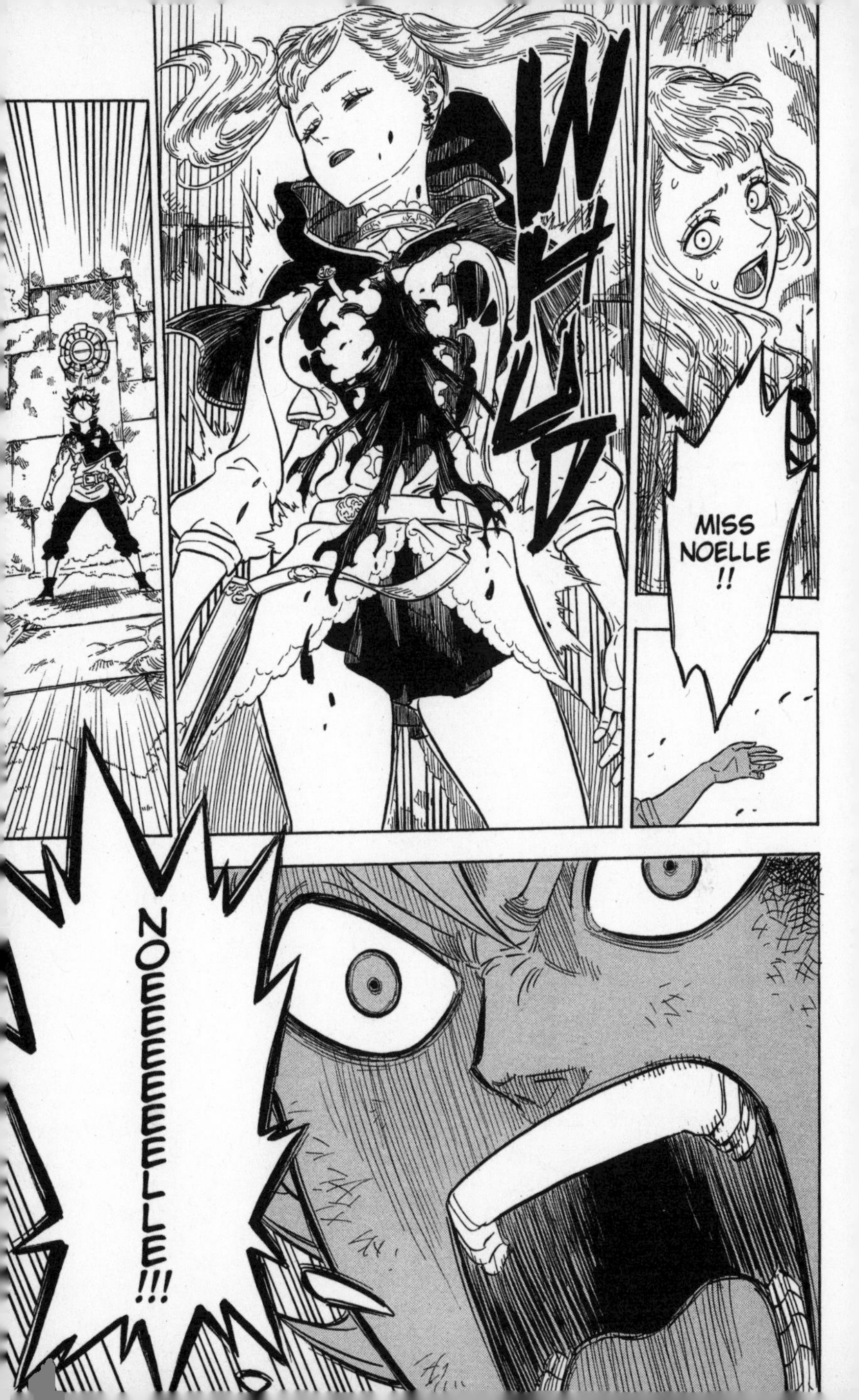
MISS NOELLE !!
WHUD
NOEEEEEEELLE!!!

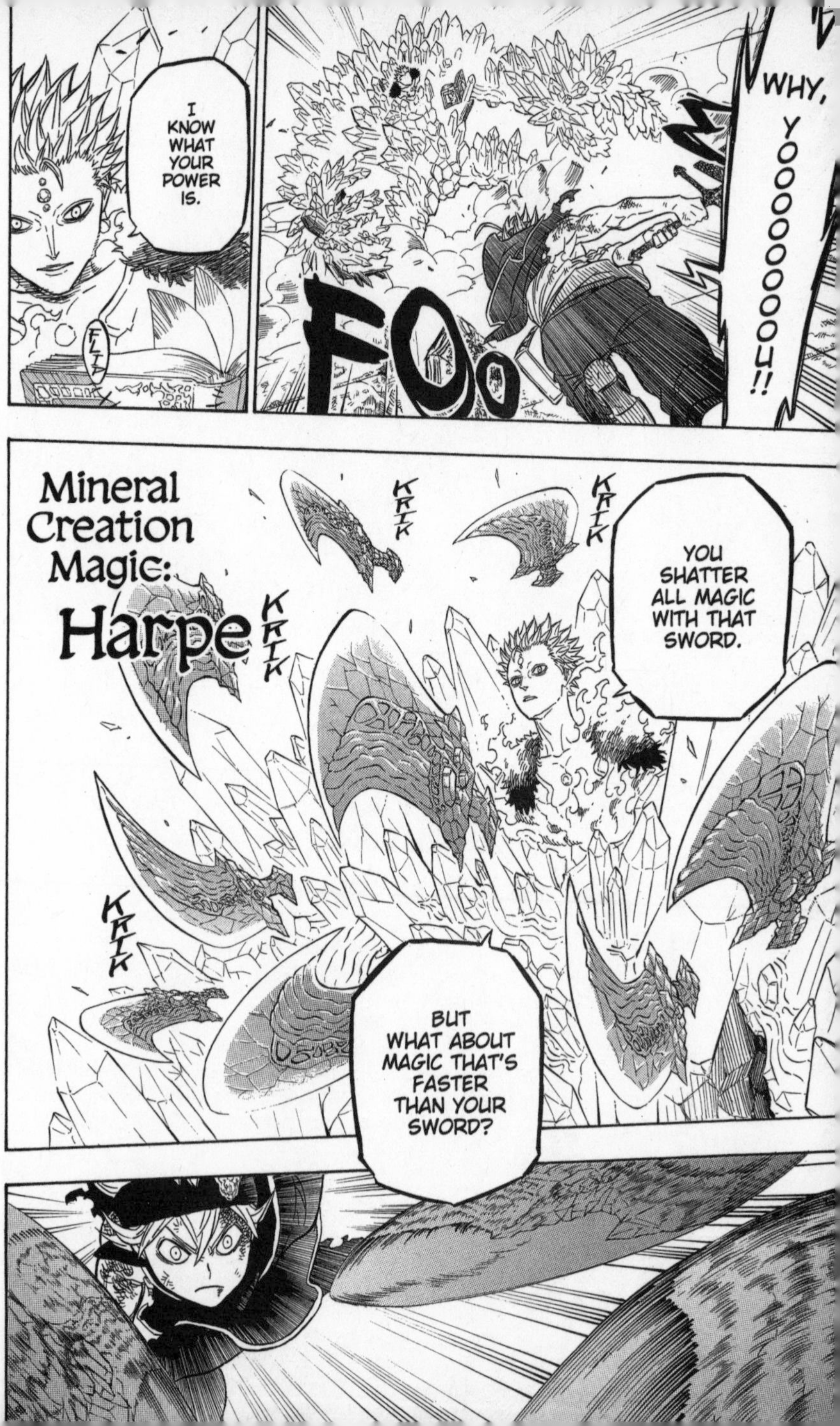
WHY, YOOOOOOOOU!!
FOO
I KNOW WHAT YOUR POWER IS.
FLIP
Mineral Creation Magic: Harpe
KRIK
KRIK
KRIK
YOU SHATTER ALL MAGIC WITH THAT SWORD.
KRIK
BUT WHAT ABOUT MAGIC THAT'S FASTER THAN YOUR SWORD?

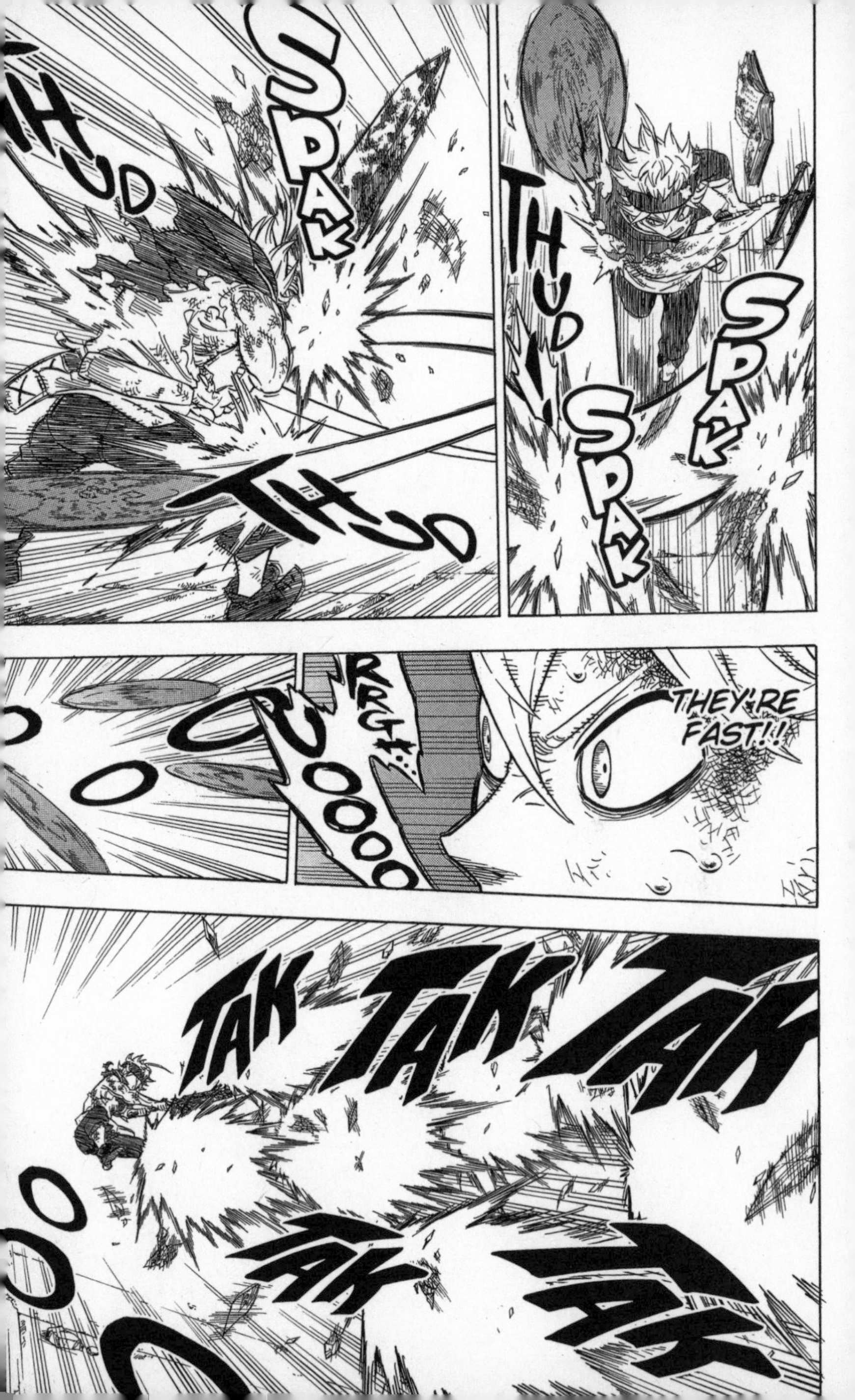
THUD!!
SPAK
SPAK
THUD
SPAK
THUD
THEY'RE FAST!!
RRGH...
GUOOOOO
OO
TAK
TAK
TAK
TAK
TAK
OOO

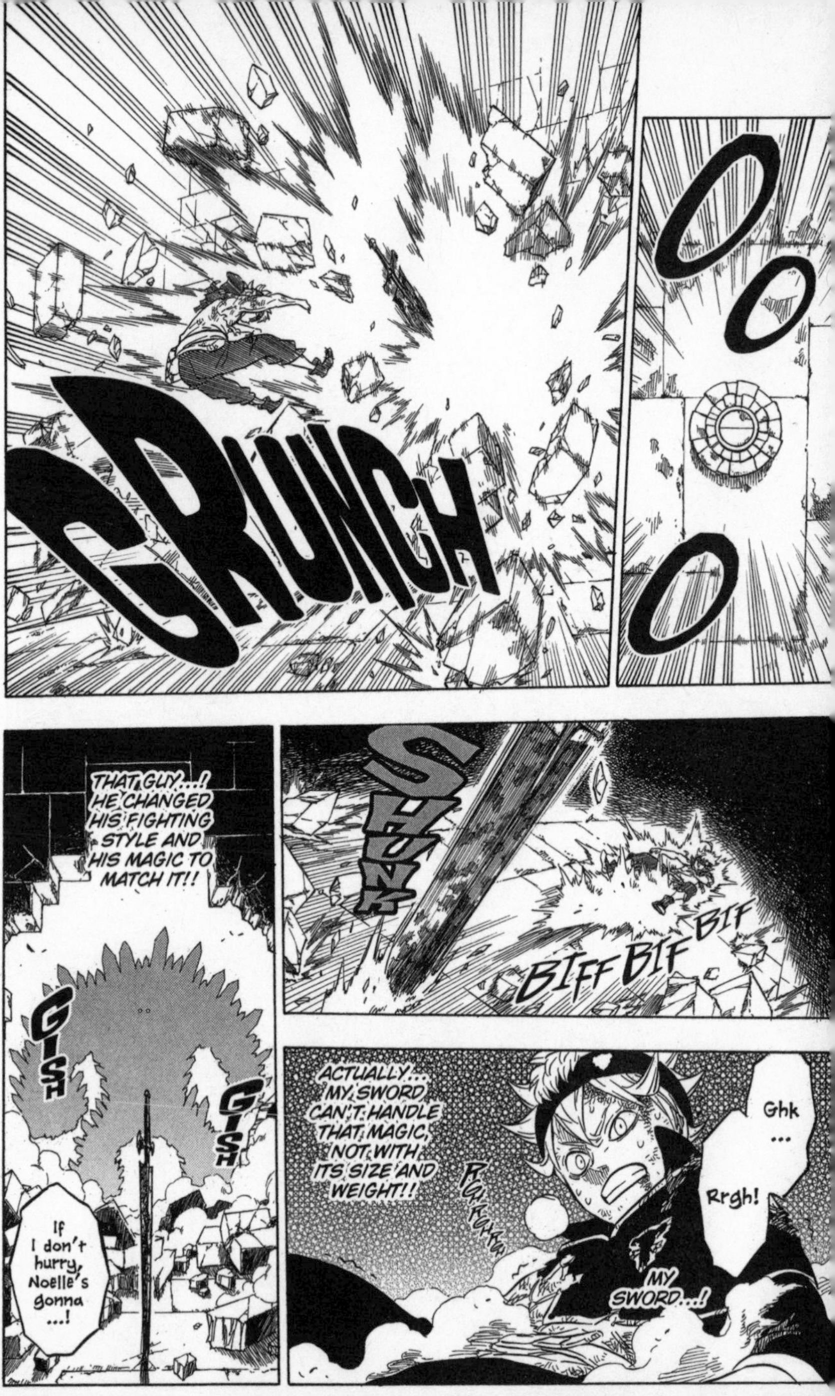
OOO
CRUNCH
SHUNK
BIFF BIF BIF
Ghk...
Rrgh!
ACTUALLY... MY SWORD CAN'T HANDLE THAT MAGIC, NOT WITH ITS SIZE AND WEIGHT!!
MY SWORD...!
THAT GUY...! HE CHANGED HIS FIGHTING STYLE AND HIS MAGIC TO MATCH IT!!
GISH
GISH
If I don't hurry, Noelle's gonna ...!

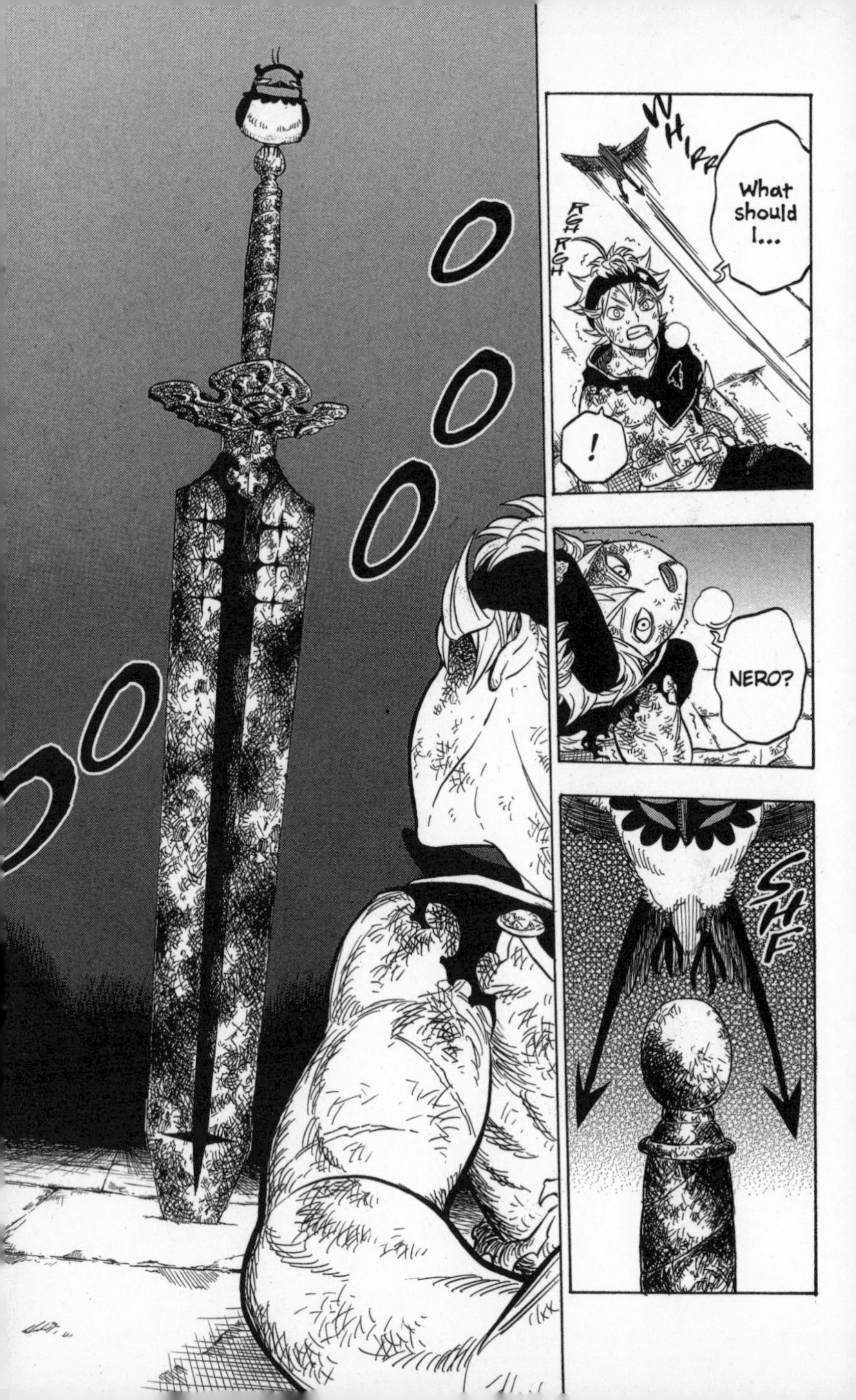
WHIRR
RGHRGH
What should I...
!
NERO?
SHF
OOOOO

Klaus
Lunettes

Age: 18
Height: 176 cm
Birthday: April 19
Sign: Aries
Blood Type: A
Likes: Reading,
     appreciating
     architecture

C h a r a c t e r   P r o f i l e

Page 19: Memories of You

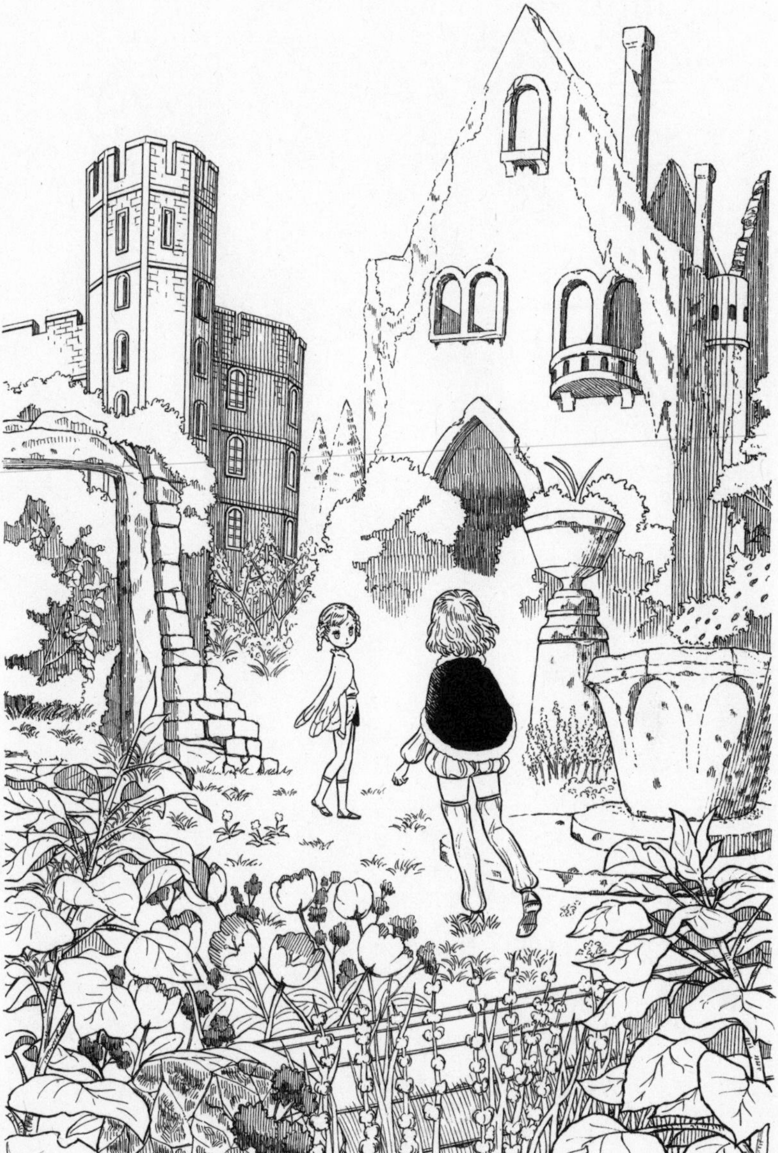

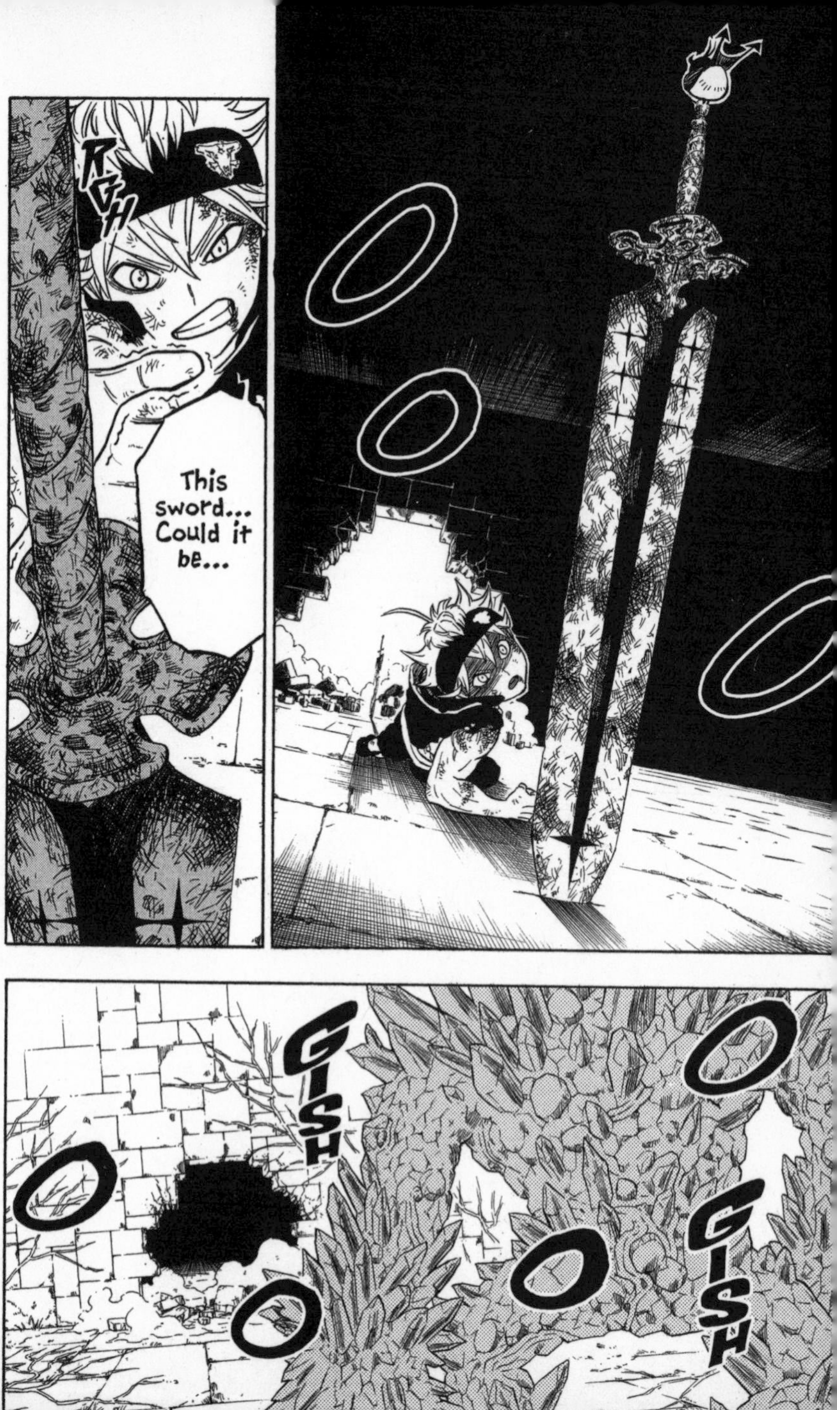
RGH
This sword... Could it be...
GISH
GISH

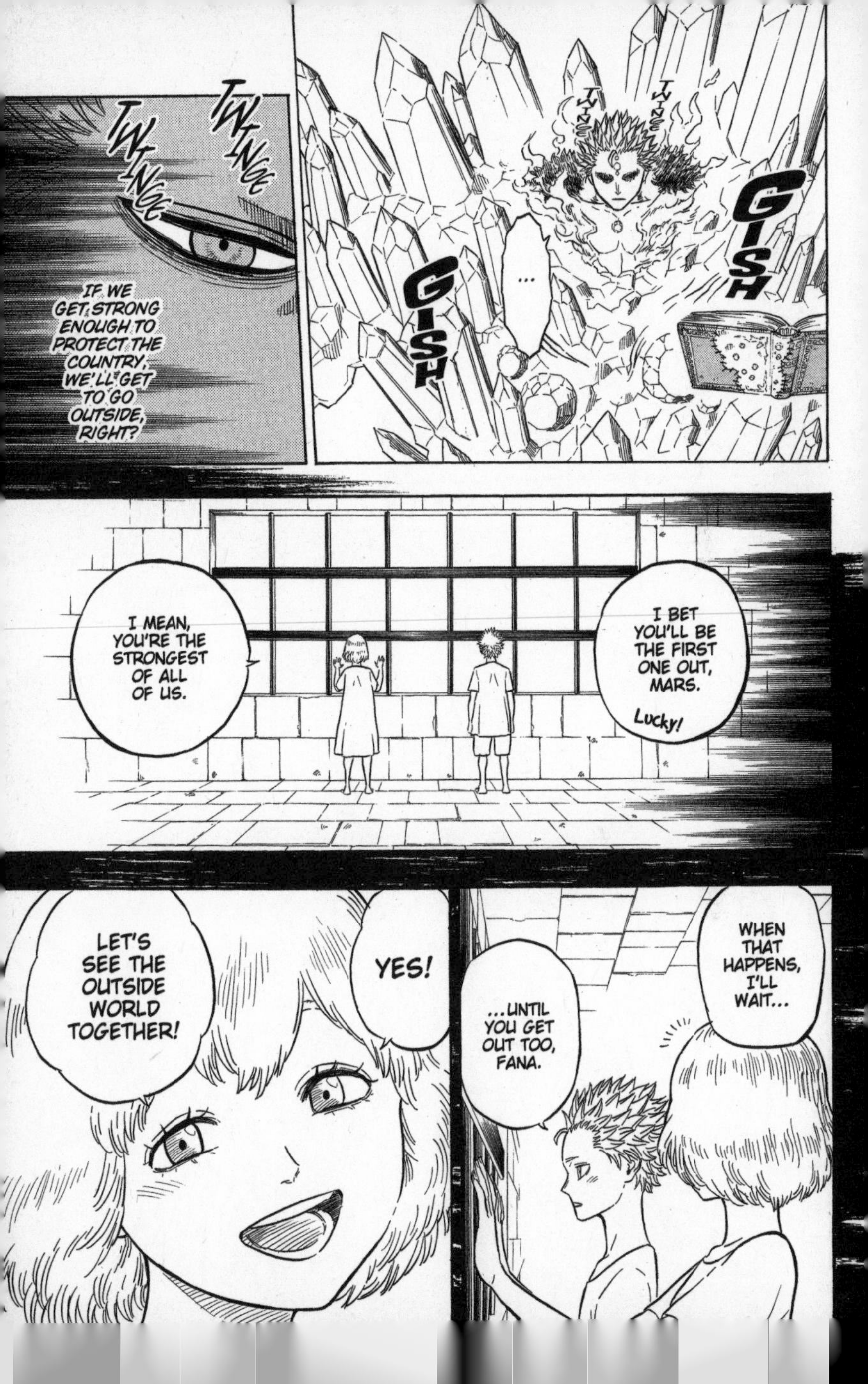
TWINGE
TWINGE
...
GISH
GISH
TWINGE
TWINGE
IF WE GET STRONG ENOUGH TO PROTECT THE COUNTRY, WE'LL GET TO GO OUTSIDE, RIGHT?
I BET YOU'LL BE THE FIRST ONE OUT, MARS.
Lucky!
I MEAN, YOU'RE THE STRONGEST OF ALL OF US.
WHEN THAT HAPPENS, I'LL WAIT...
...UNTIL YOU GET OUT TOO, FANA.
YES!
LET'S SEE THE OUTSIDE WORLD TOGETHER!

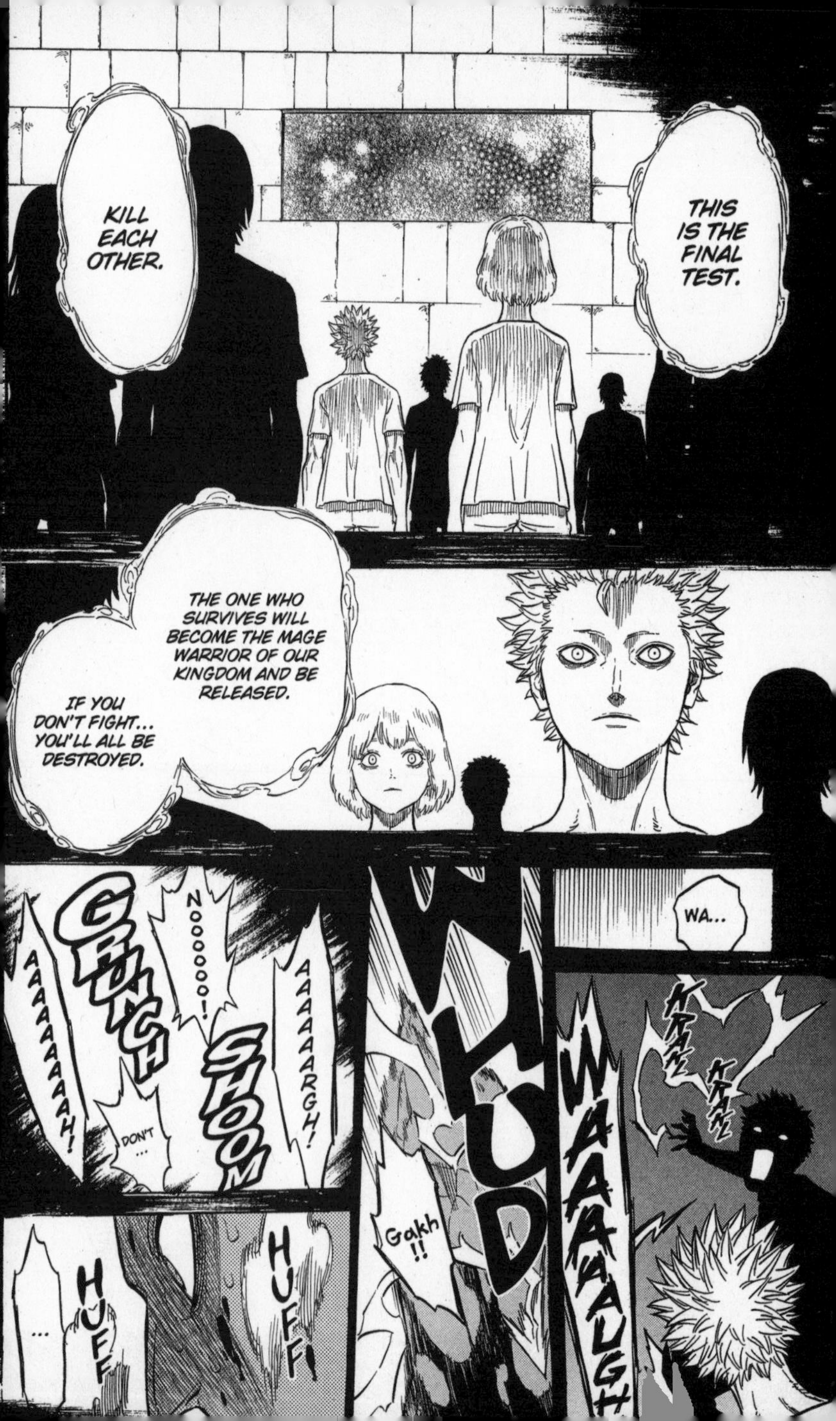
THIS IS THE FINAL TEST.
KILL EACH OTHER.
THE ONE WHO SURVIVES WILL BECOME THE MAGE WARRIOR OF OUR KINGDOM AND BE RELEASED.
IF YOU DON'T FIGHT... YOU'LL ALL BE DESTROYED.
WA...
KRAM
KRAM
WAAAAAAAUGH
THUD
Gakh !!
AAAAAAARGH!
SHOOM
NOOOOOOO!
CRUNCH
AAAAAAAAAH!
DON'T ...
HUFF
HUFF
...

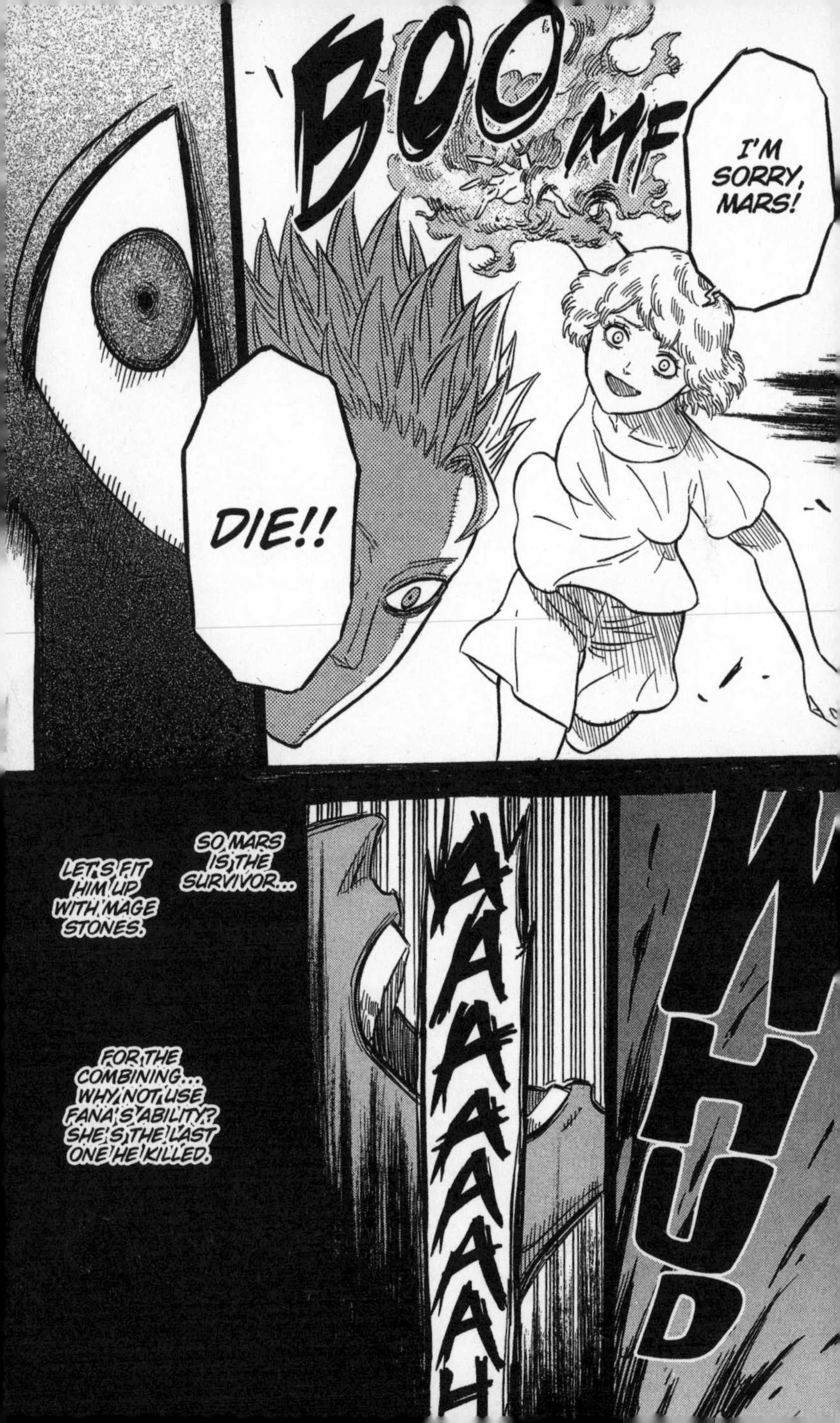
BOOMF
I'M SORRY, MARS!
DIE!!
THUD
AAAAAAAAAH
SO MARS IS THE SURVIVOR...
LET'S FIT HIM UP WITH MAGE STONES.
FOR THE COMBINING... WHY NOT USE FANA'S ABILITY? SHE'S THE LAST ONE HE KILLED.

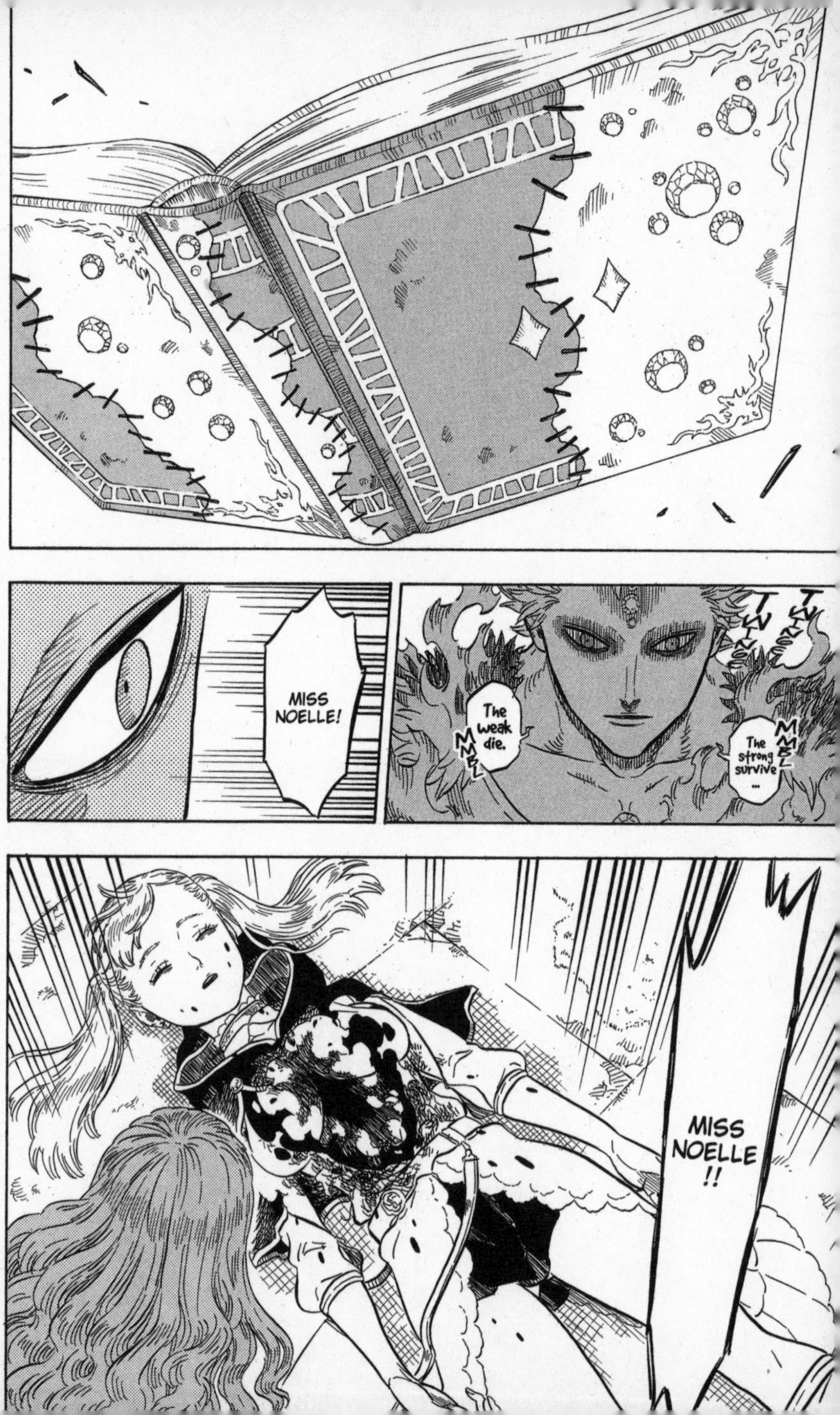
MISS NOELLE!
TWINGE
TWINGE
The weak die.
MMBL
The strong survive...
MMBL
MISS NOELLE!!

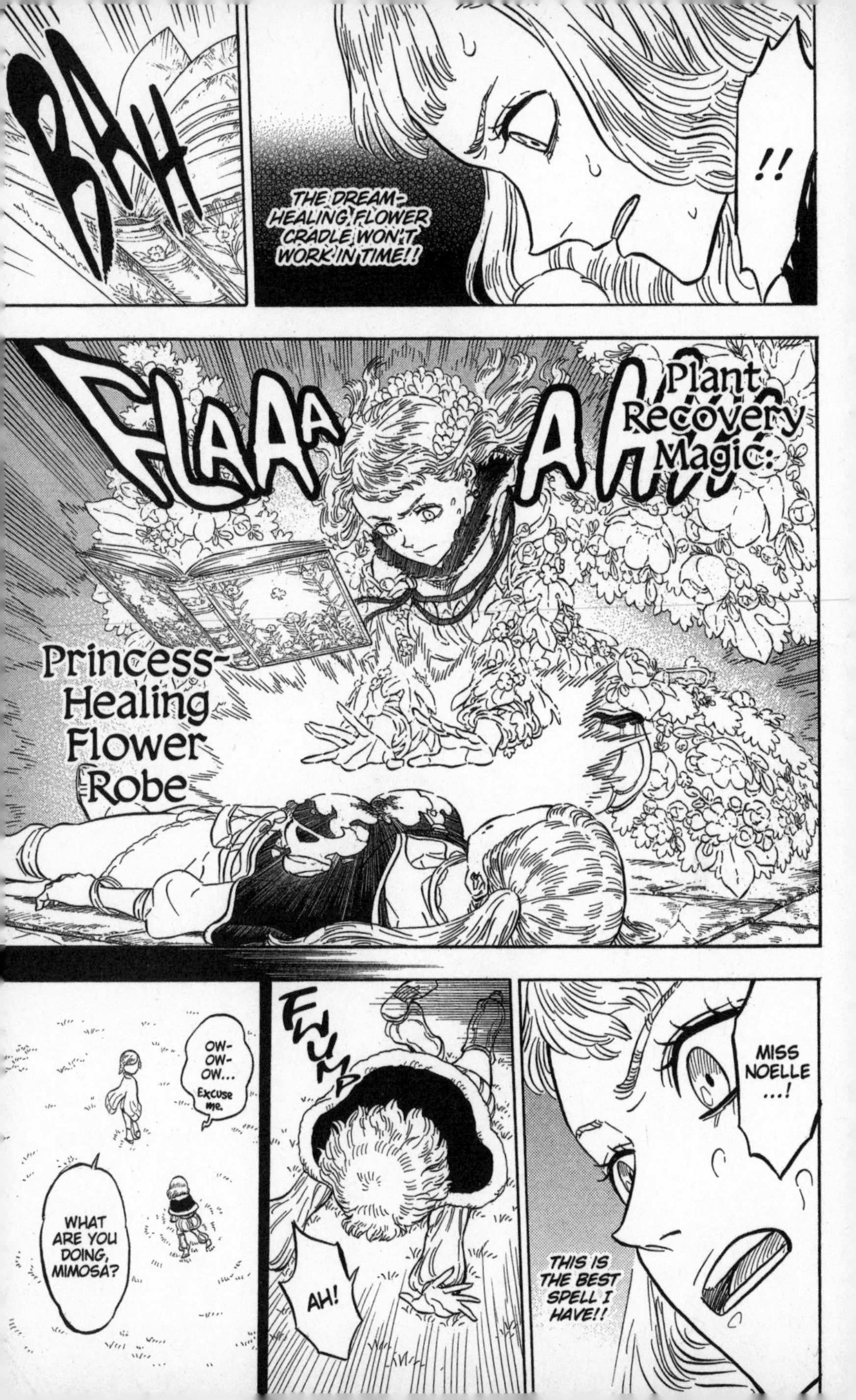
BAH
!!
THE DREAM-HEALING FLOWER CRADLE WON'T WORK IN TIME!!
FLAAAA
Plant Recovery Magic:
Princess-Healing Flower Robe
MISS NOELLE ...!
THIS IS THE BEST SPELL I HAVE!!
FWUMP
AH!
OW-OW-OW... Excuse me.
WHAT ARE YOU DOING, MIMOSA?

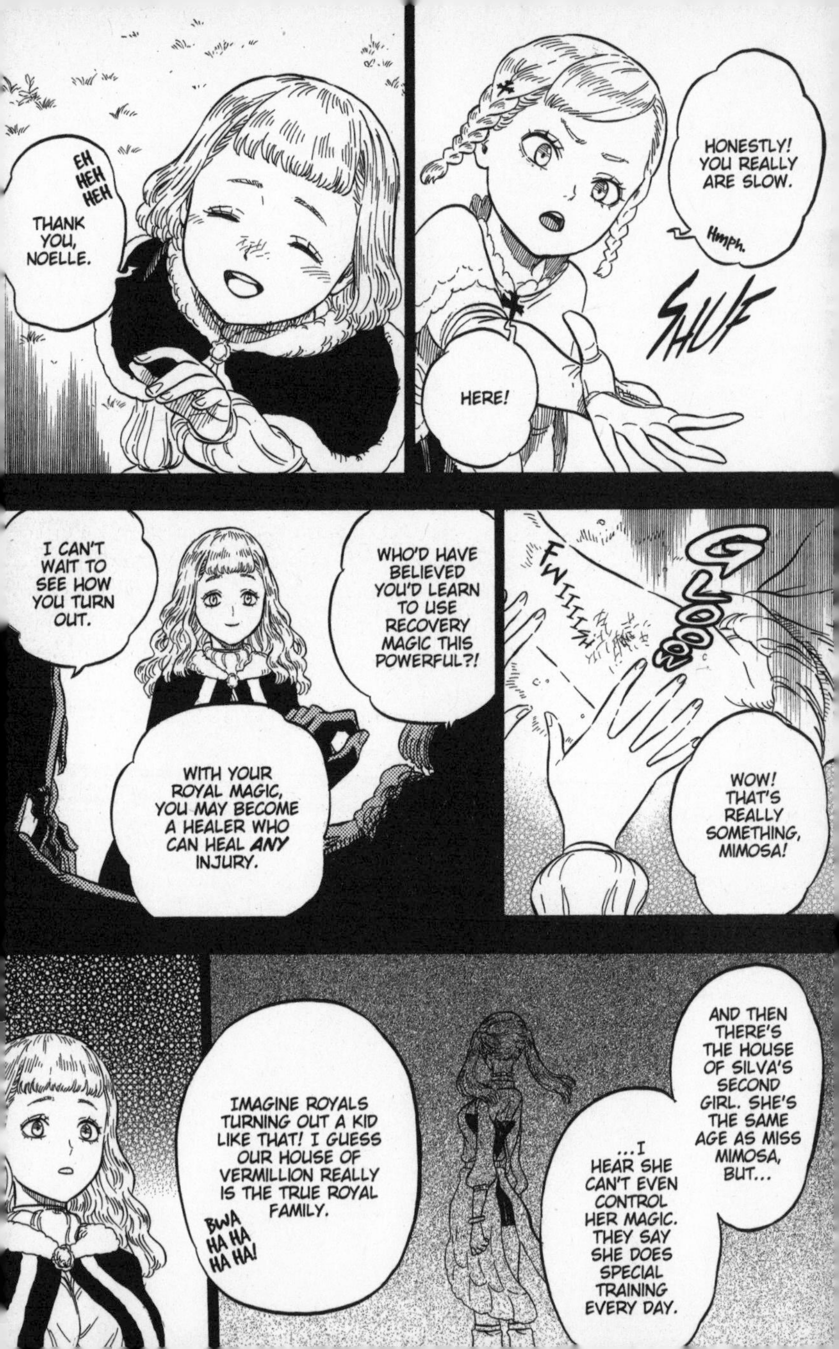
HONESTLY! YOU REALLY ARE SLOW.
Hmph.
SHUF
HERE!
EH HEH HEH
THANK YOU, NOELLE.
GLOOOW
FWIIIISH
WOW! THAT'S REALLY SOMETHING, MIMOSA!
WHO'D HAVE BELIEVED YOU'D LEARN TO USE RECOVERY MAGIC THIS POWERFUL?!
I CAN'T WAIT TO SEE HOW YOU TURN OUT.
WITH YOUR ROYAL MAGIC, YOU MAY BECOME A HEALER WHO CAN HEAL ANY INJURY.
AND THEN THERE'S THE HOUSE OF SILVA'S SECOND GIRL. SHE'S THE SAME AGE AS MISS MIMOSA, BUT...
...I HEAR SHE CAN'T EVEN CONTROL HER MAGIC. THEY SAY SHE DOES SPECIAL TRAINING EVERY DAY.
IMAGINE ROYALS TURNING OUT A KID LIKE THAT! I GUESS OUR HOUSE OF VERMILLION REALLY IS THE TRUE ROYAL FAMILY.
BWA HA HA HA HA!

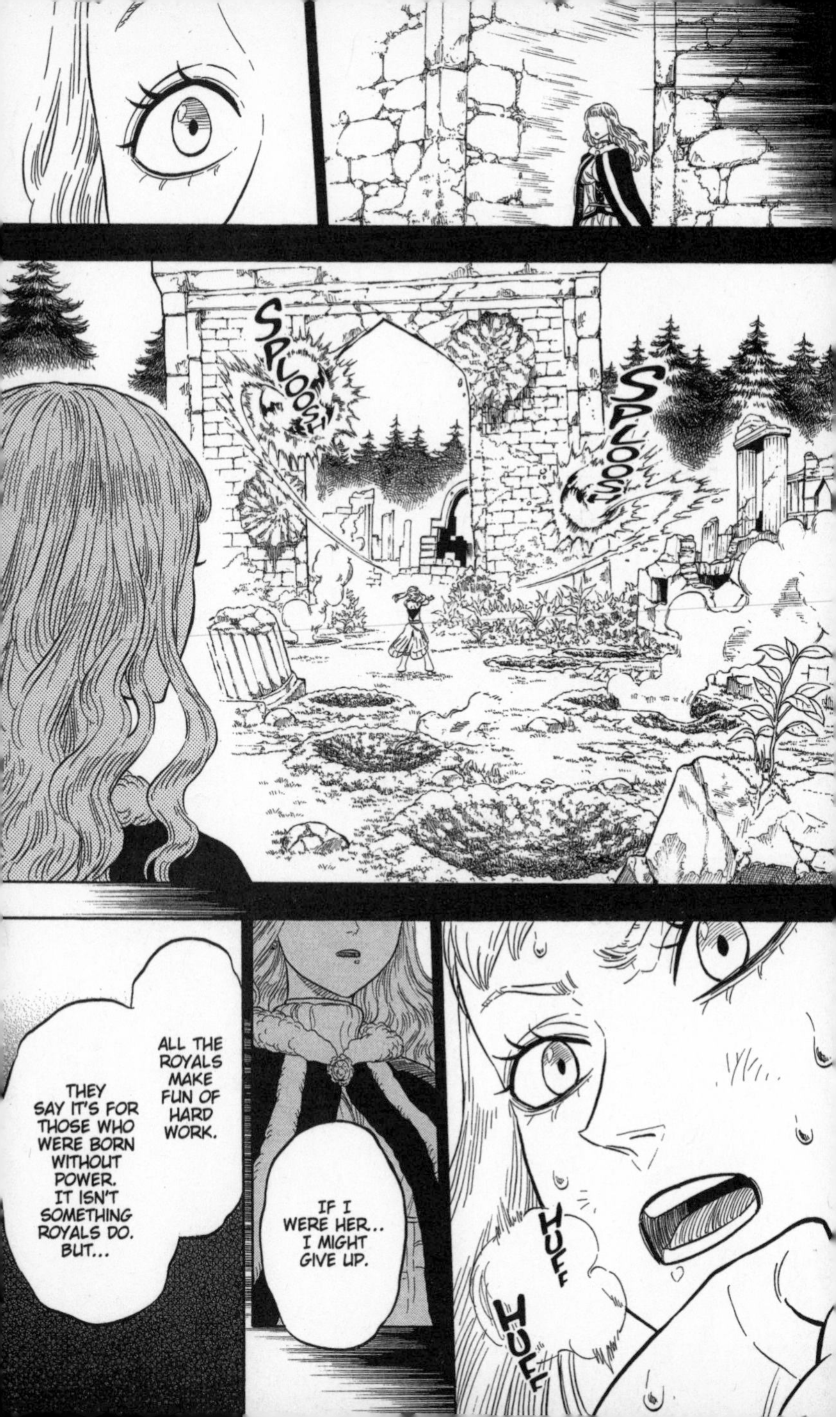
SPLOOSH
SPLOOSH
HUFF
HUFF
IF I WERE HER... I MIGHT GIVE UP.
ALL THE ROYALS MAKE FUN OF HARD WORK.
THEY SAY IT'S FOR THOSE WHO WERE BORN WITHOUT POWER. IT ISN'T SOMETHING ROYALS DO. BUT...

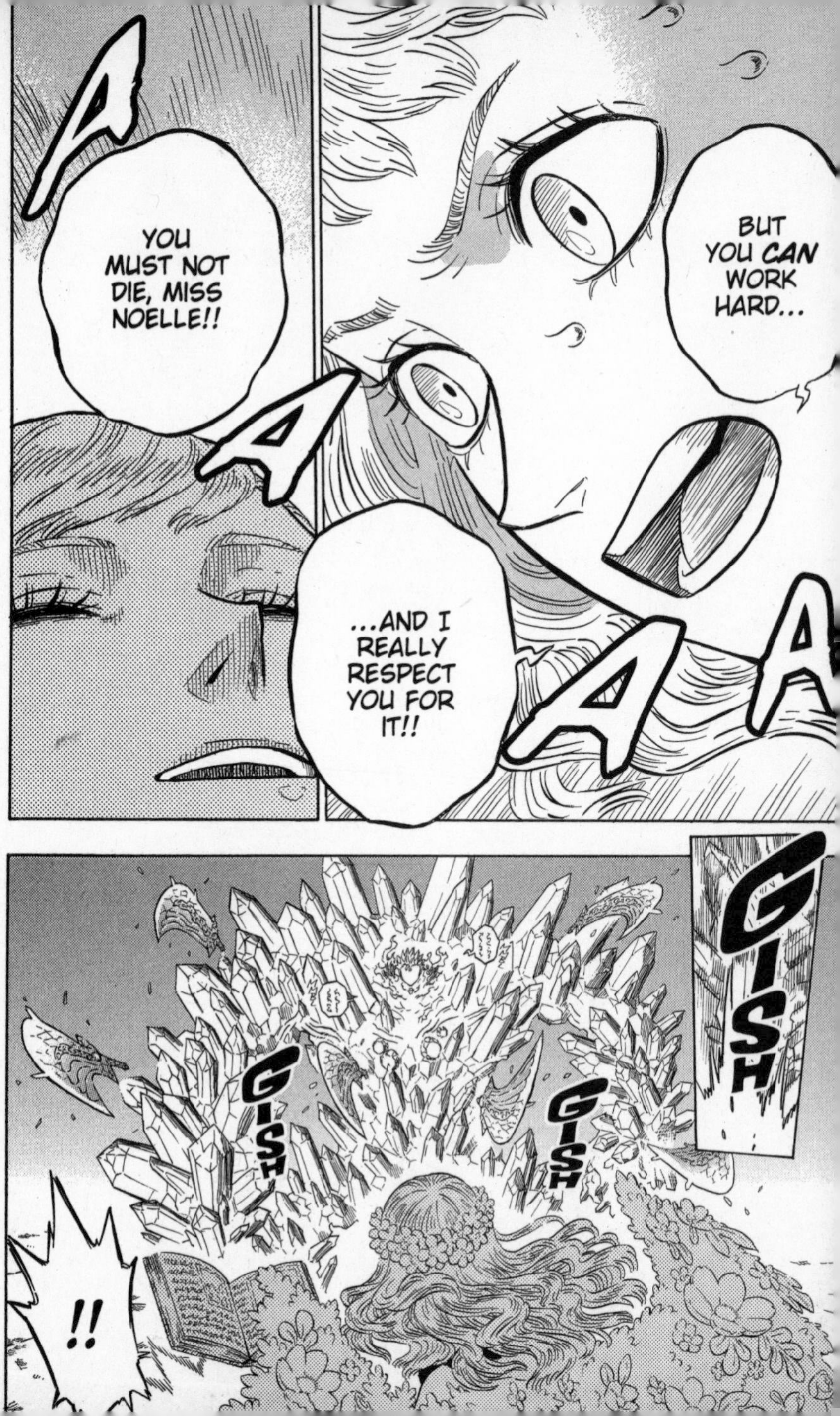
BUT YOU CAN WORK HARD...
...AND I REALLY RESPECT YOU FOR IT!!
YOU MUST NOT DIE, MISS NOELLE!!
AAAA
GISH
GISH
GISH
!!

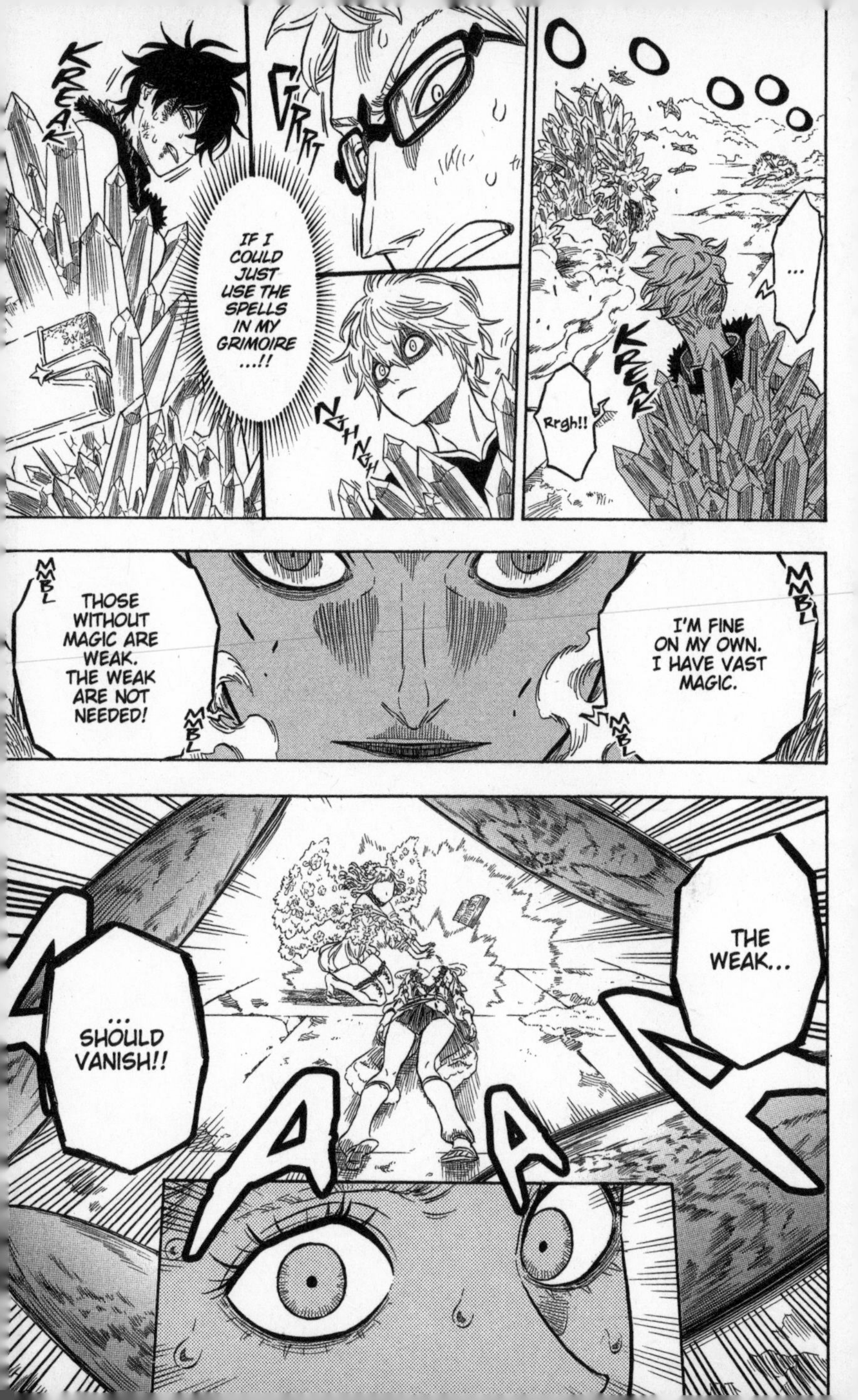
OOOOOO
...
KREAK
Rrgh!!
GRRRT
NGH NGH
KREAK
IF I COULD JUST USE THE SPELLS IN MY GRIMOIRE ...!!
MMBL
I'M FINE ON MY OWN. I HAVE VAST MAGIC.
MMBL
MMBL
THOSE WITHOUT MAGIC ARE WEAK. THE WEAK ARE NOT NEEDED!
MMBL
THE WEAK...
... SHOULD VANISH!!
AAA

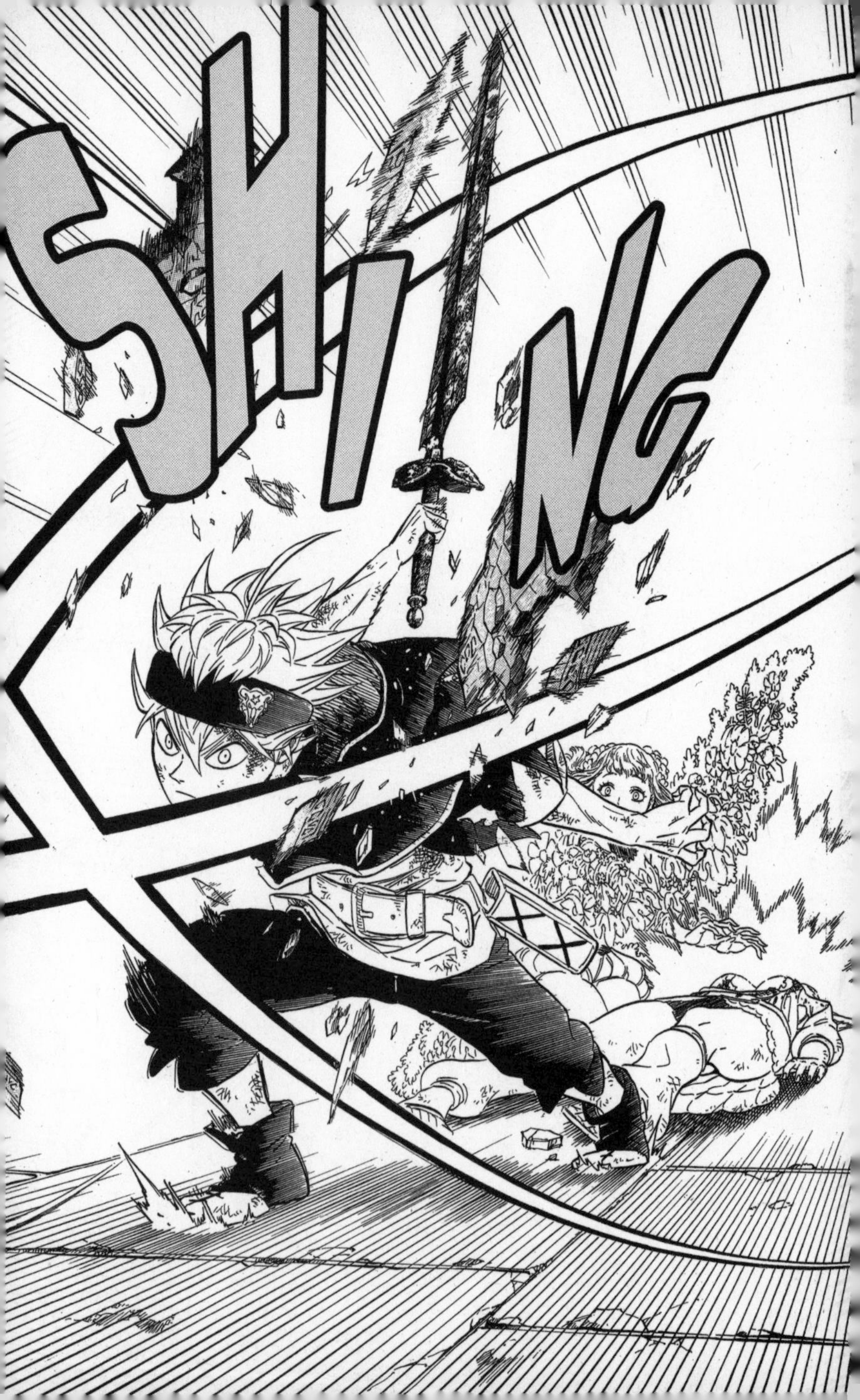
SHIING

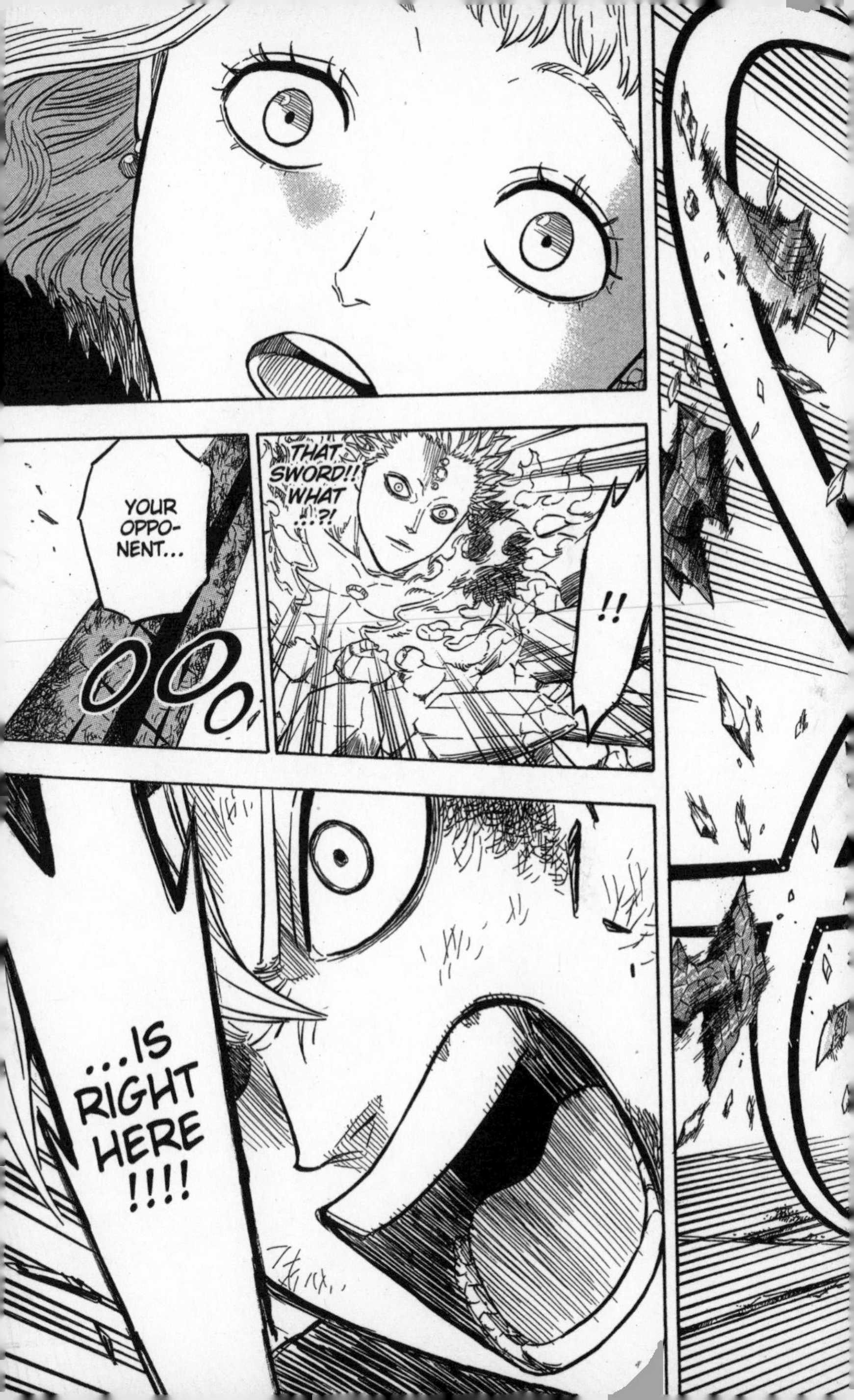
!!
THAT SWORD!! WHAT ...?!
YOUR OPPO-NENT...
...IS RIGHT HERE!!!!

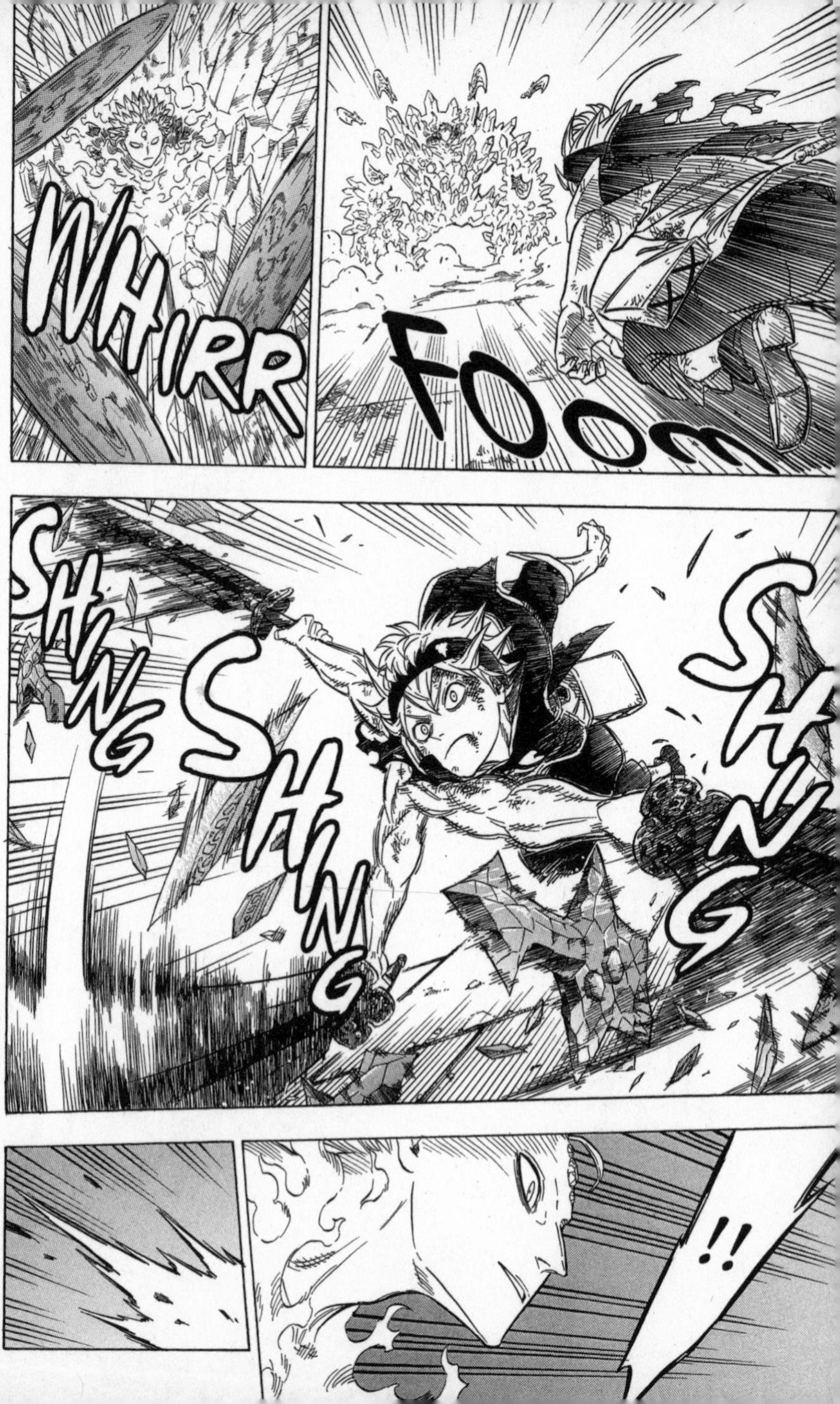
FOOOM
WHIRR
SHING
SHING
SHING
!!

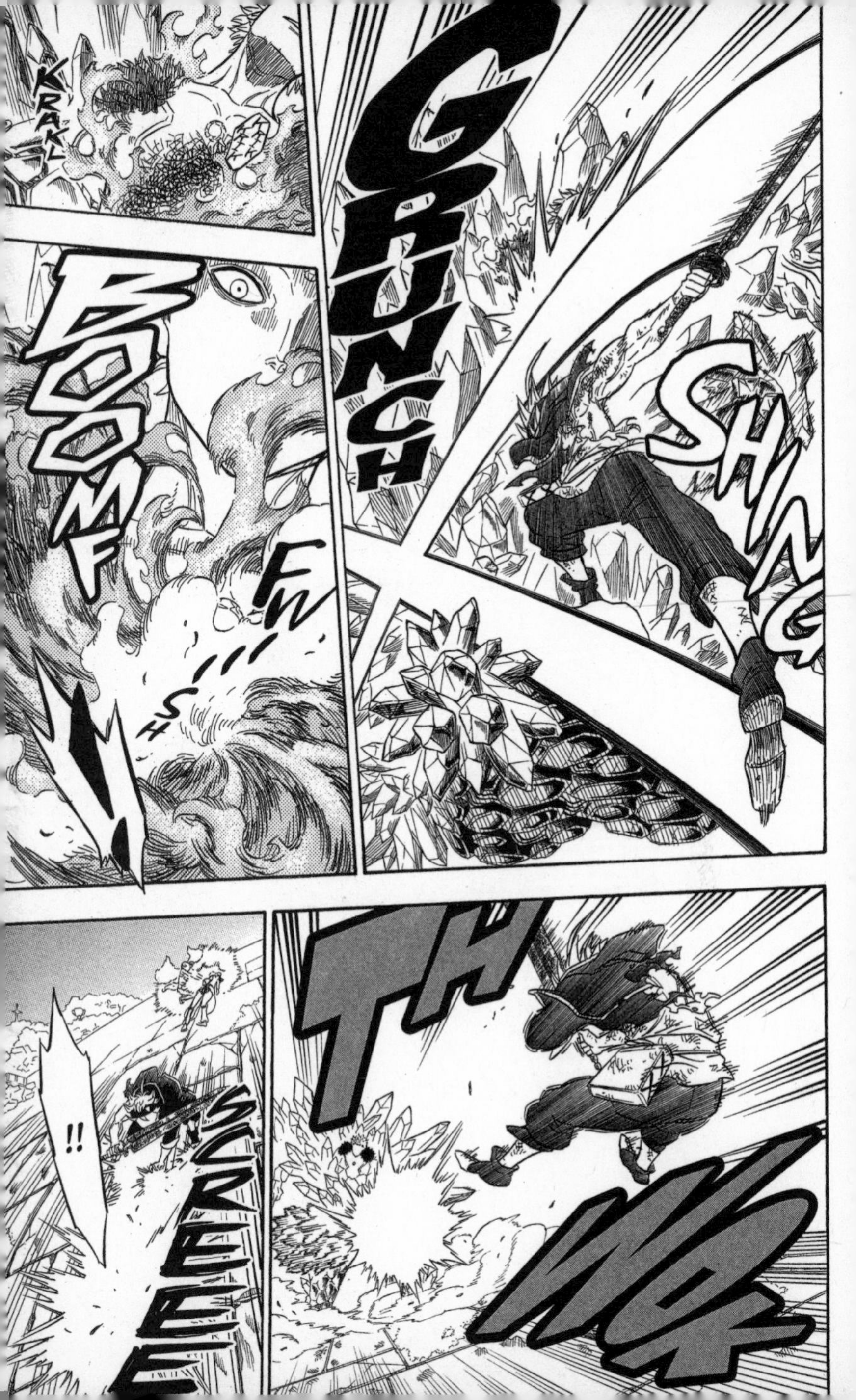
KRAKL
GBUNCH
SHING
BOOMF
FWSH
!!
SCREEEE
THWAK

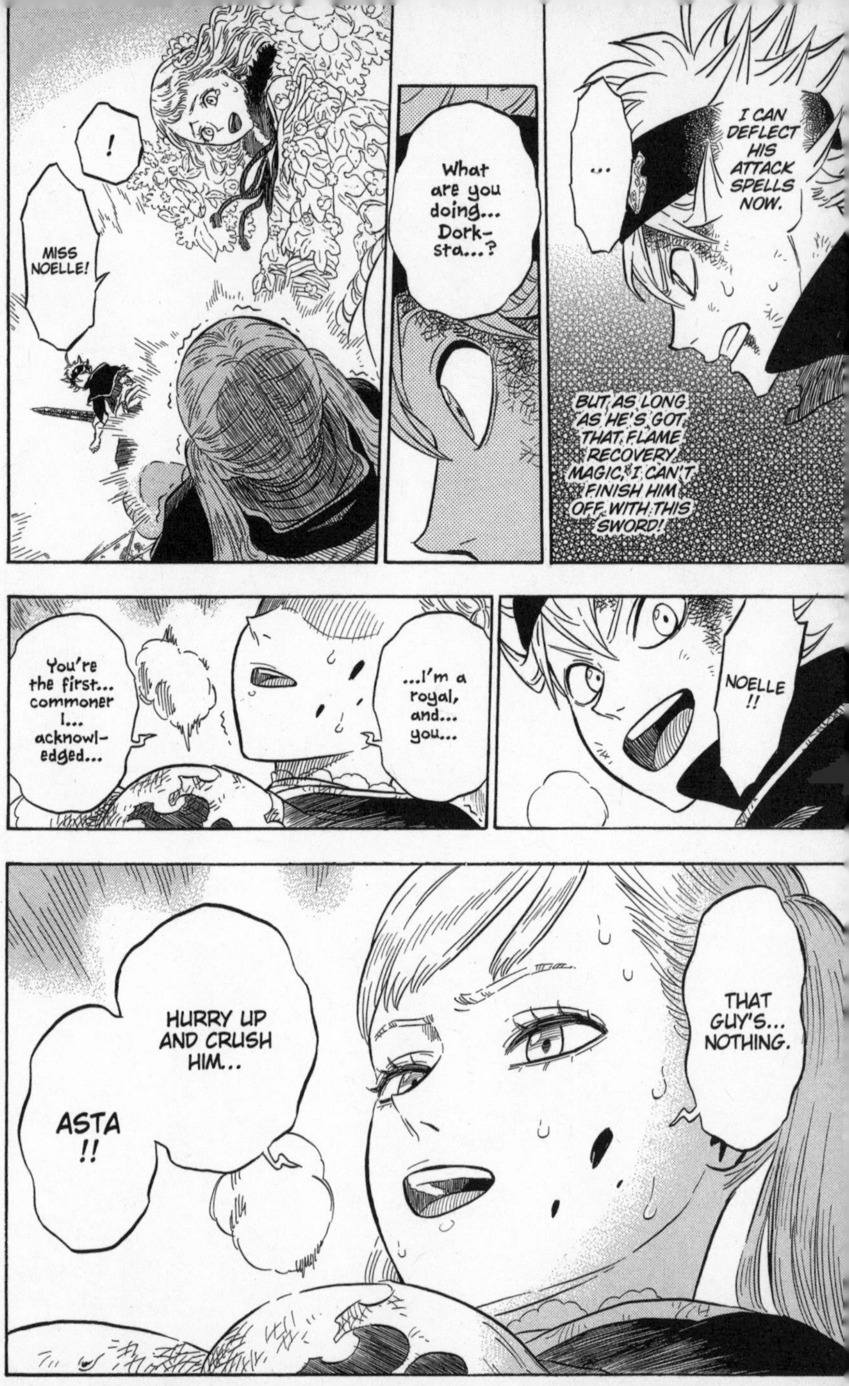
...
I CAN DEFLECT HIS ATTACK SPELLS NOW.
BUT AS LONG AS HE'S GOT THAT FLAME RECOVERY MAGIC, I CAN'T FINISH HIM OFF WITH THIS SWORD!
What are you doing... Dork-sta...?
!
MISS NOELLE!
NOELLE !!
...I'm a royal, and... you...
You're the first... commoner I... acknowledged...
THAT GUY'S... NOTHING.
HURRY UP AND CRUSH HIM...
ASTA !!

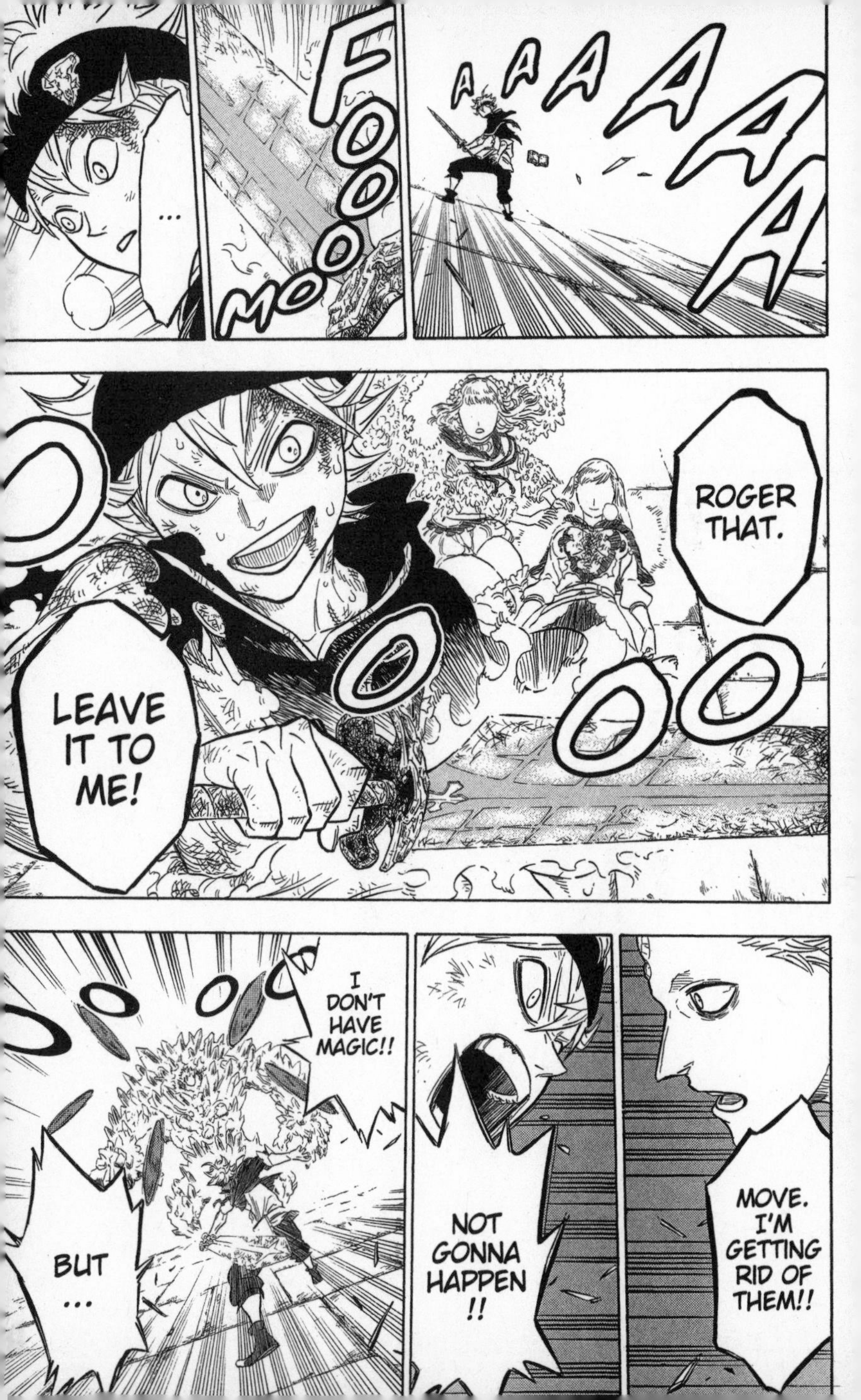

AAAAAAAA
FOOOOOM
...
ROGER THAT.
LEAVE IT TO ME!
OOOOO
MOVE. I'M GETTING RID OF THEM!!
NOT GONNA HAPPEN!!
I DON'T HAVE MAGIC!!
BUT...

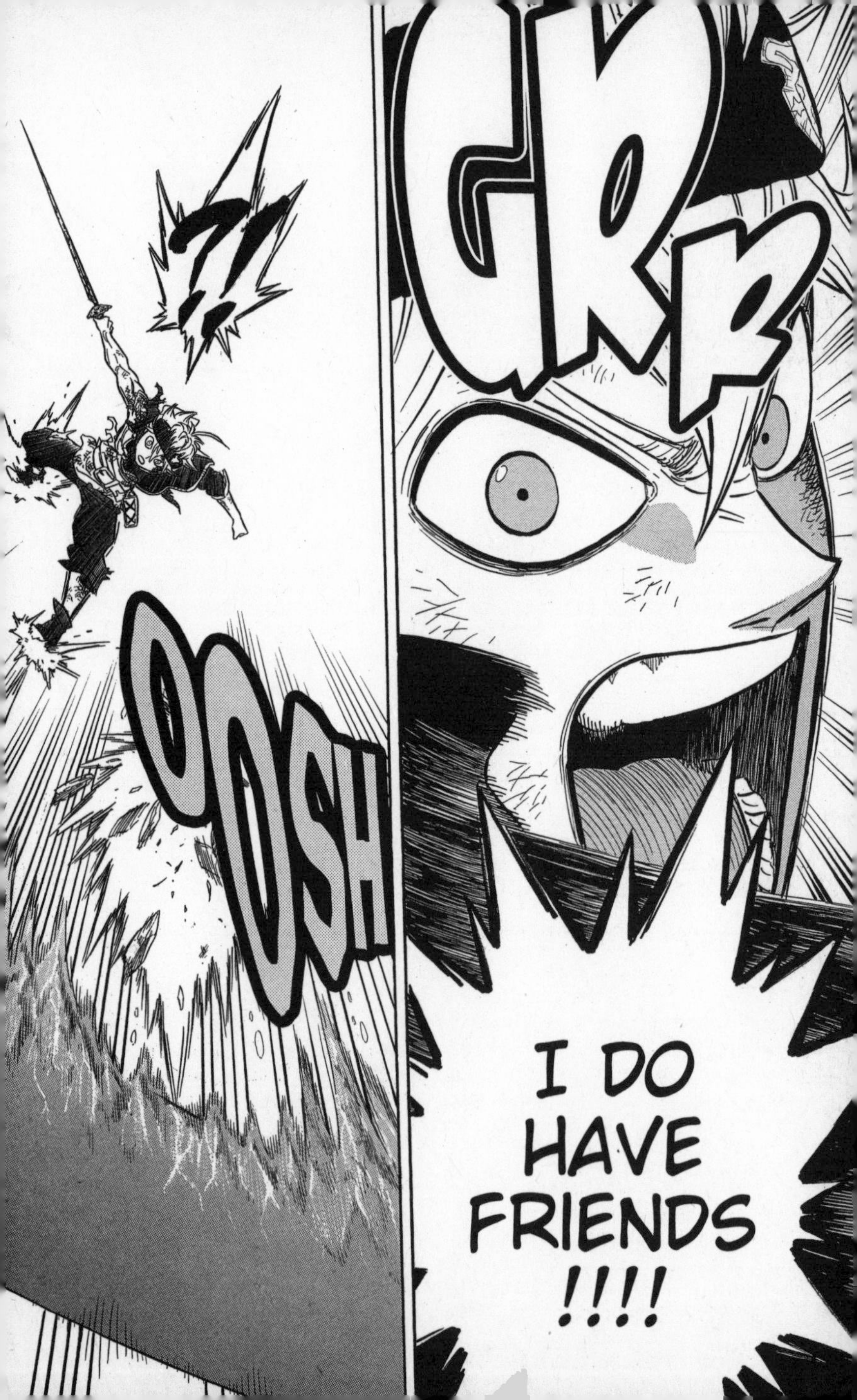
I DO HAVE FRIENDS !!!!
?!
OOSH

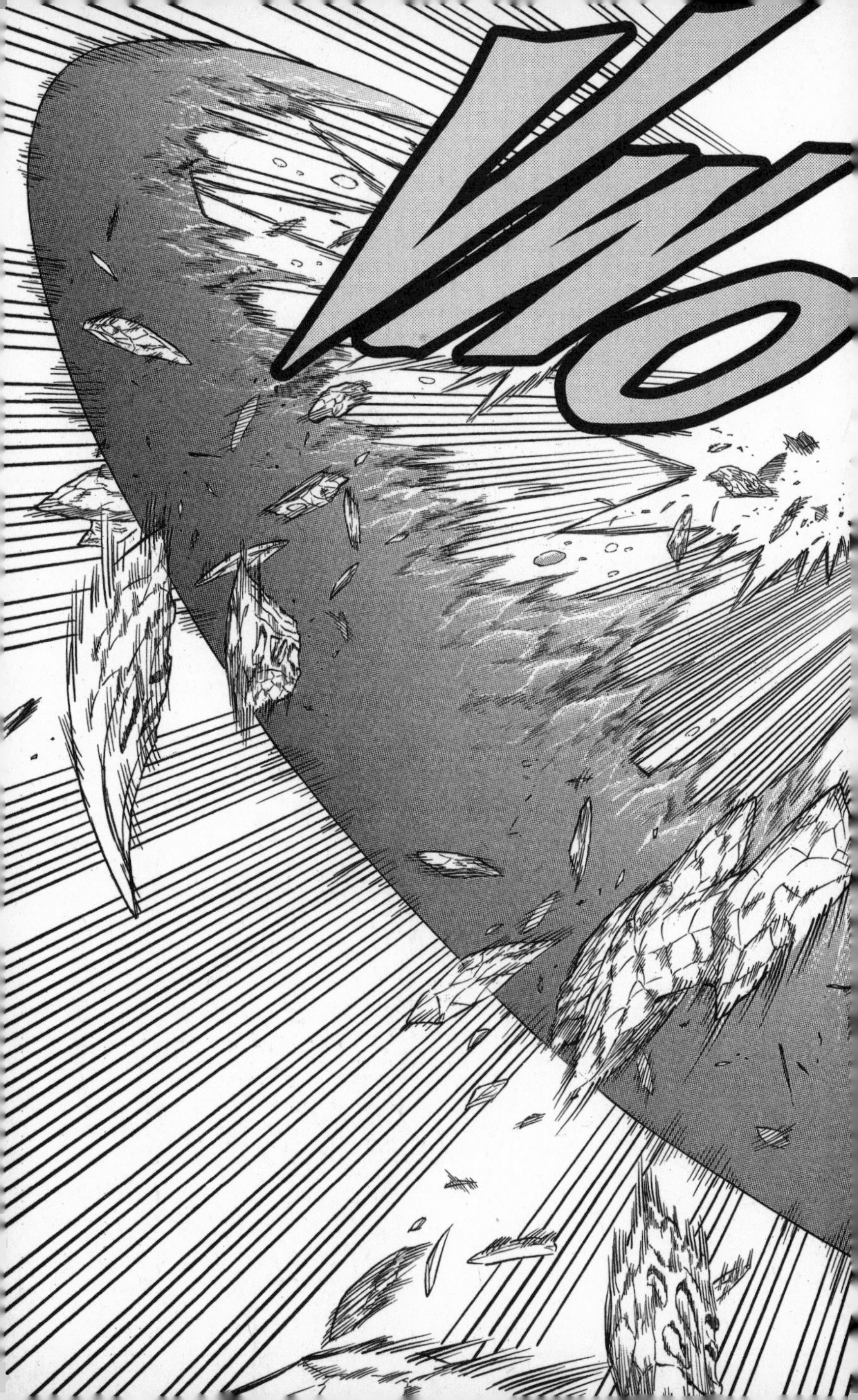

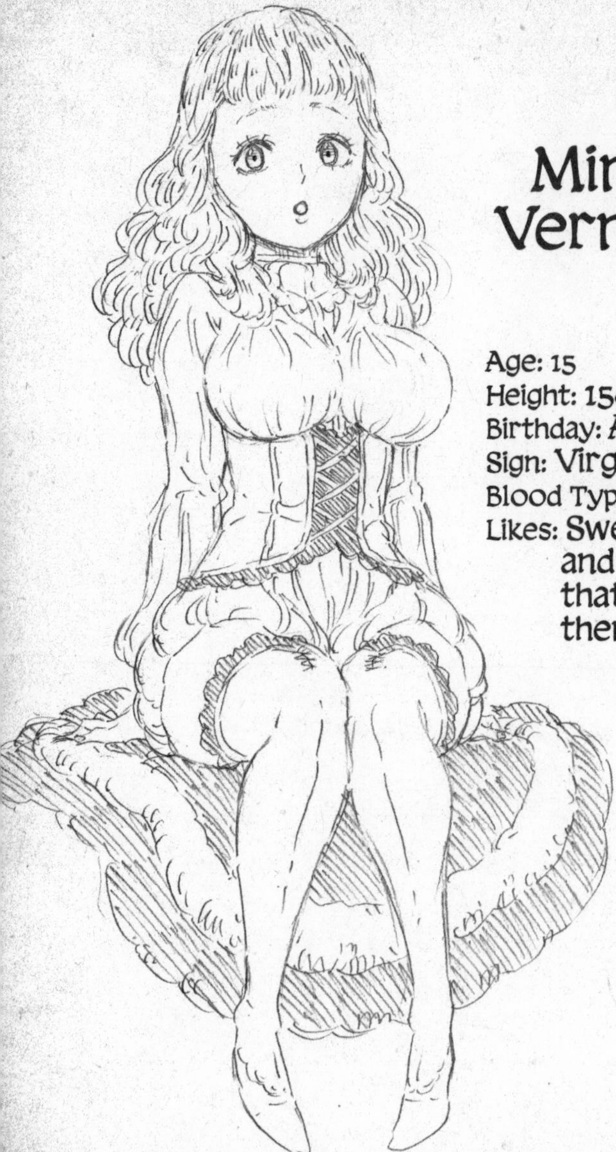

Mimosa Vermillion

Age: 15
Height: 158 cm
Birthday: August 26
Sign: Virgo
Blood Type: O
Likes: Sweets, and black teas that complement them

Character Profile

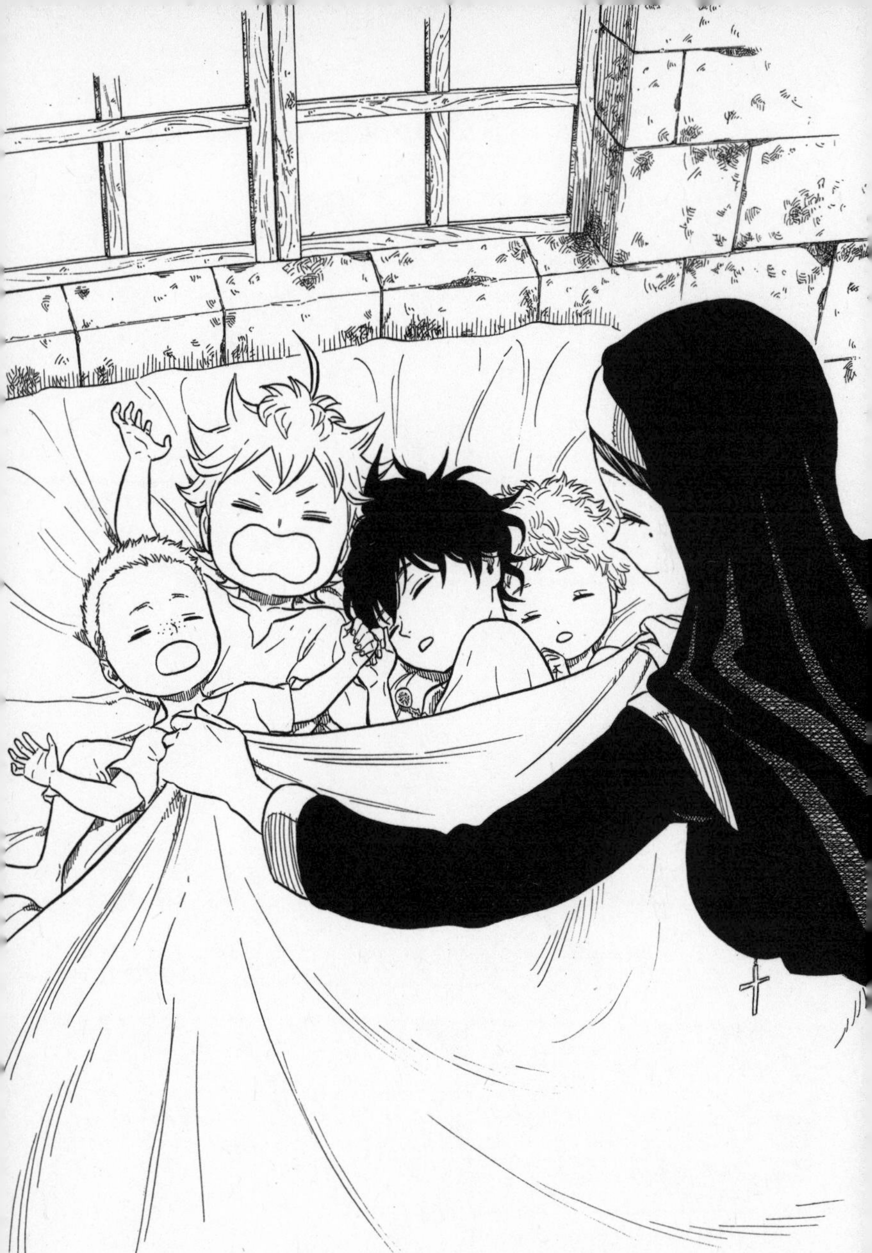

Page 20: One Instant

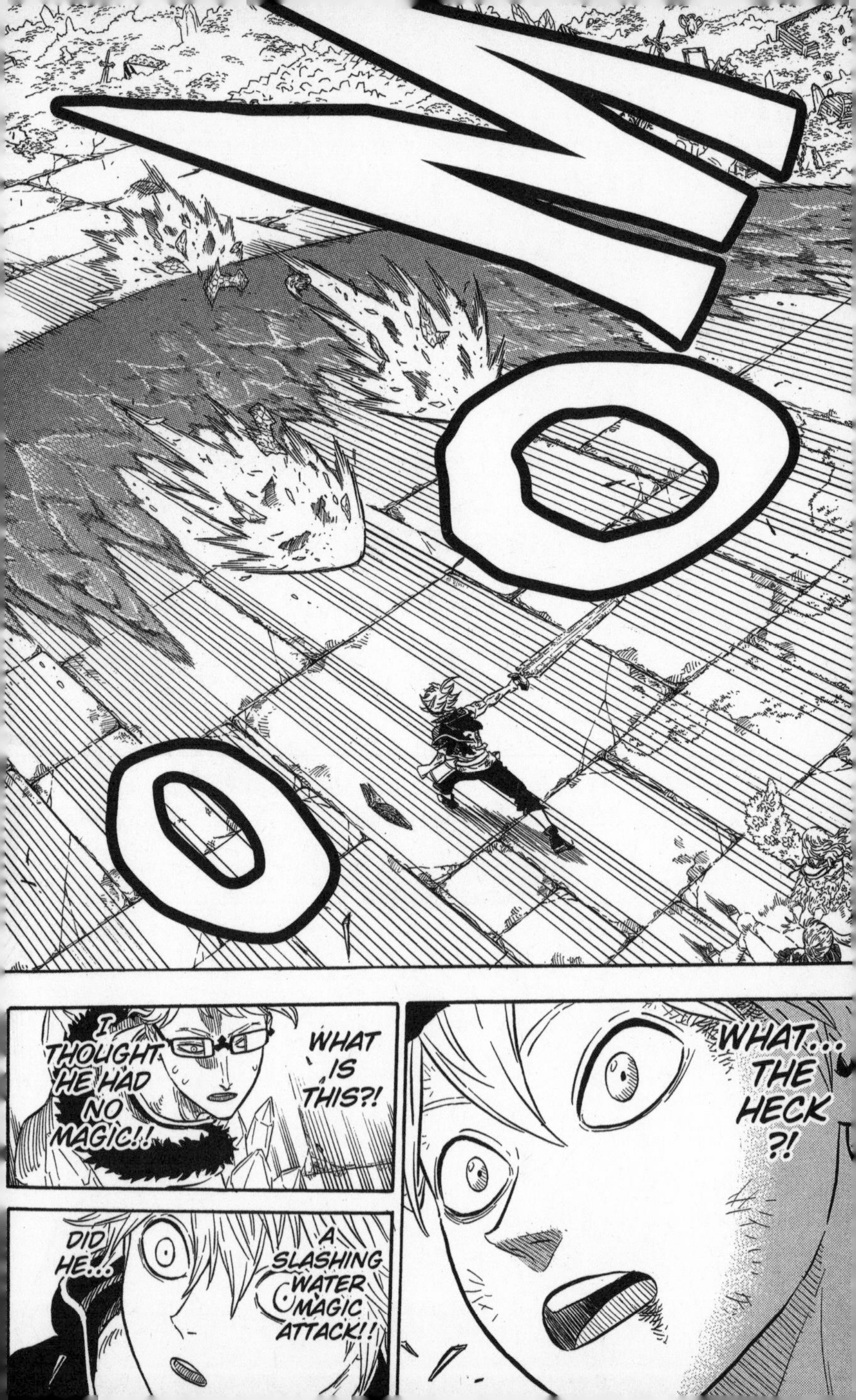
WHAT... THE HECK?!
WHAT IS THIS?!
I THOUGHT HE HAD NO MAGIC!!
A SLASHING WATER MAGIC ATTACK!!
DID HE...

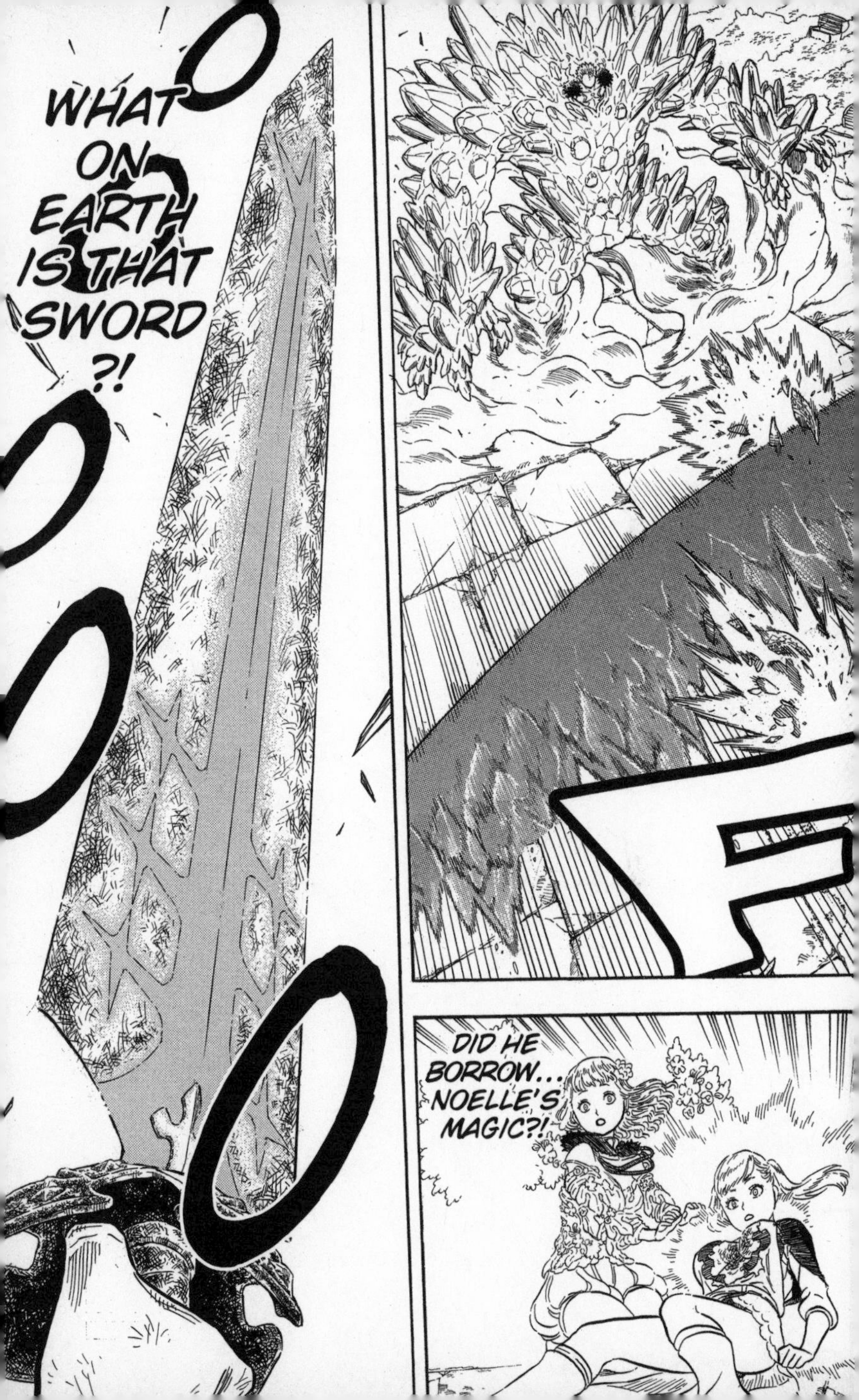
DID HE BORROW... NOELLE'S MAGIC?!
WHAT ON EARTH IS THAT SWORD ?!

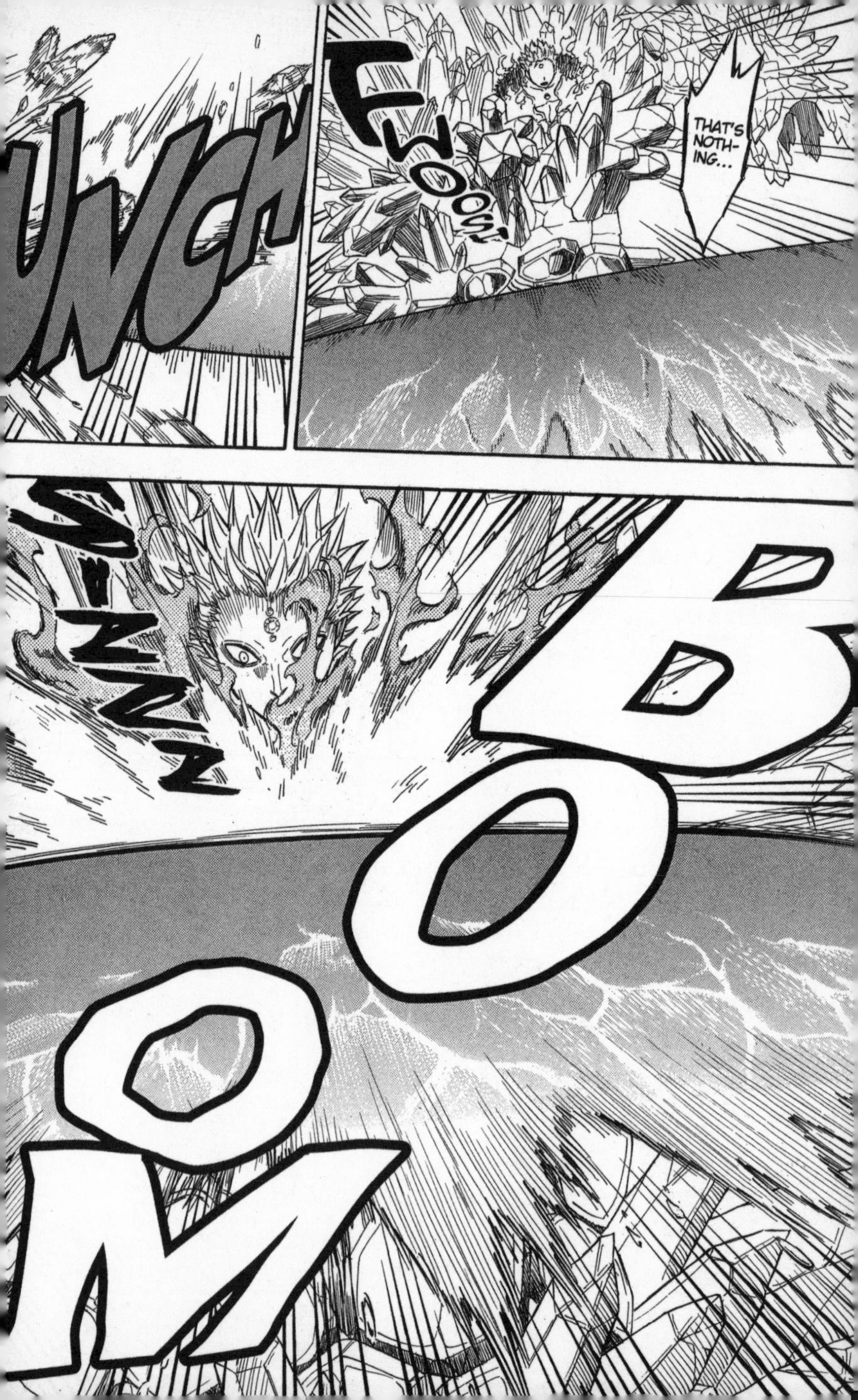
FWOOSH!
THAT'S NOTH-ING...
UNCH
BOOM

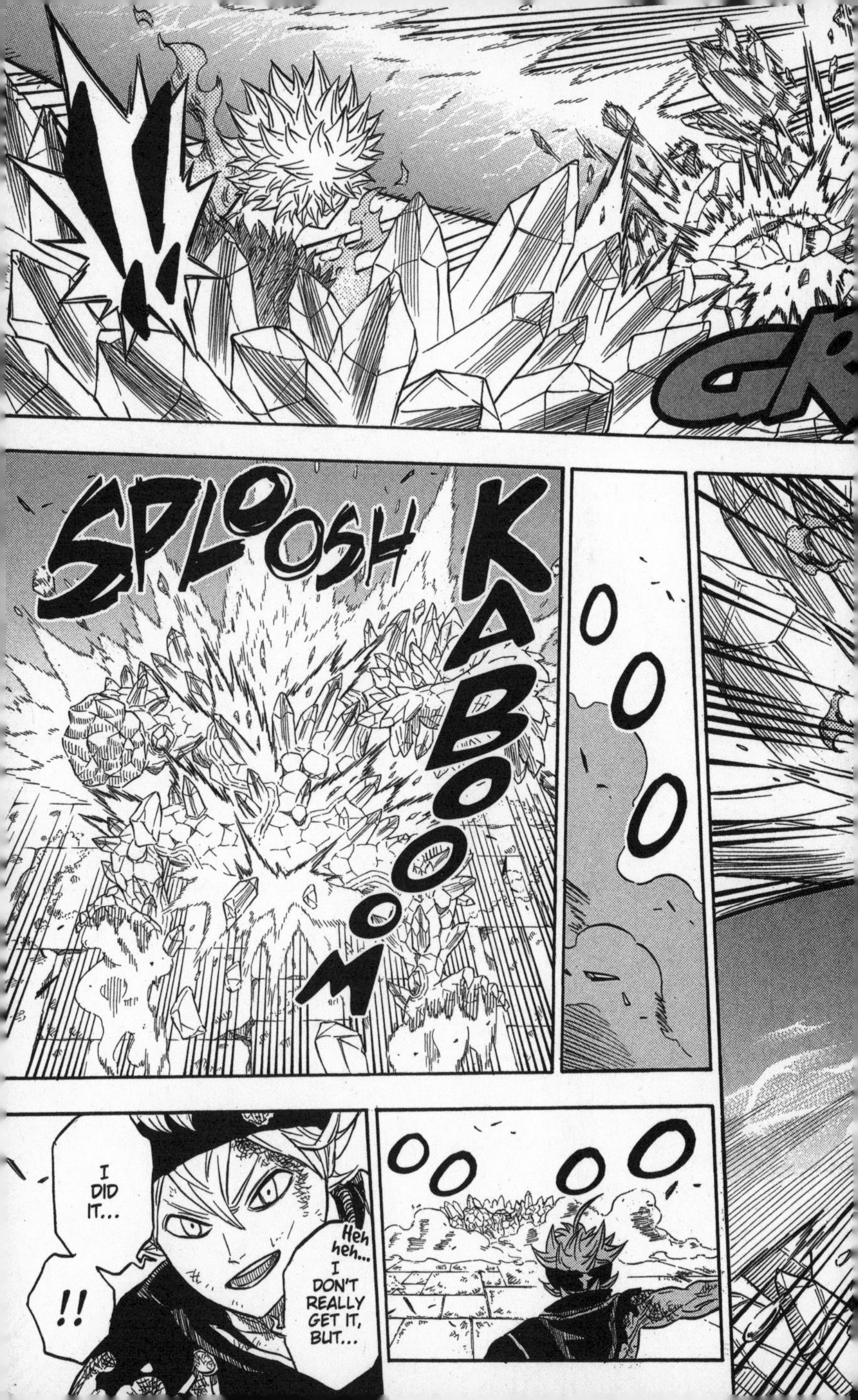

!
CR
OOOO
SPLOOSH
KABOOOOM
OOOOO
Heh heh... I DON'T REALLY GET IT, BUT...
I DID IT...
!!

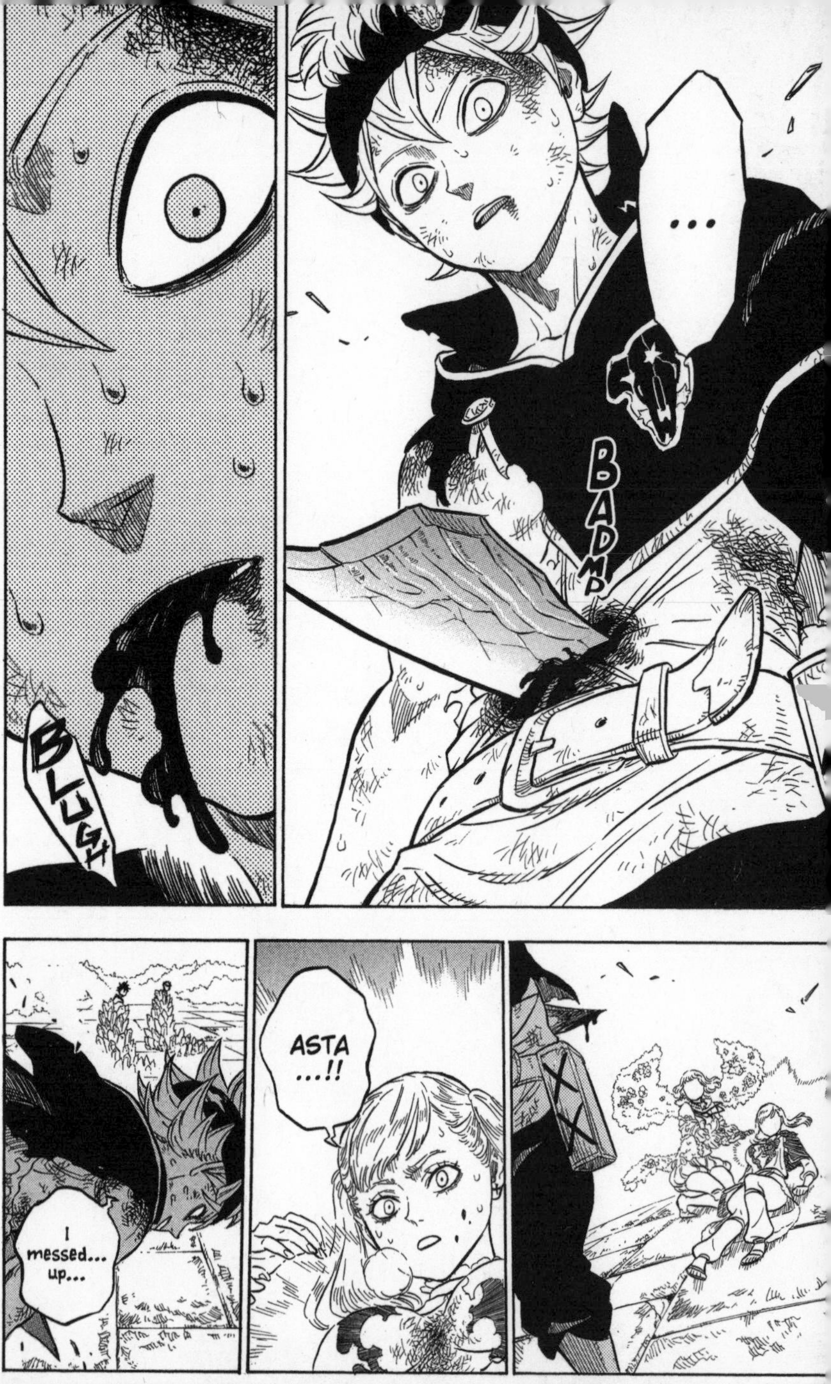
...
BADMP
BLUGH
ASTA ...!!
I messed... up...

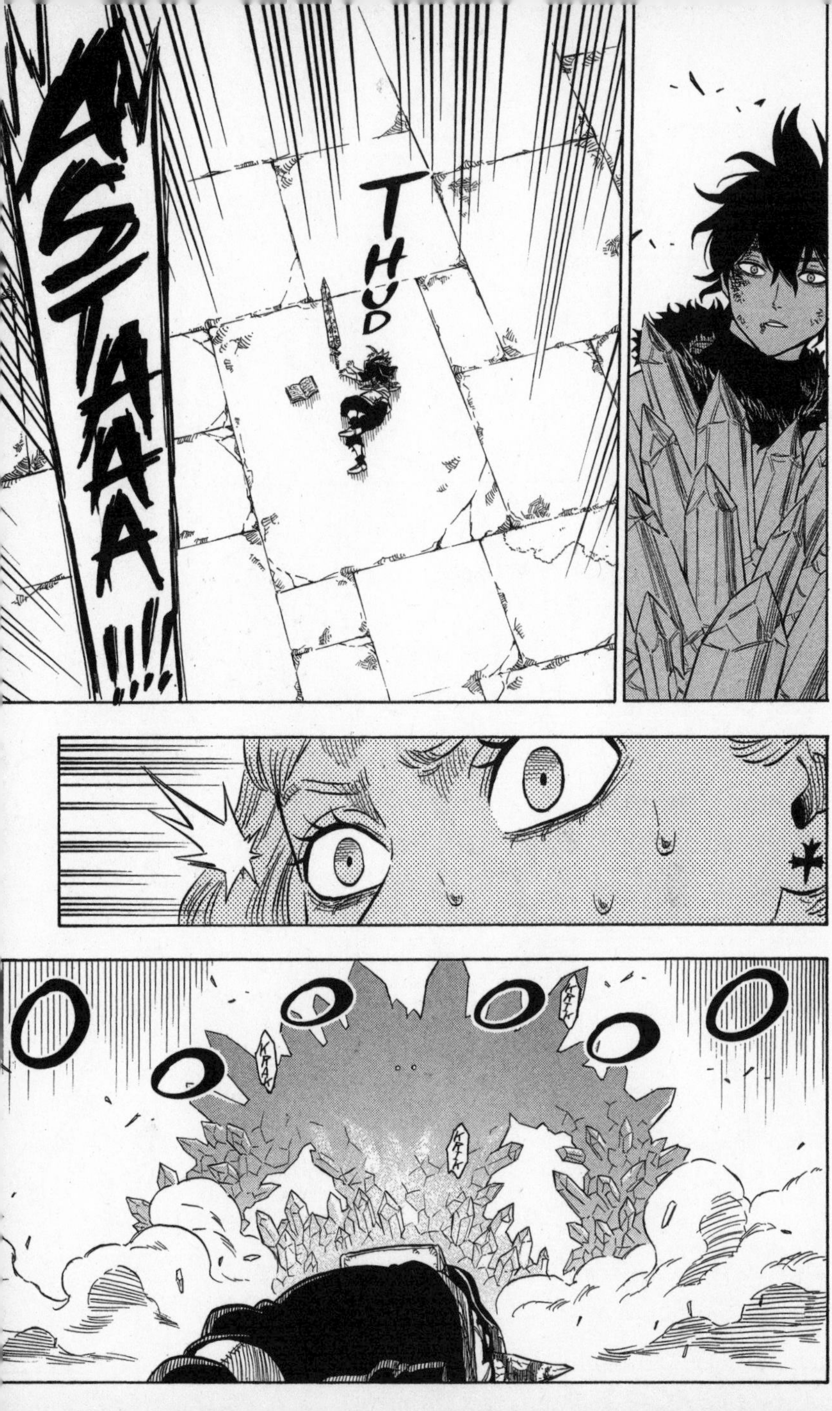
ASTAAA!!!!
THUD
OOOOOOO
KRAK
KRAK
KRAK

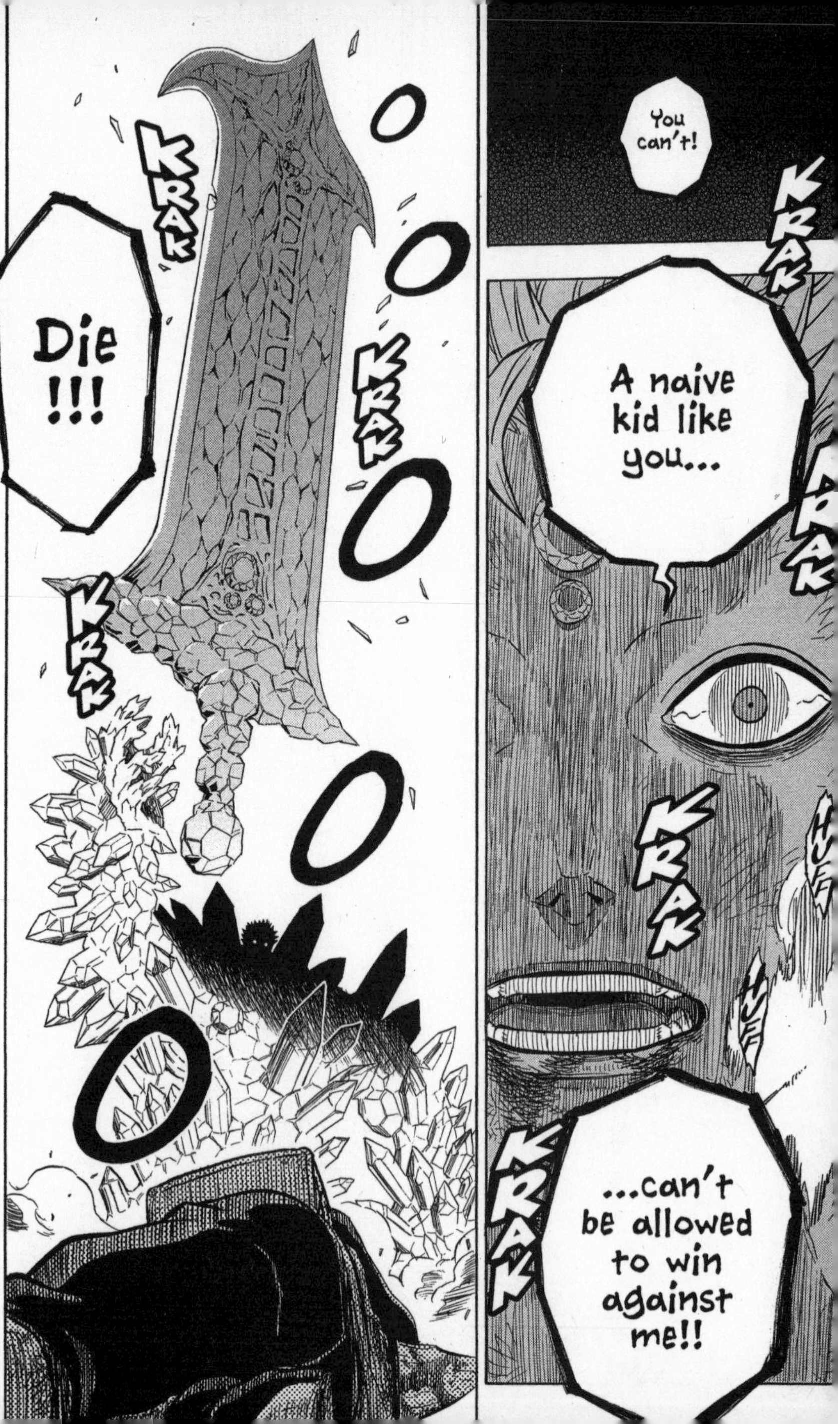
You can't!
KRAK
A naive kid like you...
KRAK
KRAK
HUFF
KRAK
...can't be allowed to win against me!!
KRAK
Die!!!
KRAK
KRAK
OOOOOO

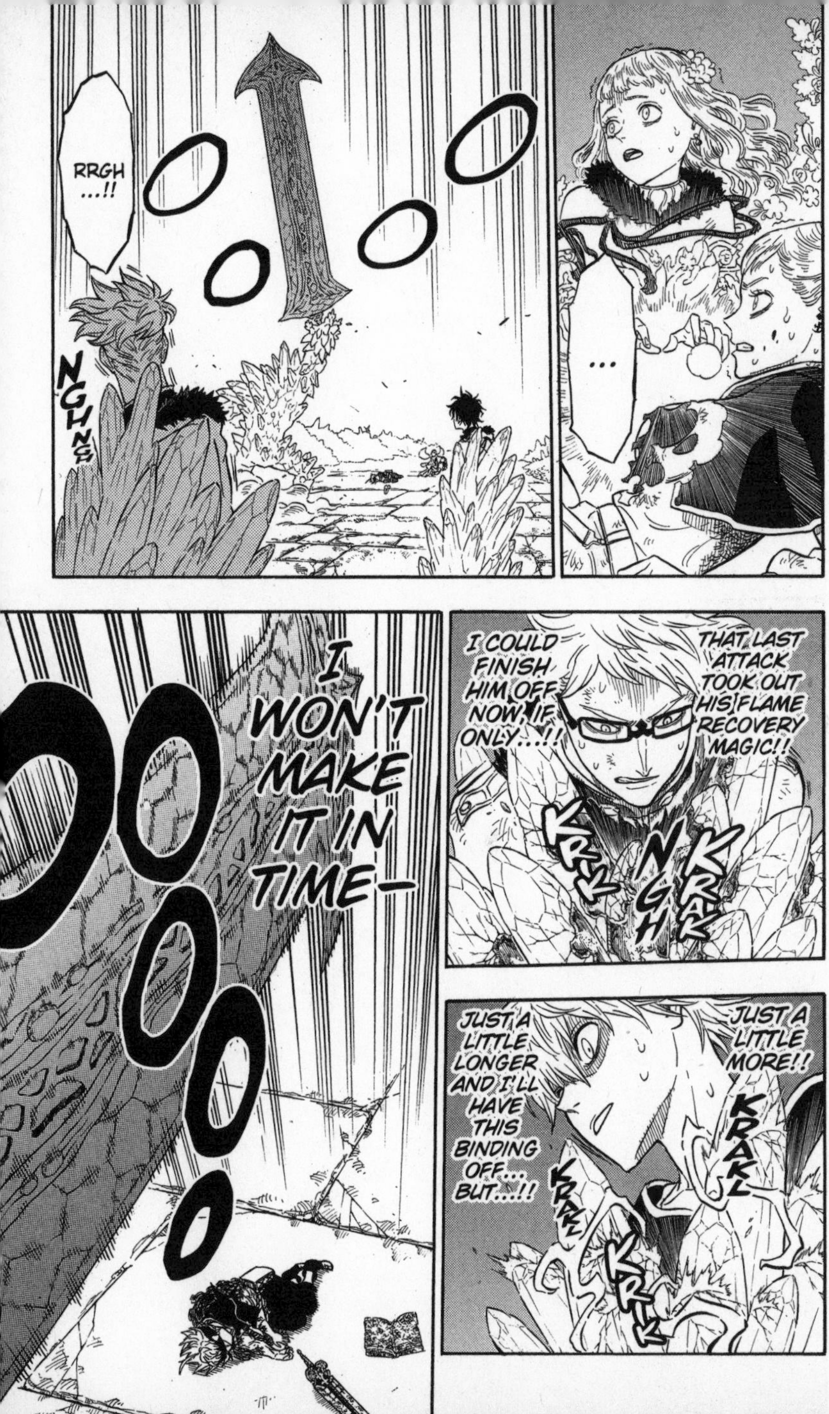
...
RRGH ...!!
NGHNGH
THAT LAST ATTACK TOOK OUT HIS FLAME RECOVERY MAGIC!!
I COULD FINISH HIM OFF NOW, IF ONLY...!!
KRAK
NGH
KRYK
JUST A LITTLE MORE!!
JUST A LITTLE LONGER AND I'LL HAVE THIS BINDING OFF... BUT...!!
KRAK
KRAK
KRIK
I WON'T MAKE IT IN TIME—

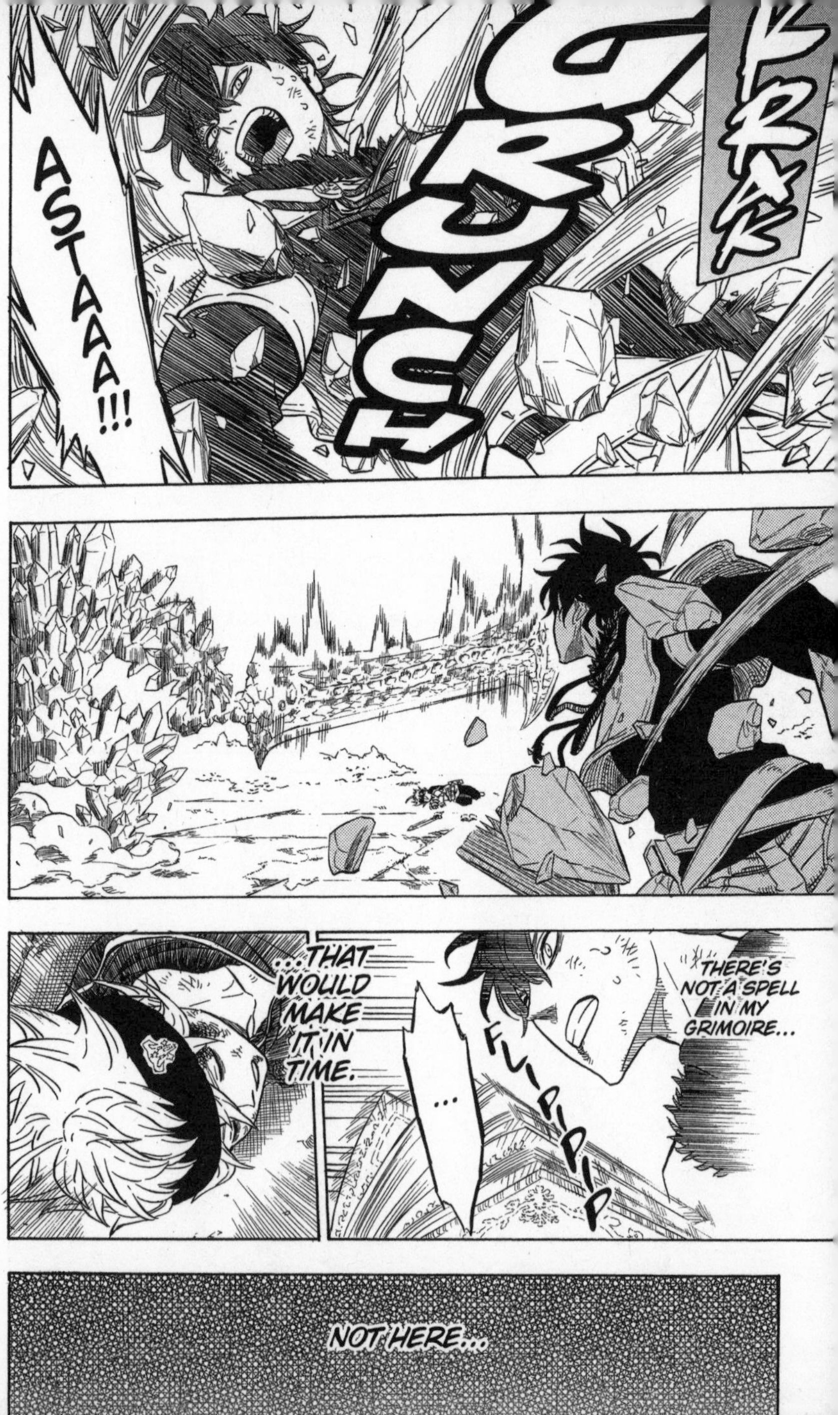
CRUNCH
ASTAAAA!!!
THERE'S NOT A SPELL IN MY GRIMOIRE...
FLIPIPIPIP
...
...THAT WOULD MAKE IT IN TIME.
NOT HERE...

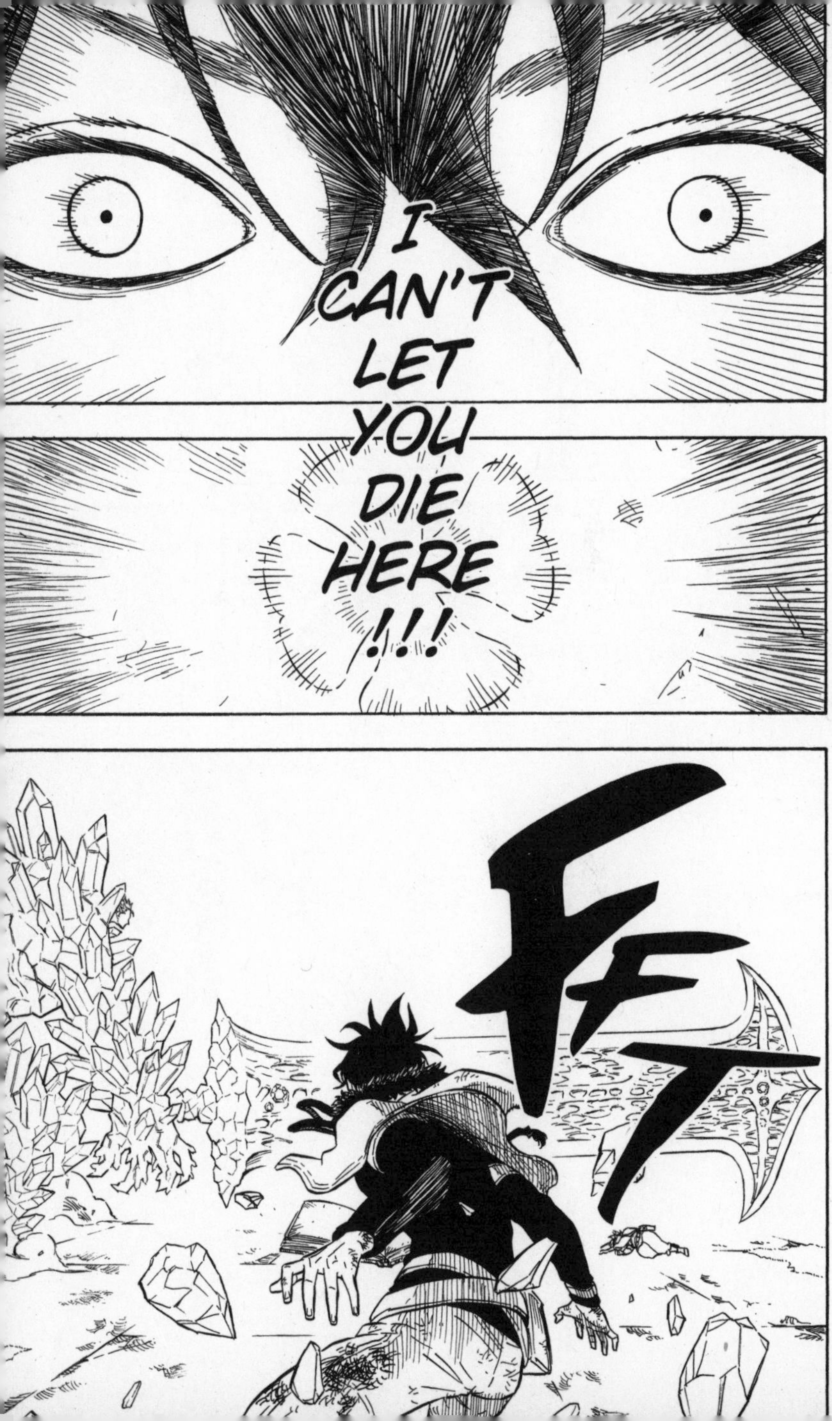
I CAN'T LET YOU DIE HERE!!!
FFT

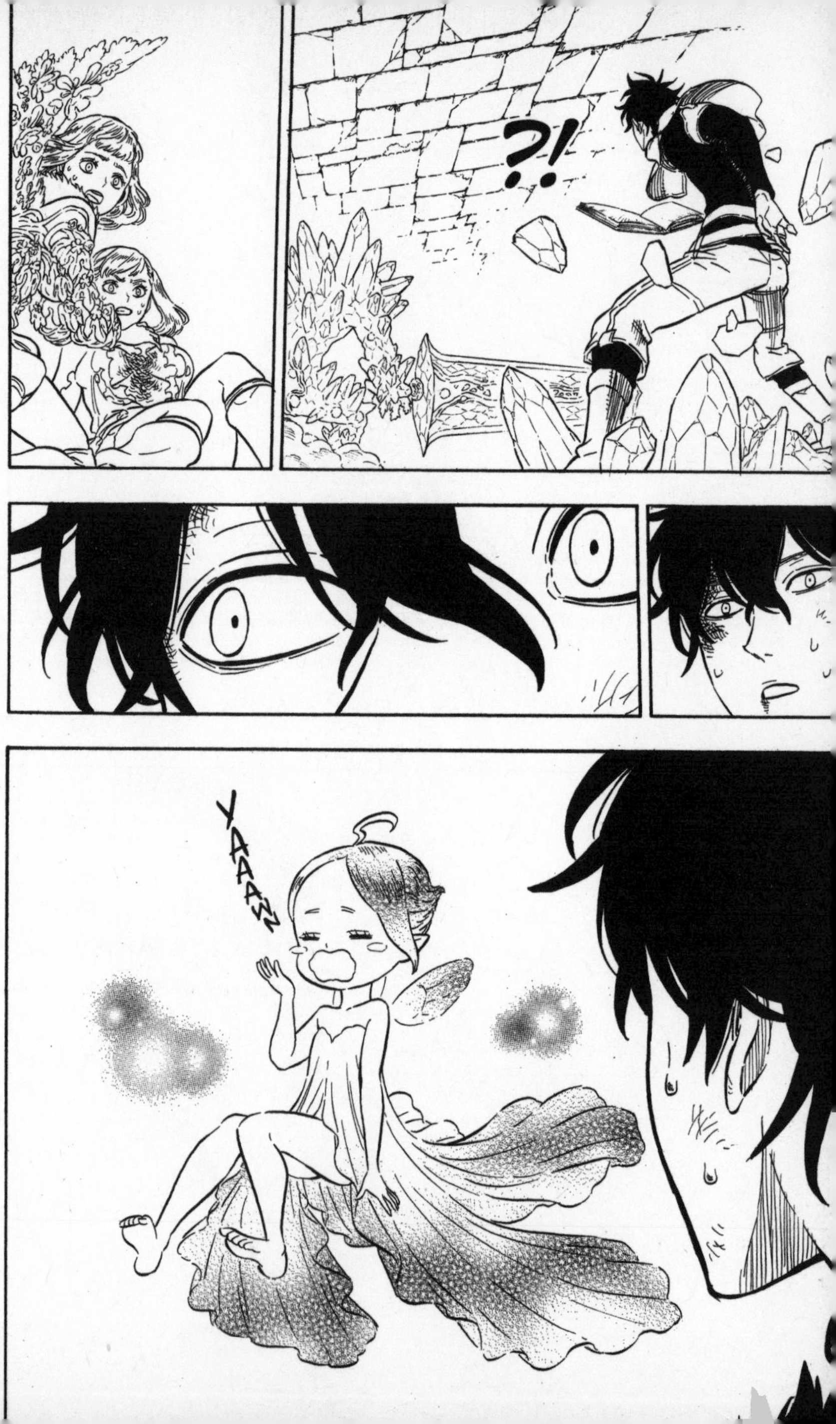
?!
YAAAWN

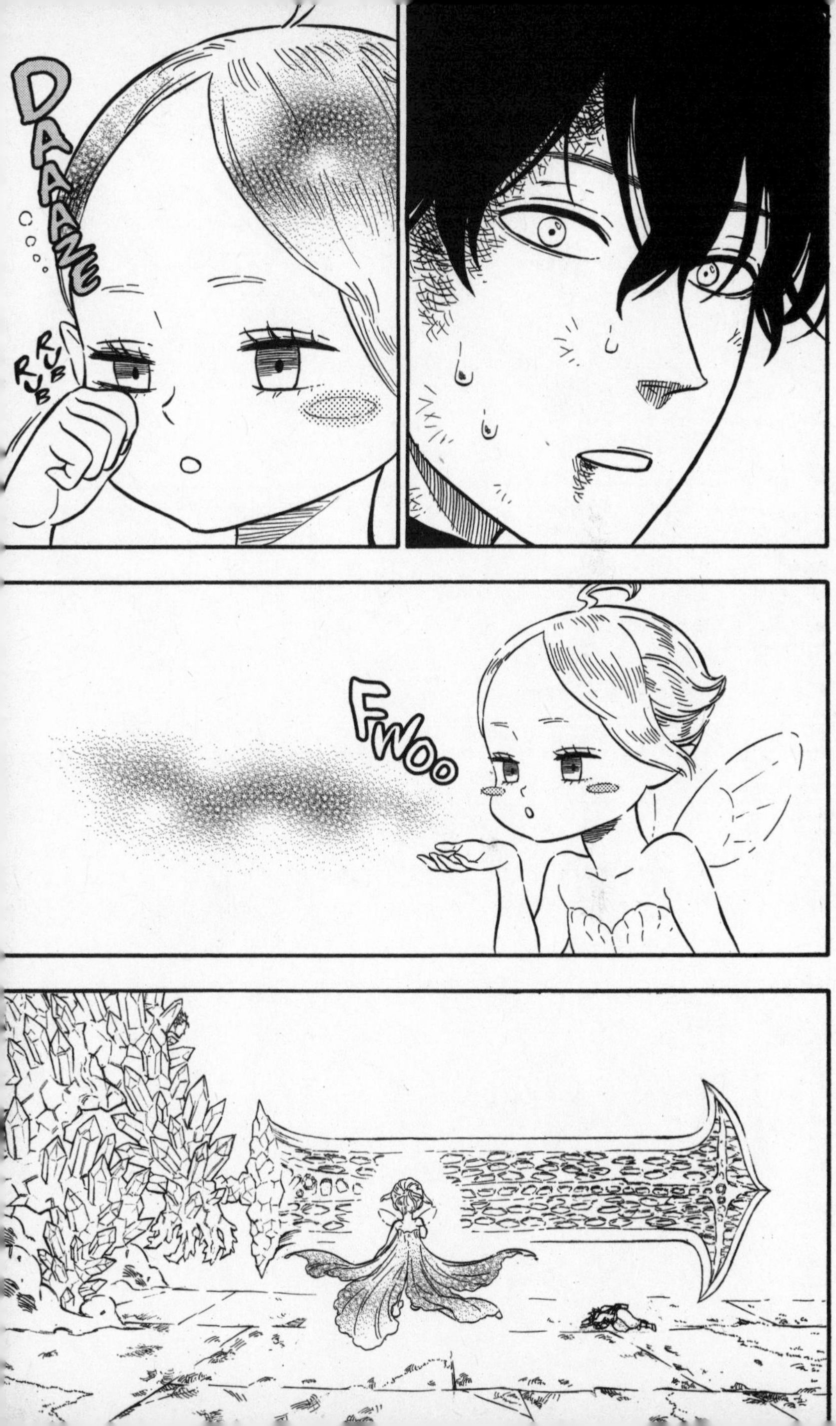
DAAAAZE
RUB RUB
FWOO

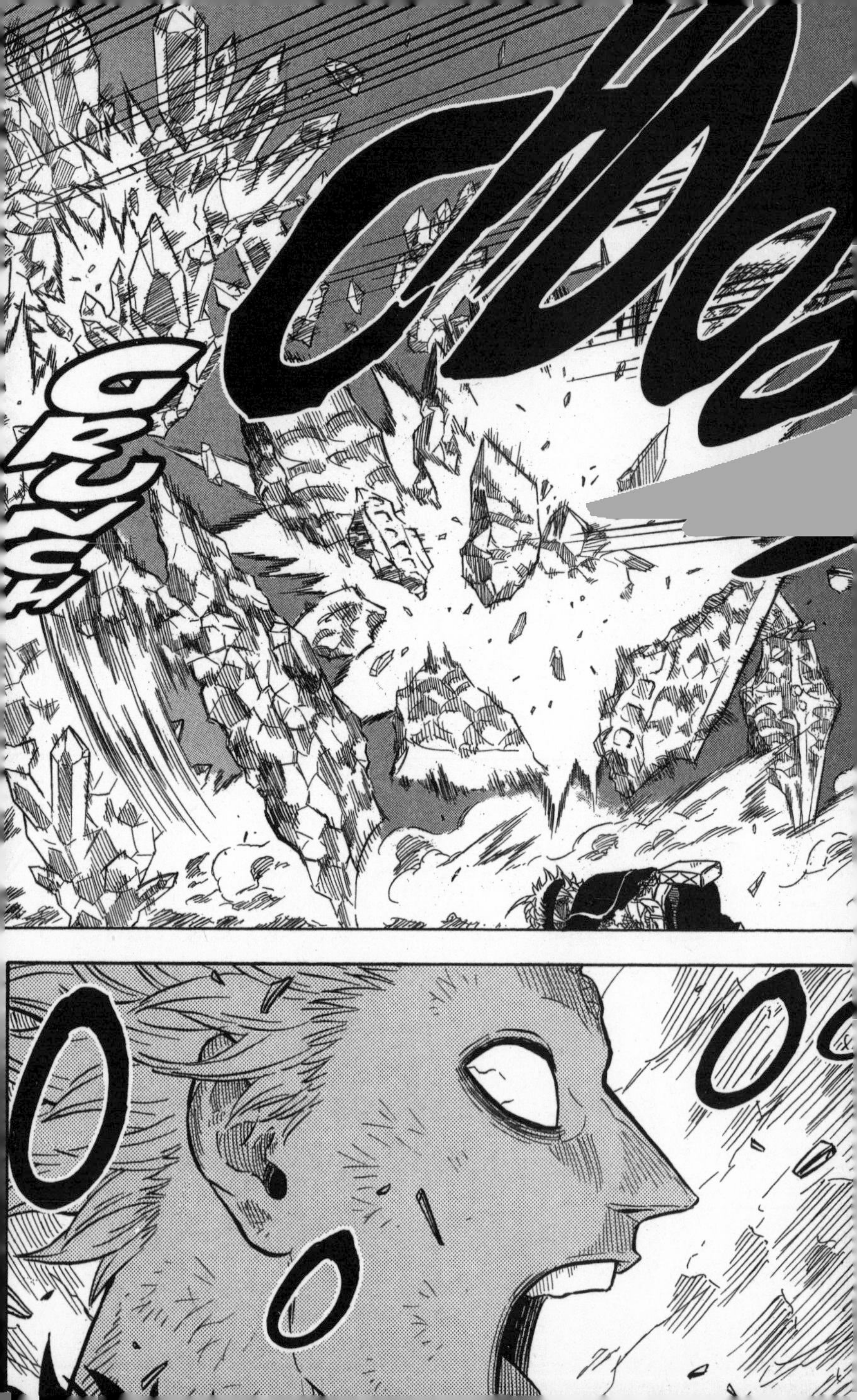
CRUNCH

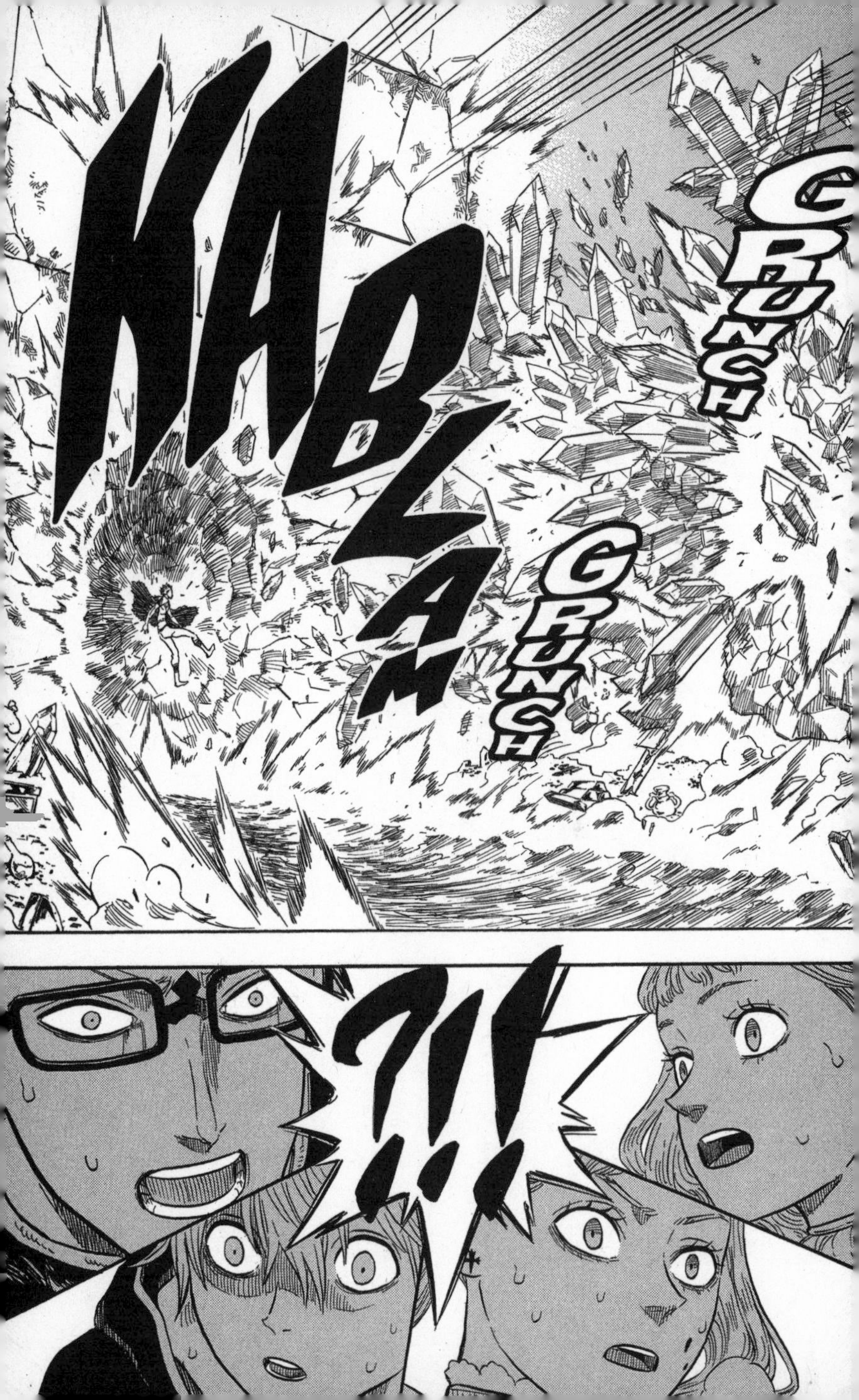
KABLAM
CRUNCH
CRUNCH
?!!
!!!

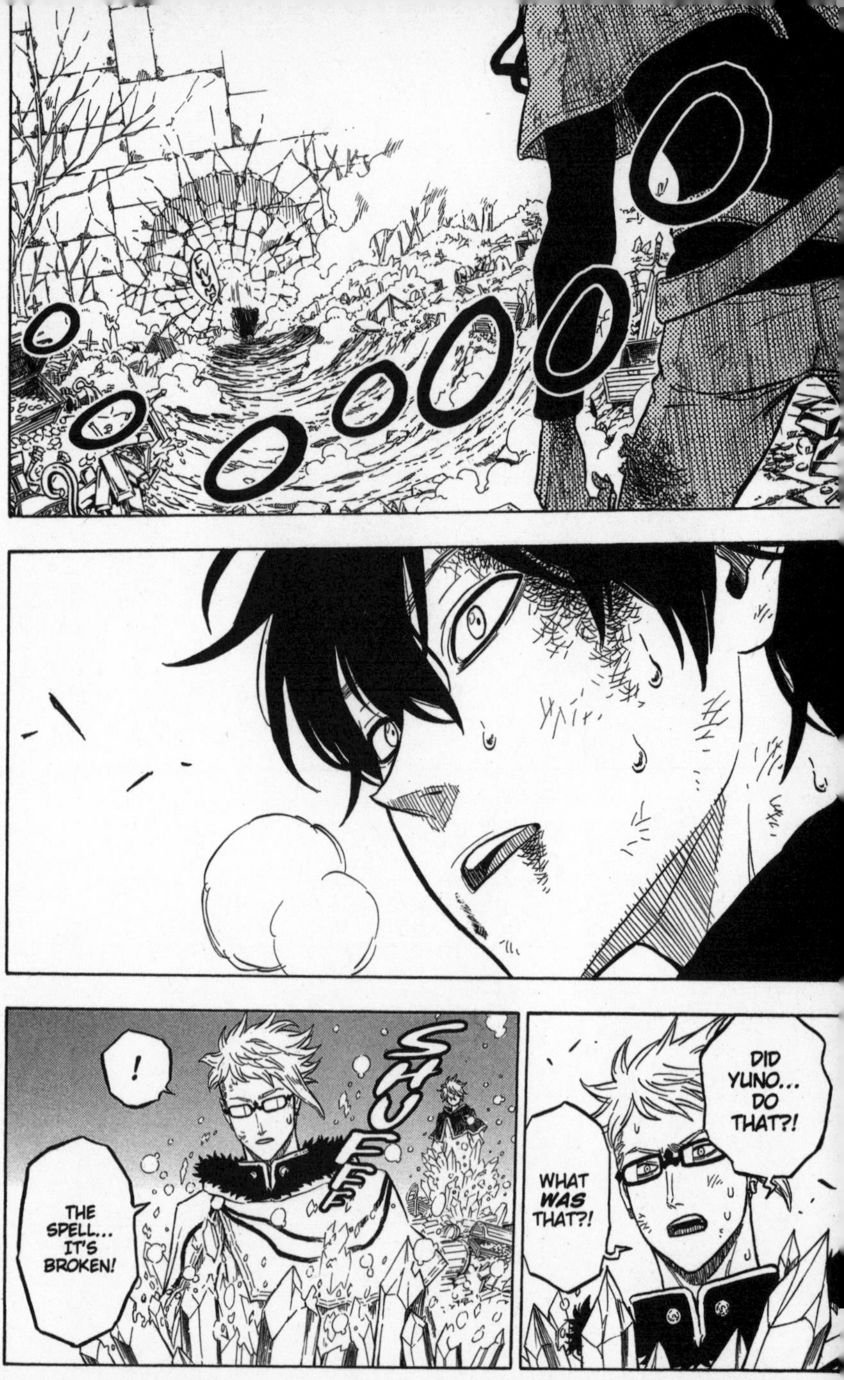
FWUMP
!
SHUFFF
THE SPELL... IT'S BROKEN!
DID YUNO... DO THAT?!
WHAT WAS THAT?!

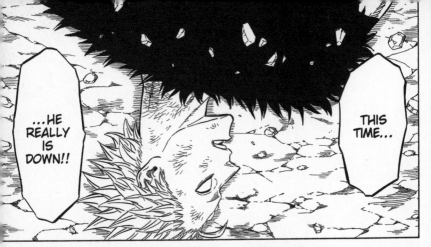

...HE REALLY IS DOWN!!

THIS TIME...

...THE WRITING FROM THAT SCROLL?!

ISN'T THIS...

!

FFT

OO

ZZT
ZZT

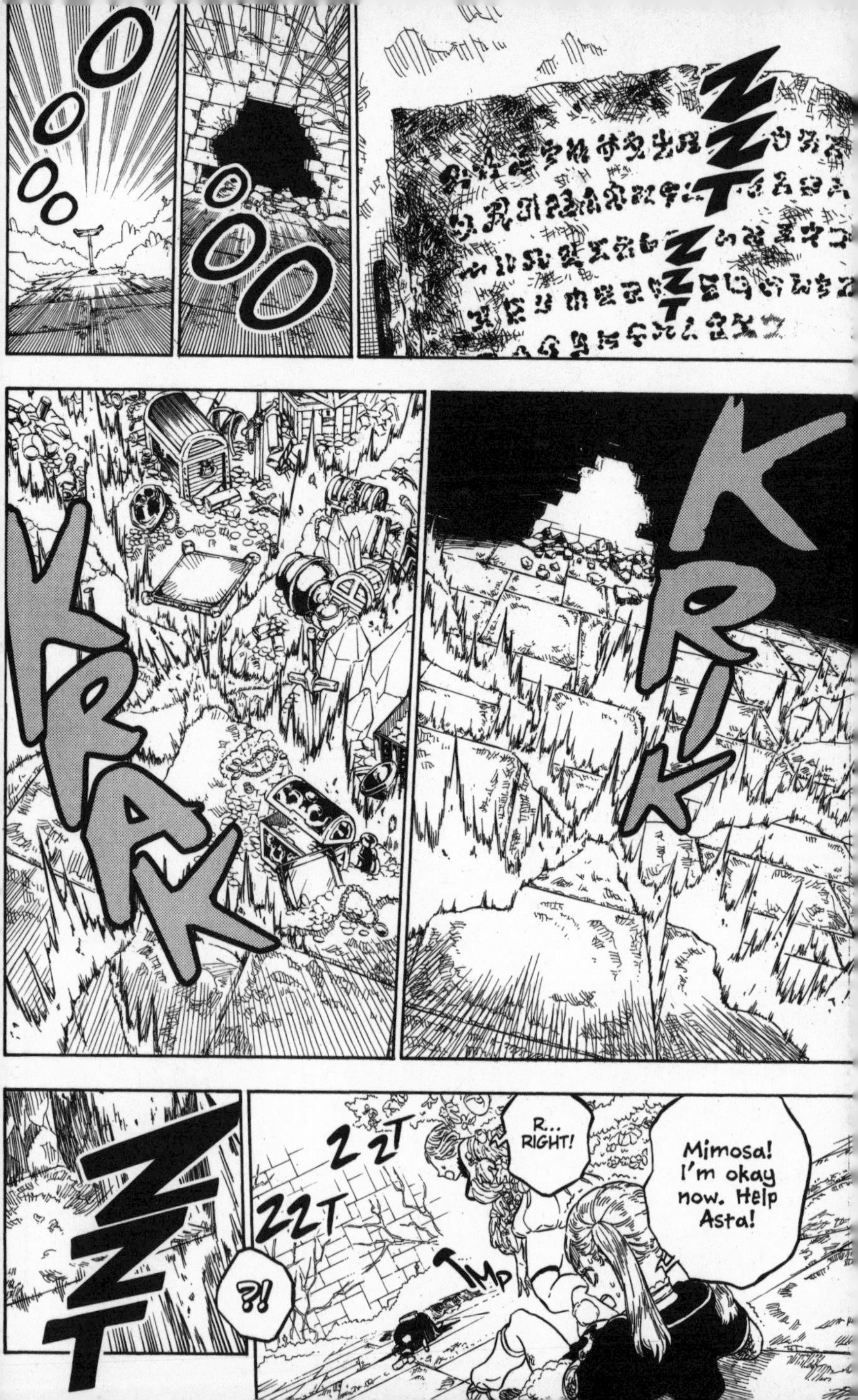
ZZT
ZZT
OOOO
OOOOO
KRIK
KRAK
Mimosa! I'm okay now. Help Asta!
R... RIGHT!
ZZT
ZZT
TMP
?!
ZZT

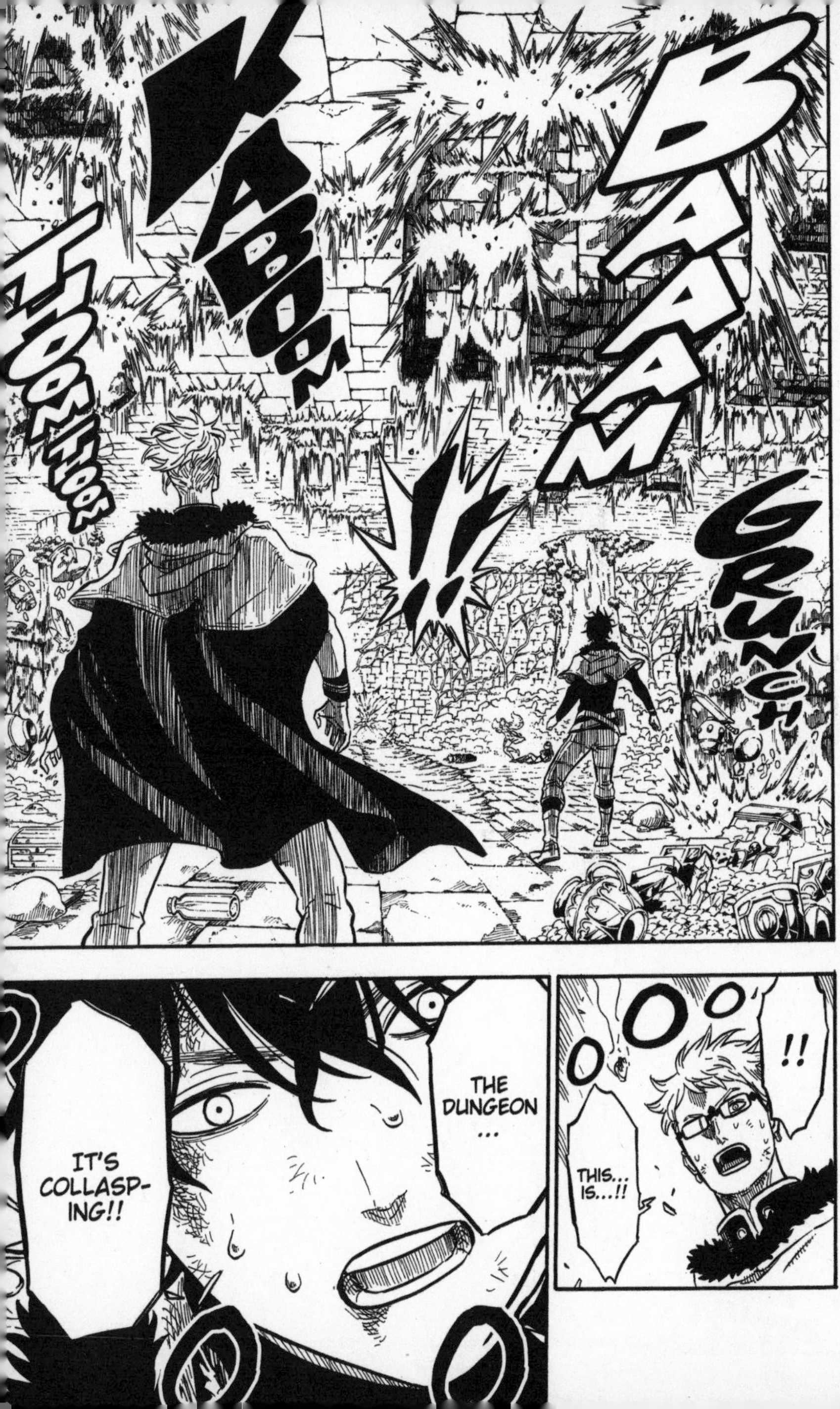
BAAM
CRUNCH
KABOOM
THOOM THOOM
!!
THIS... IS...!!
THE DUNGEON...
IT'S COLLASPING!!

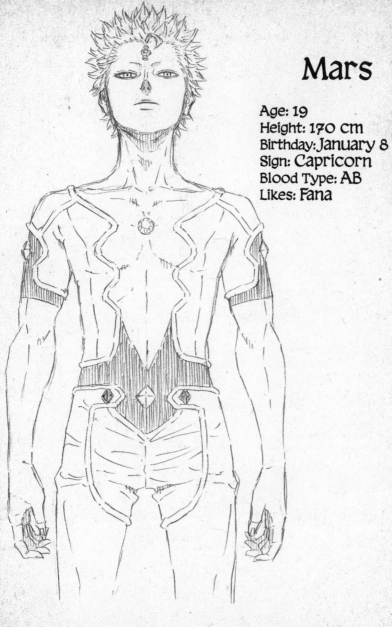

Mars

Age: 19
Height: 170 cm
Birthday: January 8
Sign: Capricorn
Blood Type: AB
Likes: Fana

Character Profile

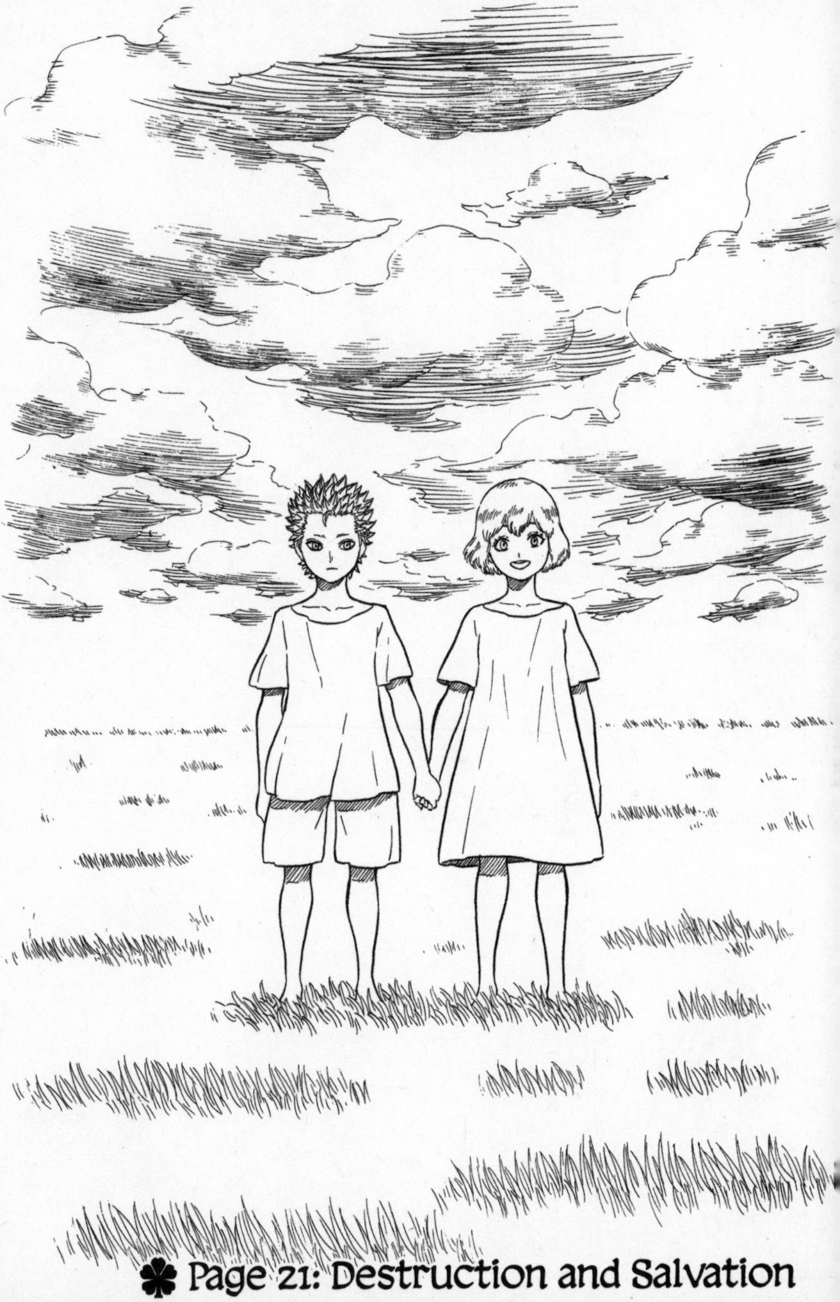

Page 21: Destruction and Salvation

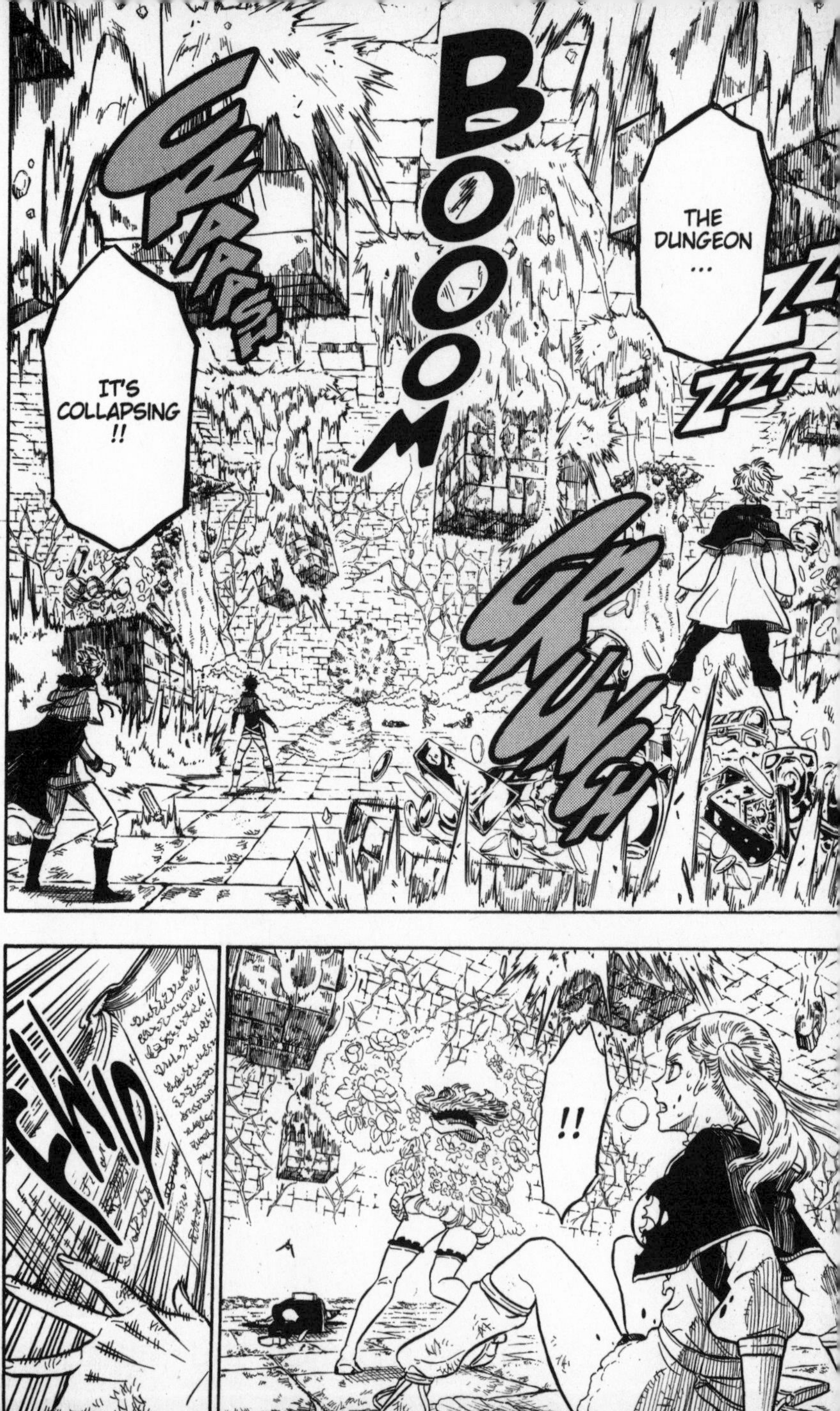
THE DUNGEON ...
ZZZT
BOOOOM
IT'S COLLAPSING !!
!!

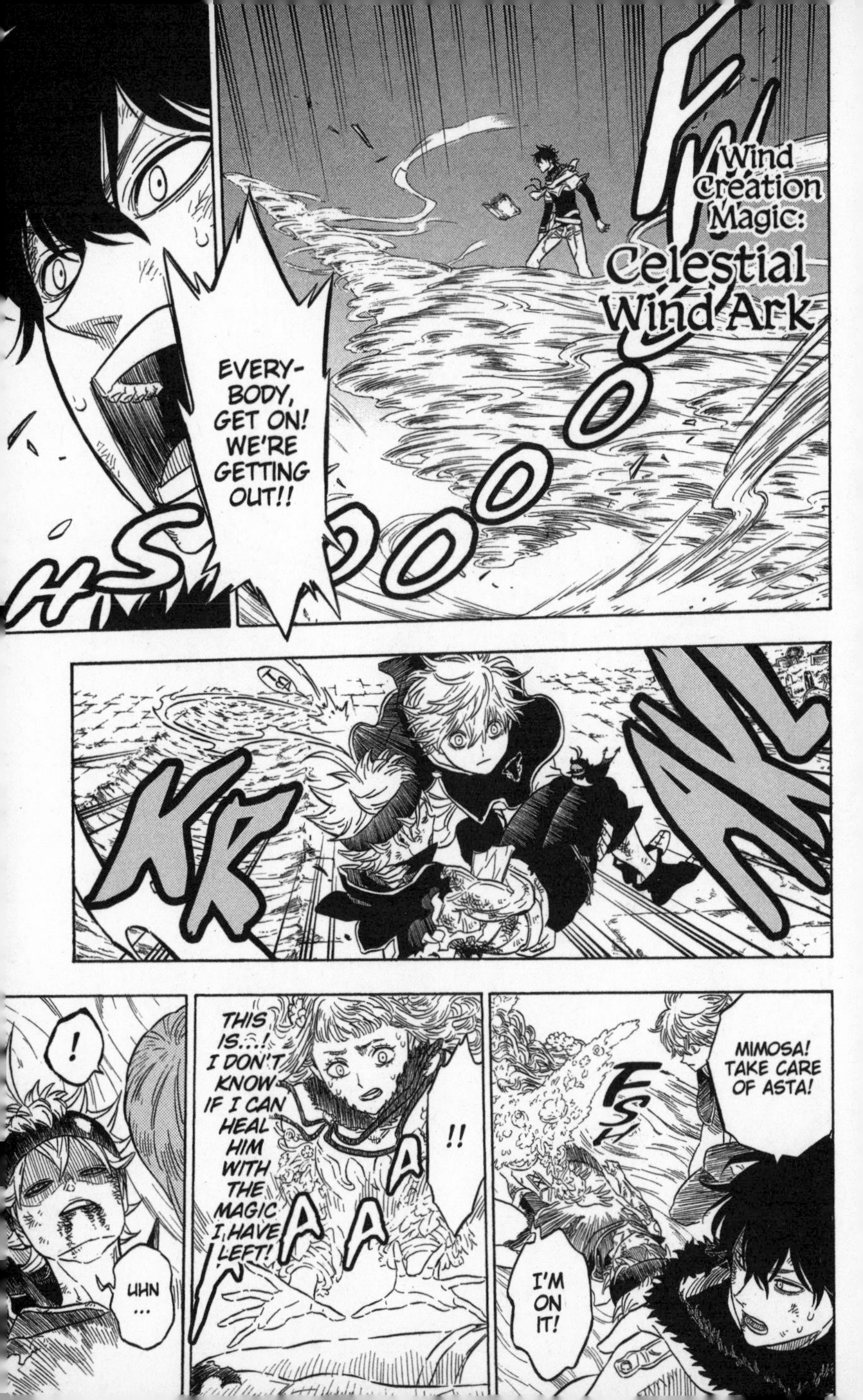
Wind Creation Magic:
Celestial Wind Ark
HSOOOOOO
EVERY-BODY, GET ON! WE'RE GETTING OUT!!
KR
MIMOSA! TAKE CARE OF ASTA!
FSH
I'M ON IT!
!!
THIS IS...! I DON'T KNOW IF I CAN HEAL HIM WITH THE MAGIC I HAVE LEFT!
AAA
!
UHN ...

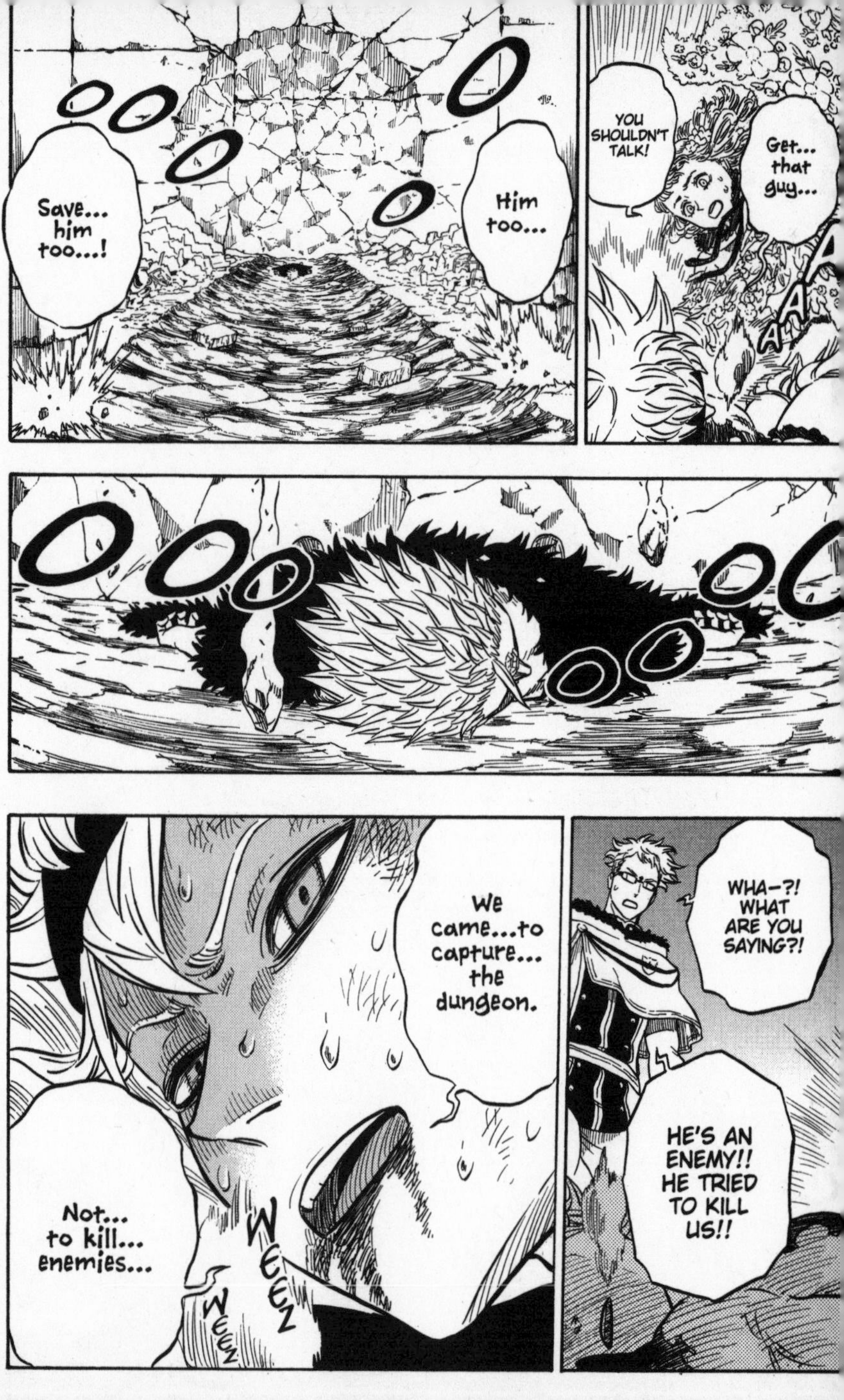
Get... that guy...
YOU SHOULDN'T TALK!
Him too...
Save... him too...!
WHA-?! WHAT ARE YOU SAYING?!
HE'S AN ENEMY!! HE TRIED TO KILL US!!
We came...to capture... the dungeon.
Not... to kill... enemies...
WEEZ
WEEZ

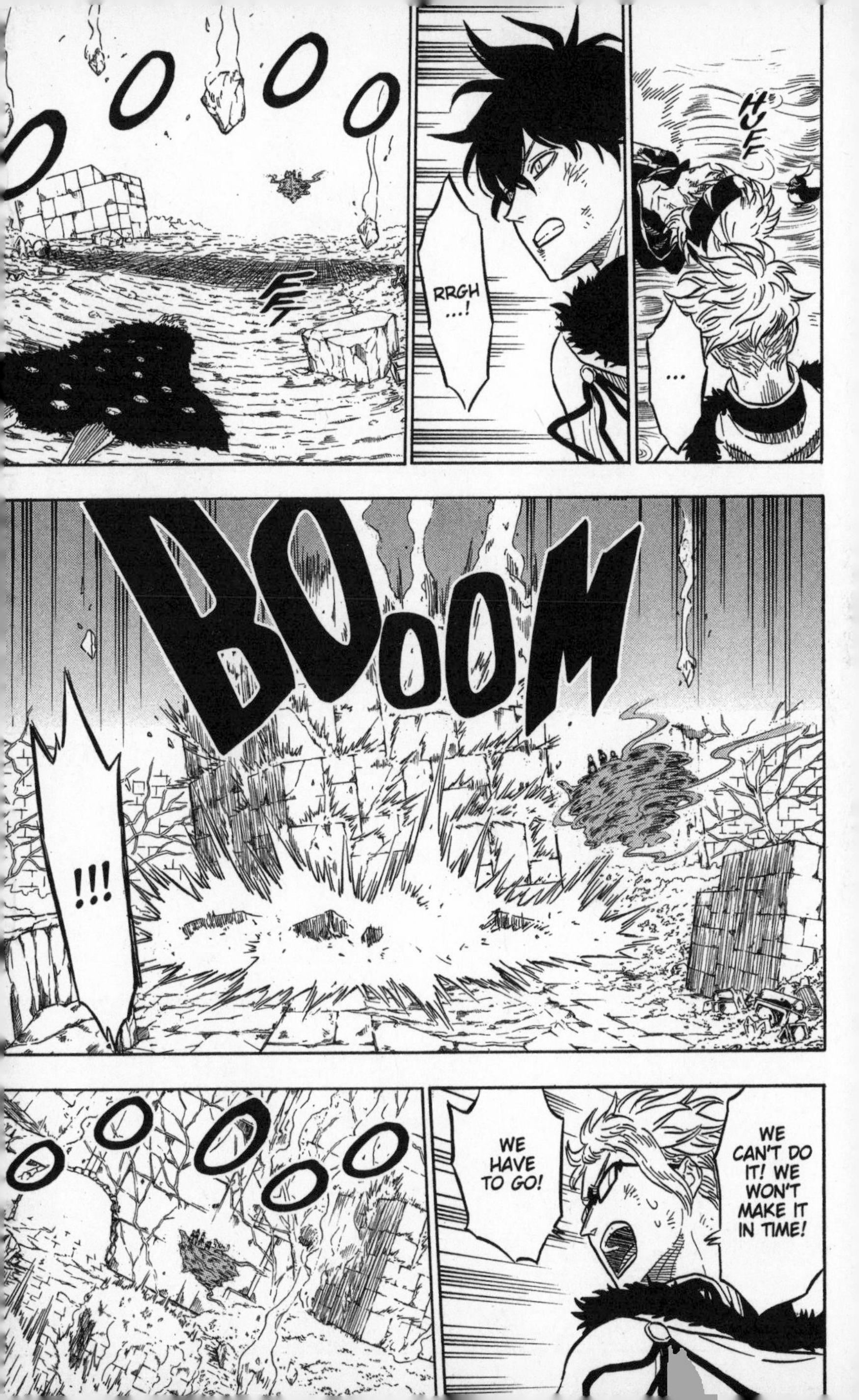
HUFF
...
RRGH ...!
OOOOO
FFT
BOOOM
!!!
WE CAN'T DO IT! WE WON'T MAKE IT IN TIME!
WE HAVE TO GO!
OOOOOO

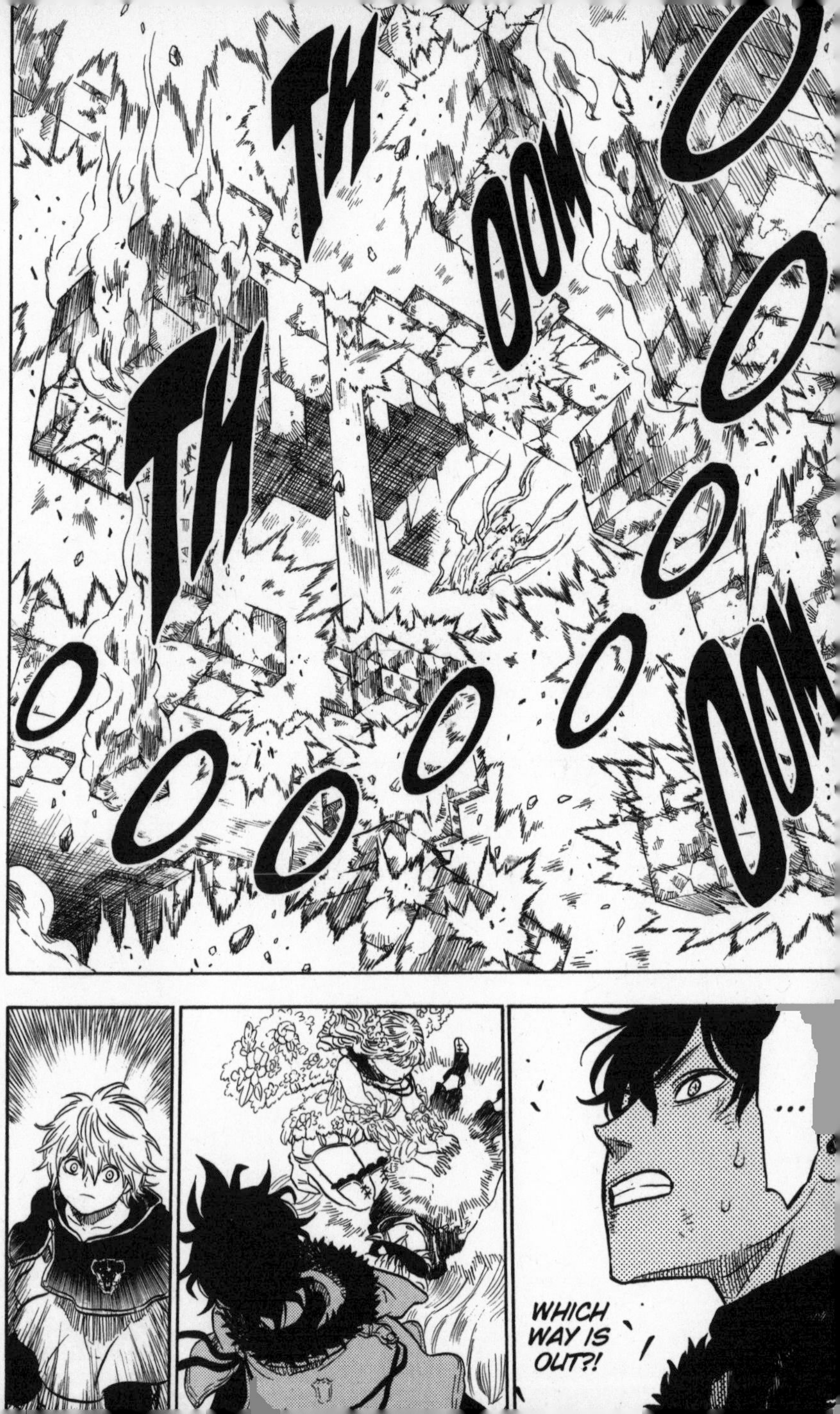
THOOOOOOOM
THOOOOOOOM
...
WHICH WAY IS OUT?!

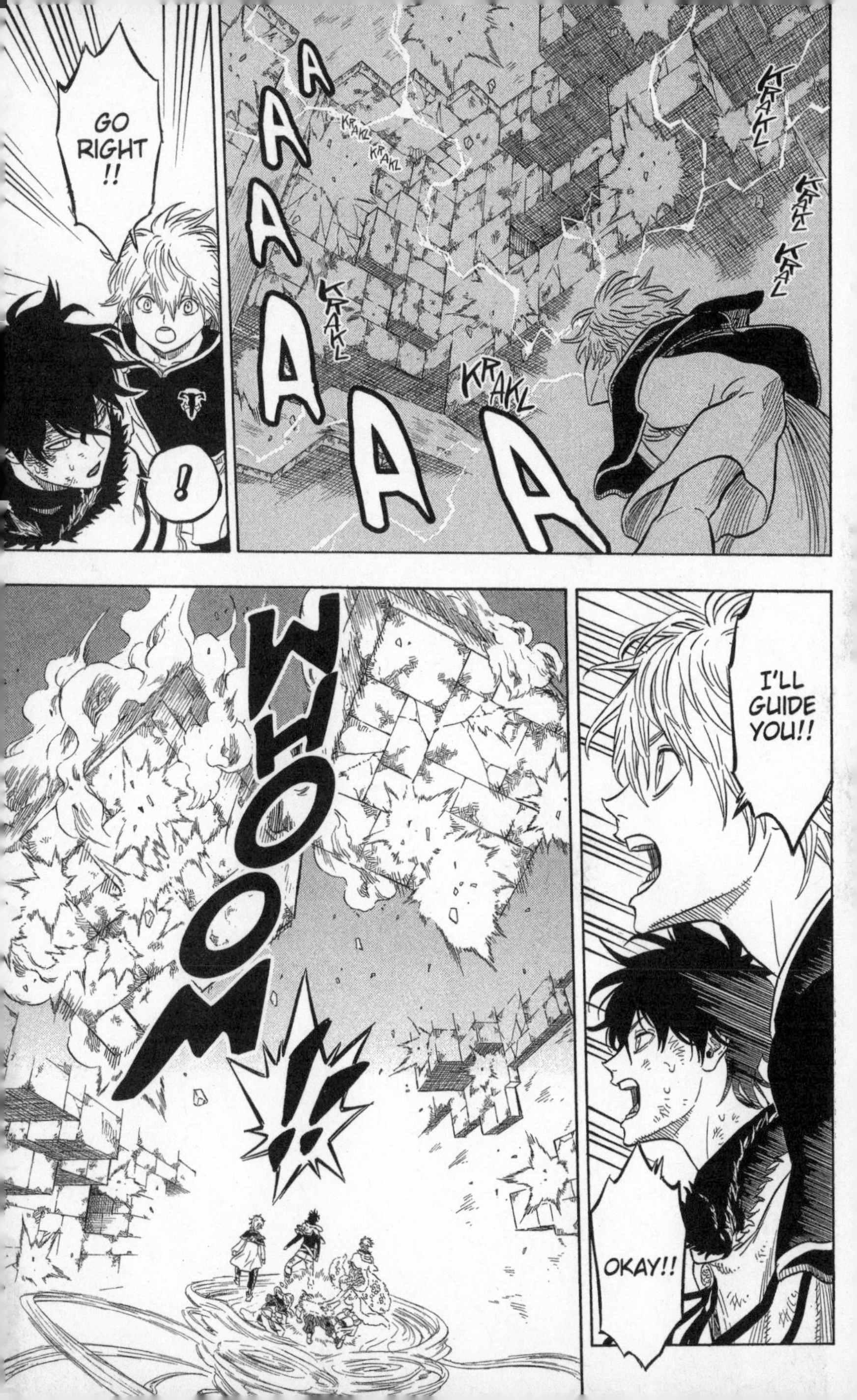
KRAKL
KRAKL
KRAKL
KRAKL
KRAKL
AAAAAAA
KRAKL
KRAKL
GO RIGHT!!
!
I'LL GUIDE YOU!!
OKAY!!
WHOOOM!!

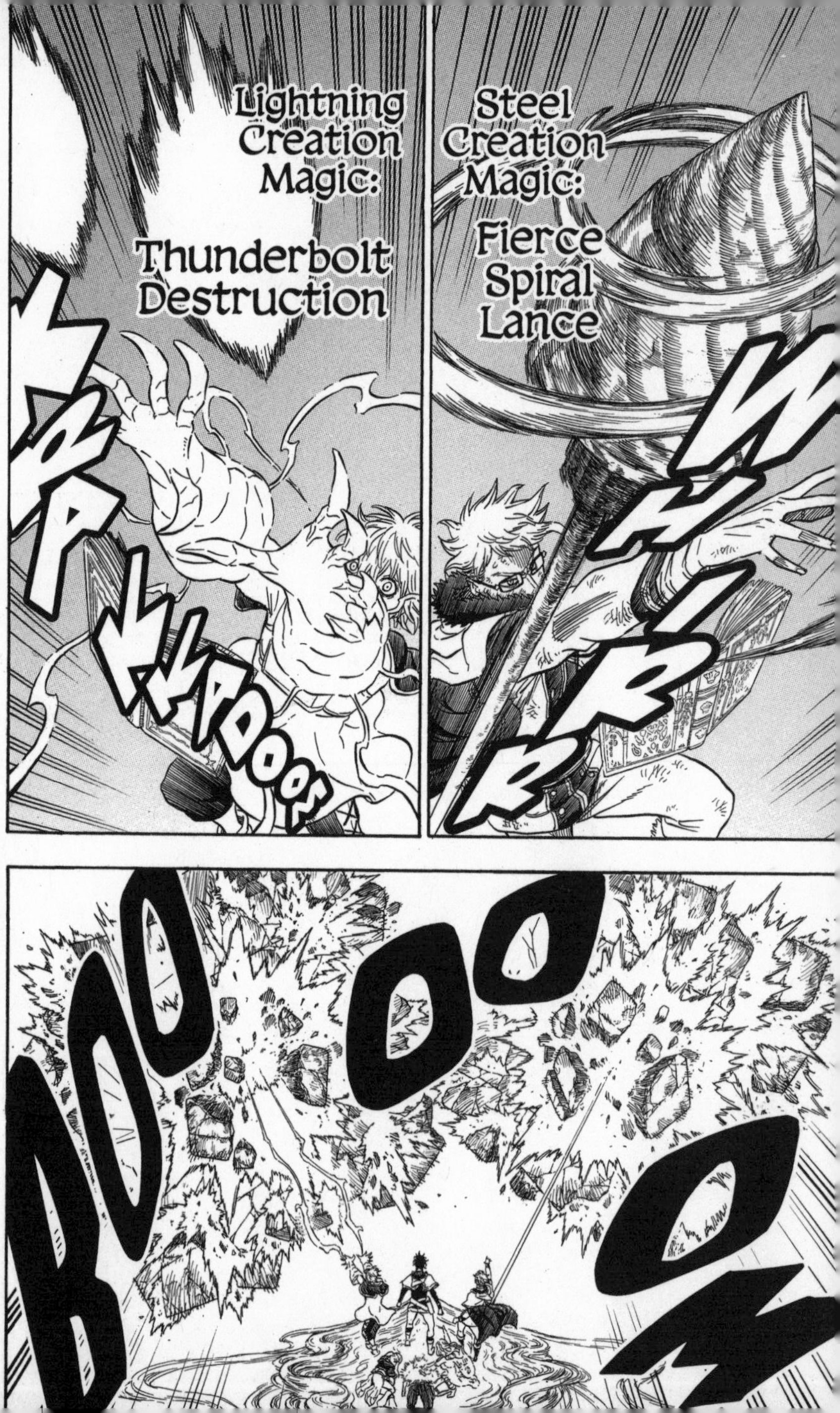
Steel Creation Magic:
Fierce Spiral Lance
WHIRR
Lightning Creation Magic:
Thunderbolt Destruction
KRAKADOOM
BOOOOOM

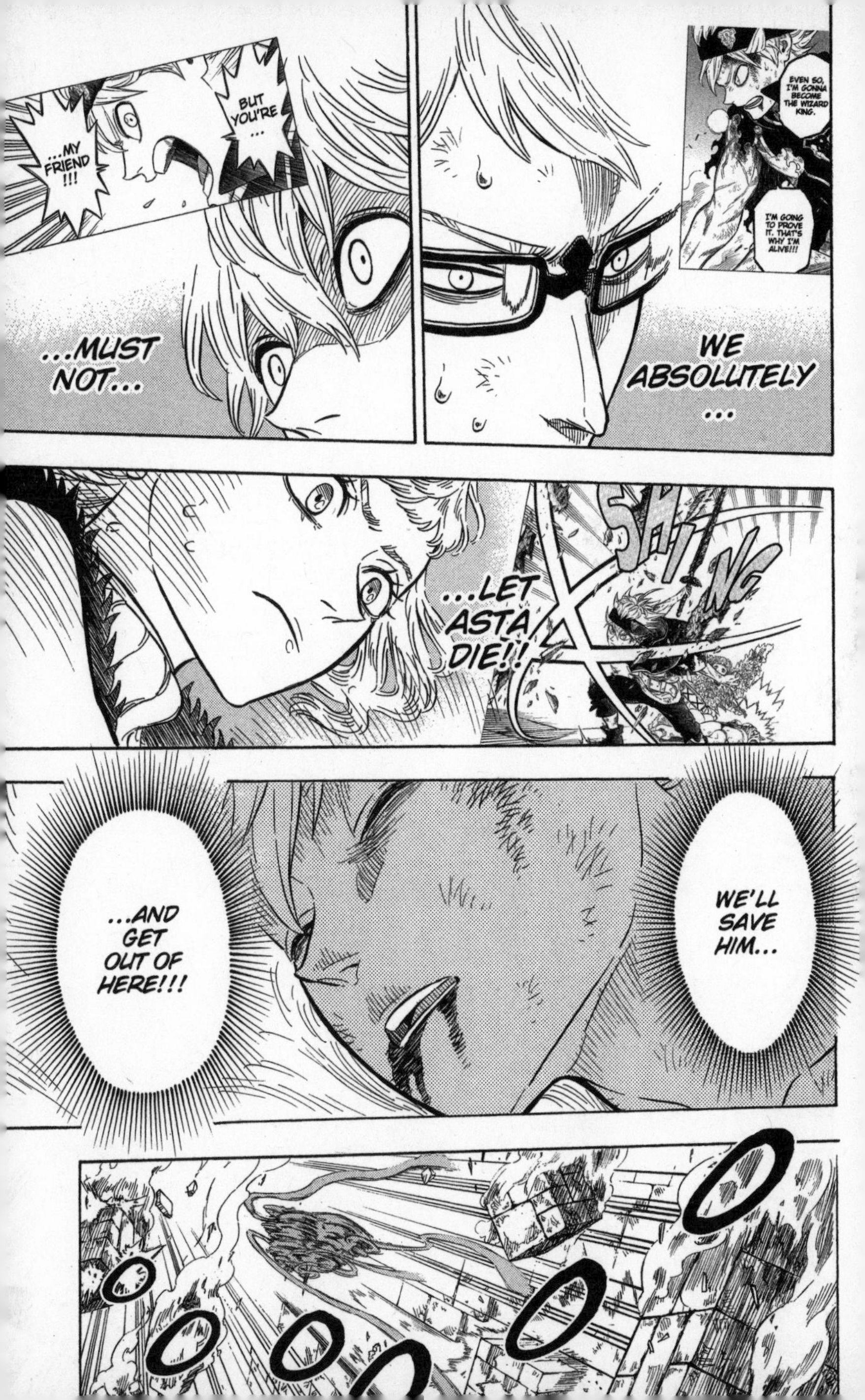
EVEN SO, I'M GONNA BECOME THE WIZARD KING.
I'M GOING TO PROVE IT. THAT'S WHY I'M ALIVE!!!
WE ABSOLUTELY ...
BUT YOU'RE ...
...MY FRIEND !!!
...MUST NOT...
SHING
...LET ASTA DIE!!
WE'LL SAVE HIM...
...AND GET OUT OF HERE!!!

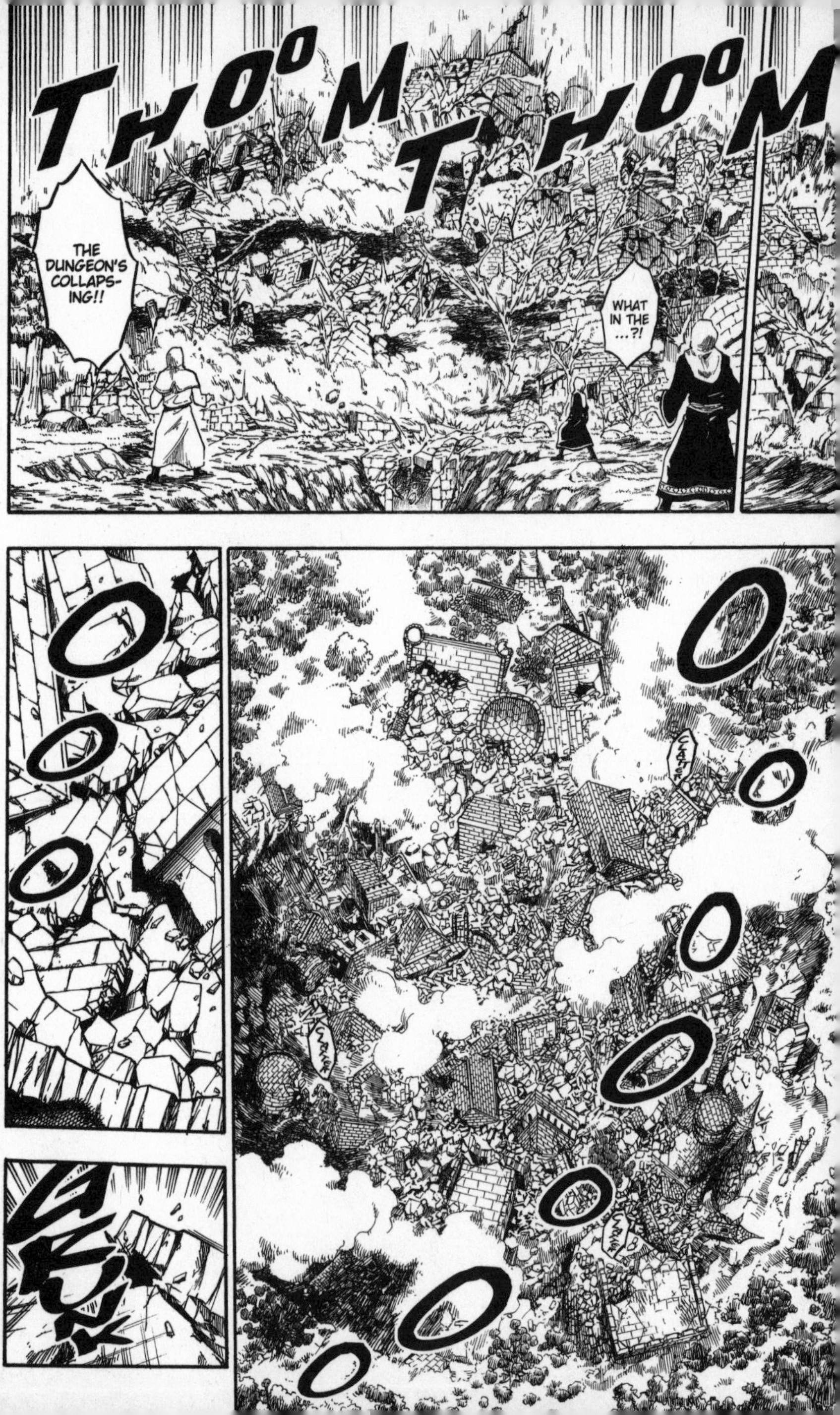
THOOM THOOM
WHAT IN THE ...?!
THE DUNGEON'S COLLAPSING!!
CLATTER
CLATTER

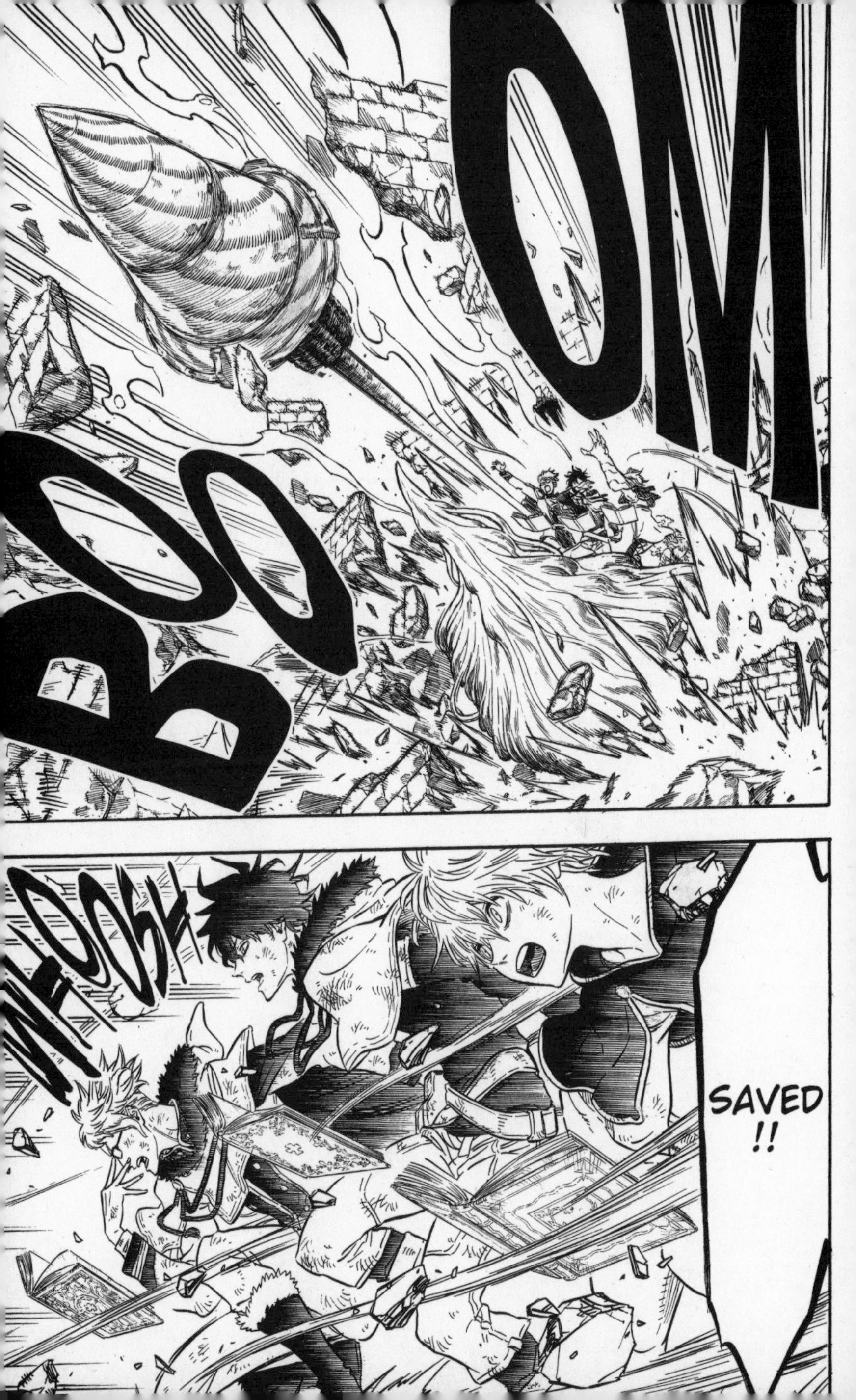
BOOOM
SAVED !!
WHOOSH

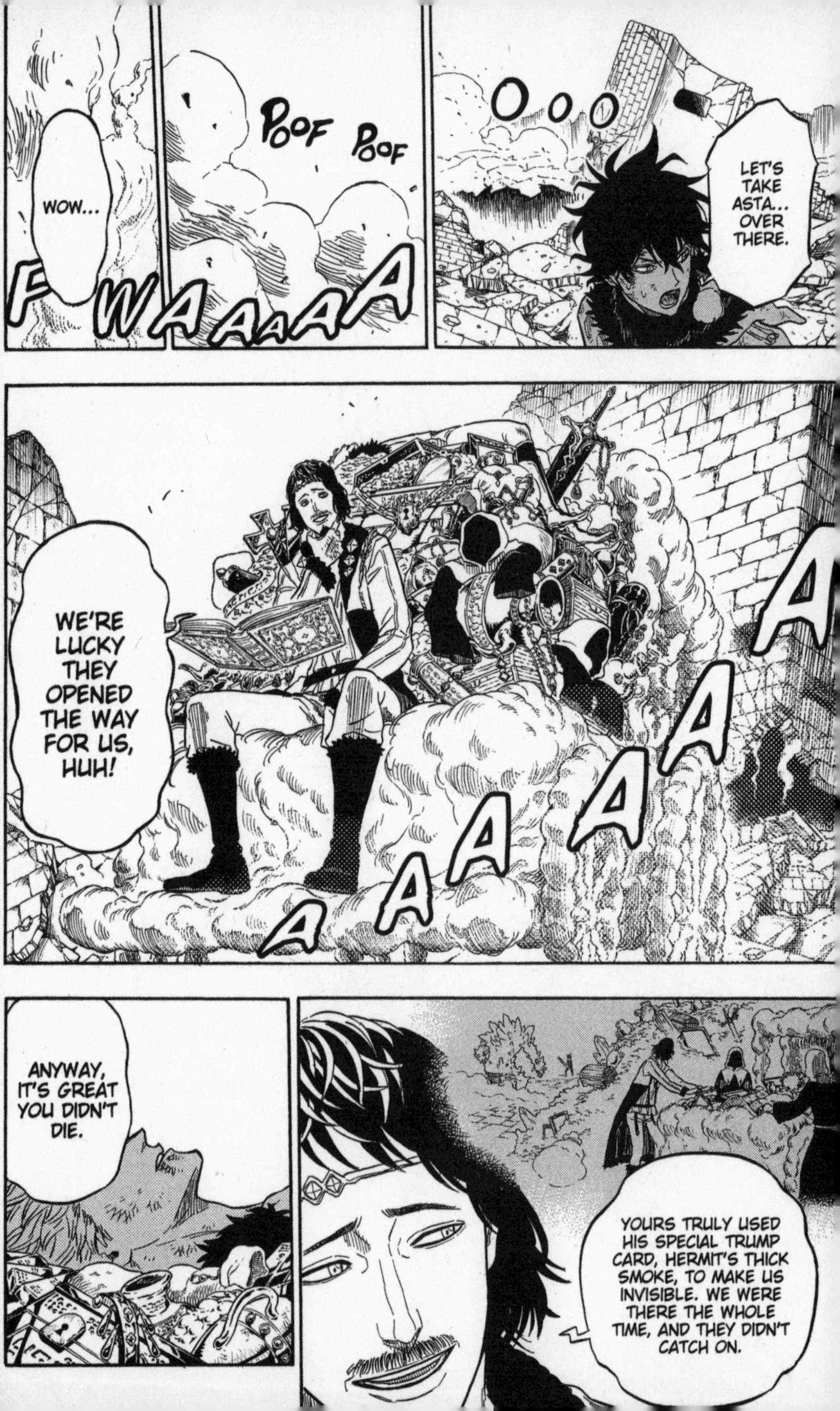
OOO
LET'S TAKE ASTA... OVER THERE.
POOF POOF
WOW...
FWAAAAAA
WE'RE LUCKY THEY OPENED THE WAY FOR US, HUH!
AAAAAAAAA
YOURS TRULY USED HIS SPECIAL TRUMP CARD, HERMIT'S THICK SMOKE, TO MAKE US INVISIBLE. WE WERE THERE THE WHOLE TIME, AND THEY DIDN'T CATCH ON.
ANYWAY, IT'S GREAT YOU DIDN'T DIE.

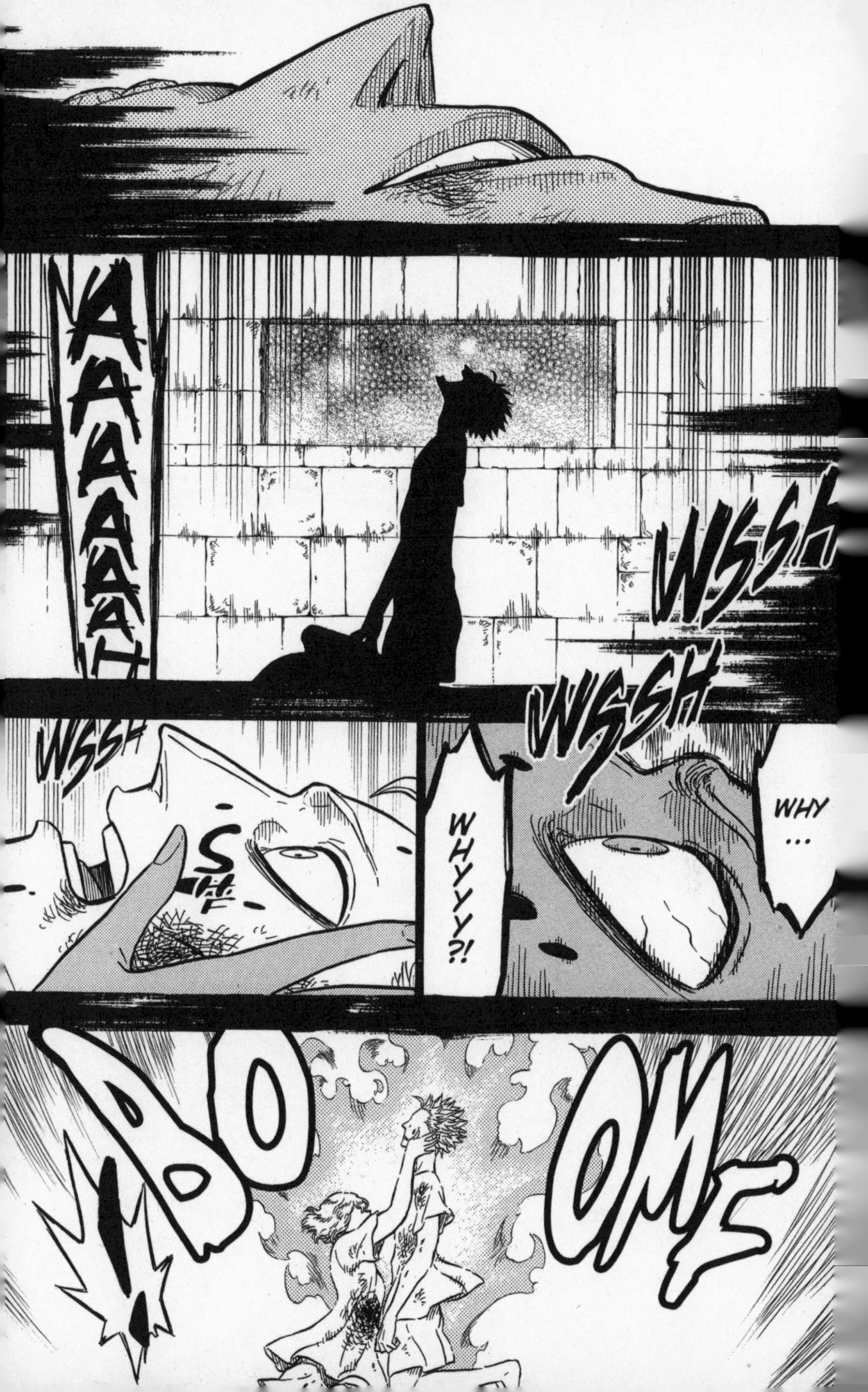
WSSH
AAAAAAH
WSSH
WHY...
WHYYYY?!
WSSH
SHF
BOOM

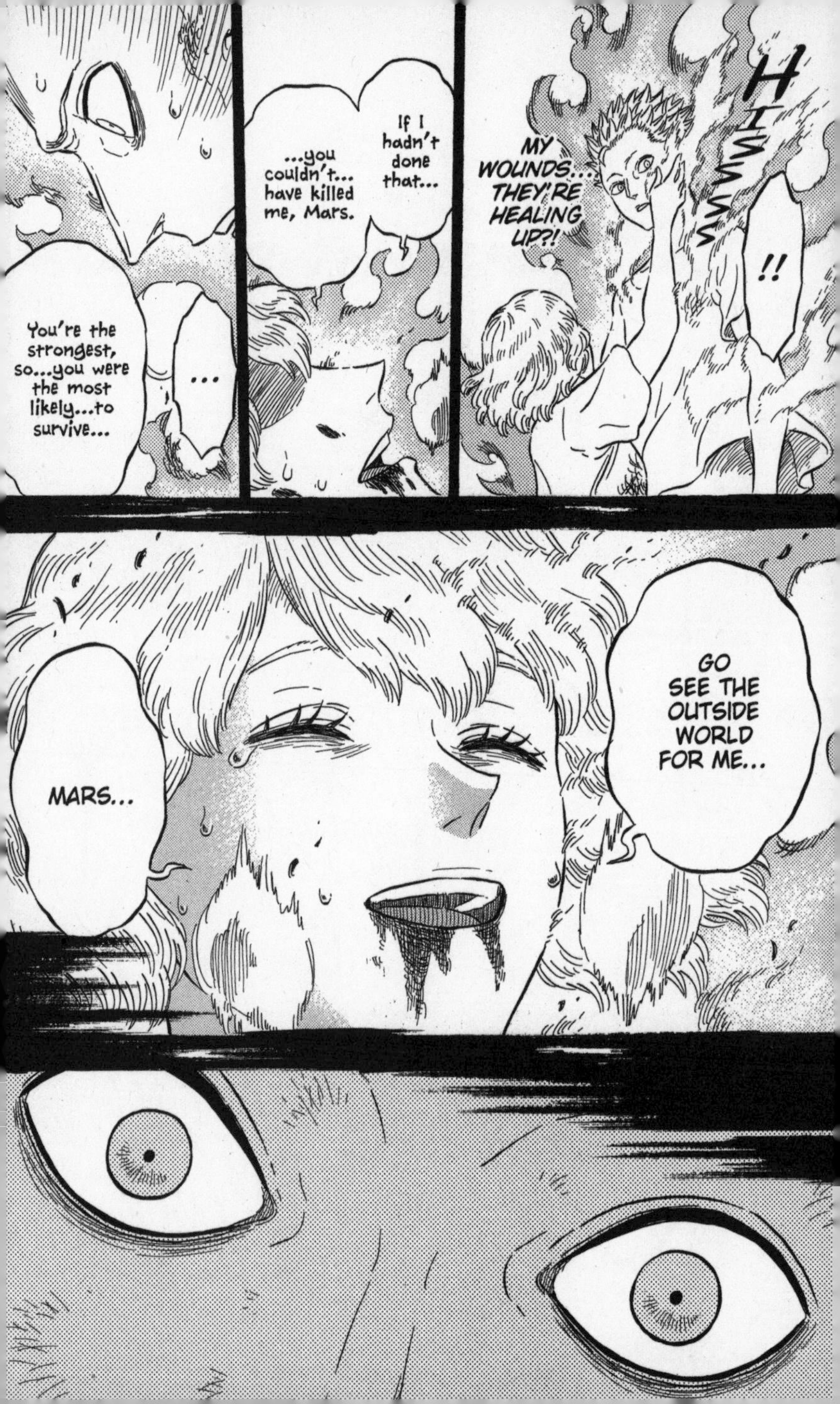
HISSSSS
!!
MY WOUNDS... THEY'RE HEALING UP?!
If I hadn't done that...
...you couldn't... have killed me, Mars.
You're the strongest, so...you were the most likely...to survive...
...
GO SEE THE OUTSIDE WORLD FOR ME...
MARS...

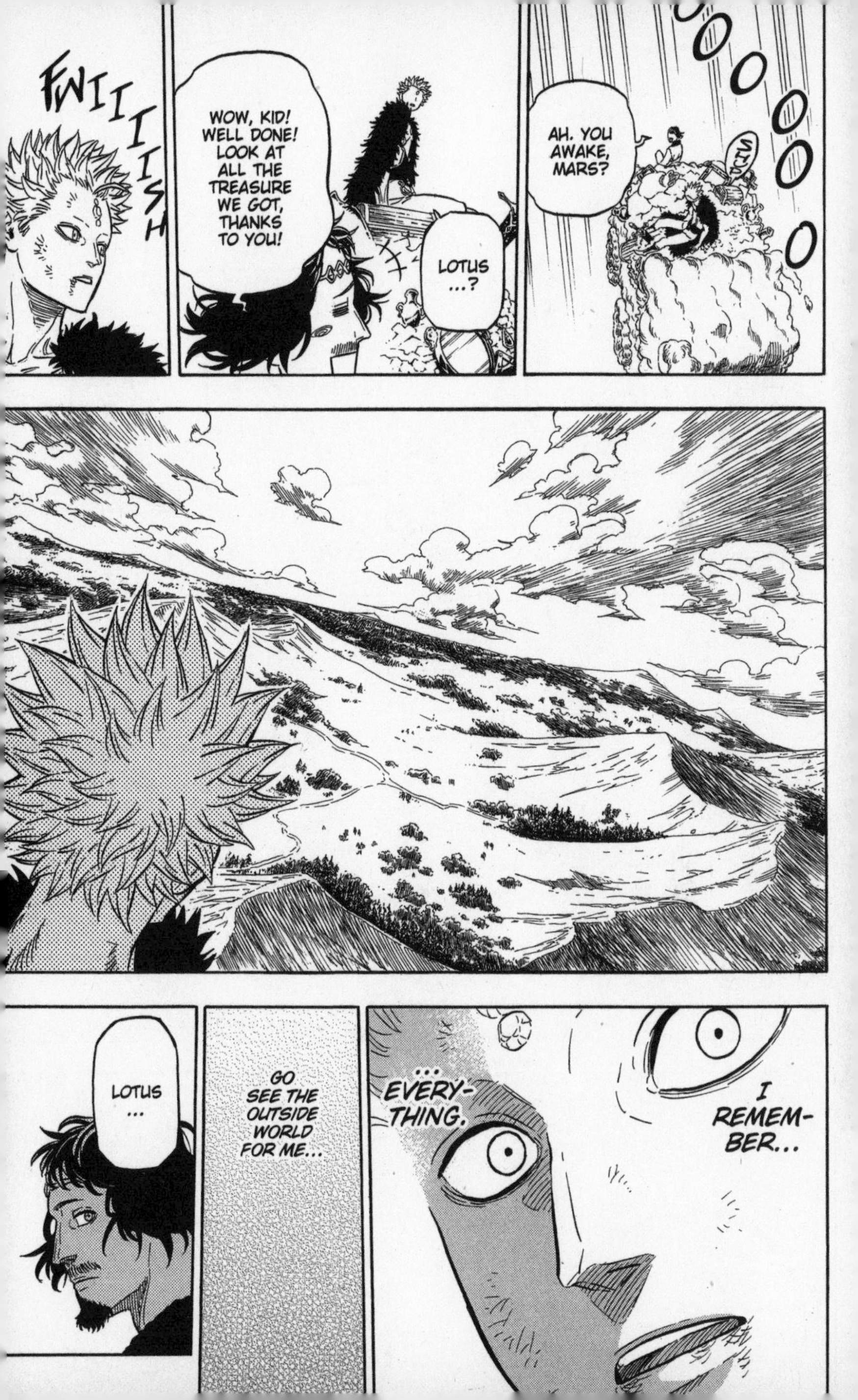
OOOOOOO
AH. YOU AWAKE, MARS?
LOTUS ...?
WOW, KID! WELL DONE! LOOK AT ALL THE TREASURE WE GOT, THANKS TO YOU!
FWIIIISH
I REMEMBER...
... EVERYTHING.
GO SEE THE OUTSIDE WORLD FOR ME...
LOTUS ...

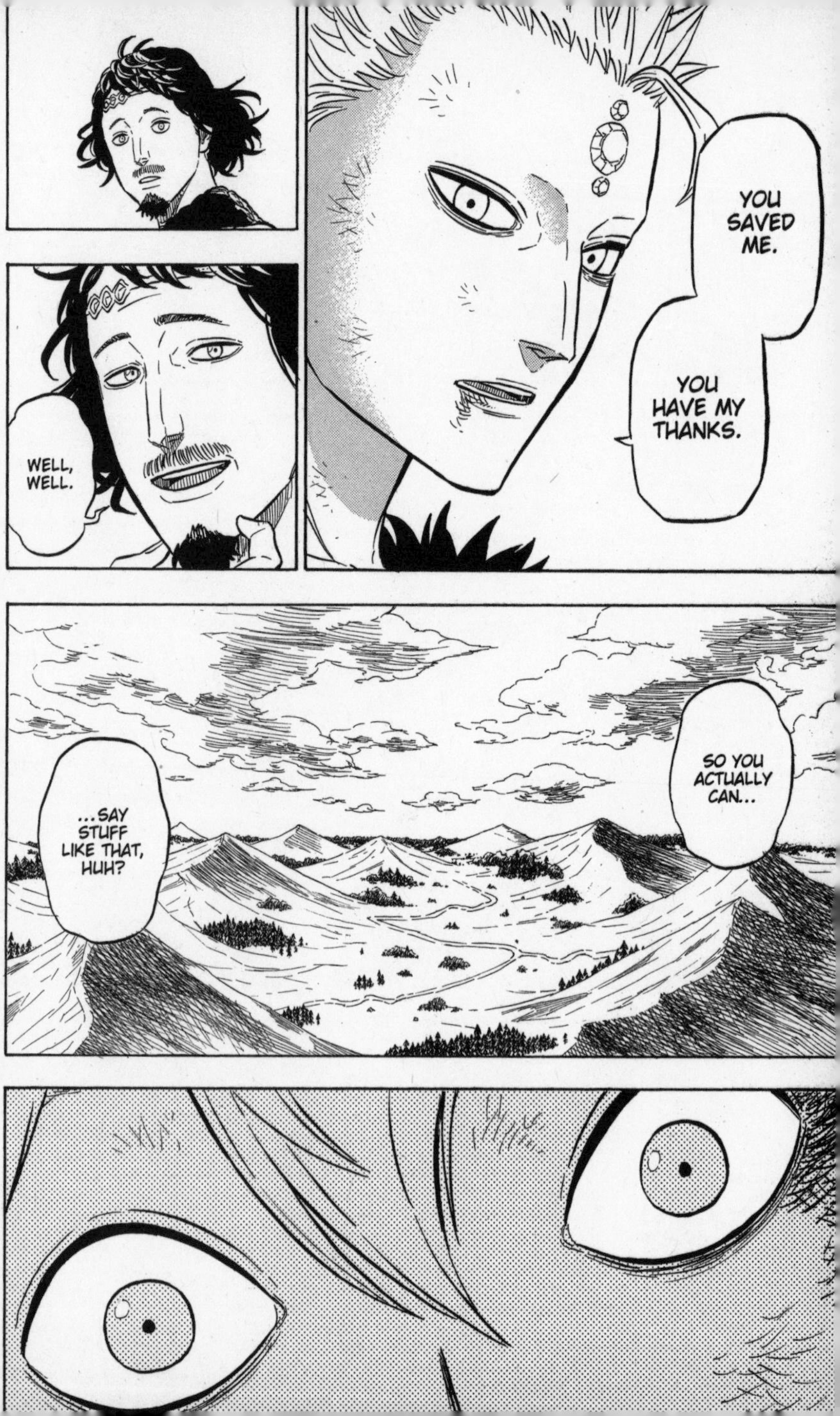
YOU SAVED ME.
YOU HAVE MY THANKS.
WELL, WELL.
SO YOU ACTUALLY CAN...
...SAY STUFF LIKE THAT, HUH?

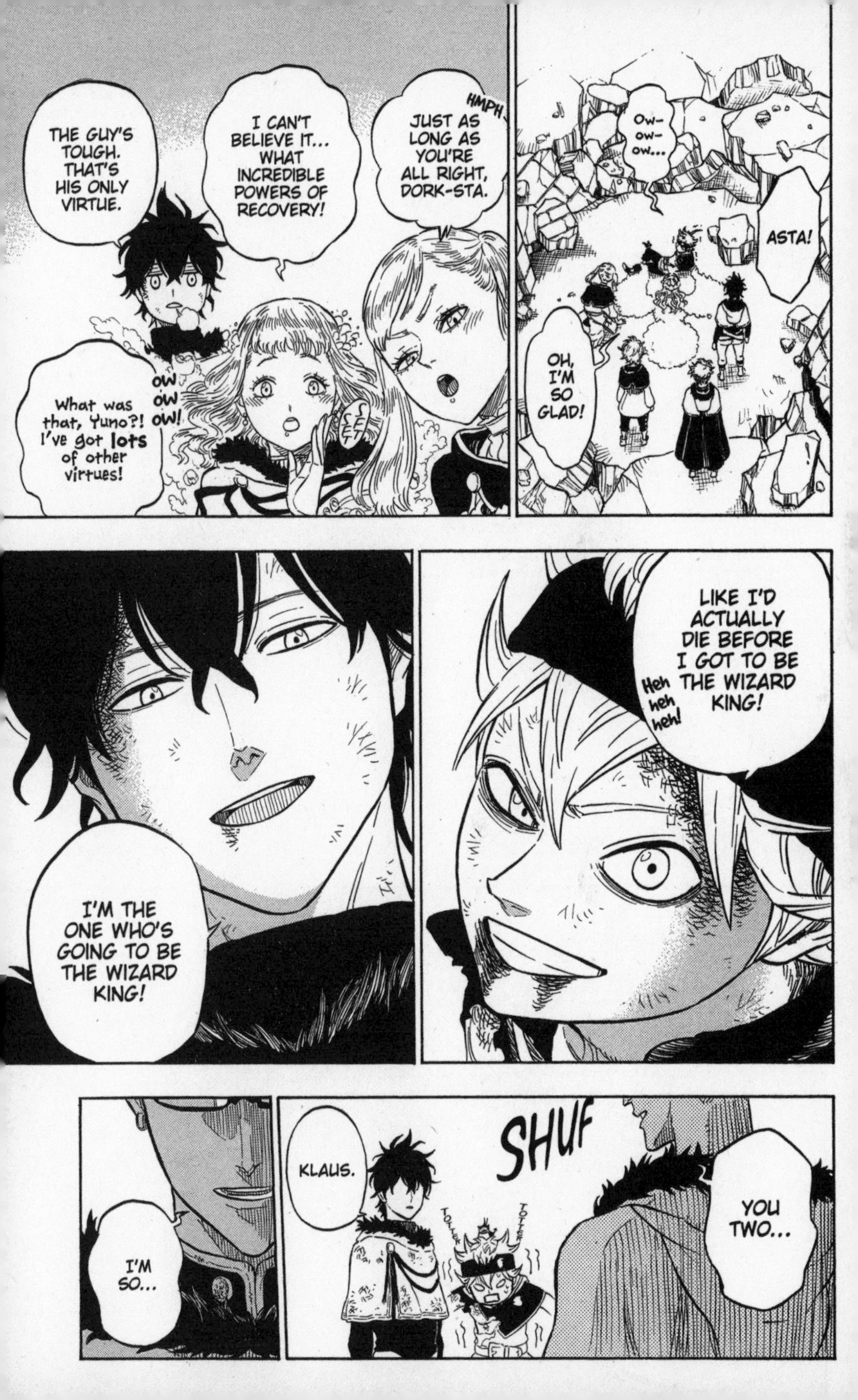
Ow-ow-ow...
ASTA!
OH, I'M SO GLAD!
HMPH
JUST AS LONG AS YOU'RE ALL RIGHT, DORK-STA.
I CAN'T BELIEVE IT... WHAT INCREDIBLE POWERS OF RECOVERY!
THE GUY'S TOUGH. THAT'S HIS ONLY VIRTUE.
SET
OW OW OW!
What was that, Yuno?! I've got lots of other virtues!
LIKE I'D ACTUALLY DIE BEFORE I GOT TO BE THE WIZARD KING!
Heh heh heh!
I'M THE ONE WHO'S GOING TO BE THE WIZARD KING!
SHUF
YOU TWO...
KLAUS.
TOTTER
TOTTER
I'M SO...

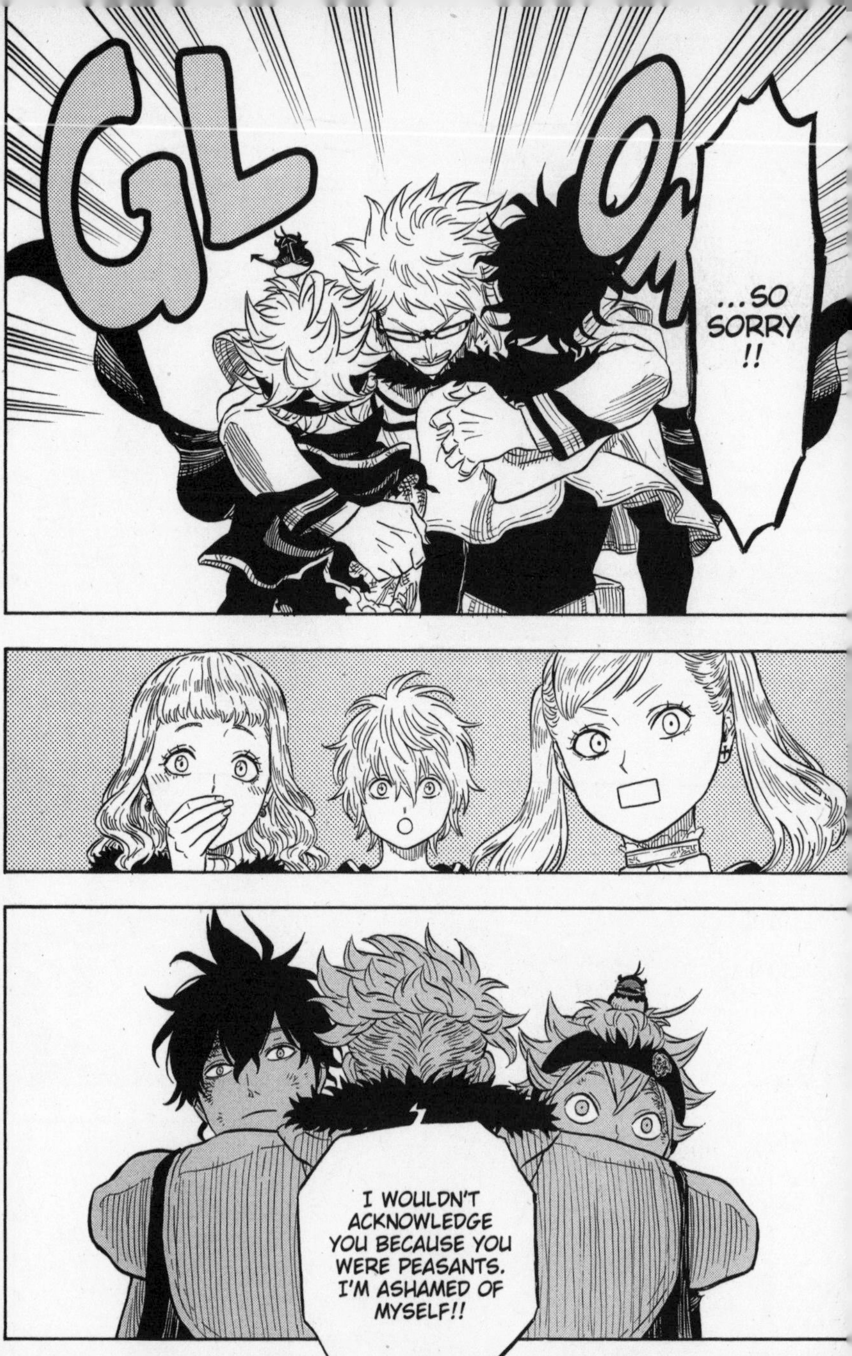
...SO SORRY !!
I WOULDN'T ACKNOWLEDGE YOU BECAUSE YOU WERE PEASANTS. I'M ASHAMED OF MYSELF!!

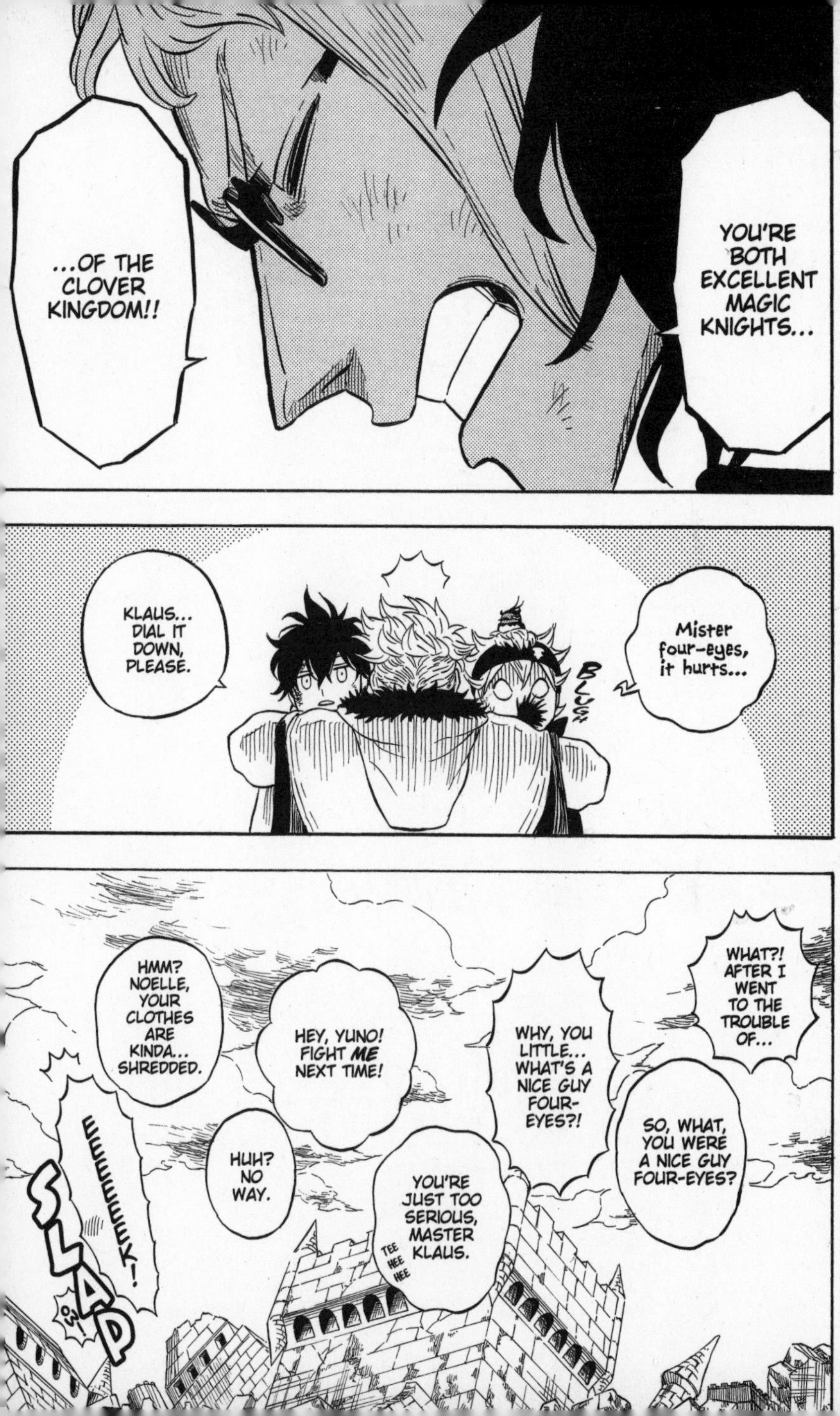
YOU'RE BOTH EXCELLENT MAGIC KNIGHTS...
...OF THE CLOVER KINGDOM!!
Mister four-eyes, it hurts...
BLUGH
KLAUS... DIAL IT DOWN, PLEASE.
WHAT?! AFTER I WENT TO THE TROUBLE OF...
WHY, YOU LITTLE... WHAT'S A NICE GUY FOUR-EYES?!
SO, WHAT, YOU WERE A NICE GUY FOUR-EYES?
HEY, YUNO! FIGHT ME NEXT TIME!
HMM? NOELLE, YOUR CLOTHES ARE KINDA... SHREDDED.
YOU'RE JUST TOO SERIOUS, MASTER KLAUS.
TEE HEE HEE
HUH? NO WAY.
EEEEEEEK!
SLAP
OW!

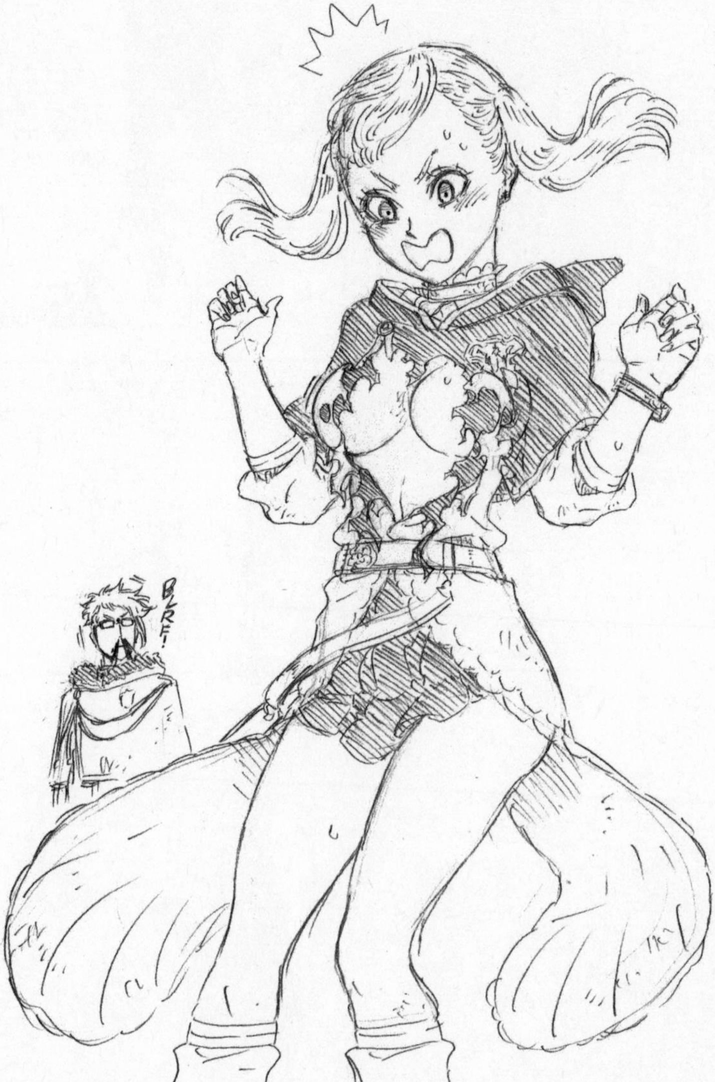
BLRF!

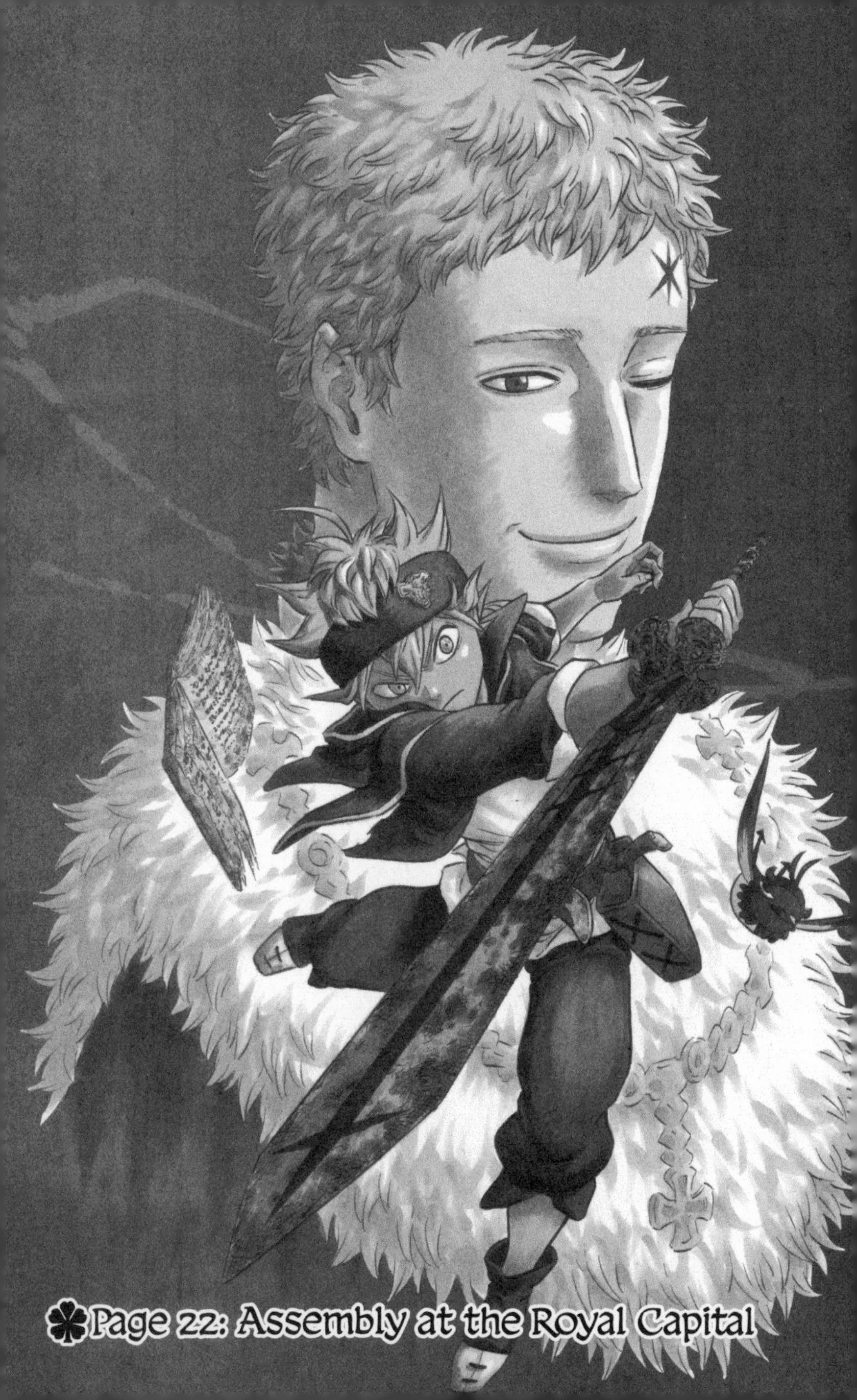

Page 22: Assembly at the Royal Capital

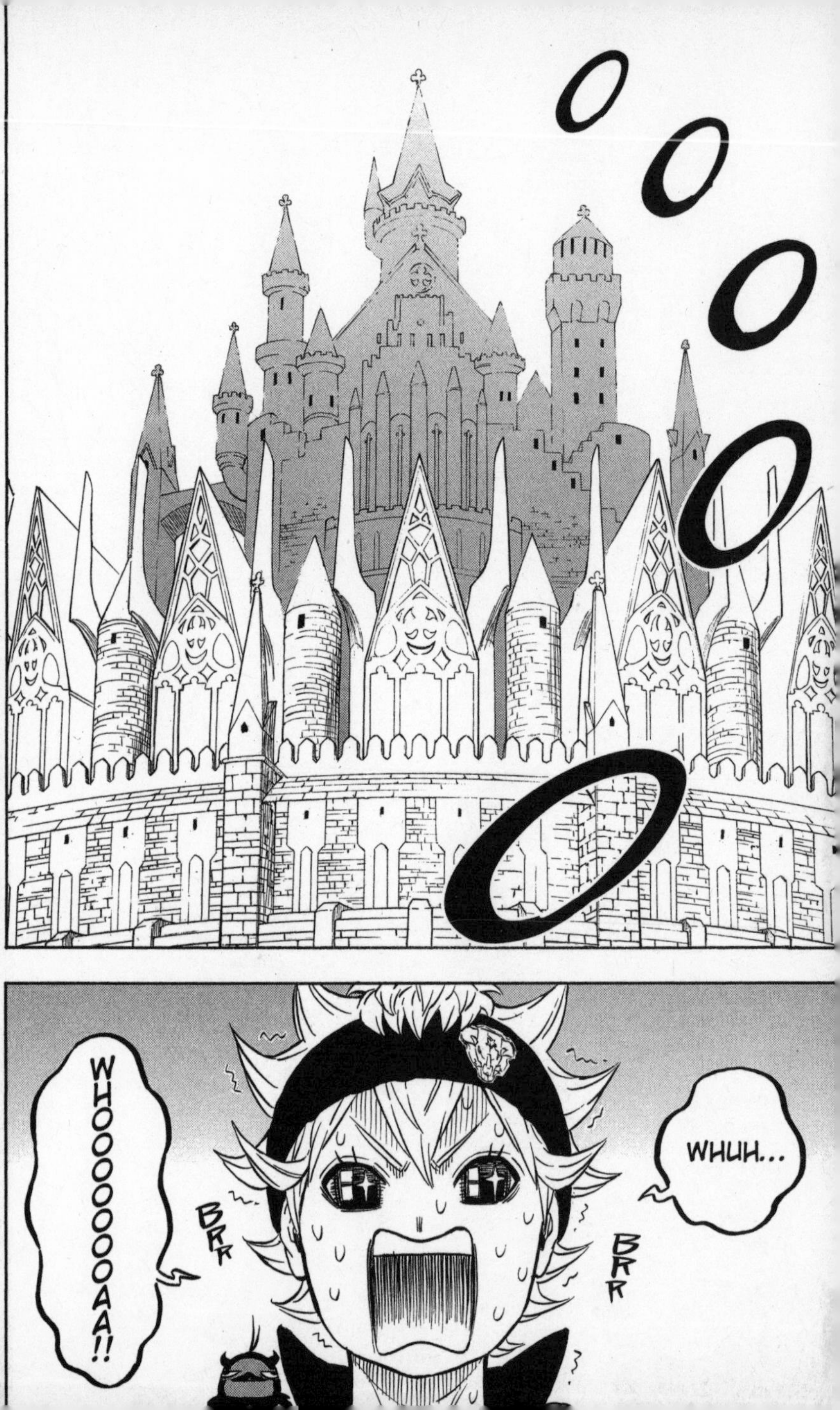
OOOOO
WHUH...
BRR
BRR
WHOOOOOOOAA!!

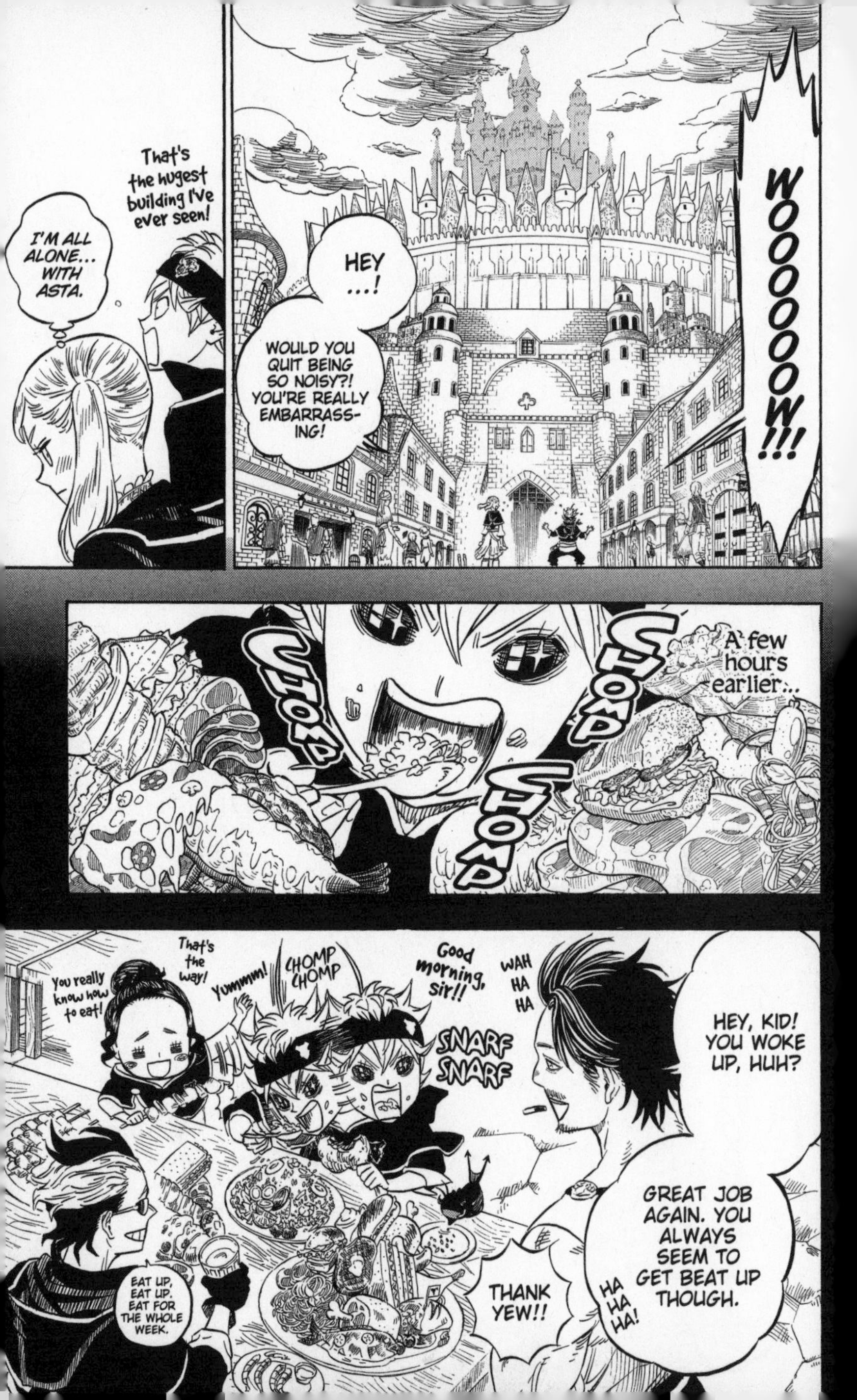
WOOOOOOOW!!!
HEY ...!
WOULD YOU QUIT BEING SO NOISY?! YOU'RE REALLY EMBARRASS-ING!
That's the hugest building I've ever seen!
I'M ALL ALONE... WITH ASTA.
A few hours earlier...
CHOMP
CHOMP
CHOMP
CHOMP
HEY, KID! YOU WOKE UP, HUH?
WAH HA HA
GREAT JOB AGAIN. YOU ALWAYS SEEM TO GET BEAT UP THOUGH.
HA HA HA!
Good morning, sir!!
SNARF SNARF
THANK YEW!!
CHOMP CHOMP
Yummm!
That's the way!
You really know how to eat!
EAT UP, EAT UP. EAT FOR THE WHOLE WEEK.

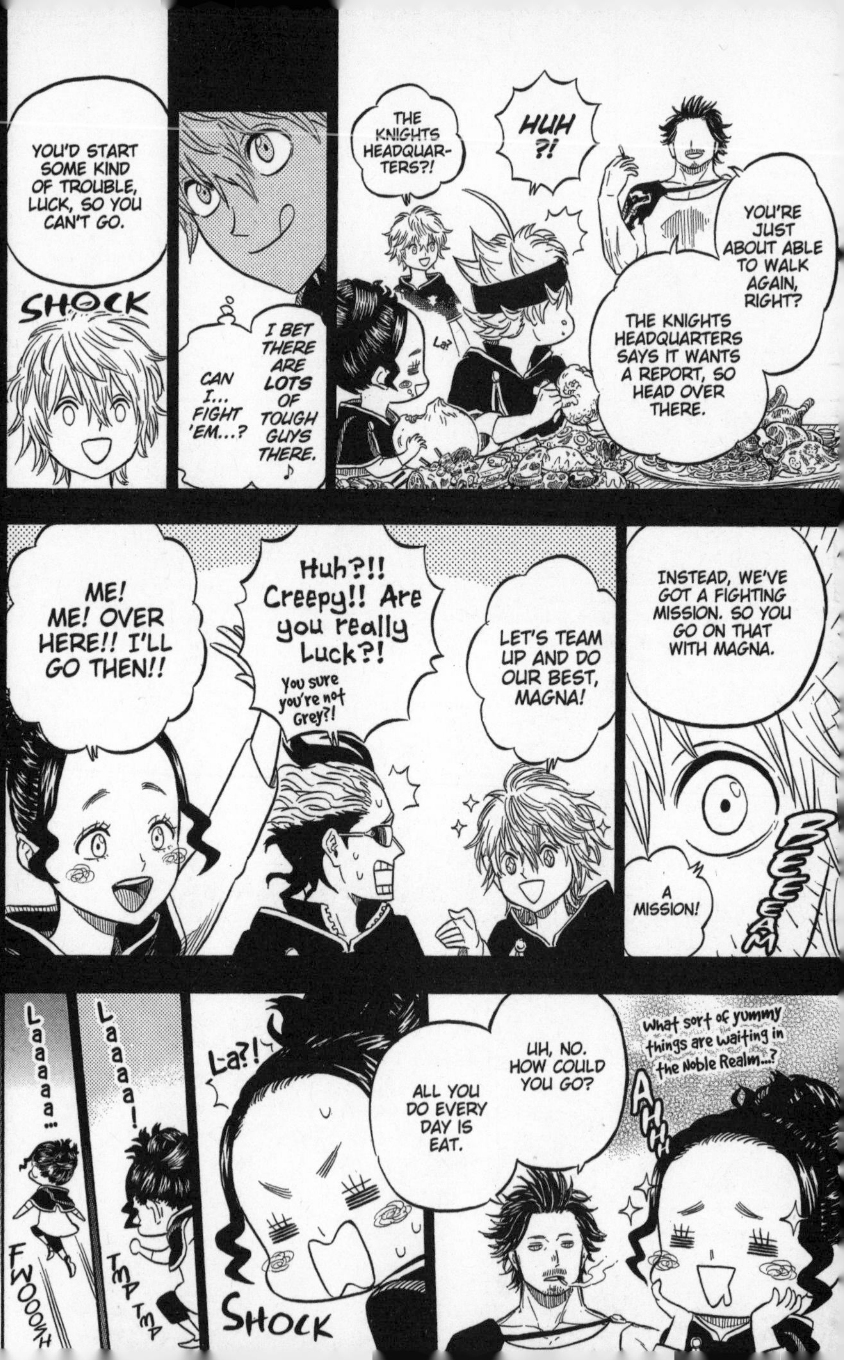
YOU'RE JUST ABOUT ABLE TO WALK AGAIN, RIGHT?
THE KNIGHTS HEADQUARTERS SAYS IT WANTS A REPORT, SO HEAD OVER THERE.
HUH ?!
THE KNIGHTS HEADQUARTERS?!
La?
I BET THERE ARE LOTS OF TOUGH GUYS THERE. ♪
CAN I... FIGHT 'EM...?
YOU'D START SOME KIND OF TROUBLE, LUCK, SO YOU CAN'T GO.
SHOCK
INSTEAD, WE'VE GOT A FIGHTING MISSION. SO YOU GO ON THAT WITH MAGNA.
A MISSION!
BEEEEAM
LET'S TEAM UP AND DO OUR BEST, MAGNA!
Huh?!! Creepy!! Are you really Luck?!
You sure you're not Grey?!
ME! ME! OVER HERE!! I'LL GO THEN!!
What sort of yummy things are waiting in the Noble Realm...?
AHHH
UH, NO. HOW COULD YOU GO?
ALL YOU DO EVERY DAY IS EAT.
L-a?!
SHOCK
Laaaa!
TMP TMP TMP
Laaaa...
FWOOOSH

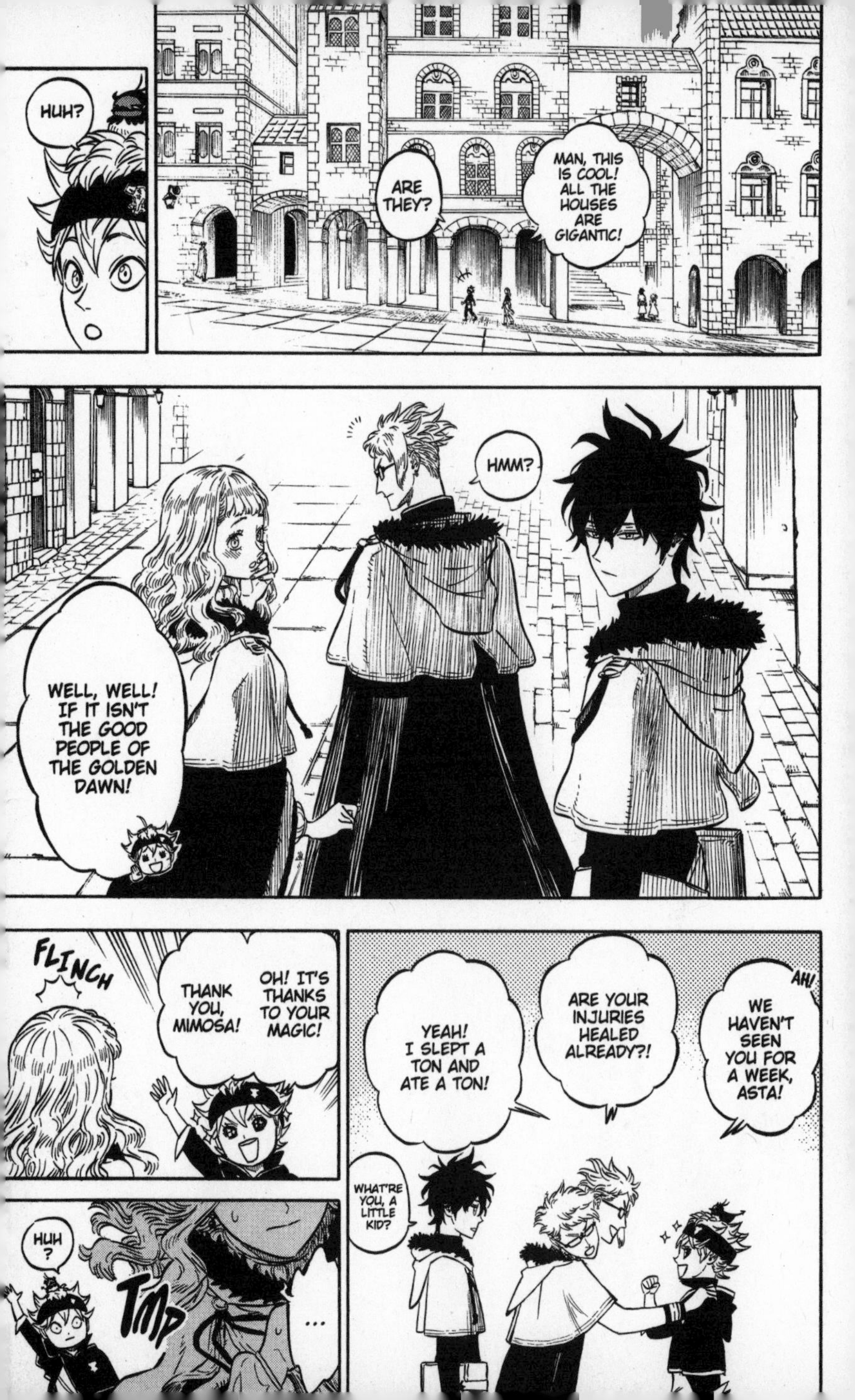
MAN, THIS IS COOL! ALL THE HOUSES ARE GIGANTIC!
ARE THEY?
HUH?
HMM?
WELL, WELL! IF IT ISN'T THE GOOD PEOPLE OF THE GOLDEN DAWN!
AH!
WE HAVEN'T SEEN YOU FOR A WEEK, ASTA!
ARE YOUR INJURIES HEALED ALREADY?!
YEAH! I SLEPT A TON AND ATE A TON!
WHAT'RE YOU, A LITTLE KID?
OH! IT'S THANKS TO YOUR MAGIC!
THANK YOU, MIMOSA!
FLINCH
TMP
...
HUH?

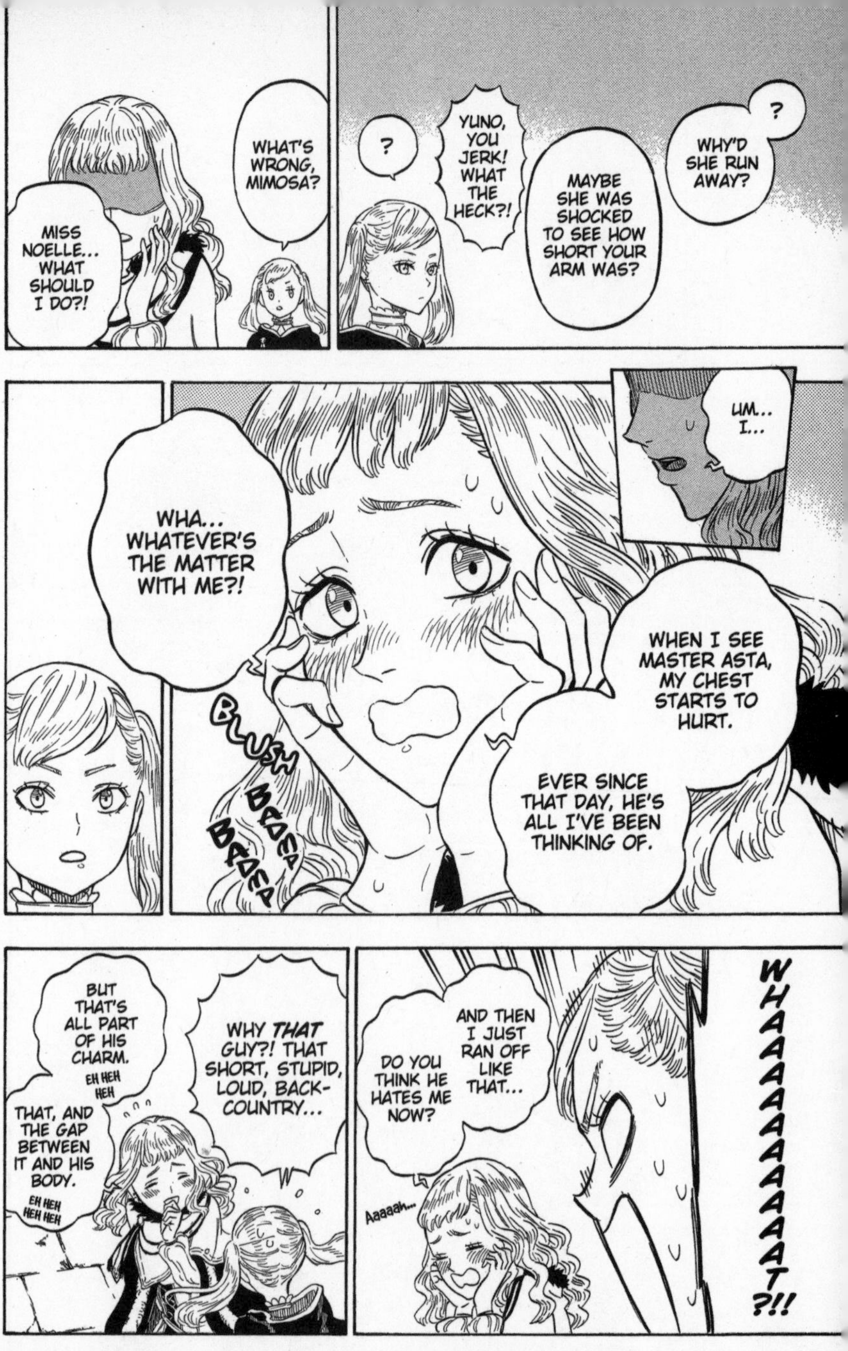
?
WHY'D SHE RUN AWAY?
MAYBE SHE WAS SHOCKED TO SEE HOW SHORT YOUR ARM WAS?
YUNO, YOU JERK! WHAT THE HECK?!
?
WHAT'S WRONG, MIMOSA?
MISS NOELLE... WHAT SHOULD I DO?!
UM... I...
WHEN I SEE MASTER ASTA, MY CHEST STARTS TO HURT.
EVER SINCE THAT DAY, HE'S ALL I'VE BEEN THINKING OF.
WHA... WHATEVER'S THE MATTER WITH ME?!
BLUSH
BADMP BADMP
WHAAAAAAAAAAAT?!!
AND THEN I JUST RAN OFF LIKE THAT...
DO YOU THINK HE HATES ME NOW?
Aaaaah...
WHY *THAT* GUY?! THAT SHORT, STUPID, LOUD, BACK-COUNTRY...
BUT THAT'S ALL PART OF HIS CHARM.
EH HEH HEH
THAT, AND THE GAP BETWEEN IT AND HIS BODY.
EH HEH HEH HEH

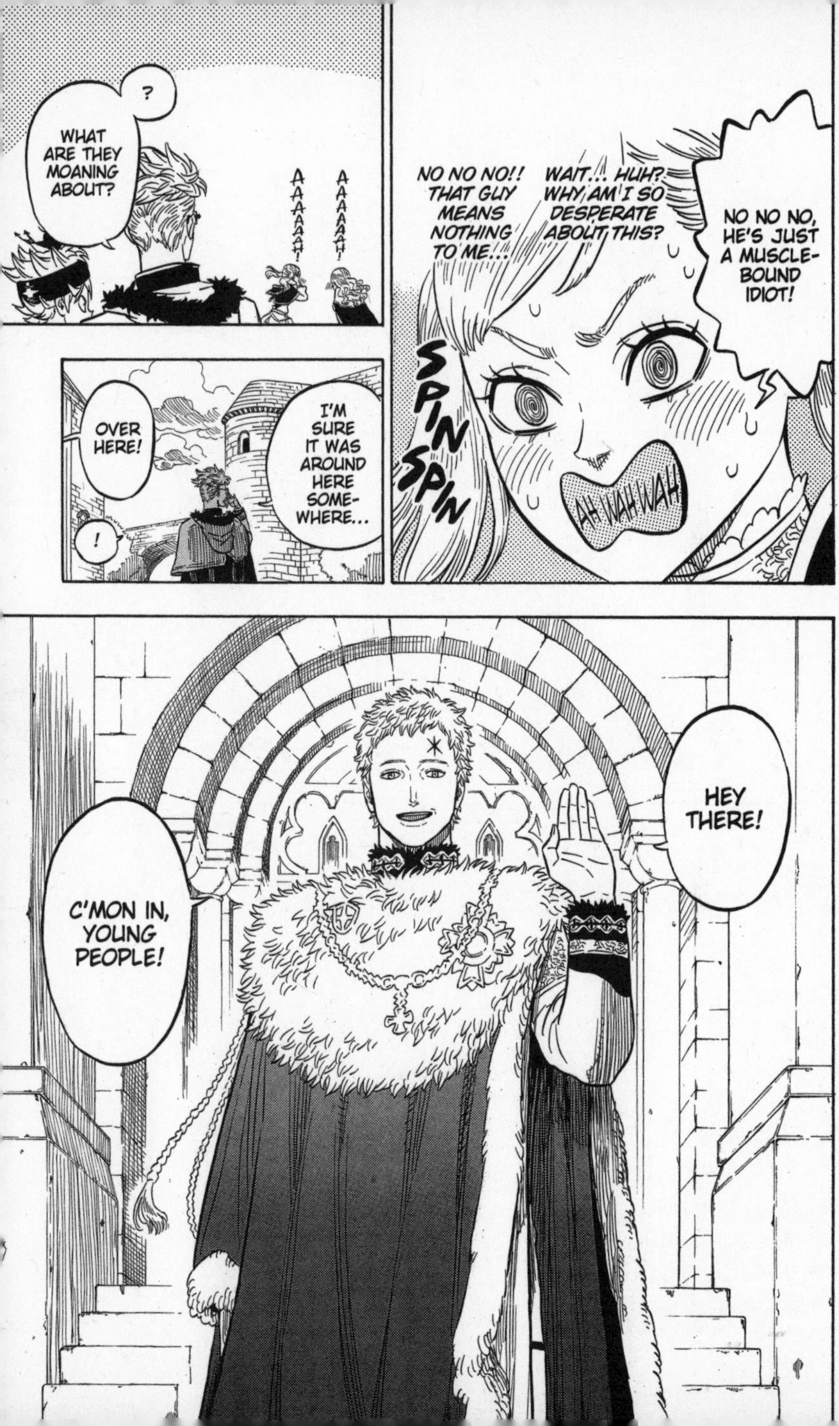
NO NO NO, HE'S JUST A MUSCLE-BOUND IDIOT!
WAIT... HUH? WHY AM I SO DESPERATE ABOUT THIS?
NO NO NO!! THAT GUY MEANS NOTHING TO ME...
SPIN SPIN
AH WAH WAH
AAAAAAH!
AAAAAAH!
?
WHAT ARE THEY MOANING ABOUT?
I'M SURE IT WAS AROUND HERE SOME-WHERE...
OVER HERE!
!
HEY THERE!
C'MON IN, YOUNG PEOPLE!

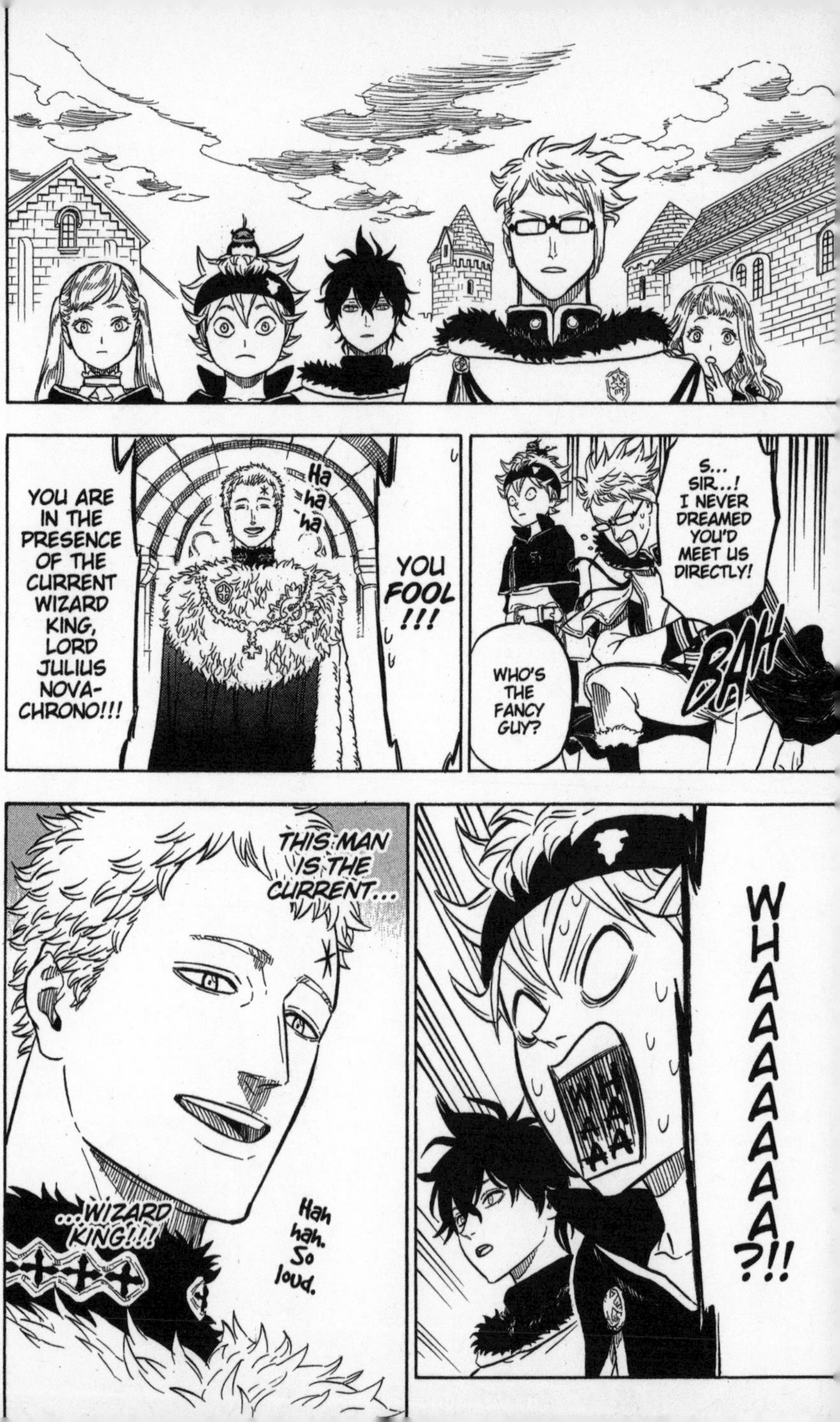
S... SIR...! I NEVER DREAMED YOU'D MEET US DIRECTLY!
BAH
WHO'S THE FANCY GUY?
YOU FOOL!!!
Ha ha ha
YOU ARE IN THE PRESENCE OF THE CURRENT WIZARD KING, LORD JULIUS NOVA-CHRONO!!!
WHAAAAAAAA?!!
WHAAA
THIS MAN IS THE CURRENT...
Hah hah. So loud.
...WIZARD KING!!!

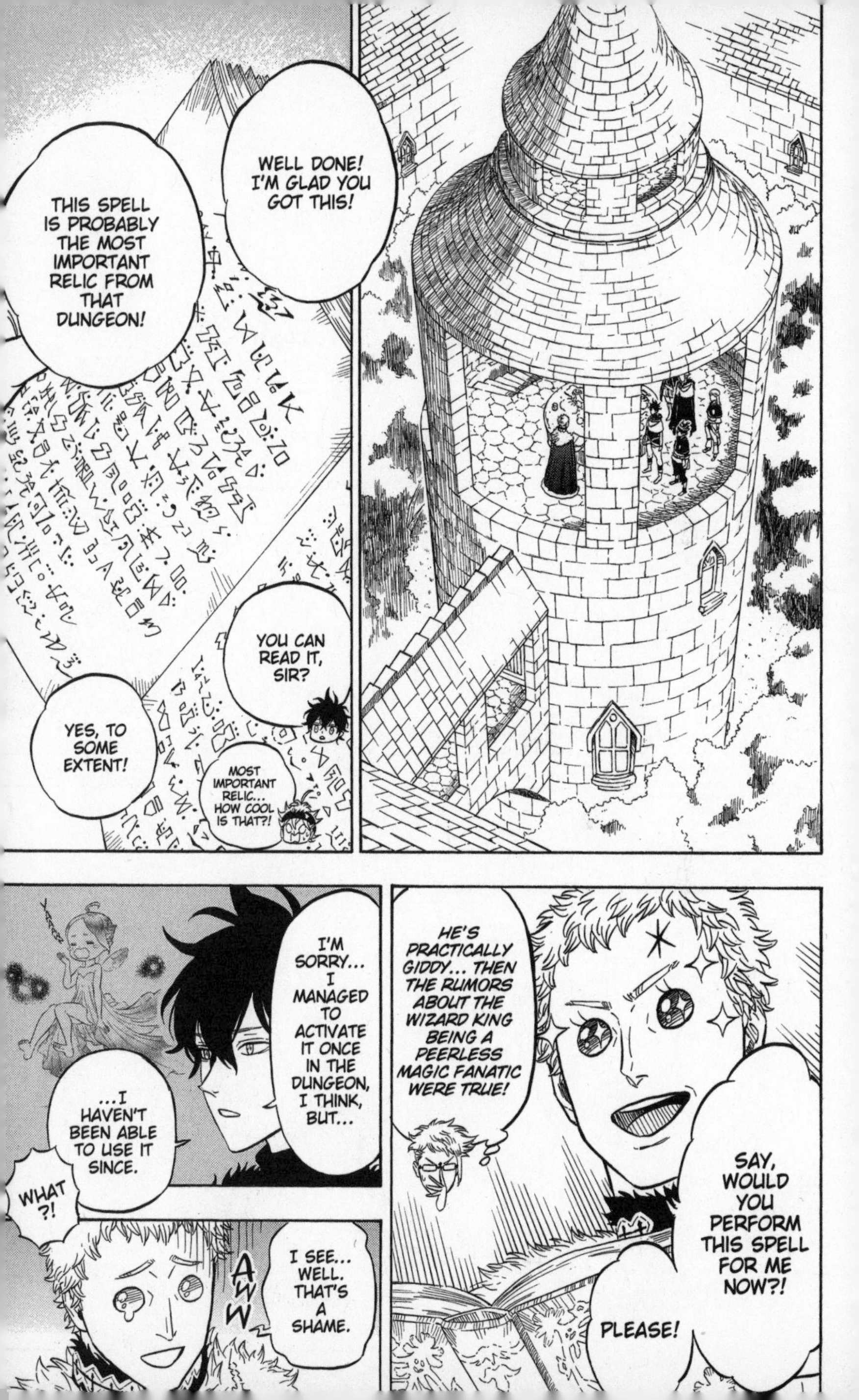
WELL DONE! I'M GLAD YOU GOT THIS!
THIS SPELL IS PROBABLY THE MOST IMPORTANT RELIC FROM THAT DUNGEON!
YOU CAN READ IT, SIR?
YES, TO SOME EXTENT!
MOST IMPORTANT RELIC... HOW COOL IS THAT?!
HE'S PRACTICALLY GIDDY... THEN THE RUMORS ABOUT THE WIZARD KING BEING A PEERLESS MAGIC FANATIC WERE TRUE!
SAY, WOULD YOU PERFORM THIS SPELL FOR ME NOW?!
PLEASE!
I'M SORRY... I MANAGED TO ACTIVATE IT ONCE IN THE DUNGEON, I THINK, BUT...
...I HAVEN'T BEEN ABLE TO USE IT SINCE.
WHAT ?!
I SEE... WELL. THAT'S A SHAME.
AWW

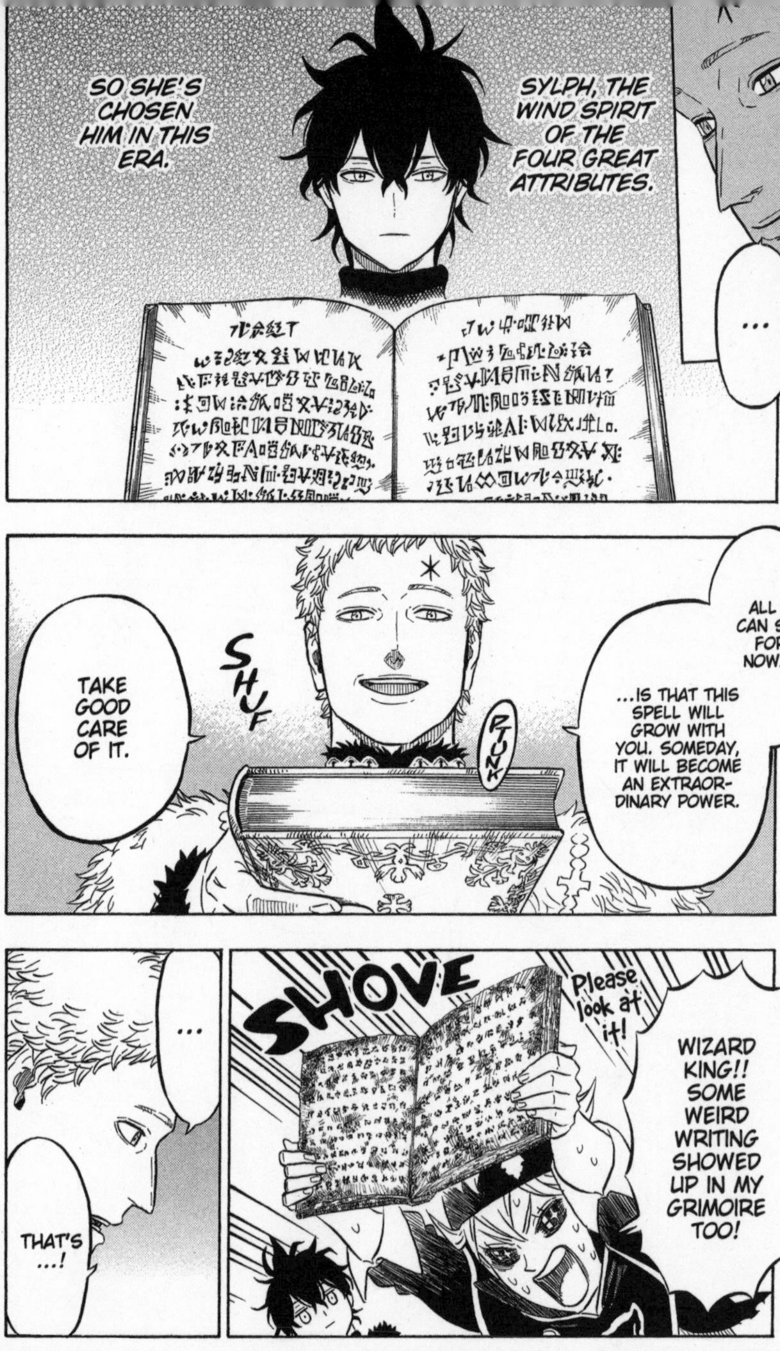
...
SYLPH, THE WIND SPIRIT OF THE FOUR GREAT ATTRIBUTES.
SO SHE'S CHOSEN HIM IN THIS ERA.
ALL I CAN SAY FOR NOW...
...IS THAT THIS SPELL WILL GROW WITH YOU. SOMEDAY, IT WILL BECOME AN EXTRAOR-DINARY POWER.
PTUNK
SHUF
TAKE GOOD CARE OF IT.
WIZARD KING!! SOME WEIRD WRITING SHOWED UP IN MY GRIMOIRE TOO!
Please look at it!
SHOVE
...
THAT'S ...!

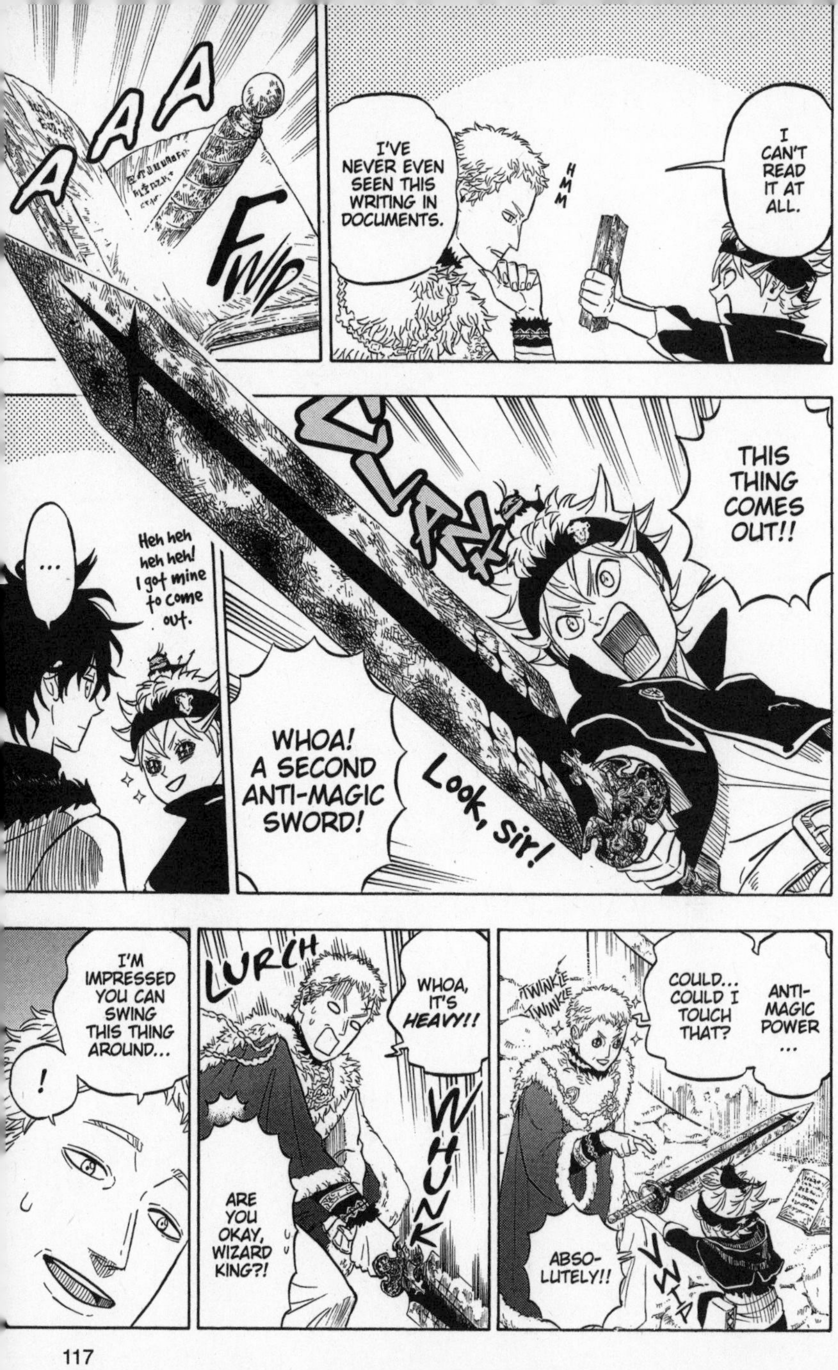
I CAN'T READ IT AT ALL.
HMM
I'VE NEVER EVEN SEEN THIS WRITING IN DOCUMENTS.
AAAA
FWIP
THIS THING COMES OUT!!
Look, sir!
WHOA! A SECOND ANTI-MAGIC SWORD!
Heh heh heh heh! I got mine to come out.
...
ANTI-MAGIC POWER...
COULD... COULD I TOUCH THAT?
TWINKLE TWINKLE
ABSO-LUTELY!!
WHOA, IT'S HEAVY!!
LURCH
WHUNK
ARE YOU OKAY, WIZARD KING?!
I'M IMPRESSED YOU CAN SWING THIS THING AROUND...
!

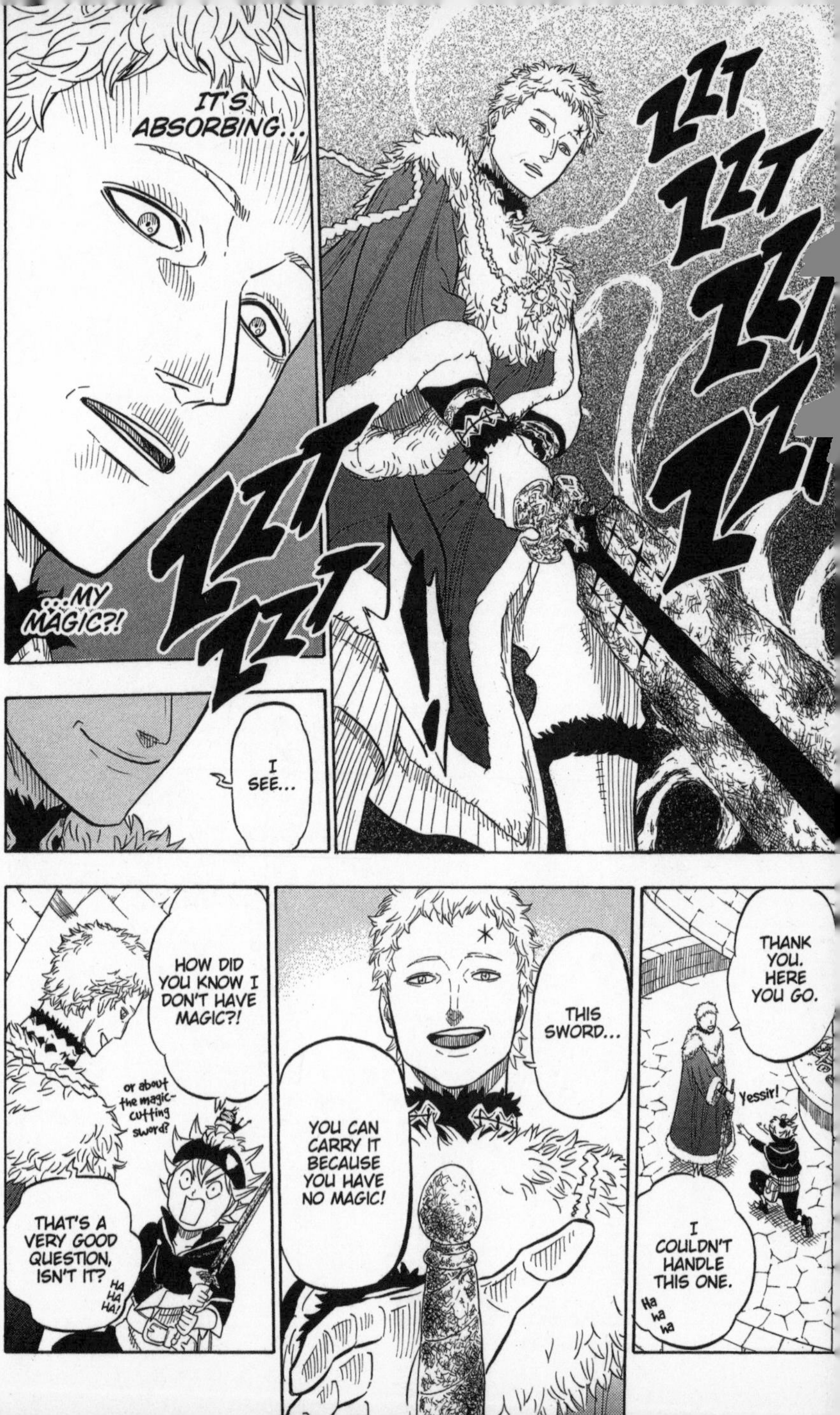
ZZZT ZZZT
ZZZT ZZZT
IT'S ABSORBING...
...MY MAGIC?!
I SEE...
THANK YOU. HERE YOU GO.
Yessir!
I COULDN'T HANDLE THIS ONE.
Ha ha ha
THIS SWORD...
YOU CAN CARRY IT BECAUSE YOU HAVE NO MAGIC!
HOW DID YOU KNOW I DON'T HAVE MAGIC?!
or about the magic-cutting sword?
THAT'S A VERY GOOD QUESTION, ISN'T IT?
HA HA HA!

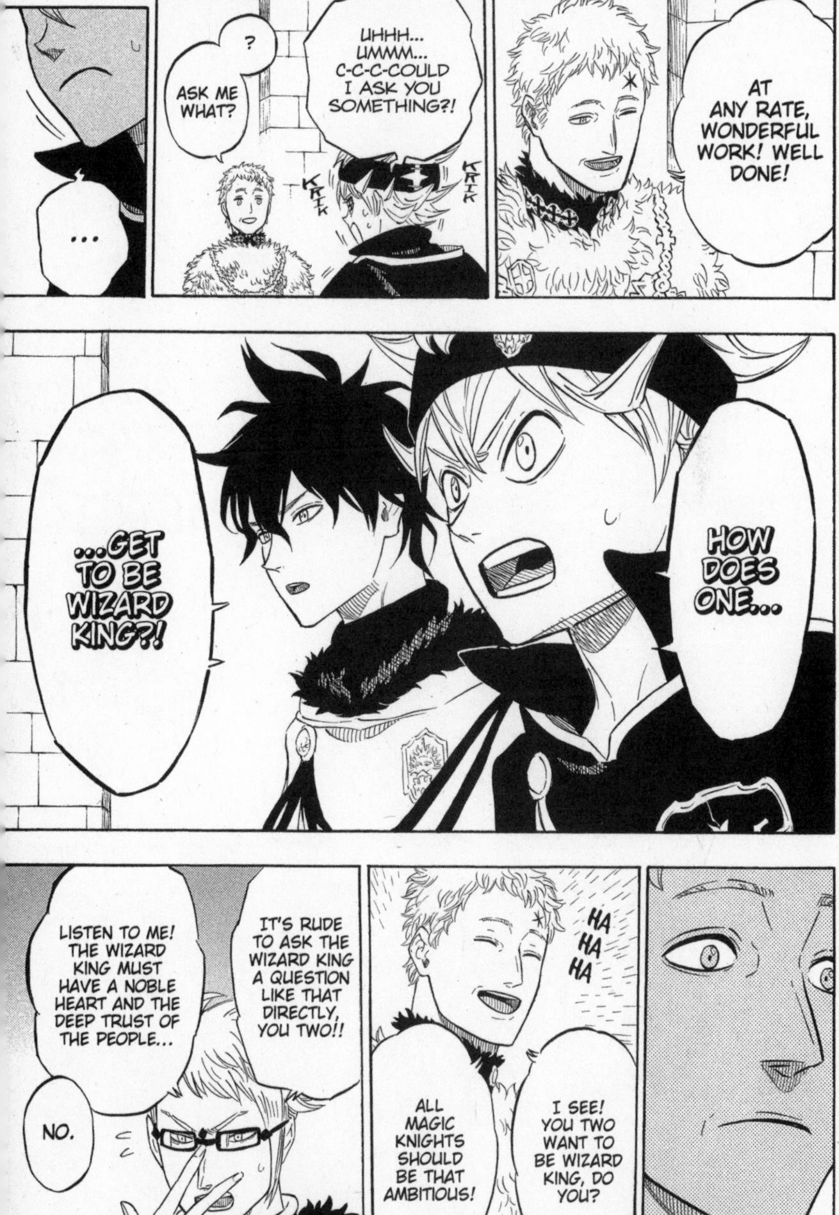
AT ANY RATE, WONDERFUL WORK! WELL DONE!
UHHH... UMMM... C-C-C-COULD I ASK YOU SOMETHING?!
KRIK
KRIK
?
ASK ME WHAT?
...
HOW DOES ONE...
...GET TO BE WIZARD KING?!
HA HA HA
I SEE! YOU TWO WANT TO BE WIZARD KING, DO YOU?
ALL MAGIC KNIGHTS SHOULD BE THAT AMBITIOUS!
IT'S RUDE TO ASK THE WIZARD KING A QUESTION LIKE THAT DIRECTLY, YOU TWO!!
LISTEN TO ME! THE WIZARD KING MUST HAVE A NOBLE HEART AND THE DEEP TRUST OF THE PEOPLE...
NO.

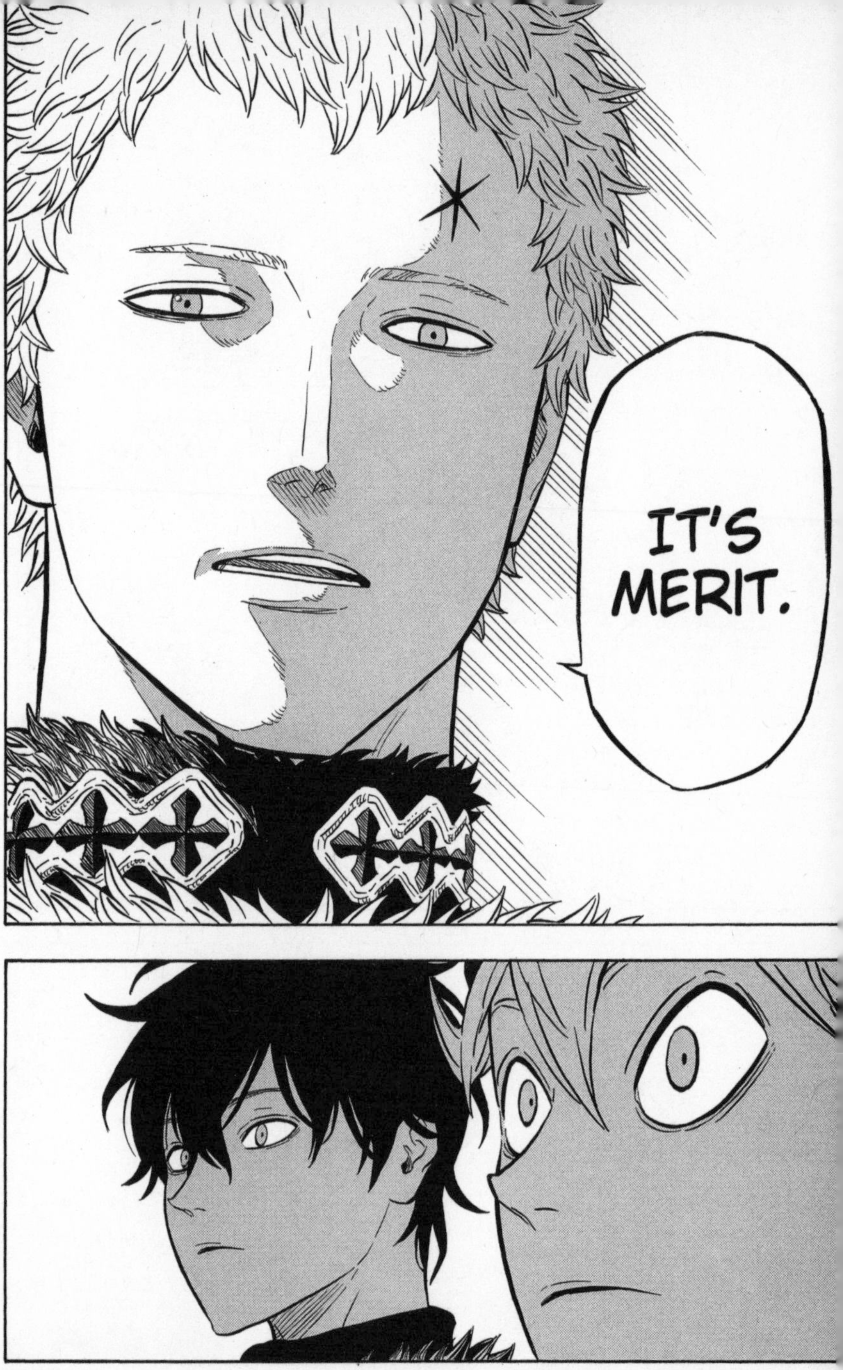
IT'S MERIT.

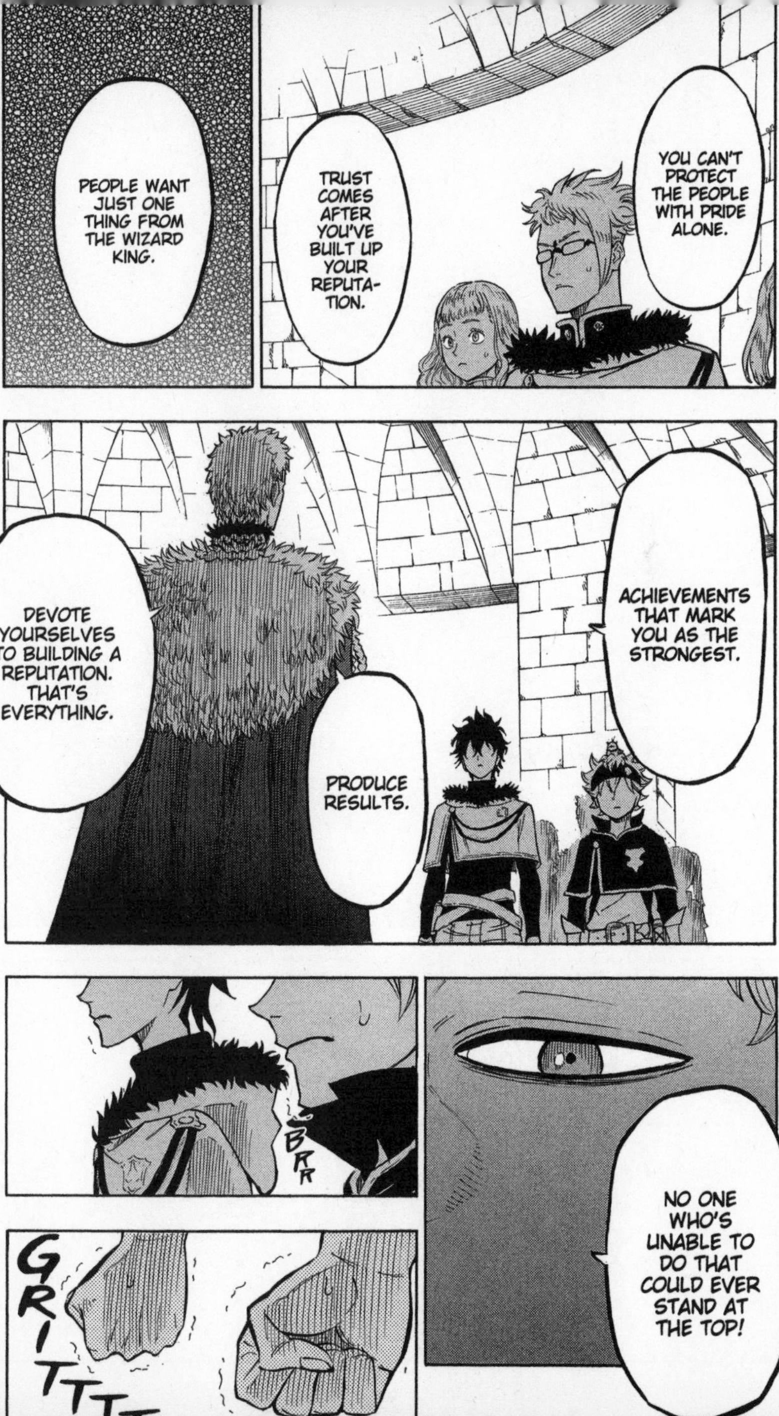
YOU CAN'T PROTECT THE PEOPLE WITH PRIDE ALONE.
TRUST COMES AFTER YOU'VE BUILT UP YOUR REPUTA-TION.
PEOPLE WANT JUST ONE THING FROM THE WIZARD KING.
ACHIEVEMENTS THAT MARK YOU AS THE STRONGEST.
PRODUCE RESULTS.
DEVOTE YOURSELVES TO BUILDING A REPUTATION. THAT'S EVERYTHING.
NO ONE WHO'S UNABLE TO DO THAT COULD EVER STAND AT THE TOP!
BRR
GRITTTT

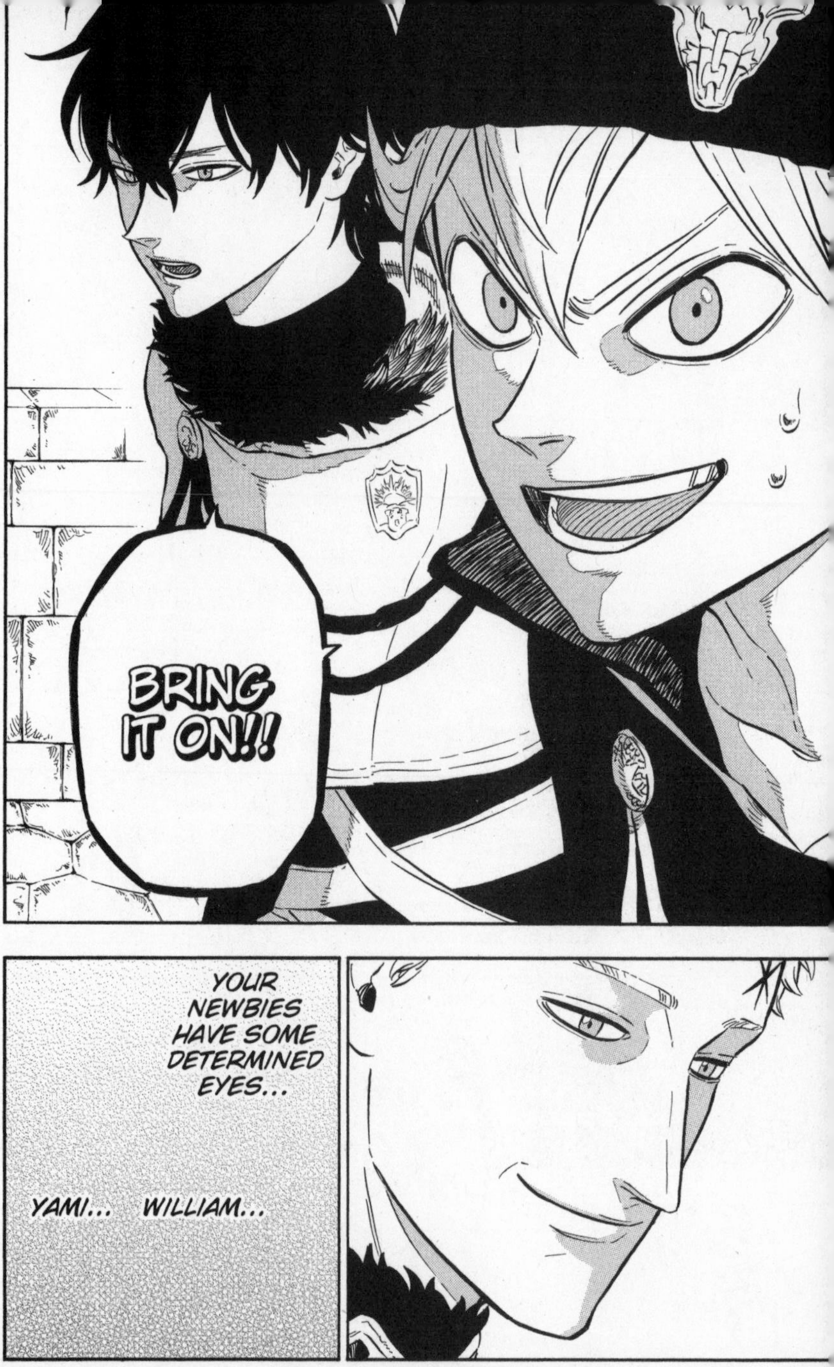
BRING IT ON!!
YOUR NEWBIES HAVE SOME DETERMINED EYES...
YAMI... WILLIAM...

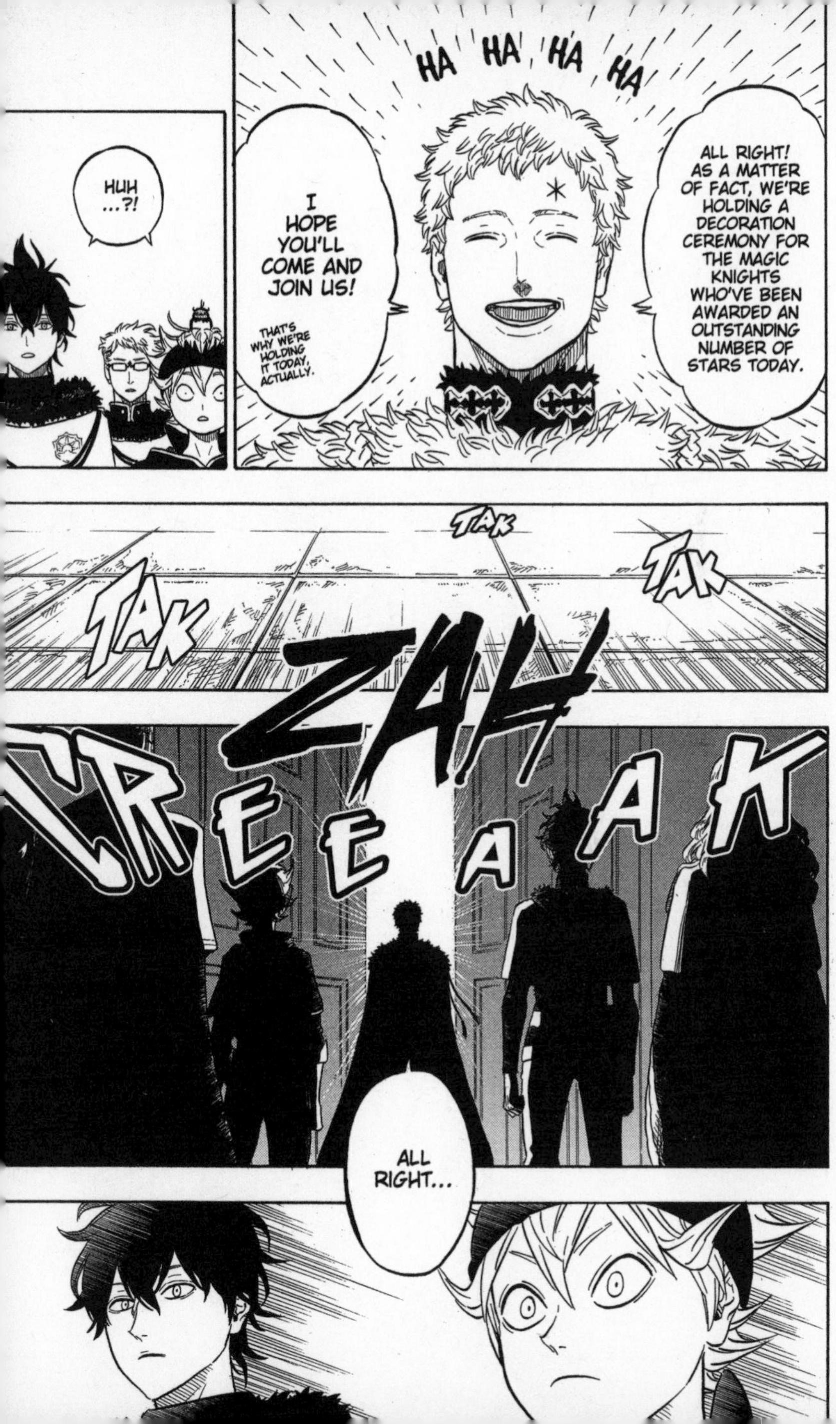
HA HA HA HA
ALL RIGHT! AS A MATTER OF FACT, WE'RE HOLDING A DECORATION CEREMONY FOR THE MAGIC KNIGHTS WHO'VE BEEN AWARDED AN OUTSTANDING NUMBER OF STARS TODAY.
I HOPE YOU'LL COME AND JOIN US!
THAT'S WHY WE'RE HOLDING IT TODAY, ACTUALLY.
HUH ...?!
TAK
TAK
TAK
ZAH
CREEAAK
ALL RIGHT...

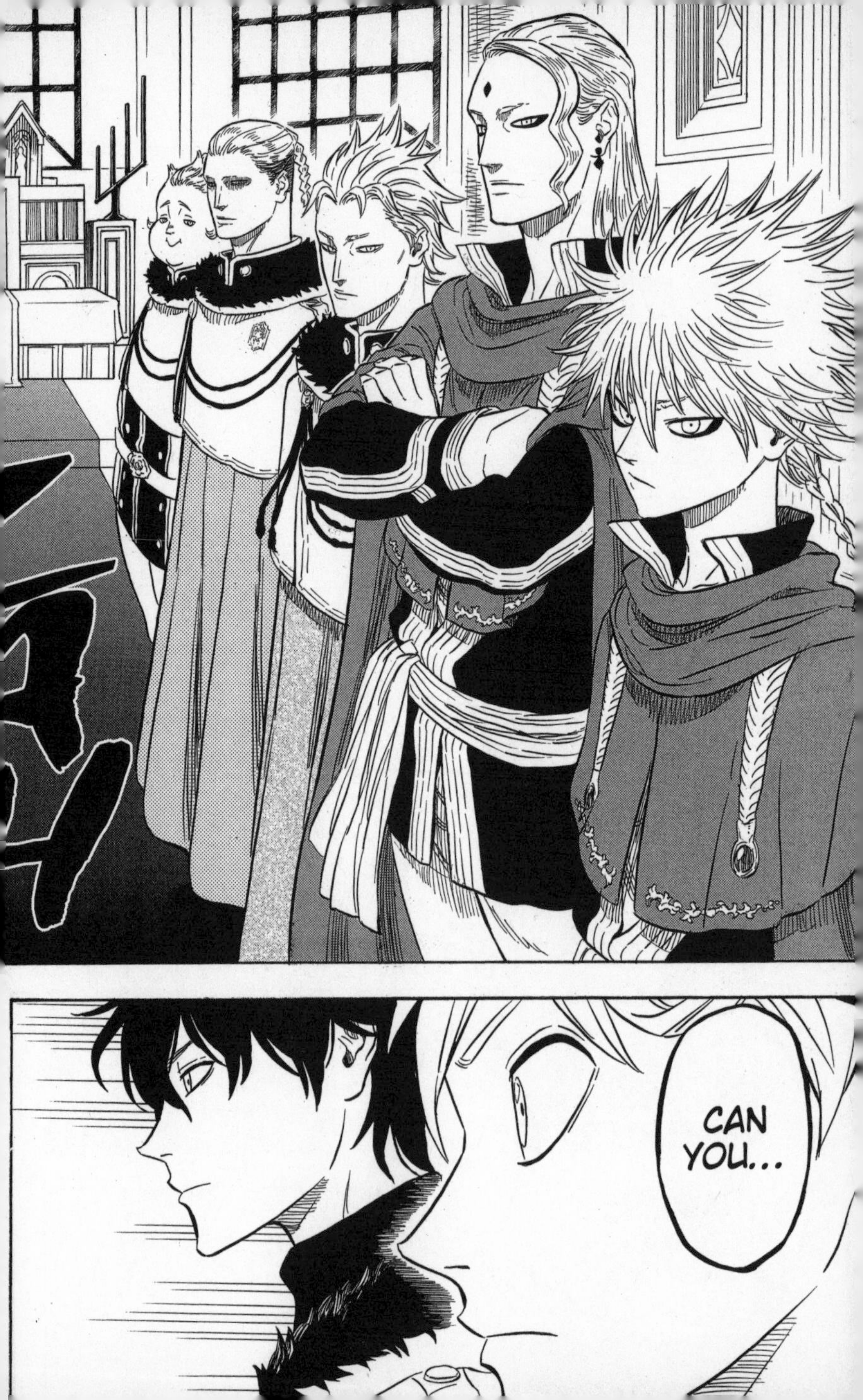
CAN YOU...

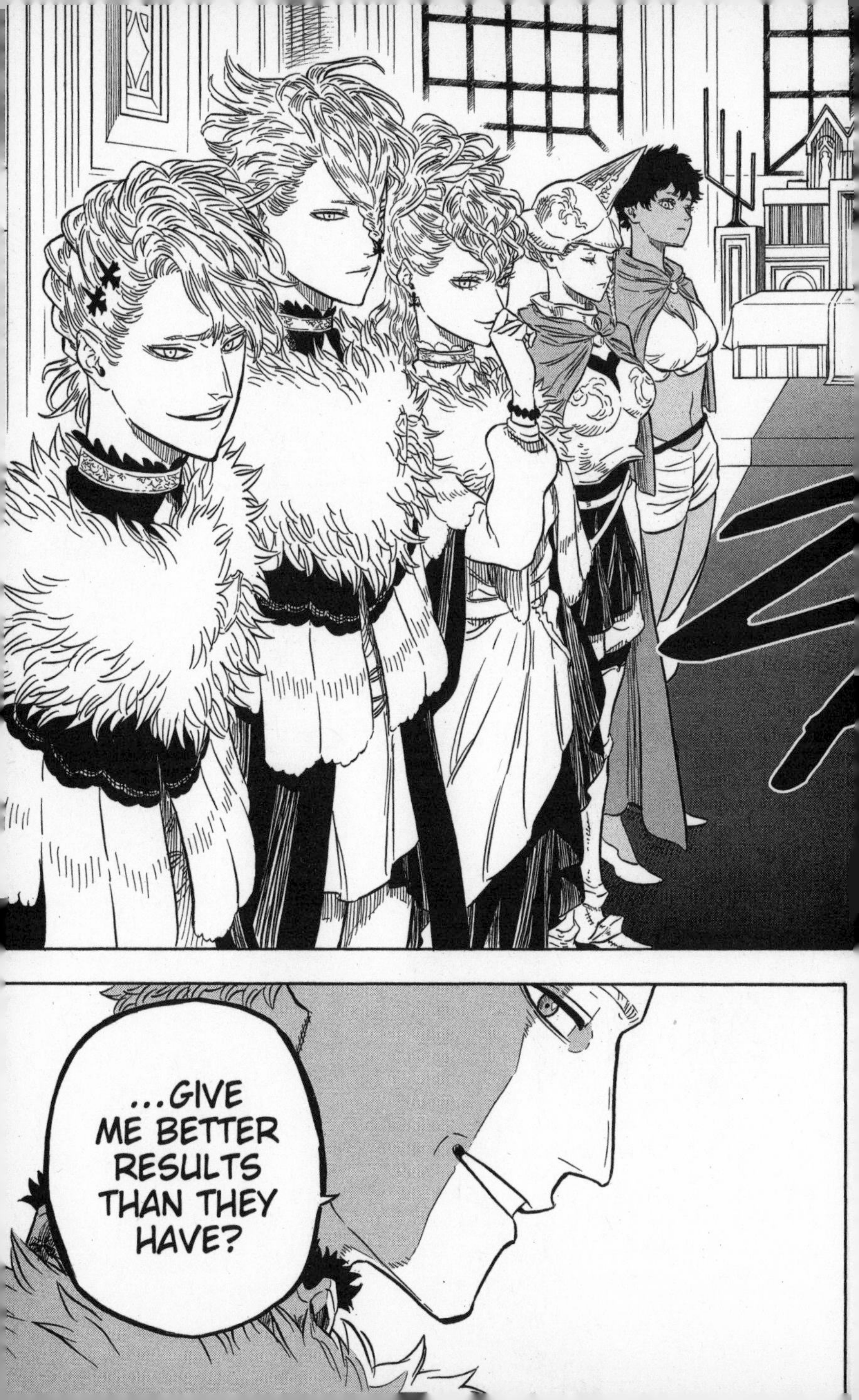
...GIVE ME BETTER RESULTS THAN THEY HAVE?

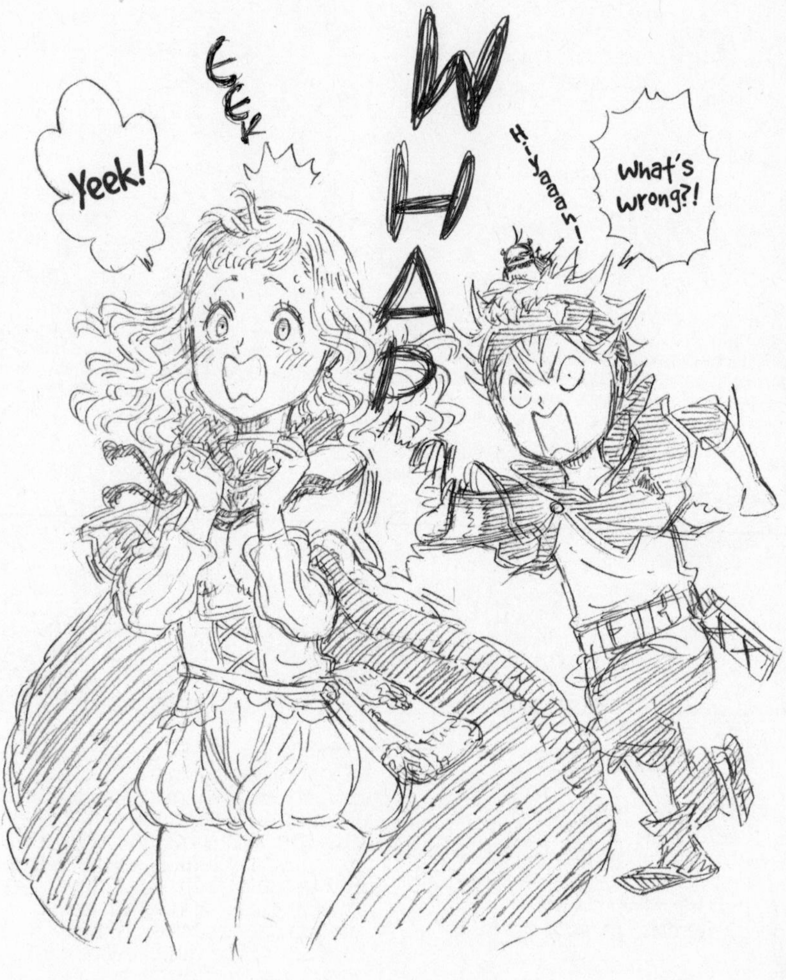
What's wrong?!
Hiyaaah!
WHAP
EEK
Yeek!

✿ Page 23: The Distinguished Service Ceremony

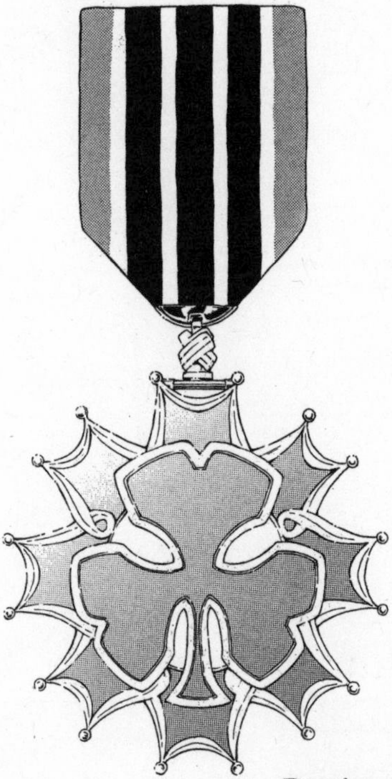

Ranks (Titles):

Rank Names
① Wizard King
② Grand Magic Knight
③ Senior Magic Knight
④ Intermediate Magic Knight
⑤ Junior Magic Knight

Magic Knights of the Clover Kingdom are given ranks to indicate each knight's ability. There are five general ranks, with the Wizard King at the top, and each rank is subdivided in five again, from first class to fifth class. If knights are awarded a prescribed number of stars in the time before the annual decoration ceremony, they are given a new rank by the Wizard King.

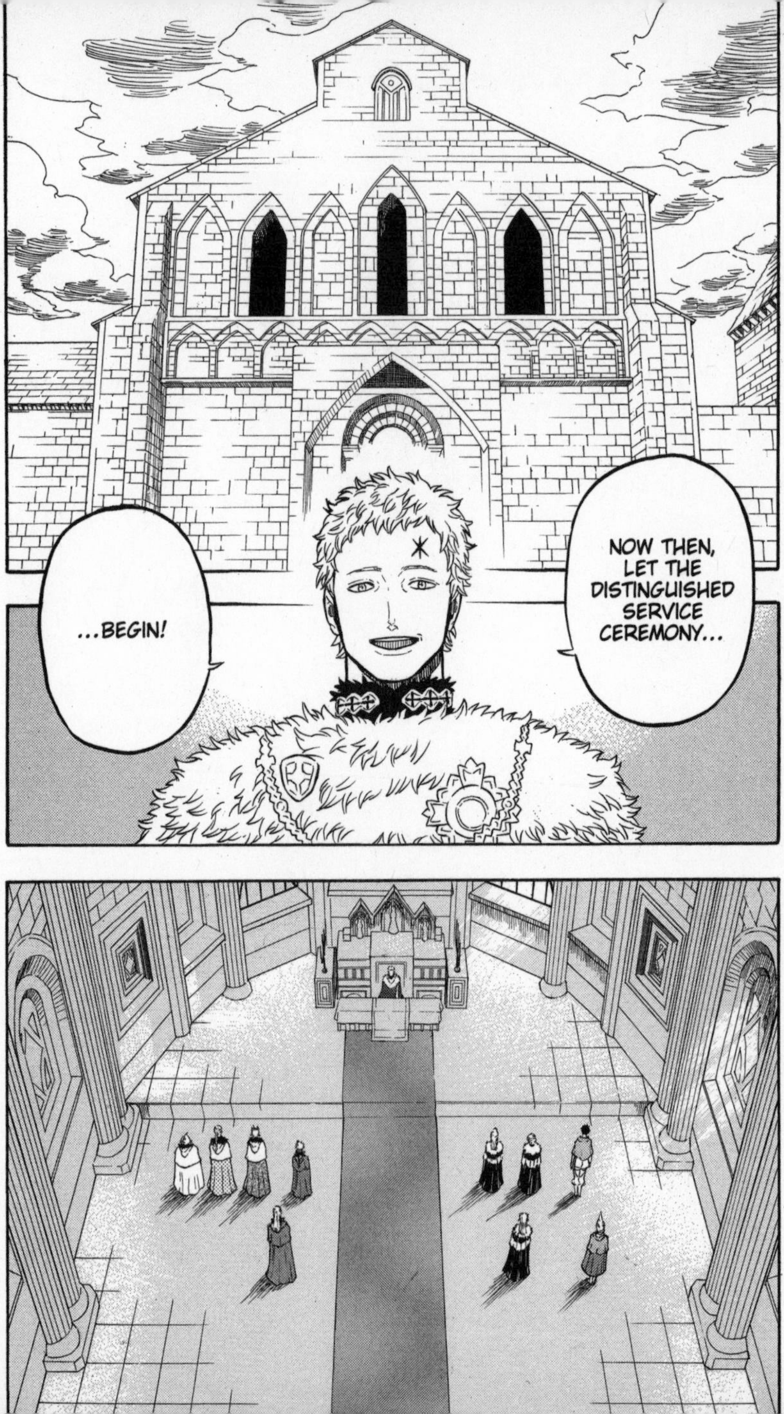
NOW THEN, LET THE DISTINGUISHED SERVICE CEREMONY...
...BEGIN!

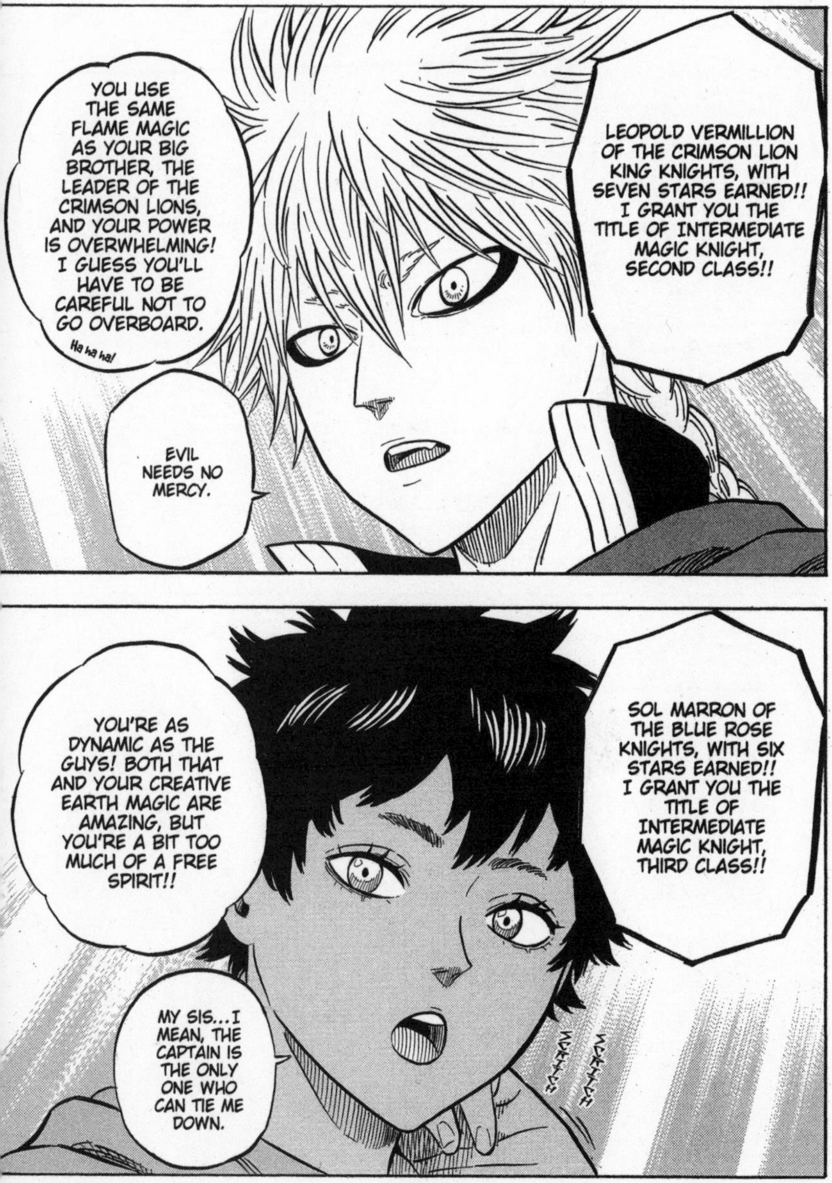
LEOPOLD VERMILLION OF THE CRIMSON LION KING KNIGHTS, WITH SEVEN STARS EARNED!! I GRANT YOU THE TITLE OF INTERMEDIATE MAGIC KNIGHT, SECOND CLASS!!
YOU USE THE SAME FLAME MAGIC AS YOUR BIG BROTHER, THE LEADER OF THE CRIMSON LIONS, AND YOUR POWER IS OVERWHELMING! I GUESS YOU'LL HAVE TO BE CAREFUL NOT TO GO OVERBOARD.
Ha ha ha!
EVIL NEEDS NO MERCY.
SOL MARRON OF THE BLUE ROSE KNIGHTS, WITH SIX STARS EARNED!! I GRANT YOU THE TITLE OF INTERMEDIATE MAGIC KNIGHT, THIRD CLASS!!
YOU'RE AS DYNAMIC AS THE GUYS! BOTH THAT AND YOUR CREATIVE EARTH MAGIC ARE AMAZING, BUT YOU'RE A BIT TOO MUCH OF A FREE SPIRIT!!
SCRITCH
SCRITCH
MY SIS...I MEAN, THE CAPTAIN IS THE ONLY ONE WHO CAN TIE ME DOWN.

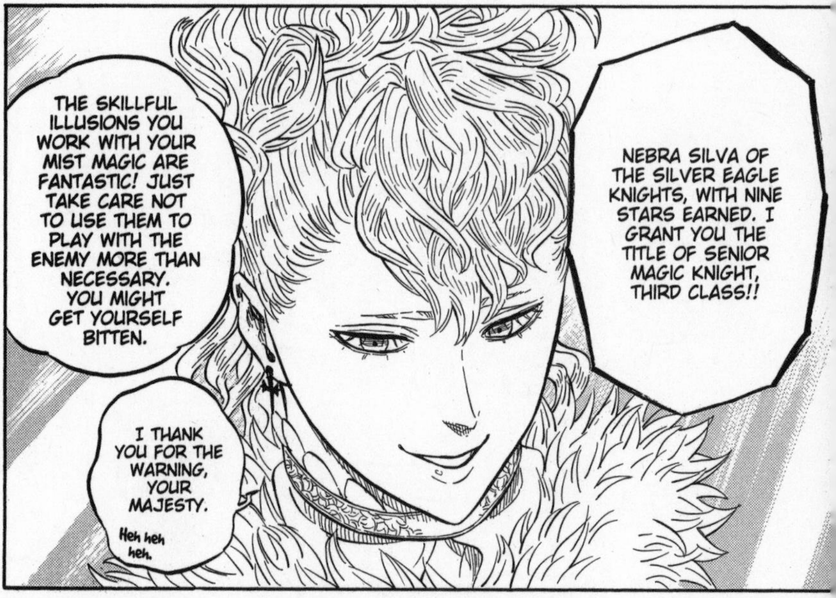
NEBRA SILVA OF THE SILVER EAGLE KNIGHTS, WITH NINE STARS EARNED. I GRANT YOU THE TITLE OF SENIOR MAGIC KNIGHT, THIRD CLASS!!
THE SKILLFUL ILLUSIONS YOU WORK WITH YOUR MIST MAGIC ARE FANTASTIC! JUST TAKE CARE NOT TO USE THEM TO PLAY WITH THE ENEMY MORE THAN NECESSARY. YOU MIGHT GET YOURSELF BITTEN.
I THANK YOU FOR THE WARNING, YOUR MAJESTY.
Heh heh heh.
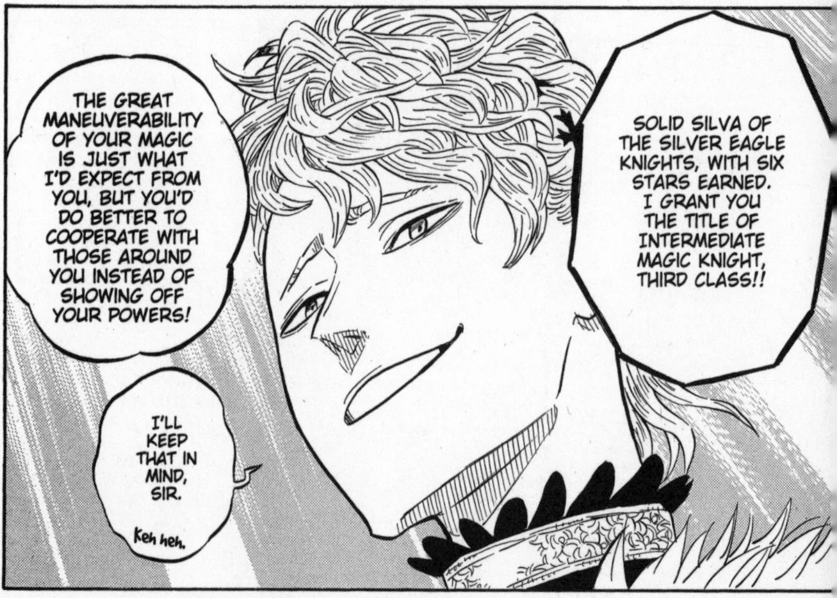
SOLID SILVA OF THE SILVER EAGLE KNIGHTS, WITH SIX STARS EARNED. I GRANT YOU THE TITLE OF INTERMEDIATE MAGIC KNIGHT, THIRD CLASS!!
THE GREAT MANEUVERABILITY OF YOUR MAGIC IS JUST WHAT I'D EXPECT FROM YOU, BUT YOU'D DO BETTER TO COOPERATE WITH THOSE AROUND YOU INSTEAD OF SHOWING OFF YOUR POWERS!
I'LL KEEP THAT IN MIND, SIR.
Keh heh.

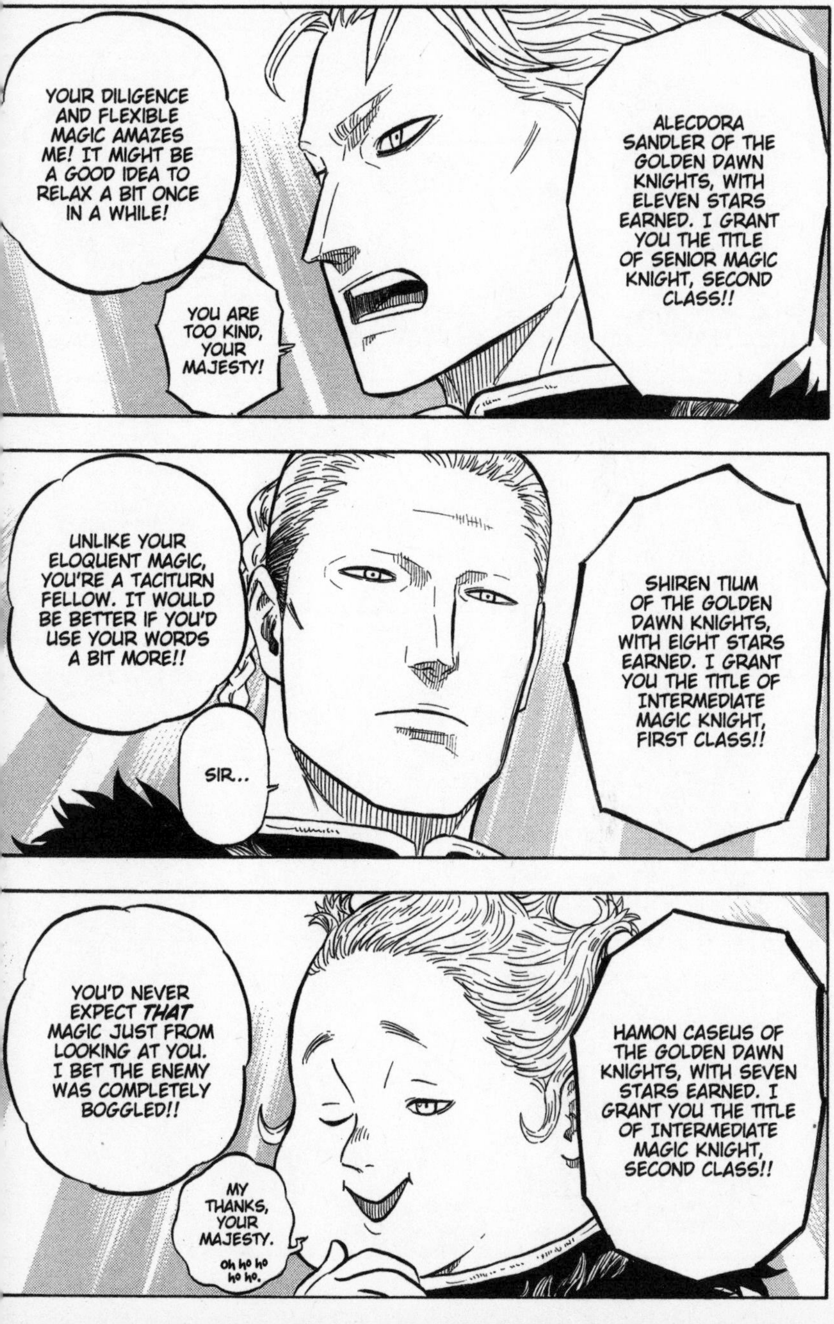
ALECDORA SANDLER OF THE GOLDEN DAWN KNIGHTS, WITH ELEVEN STARS EARNED. I GRANT YOU THE TITLE OF SENIOR MAGIC KNIGHT, SECOND CLASS!!
YOUR DILIGENCE AND FLEXIBLE MAGIC AMAZES ME! IT MIGHT BE A GOOD IDEA TO RELAX A BIT ONCE IN A WHILE!
YOU ARE TOO KIND, YOUR MAJESTY!
SHIREN TIUM OF THE GOLDEN DAWN KNIGHTS, WITH EIGHT STARS EARNED. I GRANT YOU THE TITLE OF INTERMEDIATE MAGIC KNIGHT, FIRST CLASS!!
UNLIKE YOUR ELOQUENT MAGIC, YOU'RE A TACITURN FELLOW. IT WOULD BE BETTER IF YOU'D USE YOUR WORDS A BIT MORE!!
SIR...
HAMON CASEUS OF THE GOLDEN DAWN KNIGHTS, WITH SEVEN STARS EARNED. I GRANT YOU THE TITLE OF INTERMEDIATE MAGIC KNIGHT, SECOND CLASS!!
YOU'D NEVER EXPECT *THAT* MAGIC JUST FROM LOOKING AT YOU. I BET THE ENEMY WAS COMPLETELY BOGGLED!!
MY THANKS, YOUR MAJESTY.
oh ho ho ho ho.

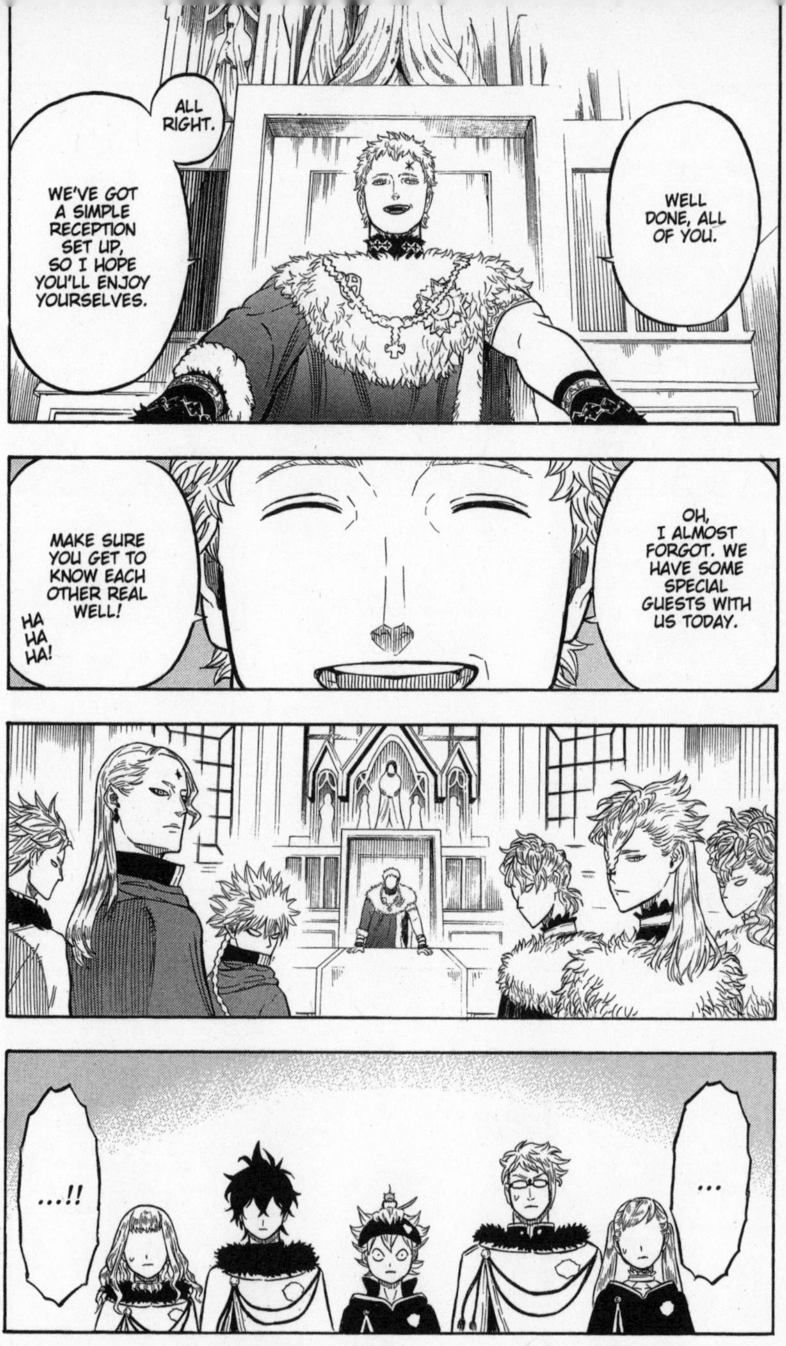
WELL DONE, ALL OF YOU.
ALL RIGHT.
WE'VE GOT A SIMPLE RECEPTION SET UP, SO I HOPE YOU'LL ENJOY YOURSELVES.
OH, I ALMOST FORGOT. WE HAVE SOME SPECIAL GUESTS WITH US TODAY.
MAKE SURE YOU GET TO KNOW EACH OTHER REAL WELL!
HA HA HA!
...
...!!

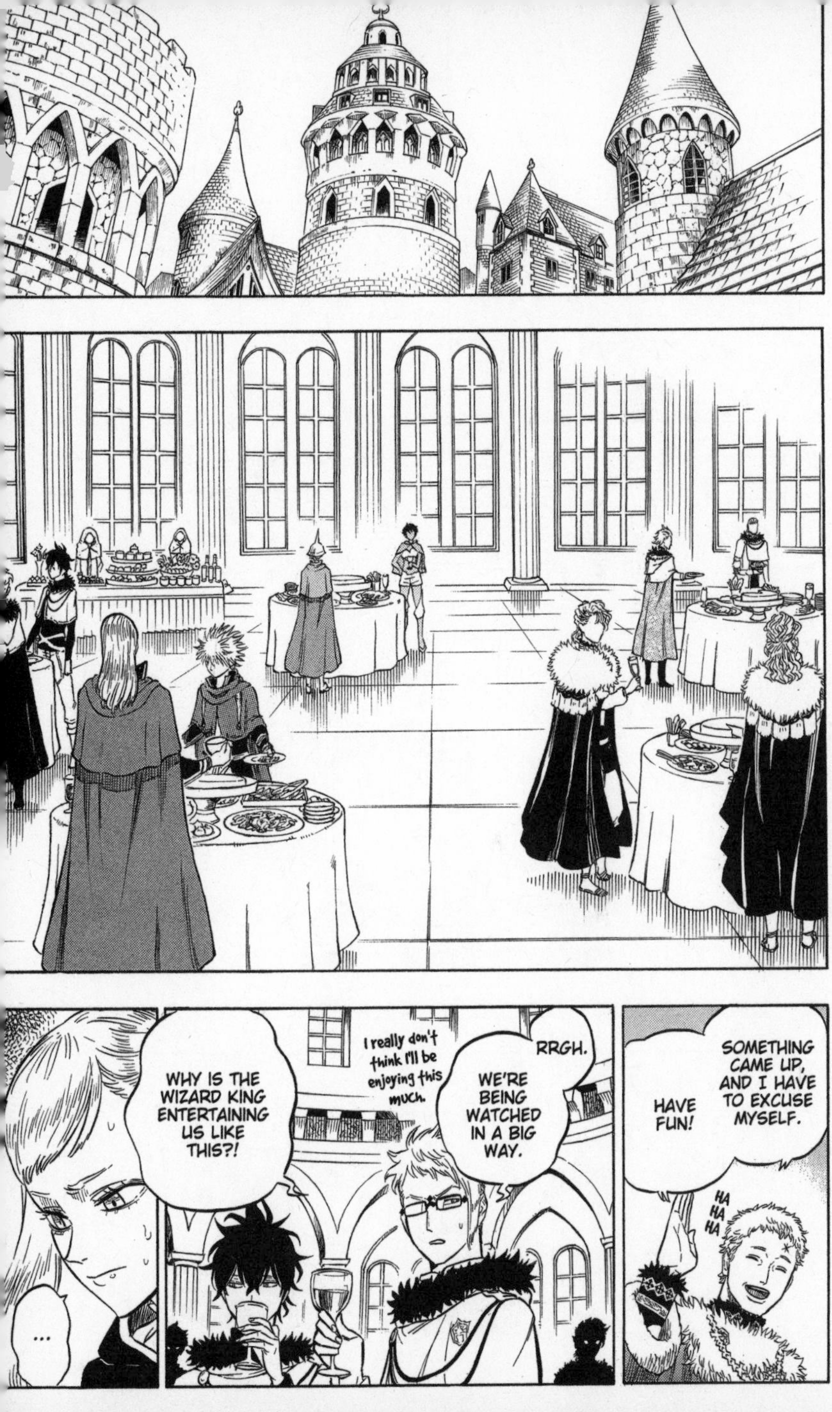
SOMETHING CAME UP, AND I HAVE TO EXCUSE MYSELF.
HAVE FUN!
HA HA HA
RRGH.
WE'RE BEING WATCHED IN A BIG WAY.
I really don't think I'll be enjoying this much.
WHY IS THE WIZARD KING ENTERTAINING US LIKE THIS?!
...

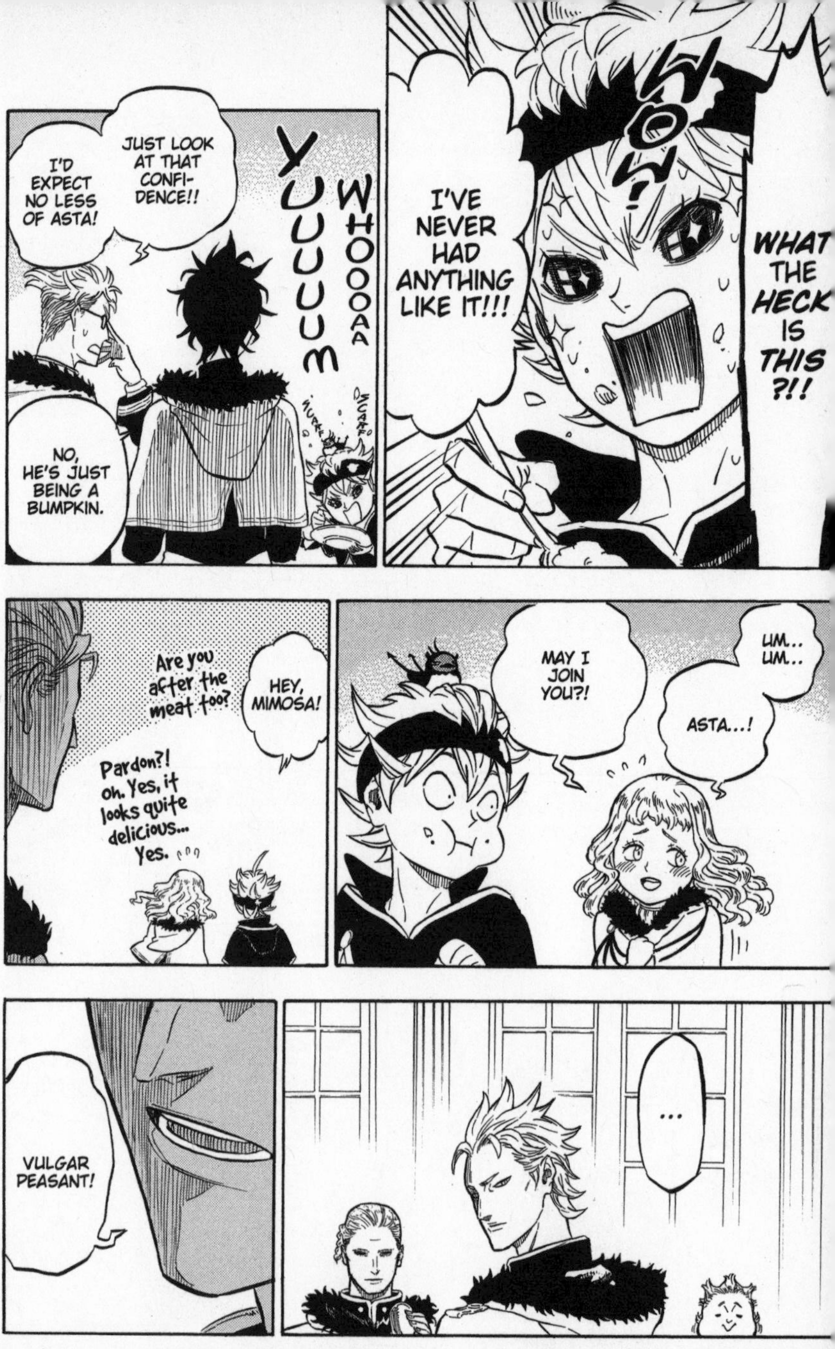
WOW!
WHAT THE HECK IS THIS?!!
I'VE NEVER HAD ANYTHING LIKE IT!!!
WHOOOOAA
YUUUUUM
SCARF
SCARF
JUST LOOK AT THAT CONFI-DENCE!!
I'D EXPECT NO LESS OF ASTA!
NO, HE'S JUST BEING A BUMPKIN.
UM... UM...
ASTA...!
MAY I JOIN YOU?!
HEY, MIMOSA!
Are you after the meat too?
Pardon?! oh. Yes, it looks quite delicious... Yes.
...
VULGAR PEASANT!

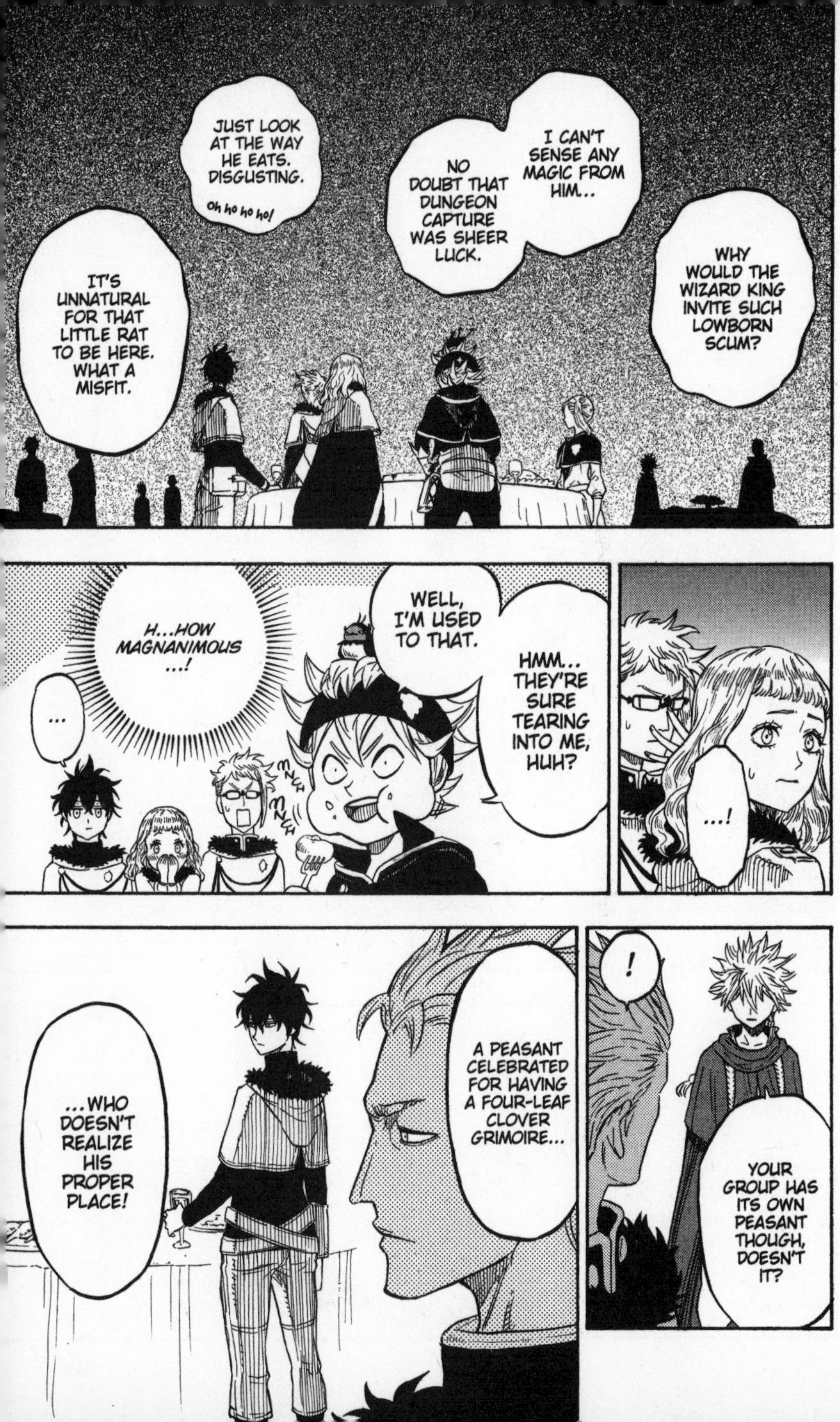
WHY WOULD THE WIZARD KING INVITE SUCH LOWBORN SCUM?
I CAN'T SENSE ANY MAGIC FROM HIM...
NO DOUBT THAT DUNGEON CAPTURE WAS SHEER LUCK.
JUST LOOK AT THE WAY HE EATS. DISGUSTING.
Oh ho ho ho!
IT'S UNNATURAL FOR THAT LITTLE RAT TO BE HERE. WHAT A MISFIT.
...!
WELL, I'M USED TO THAT.
HMM... THEY'RE SURE TEARING INTO ME, HUH?
MNCH MNCH
H...HOW MAGNANIMOUS ...!
...
!
YOUR GROUP HAS ITS OWN PEASANT THOUGH, DOESN'T IT?
A PEASANT CELEBRATED FOR HAVING A FOUR-LEAF CLOVER GRIMOIRE...
...WHO DOESN'T REALIZE HIS PROPER PLACE!

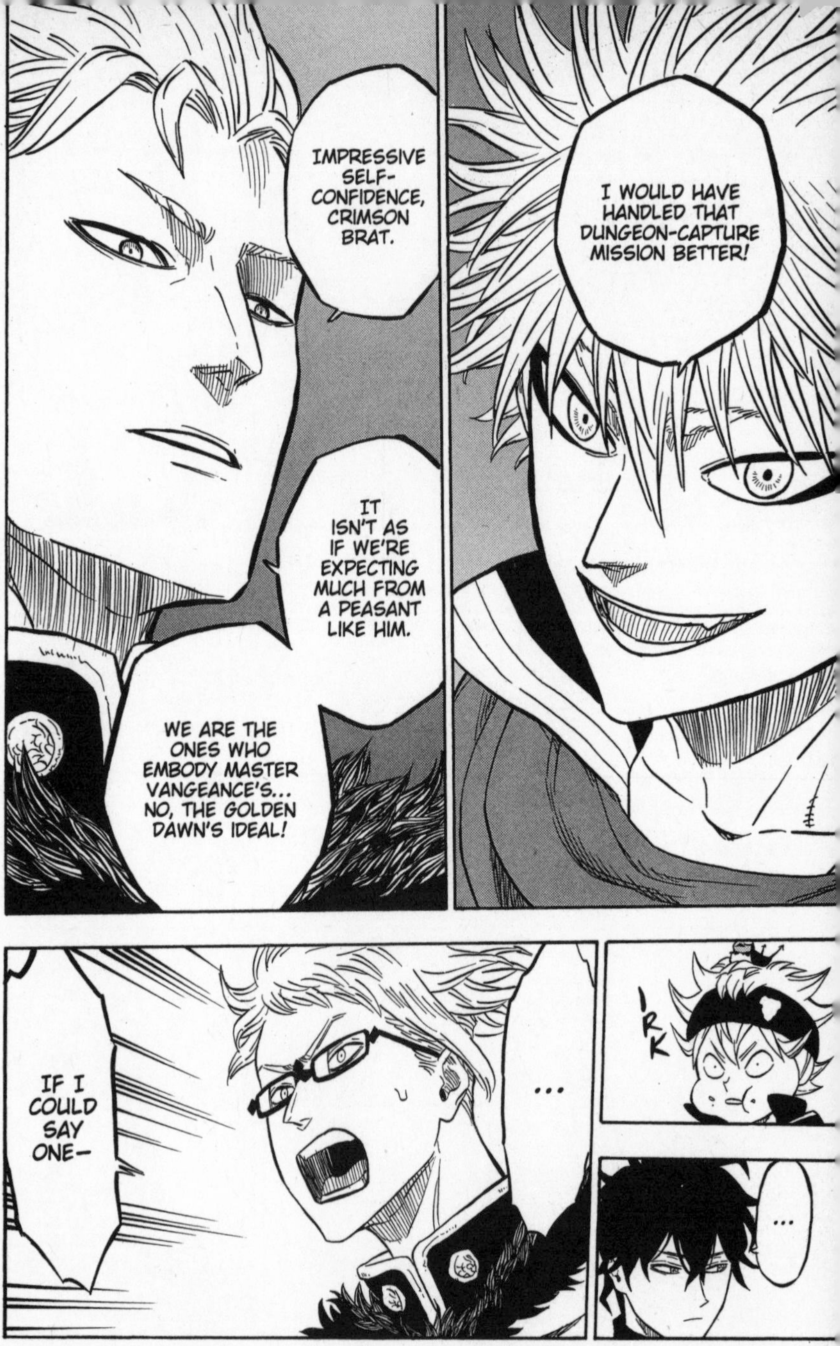
I WOULD HAVE HANDLED THAT DUNGEON-CAPTURE MISSION BETTER!
IMPRESSIVE SELF-CONFIDENCE, CRIMSON BRAT.
IT ISN'T AS IF WE'RE EXPECTING MUCH FROM A PEASANT LIKE HIM.
WE ARE THE ONES WHO EMBODY MASTER VANGEANCE'S... NO, THE GOLDEN DAWN'S IDEAL!
IRK
...
...
IF I COULD SAY ONE—

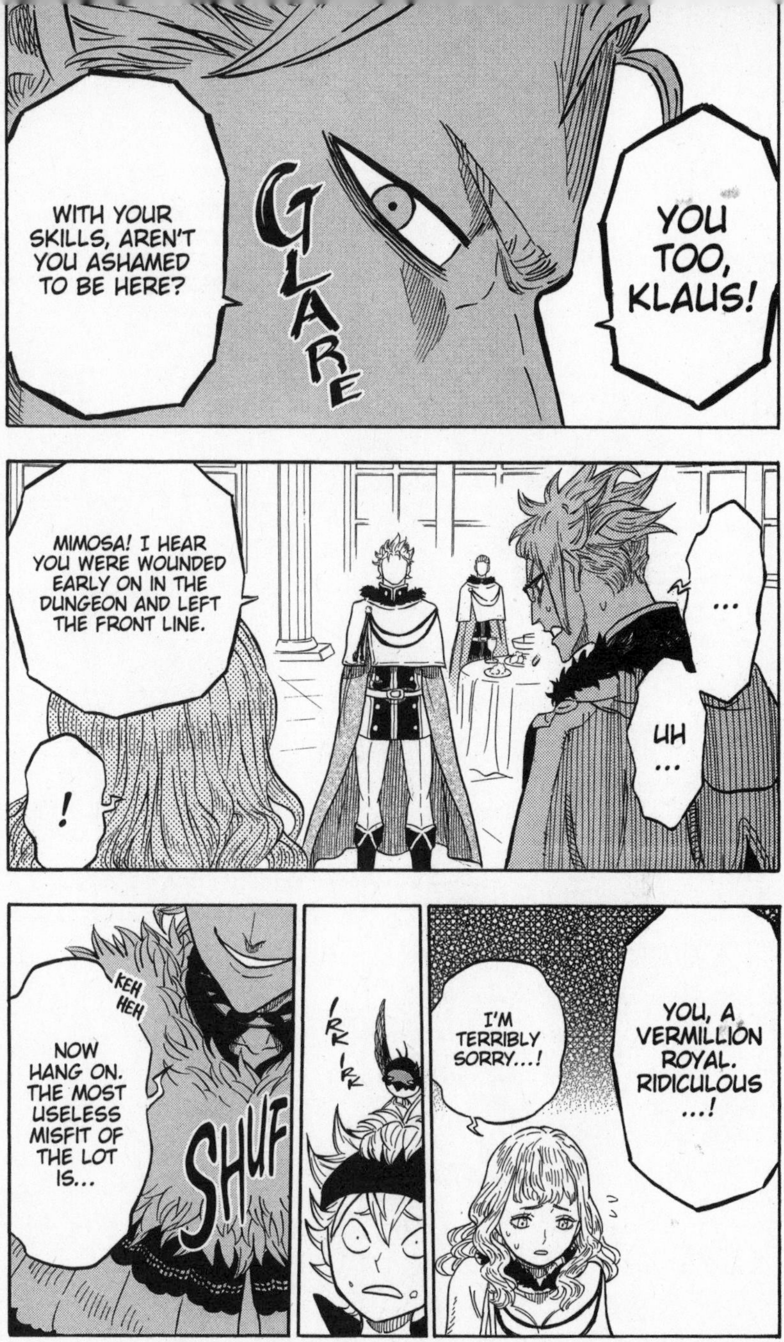
YOU TOO, KLAUS!
GLARE
WITH YOUR SKILLS, AREN'T YOU ASHAMED TO BE HERE?
...
UH ...
MIMOSA! I HEAR YOU WERE WOUNDED EARLY ON IN THE DUNGEON AND LEFT THE FRONT LINE.
!
YOU, A VERMILLION ROYAL. RIDICULOUS ...!
I'M TERRIBLY SORRY...!
IRK IRK
KEH HEH
NOW HANG ON. THE MOST USELESS MISFIT OF THE LOT IS...
SHUF

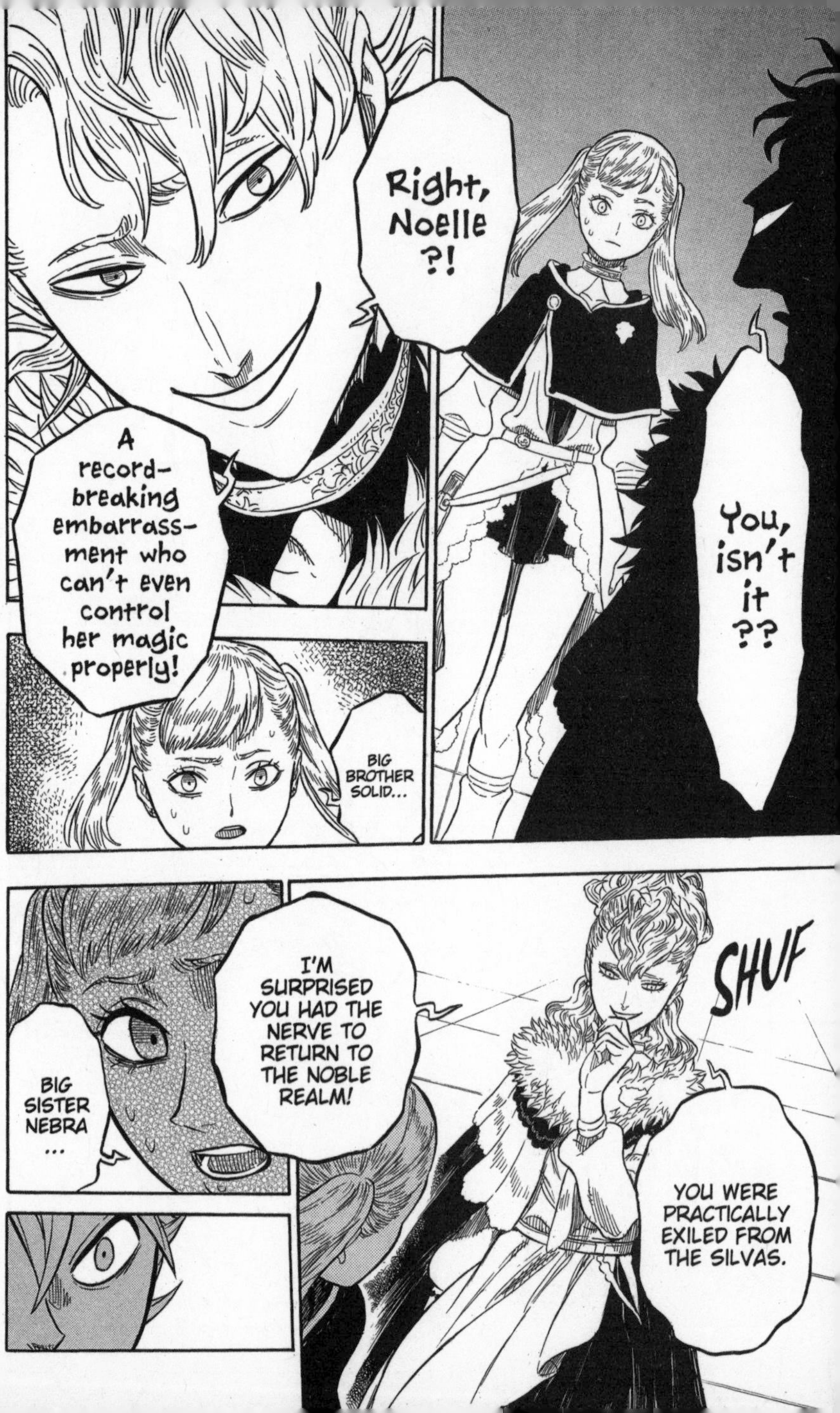
You, isn't it ??
Right, Noelle ?!
A record-breaking embarrassment who can't even control her magic properly!
BIG BROTHER SOLID...
SHUF
I'M SURPRISED YOU HAD THE NERVE TO RETURN TO THE NOBLE REALM!
YOU WERE PRACTICALLY EXILED FROM THE SILVAS.
BIG SISTER NEBRA ...

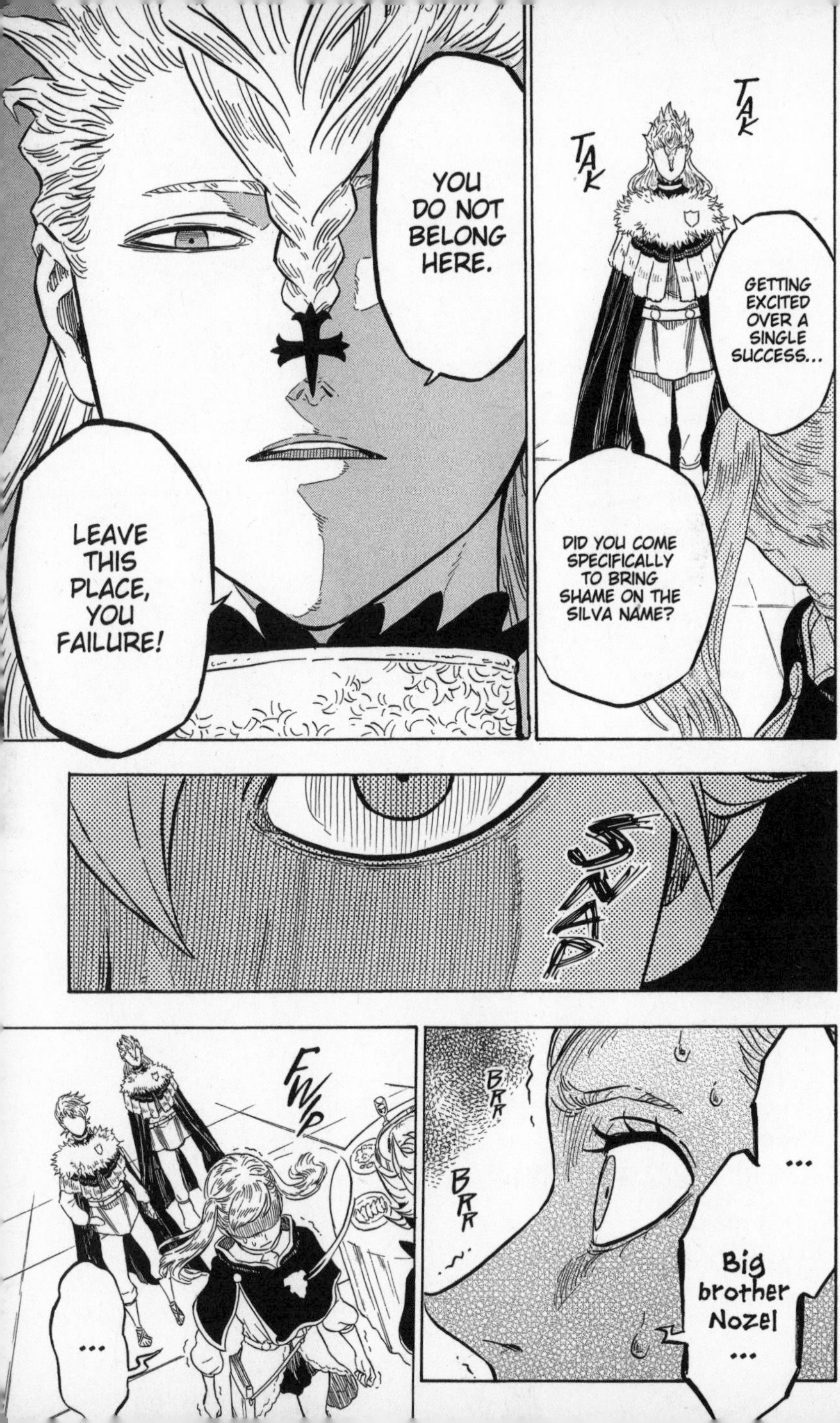
TAK
TAK
GETTING EXCITED OVER A SINGLE SUCCESS...
DID YOU COME SPECIFICALLY TO BRING SHAME ON THE SILVA NAME?
YOU DO NOT BELONG HERE.
LEAVE THIS PLACE, YOU FAILURE!
SNAP
BRR
BRR
...
Big brother Nozel ...
FWIP
...

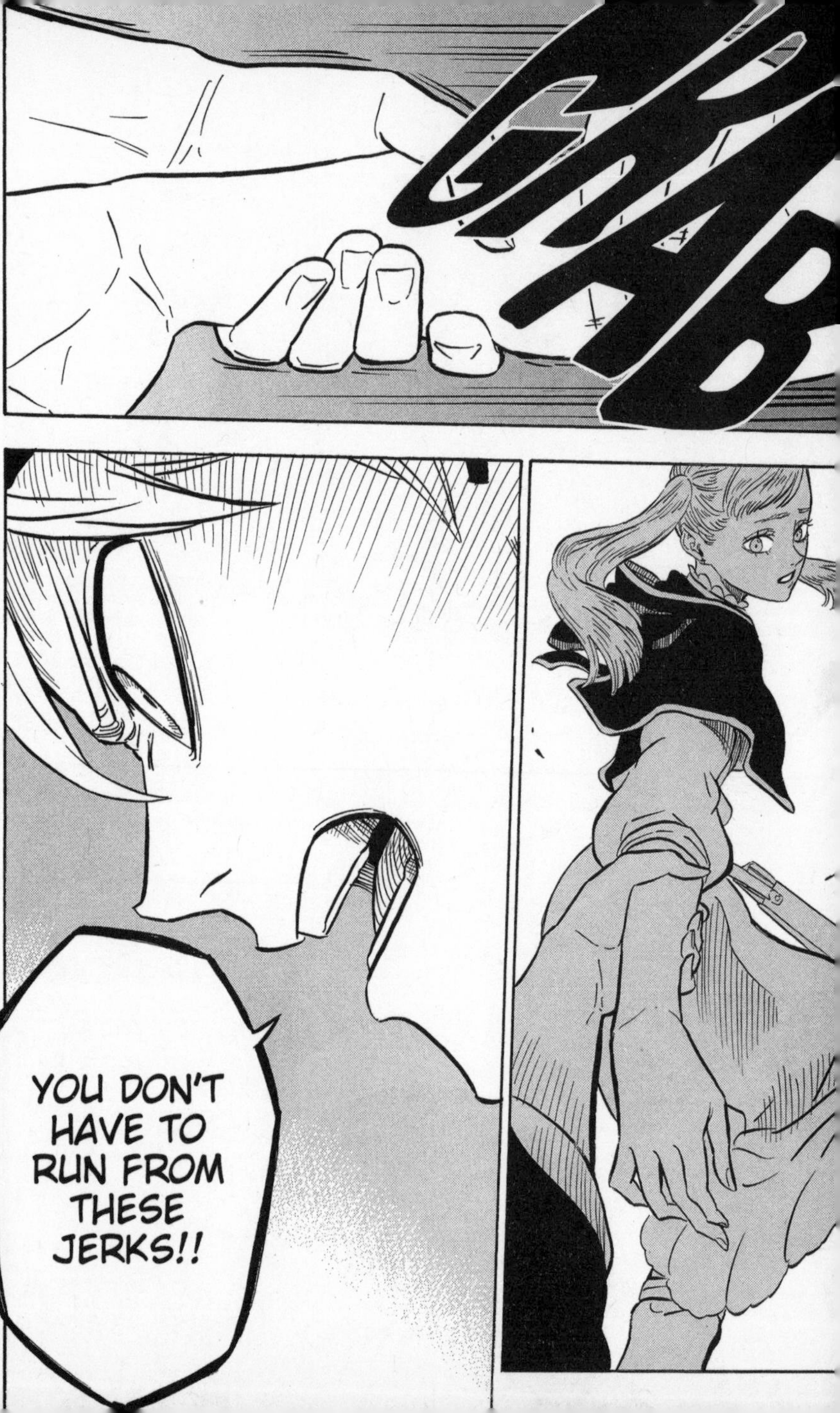
GRAB
YOU DON'T HAVE TO RUN FROM THESE JERKS!!

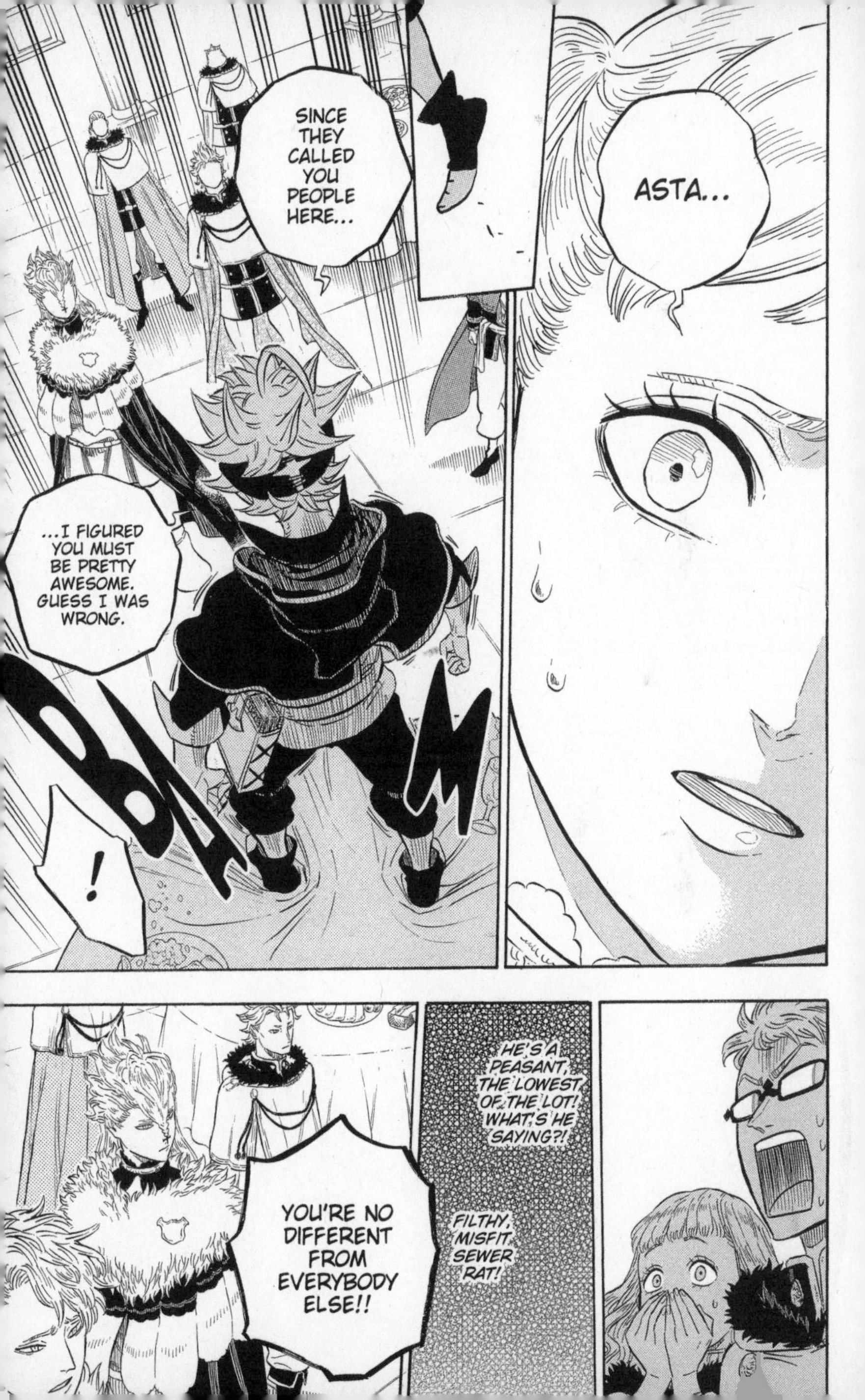
ASTA...
SINCE THEY CALLED YOU PEOPLE HERE...
...I FIGURED YOU MUST BE PRETTY AWESOME. GUESS I WAS WRONG.
BAM
!
HE'S A PEASANT, THE LOWEST OF THE LOT! WHAT'S HE SAYING?!
FILTHY, MISFIT SEWER RAT!
YOU'RE NO DIFFERENT FROM EVERYBODY ELSE!!

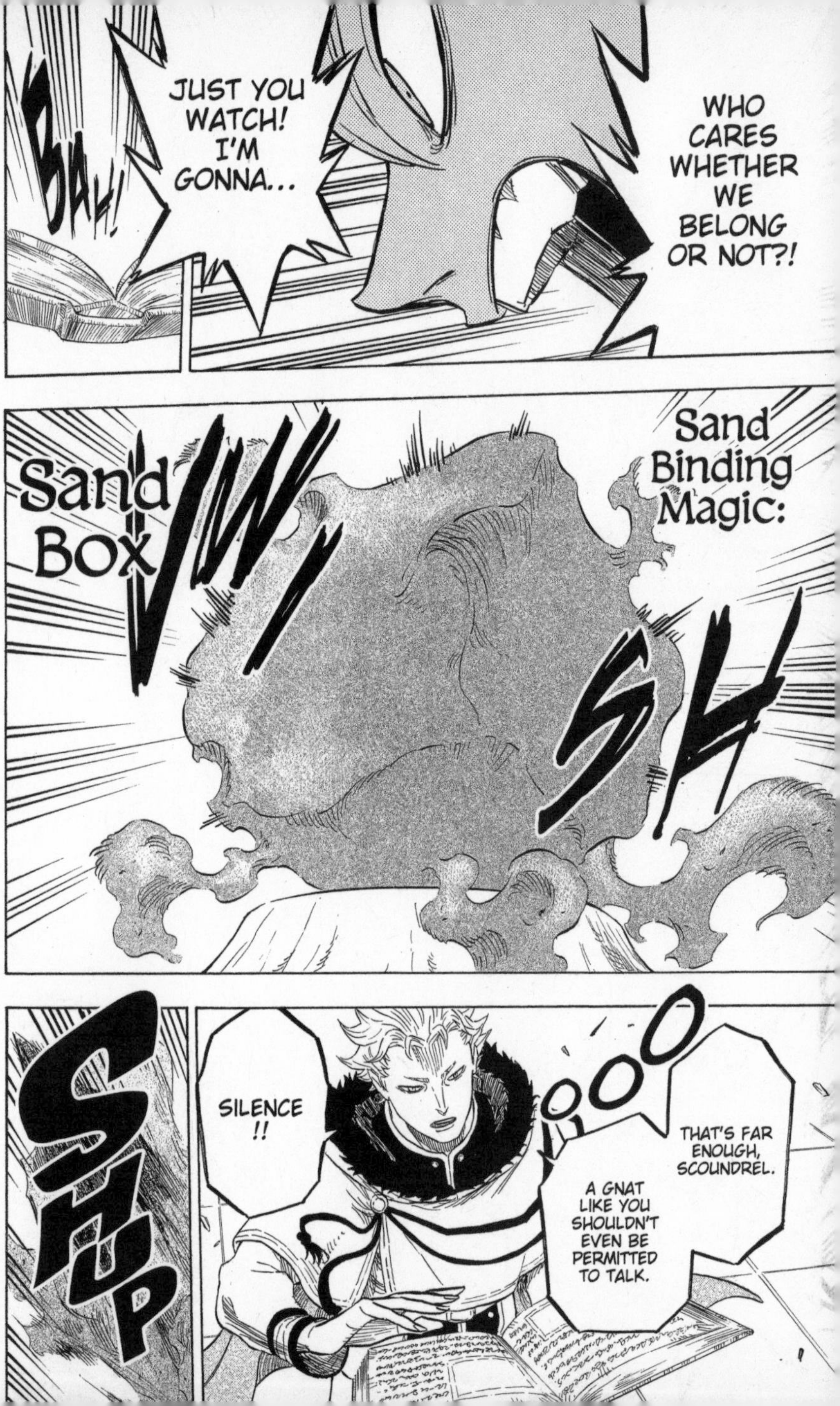
WHO CARES WHETHER WE BELONG OR NOT?!
JUST YOU WATCH! I'M GONNA...
Sand Binding Magic:
Sand Box
THAT'S FAR ENOUGH, SCOUNDREL.
A GNAT LIKE YOU SHOULDN'T EVEN BE PERMITTED TO TALK.
SILENCE !!
SHUP

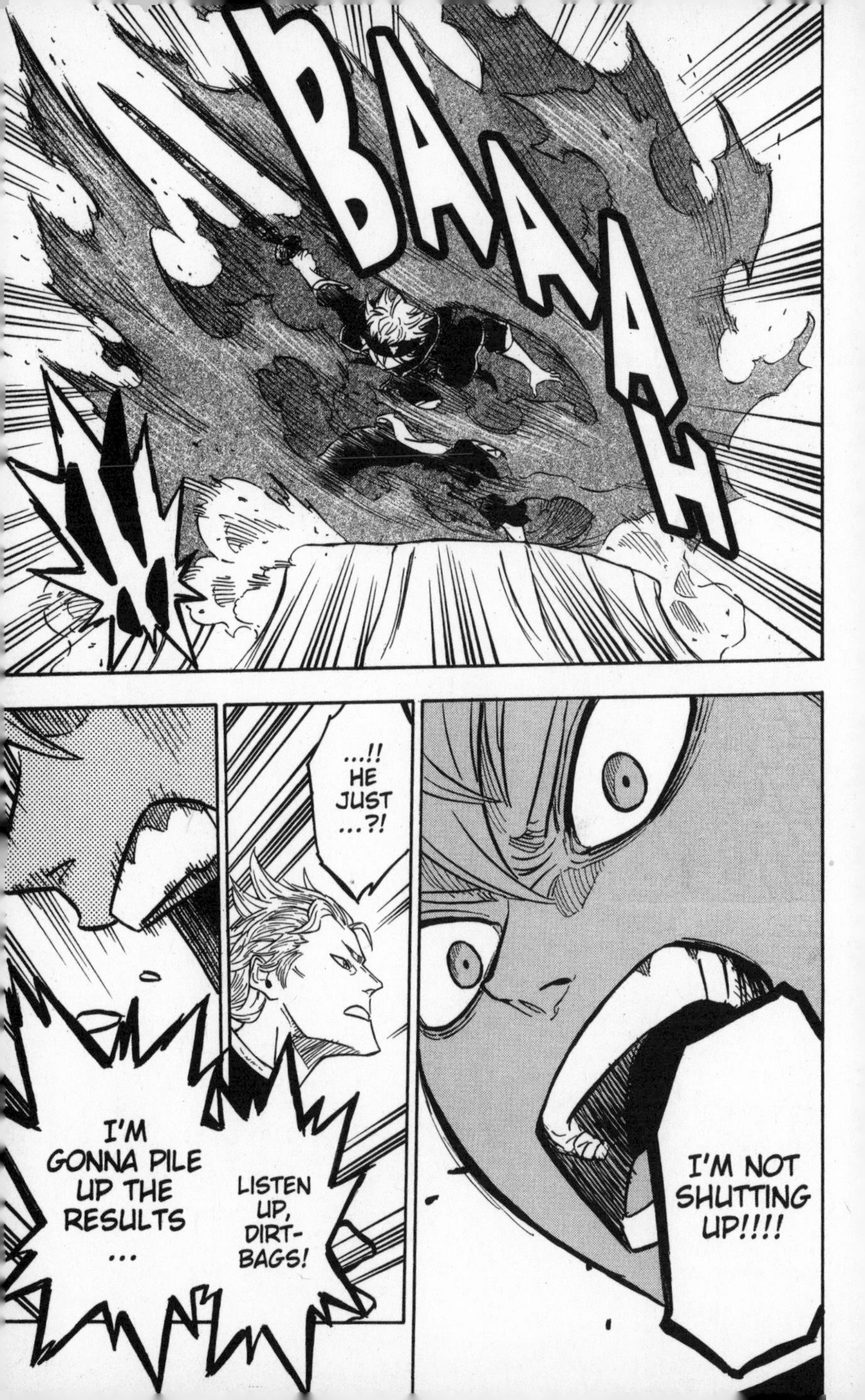
BAAAH
I'M NOT SHUTTING UP!!!!
...!! HE JUST ...?!
LISTEN UP, DIRT-BAGS!
I'M GONNA PILE UP THE RESULTS ...

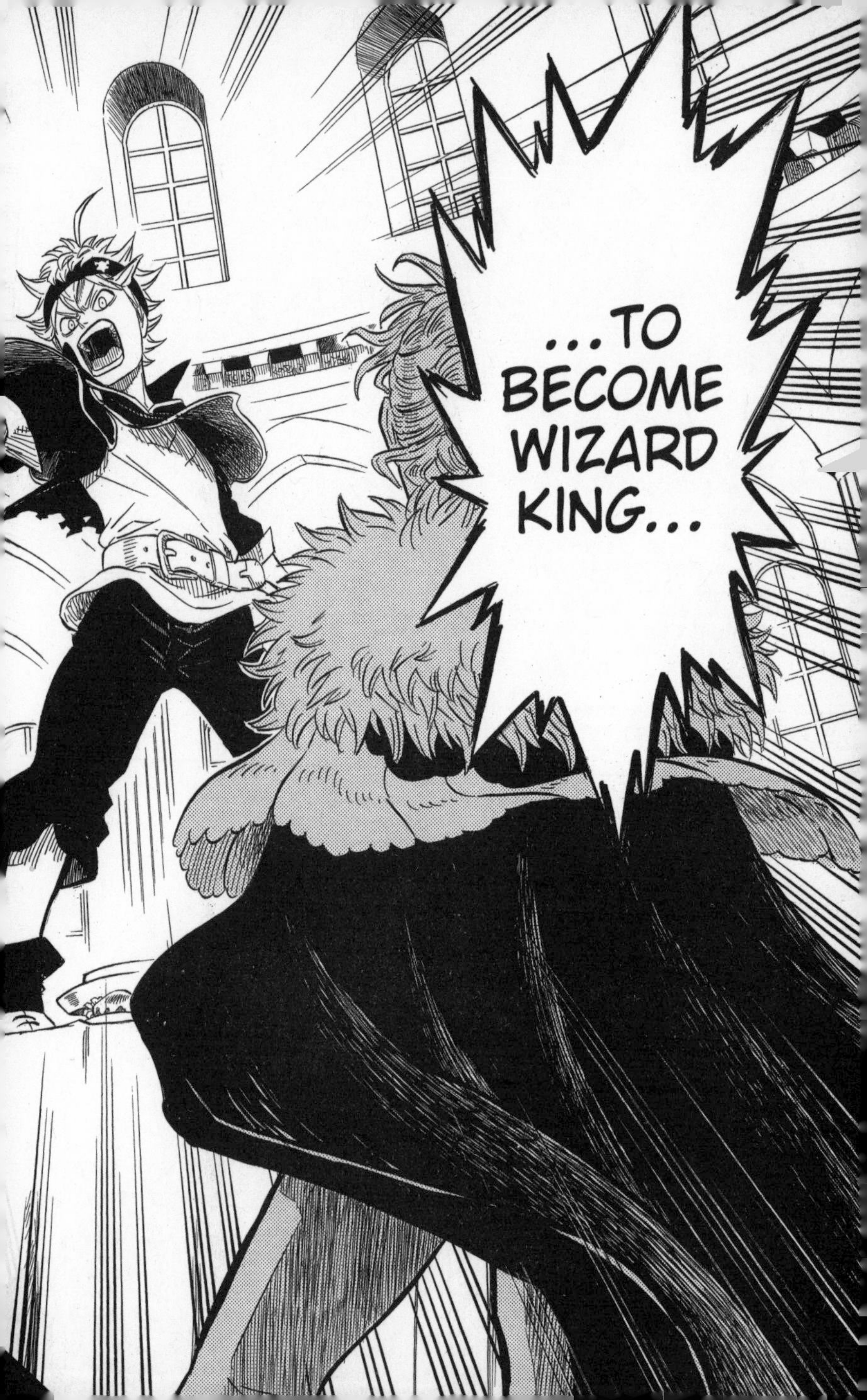
...TO BECOME WIZARD KING...

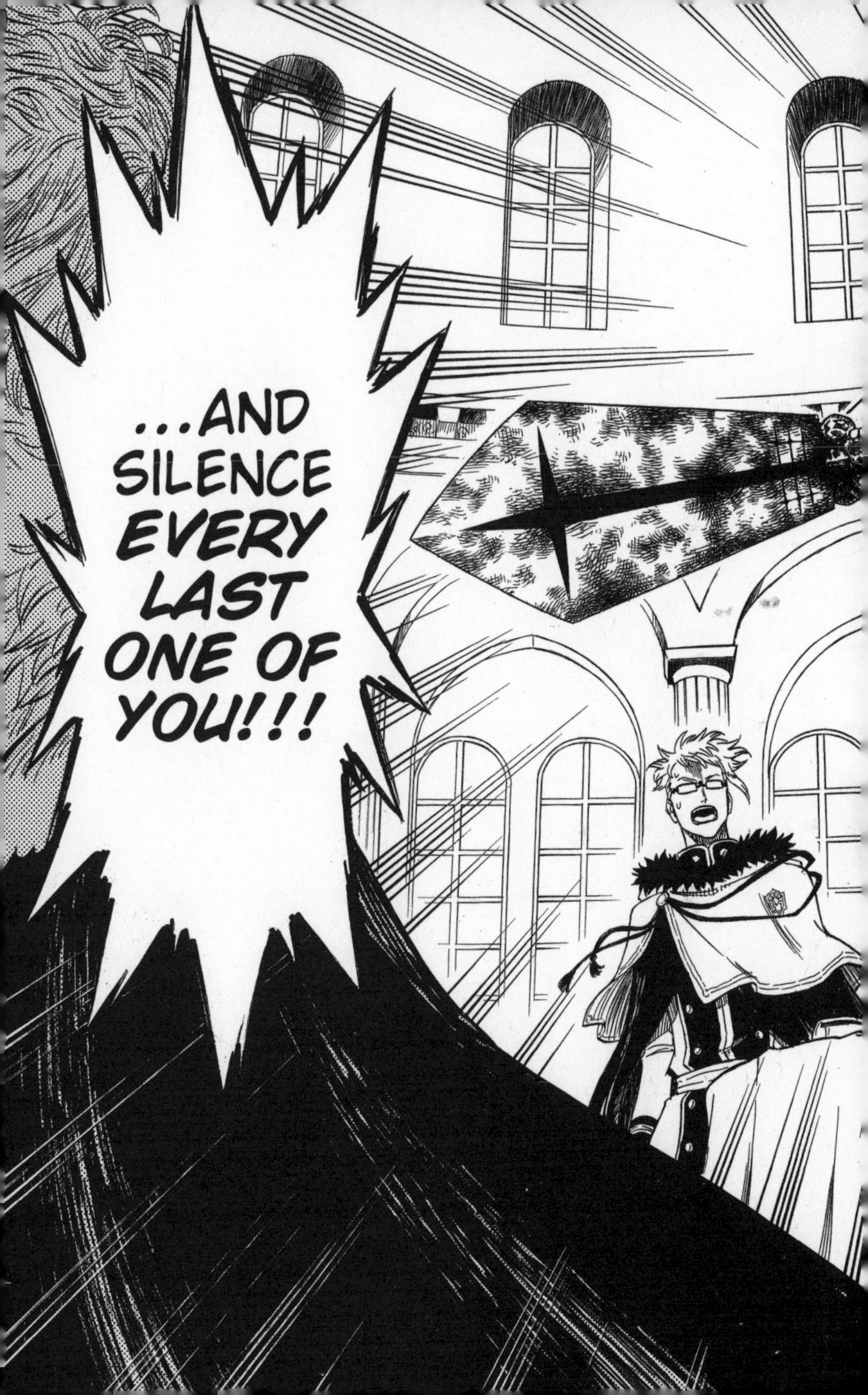
...AND SILENCE EVERY LAST ONE OF YOU!!!

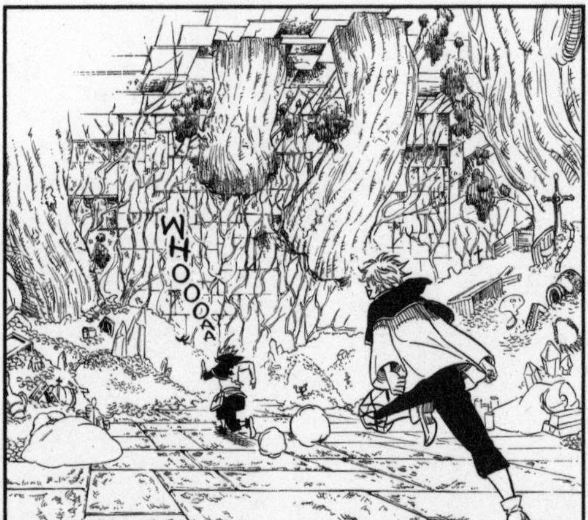
WHOOOAA

✽Page 24: Capital Riot

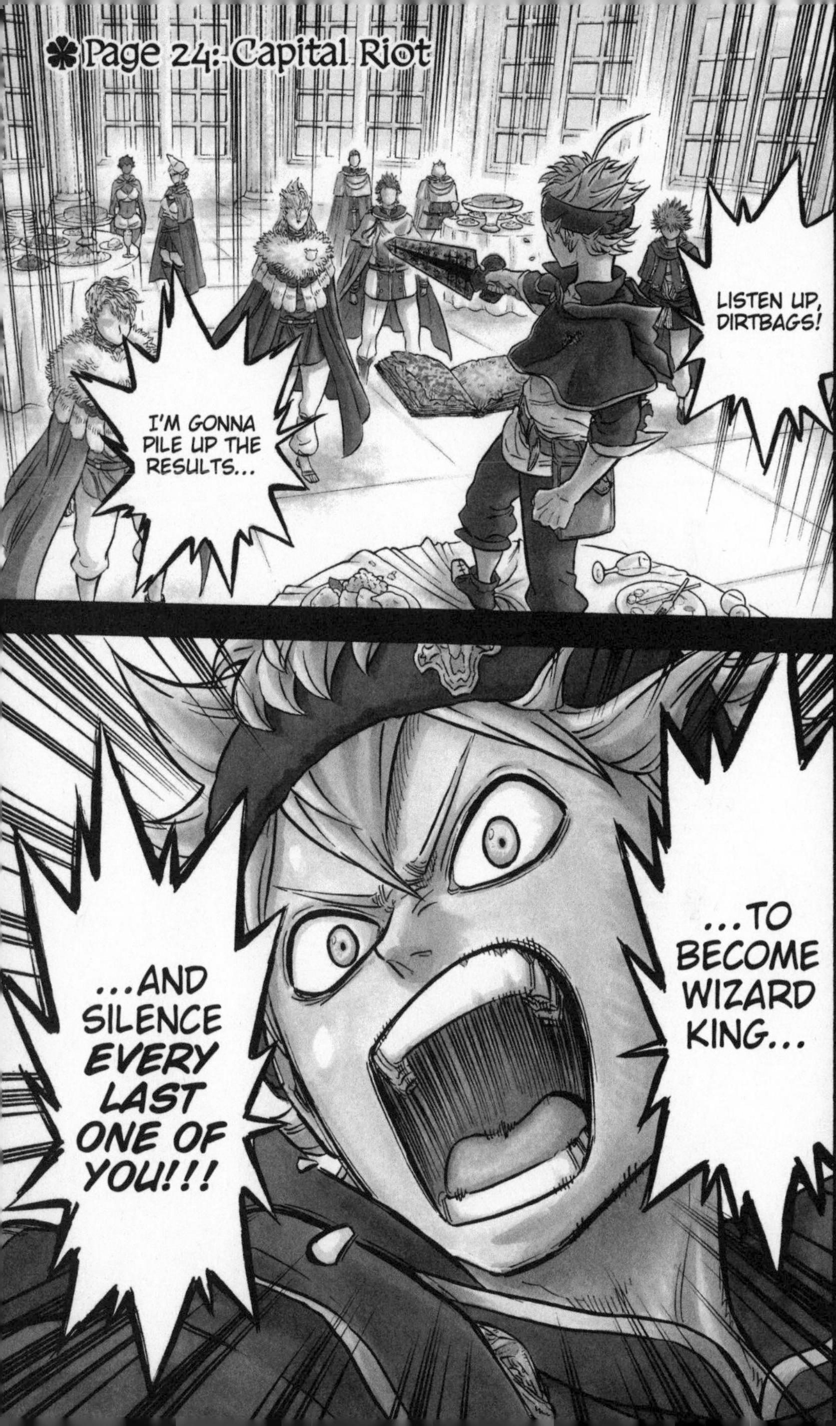
LISTEN UP, DIRTBAGS!
I'M GONNA PILE UP THE RESULTS...
...TO BECOME WIZARD KING...
...AND SILENCE *EVERY LAST ONE OF YOU!!!*

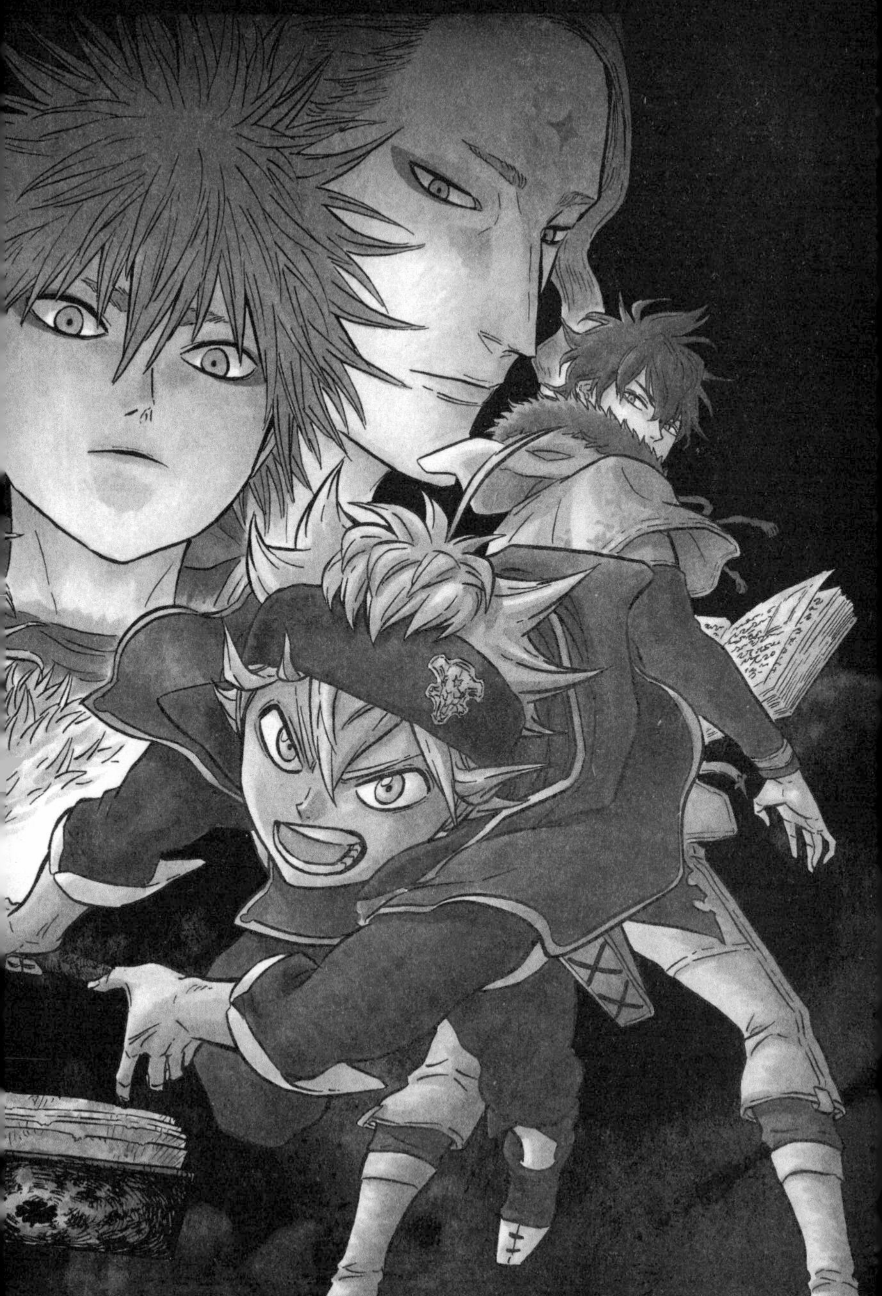

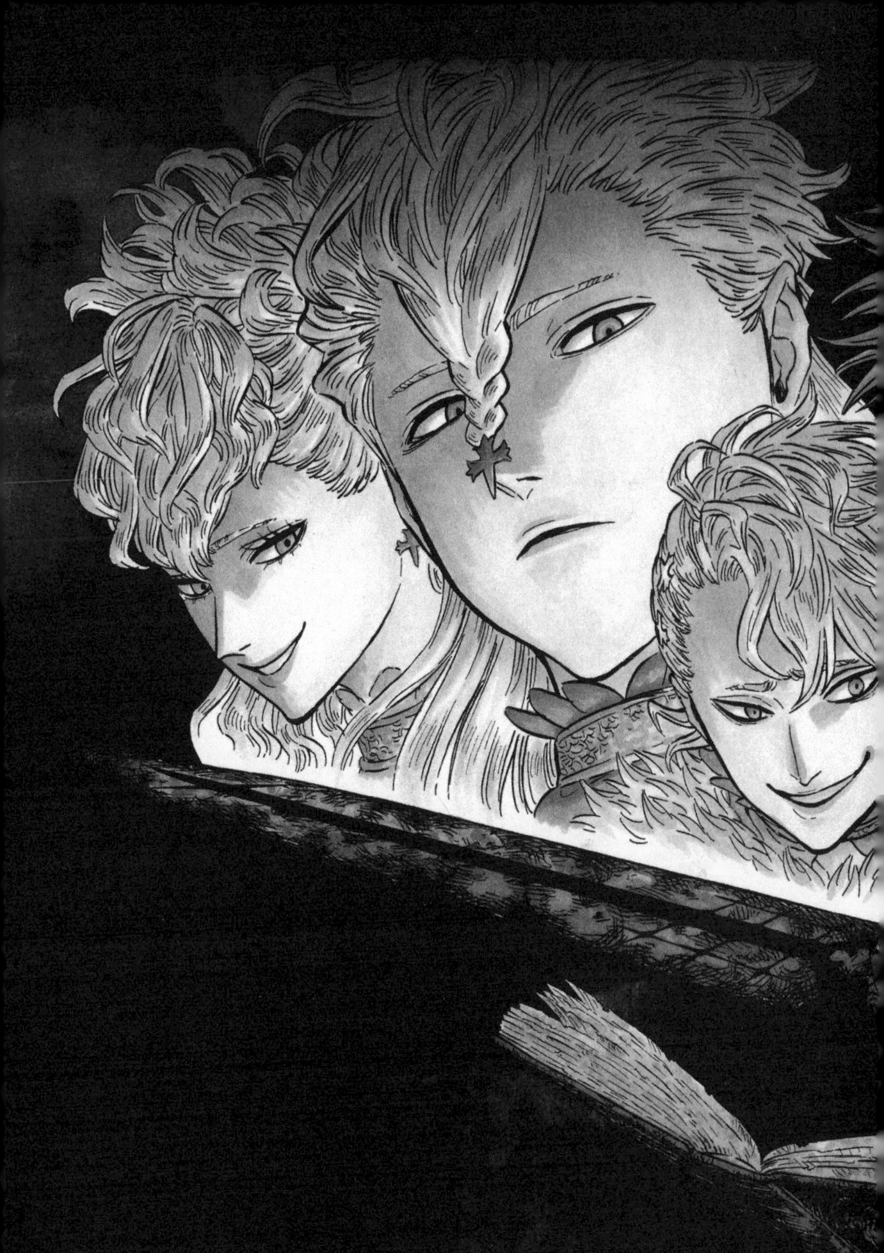

Page 24: Capital Riot

BLACK✦CLOVER

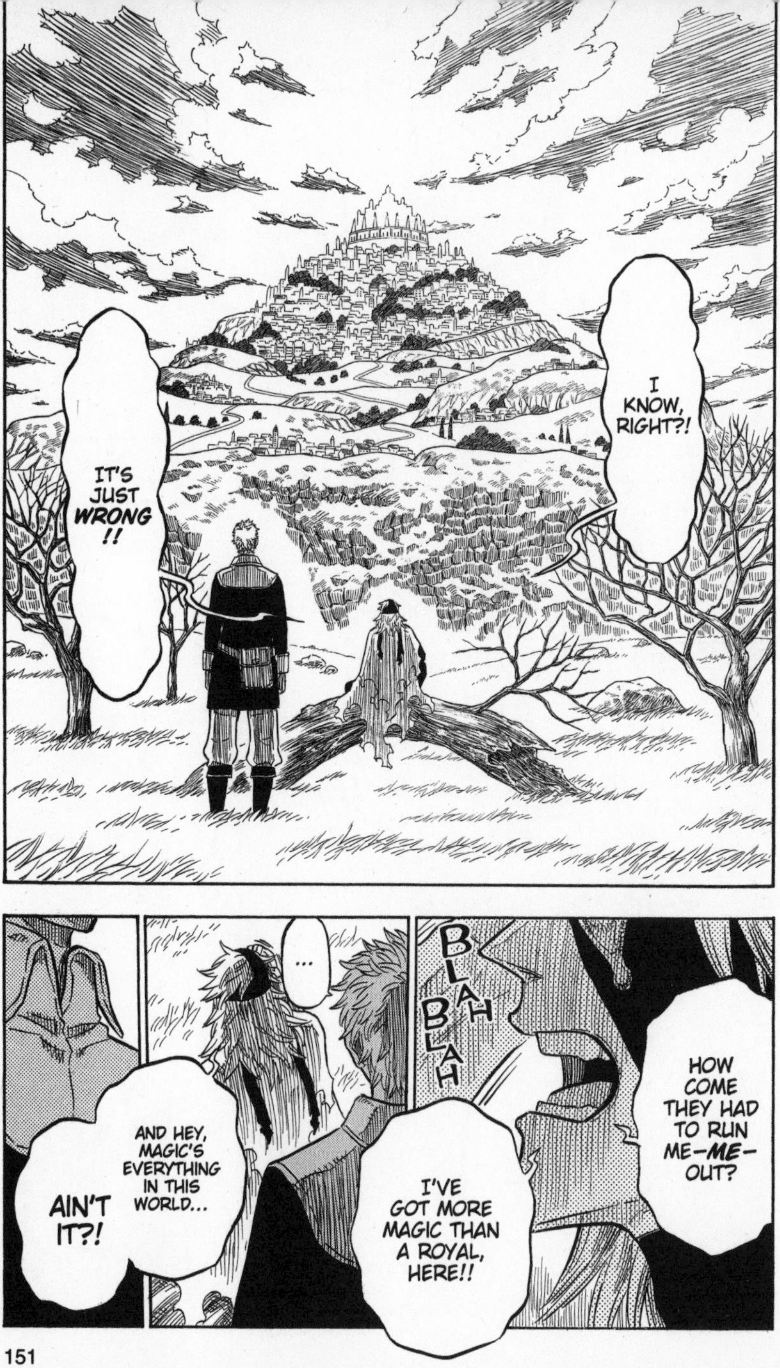
I KNOW, RIGHT?!
IT'S JUST *WRONG*!!
BLAH BLAH
HOW COME THEY HAD TO RUN ME—*ME*—OUT?
I'VE GOT MORE MAGIC THAN A ROYAL, HERE!!
...
AND HEY, MAGIC'S EVERYTHING IN THIS WORLD...
AIN'T IT?!

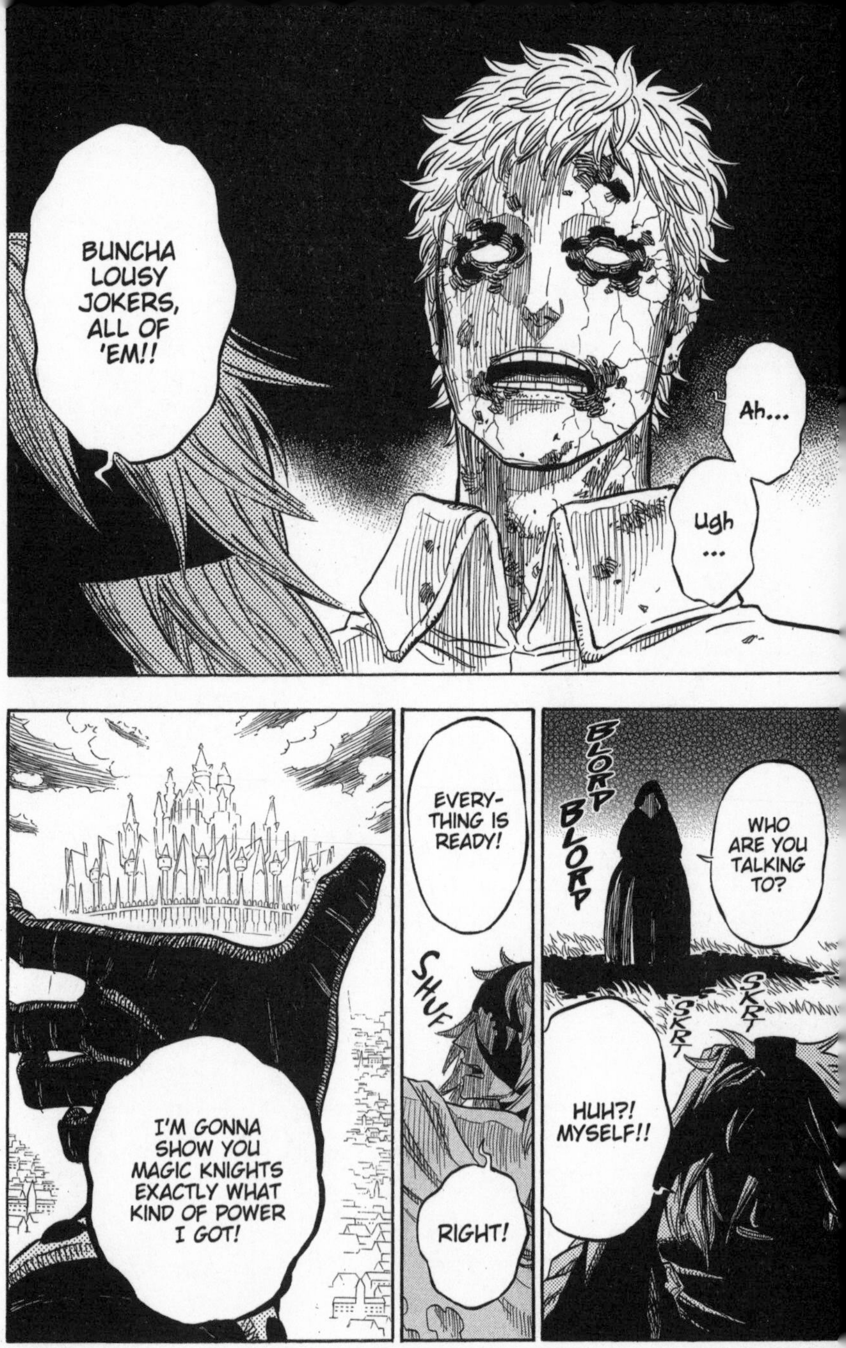
Ah...
Ugh ...
BUNCHA LOUSY JOKERS, ALL OF 'EM!!
BLORP BLORP
WHO ARE YOU TALKING TO?
SKRT SKRT
HUH?! MYSELF!!
EVERY-THING IS READY!
SHUF
RIGHT!
I'M GONNA SHOW YOU MAGIC KNIGHTS EXACTLY WHAT KIND OF POWER I GOT!

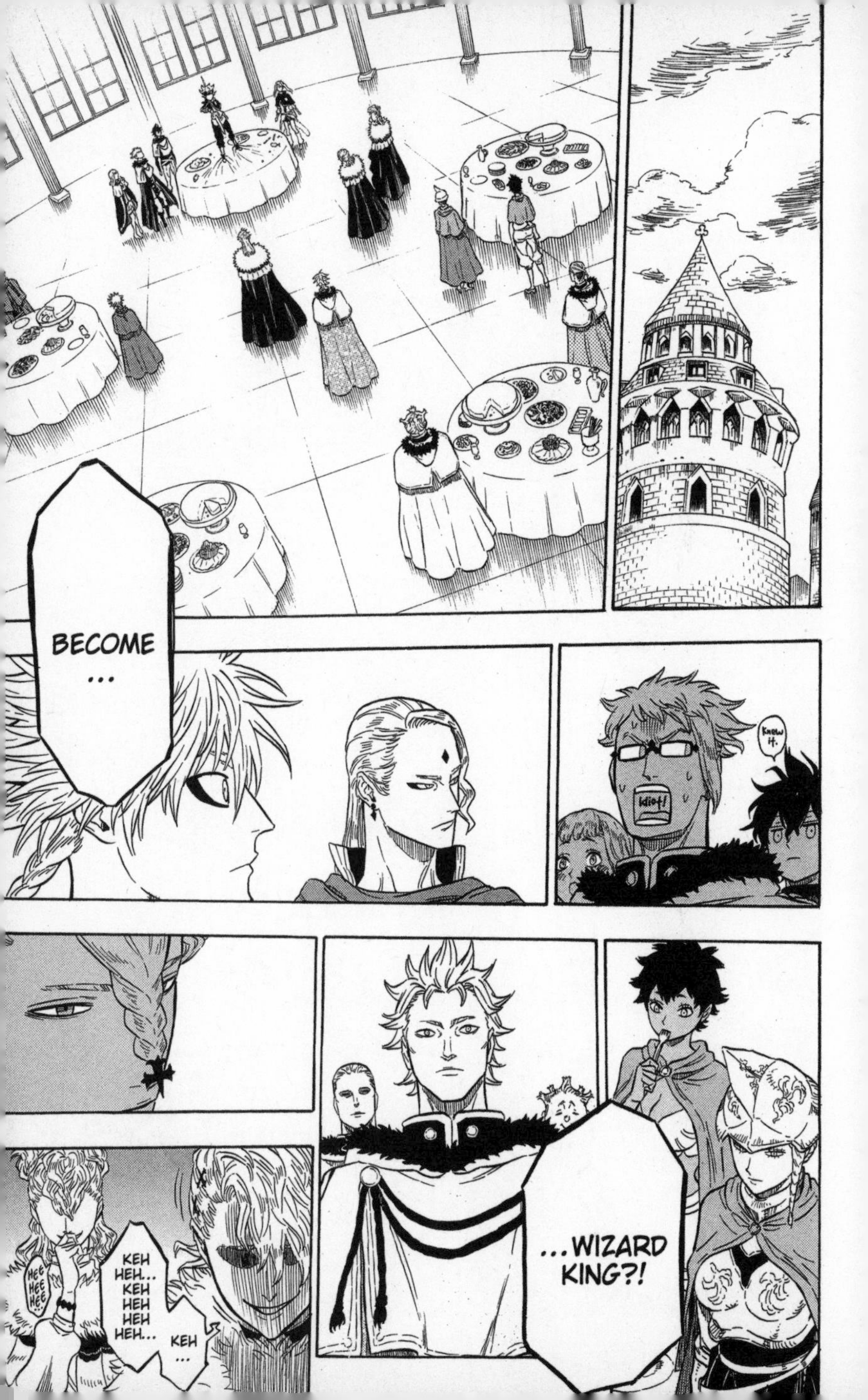
BECOME ...
Knew it.
Idiot!
...WIZARD KING?!
KEH HEH... KEH HEH HEH HEH...
HEE HEE HEE
KEH ...

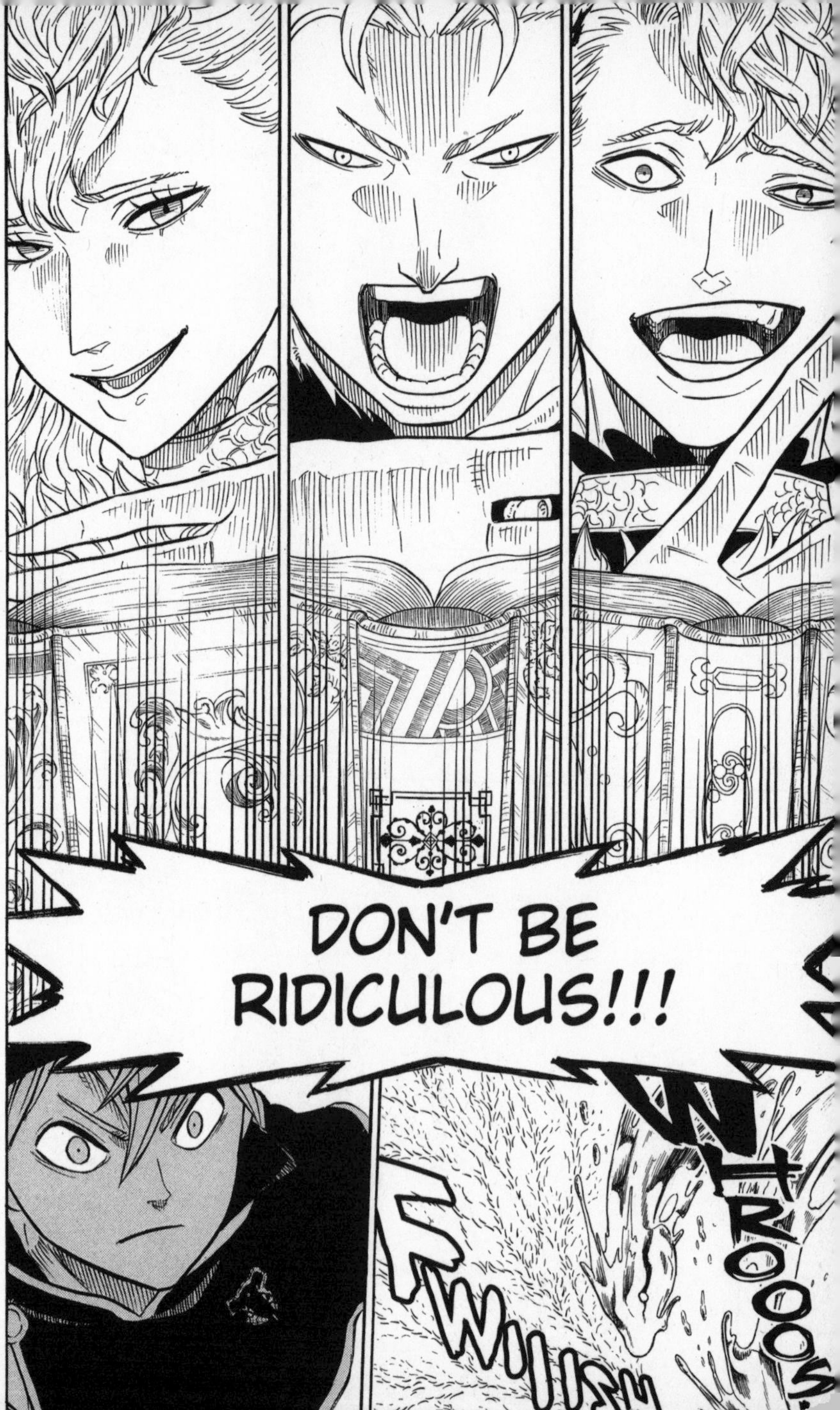
DON'T BE RIDICULOUS!!!
WHROOOSH
FWIIISH

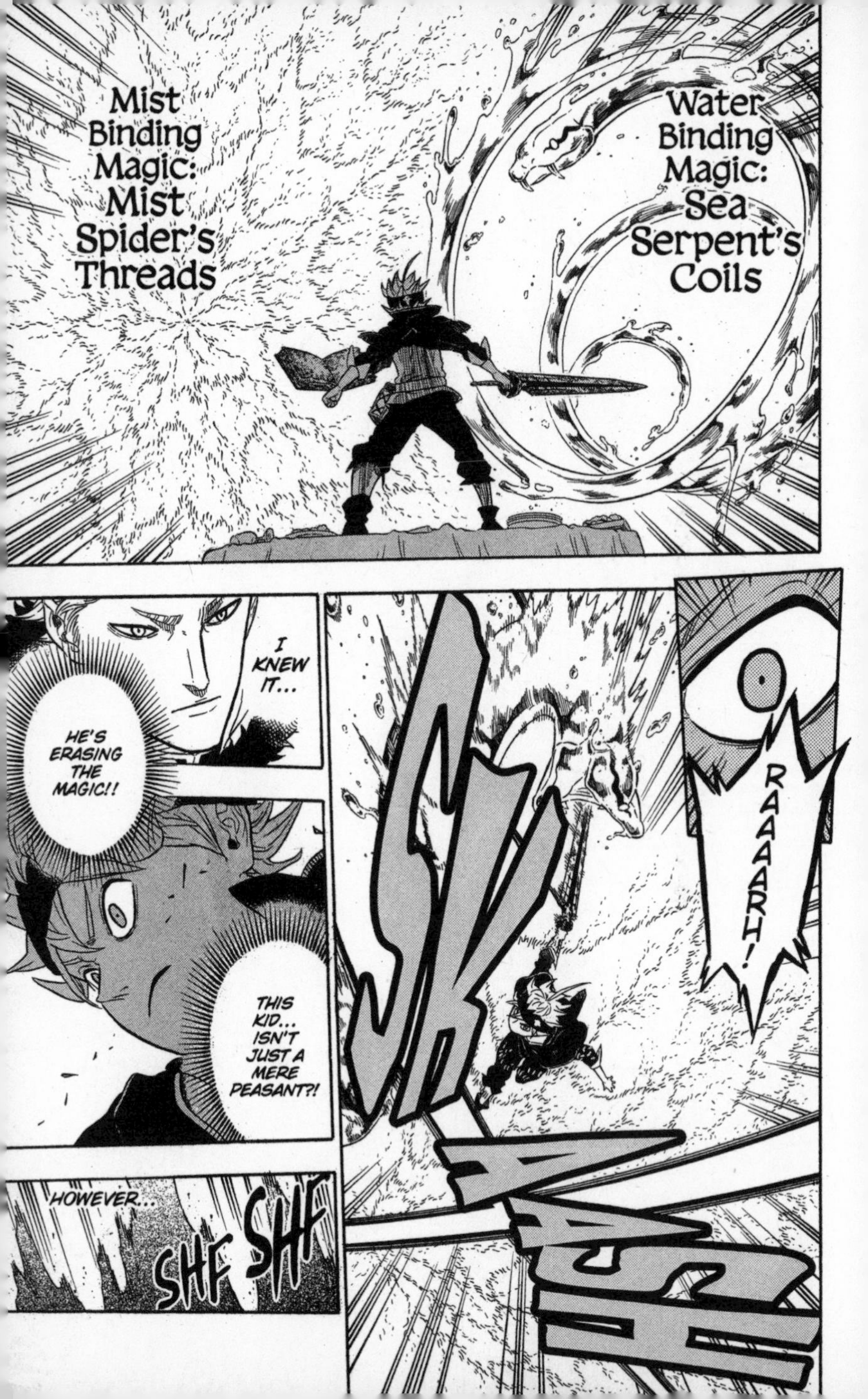

Water Binding Magic: Sea Serpent's Coils
Mist Binding Magic: Mist Spider's Threads
RAAAARH!
SKASH
I KNEW IT...
HE'S ERASING THE MAGIC!!
THIS KID... ISN'T JUST A MERE PEASANT?!
HOWEVER...
SHF SHF

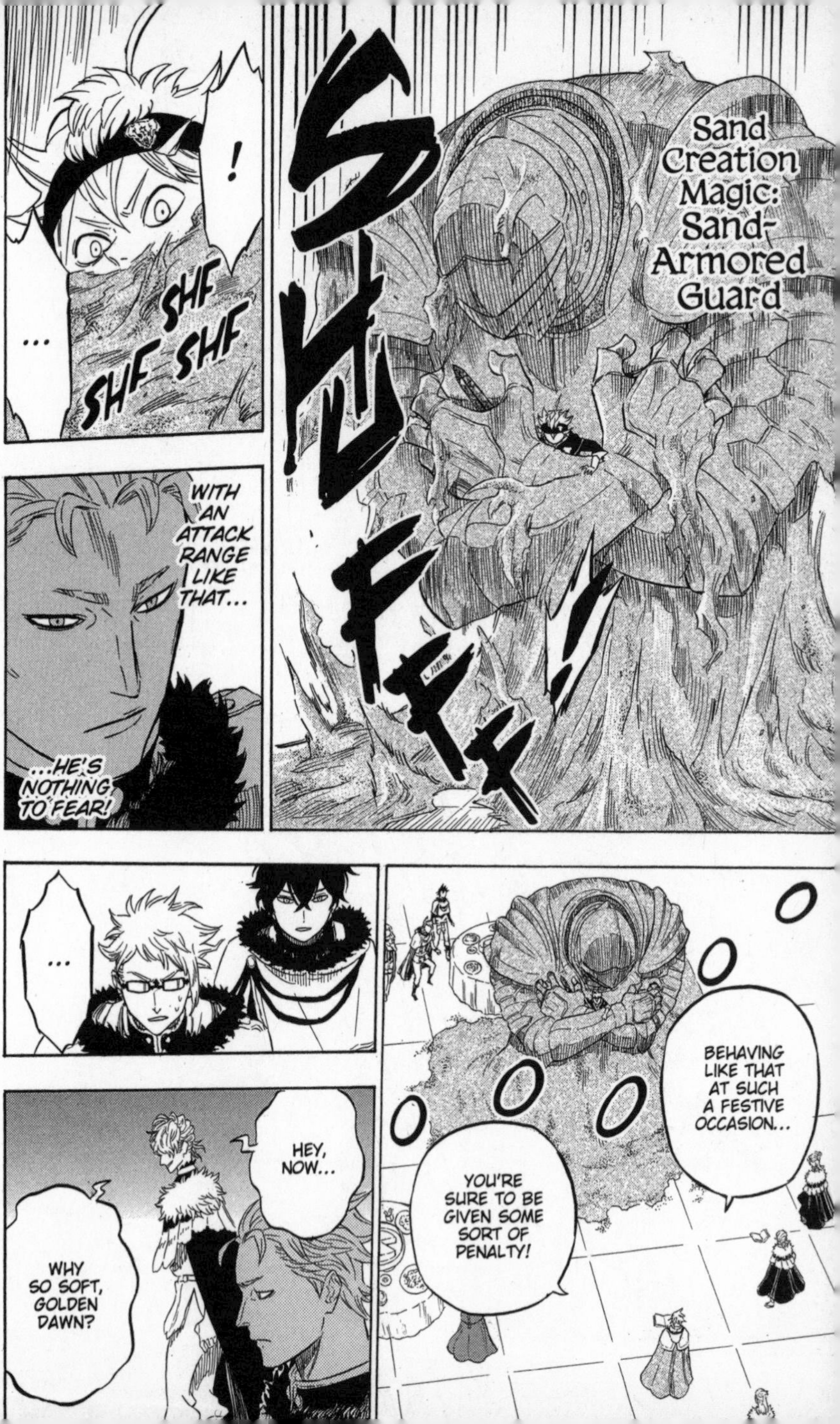
Sand Creation Magic: Sand-Armored Guard
!
...
SHF SHF SHF
WITH AN ATTACK RANGE LIKE THAT...
...HE'S NOTHING TO FEAR!
BEHAVING LIKE THAT AT SUCH A FESTIVE OCCASION...
YOU'RE SURE TO BE GIVEN SOME SORT OF PENALTY!
...
HEY, NOW...
WHY SO SOFT, GOLDEN DAWN?

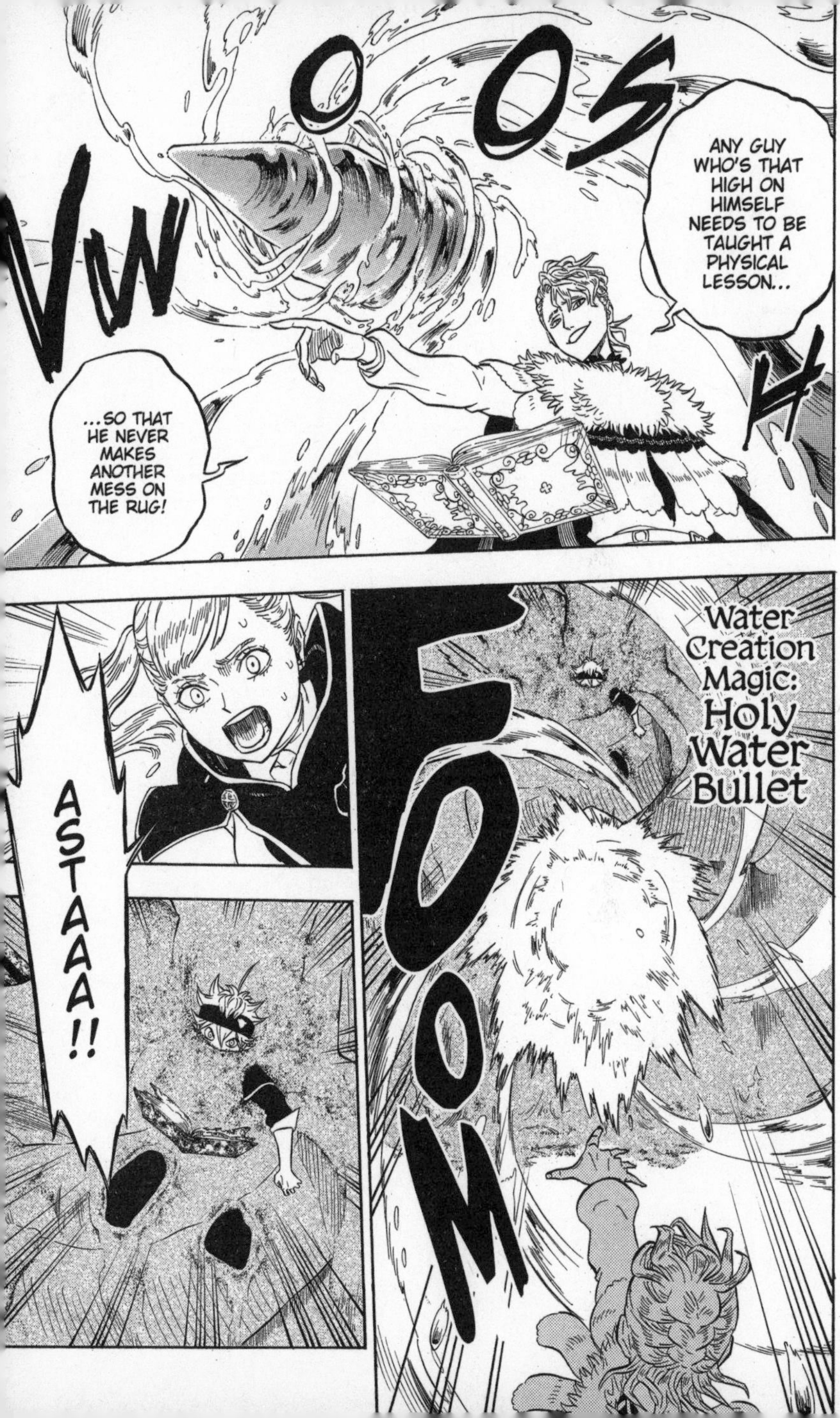
ANY GUY WHO'S THAT HIGH ON HIMSELF NEEDS TO BE TAUGHT A PHYSICAL LESSON...
...SO THAT HE NEVER MAKES ANOTHER MESS ON THE RUG!
VWOOOSH
Water Creation Magic: Holy Water Bullet
VOOOM
ASTAAA!!

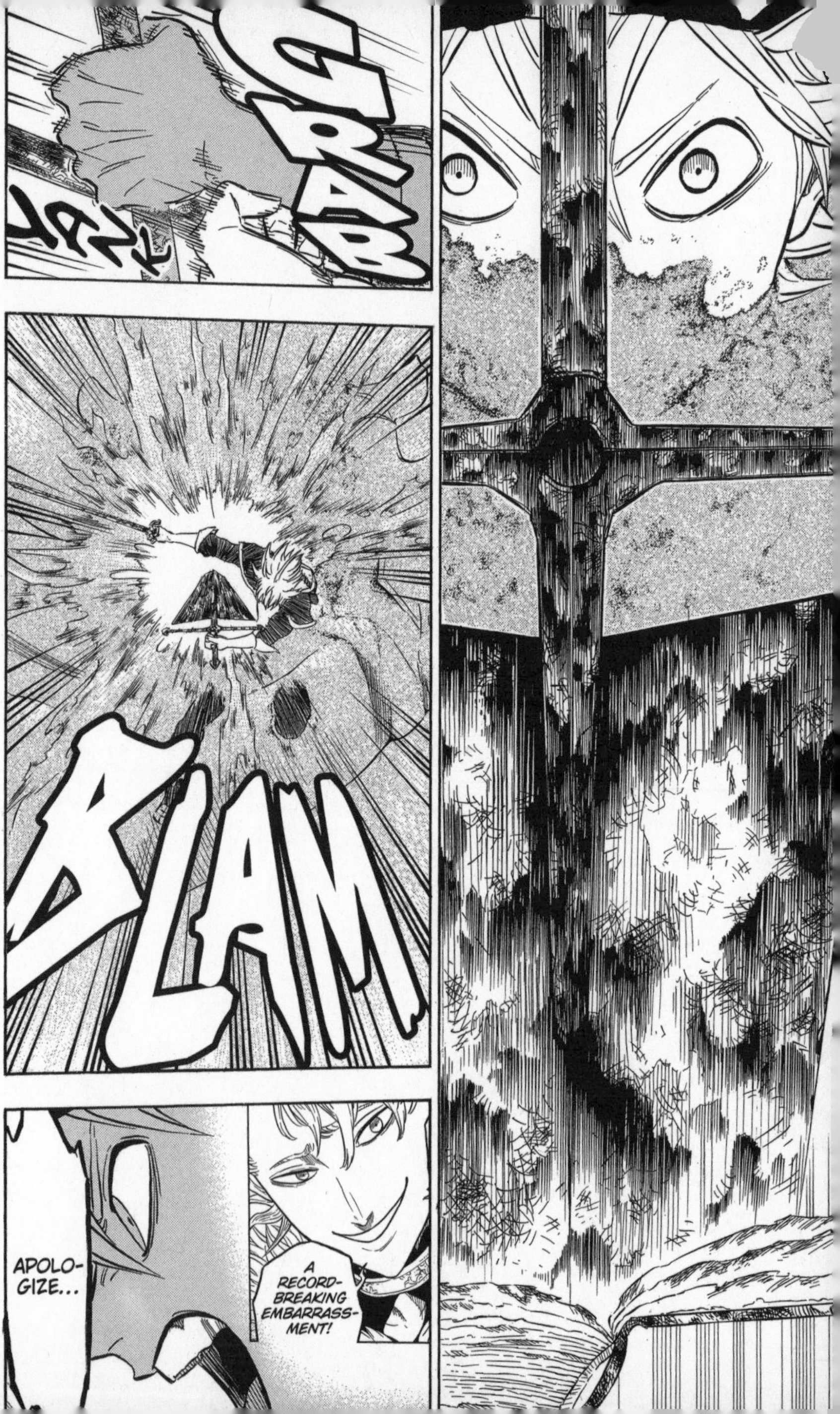
GRAB
BLAM
A RECORD-BREAKING EMBARRASSMENT!
APOLOGIZE...

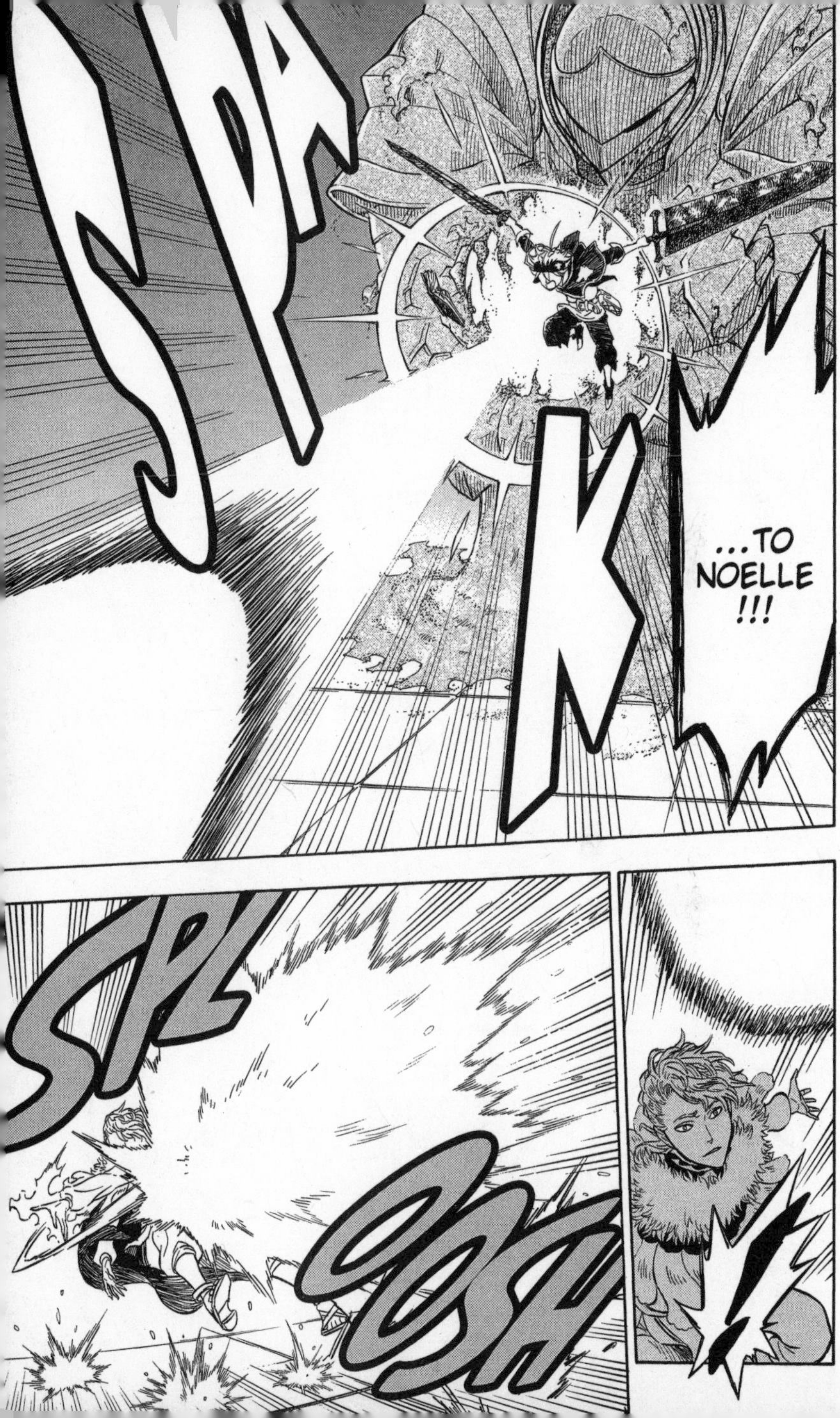
...TO NOELLE !!!
SPAK
!
SPLOOSH

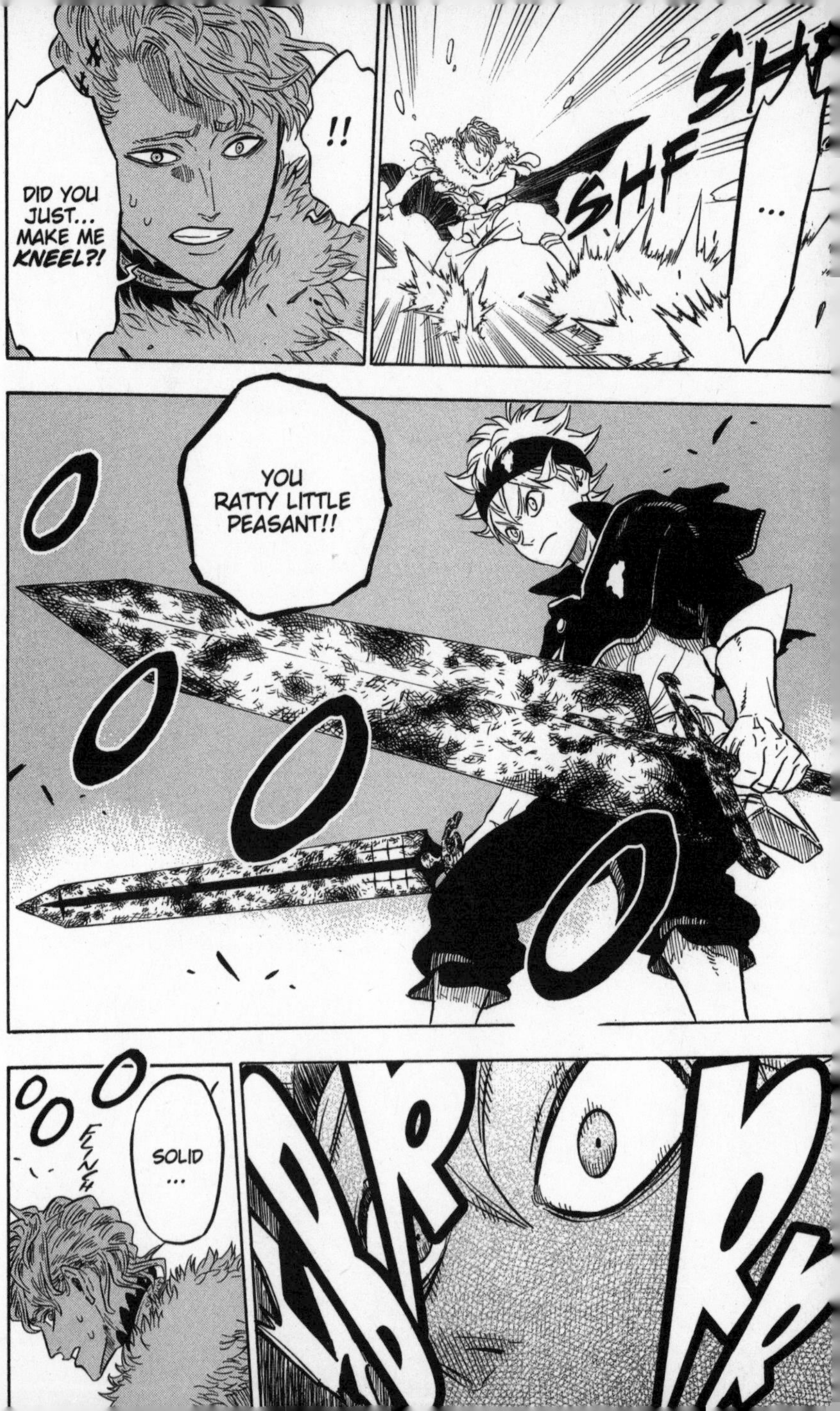
SHF SHF
...
!!
DID YOU JUST... MAKE ME KNEEL?!
YOU RATTY LITTLE PEASANT!!
FLINCH
SOLID ...

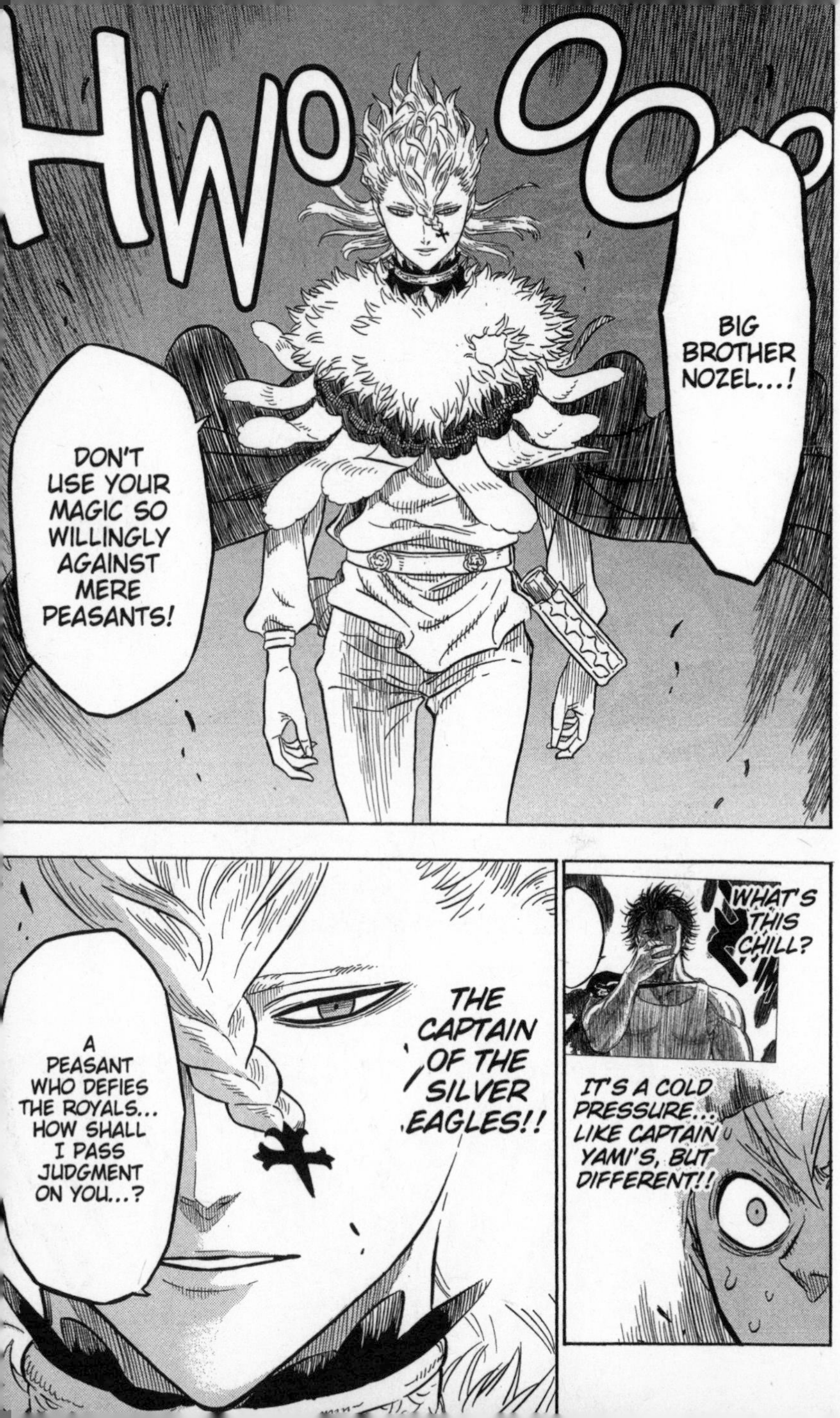
HWOOOO
BIG BROTHER NOZEL...!
DON'T USE YOUR MAGIC SO WILLINGLY AGAINST MERE PEASANTS!
WHAT'S THIS CHILL?
IT'S A COLD PRESSURE... LIKE CAPTAIN YAMI'S, BUT DIFFERENT!!
THE CAPTAIN OF THE SILVER EAGLES!!
A PEASANT WHO DEFIES THE ROYALS... HOW SHALL I PASS JUDGMENT ON YOU...?

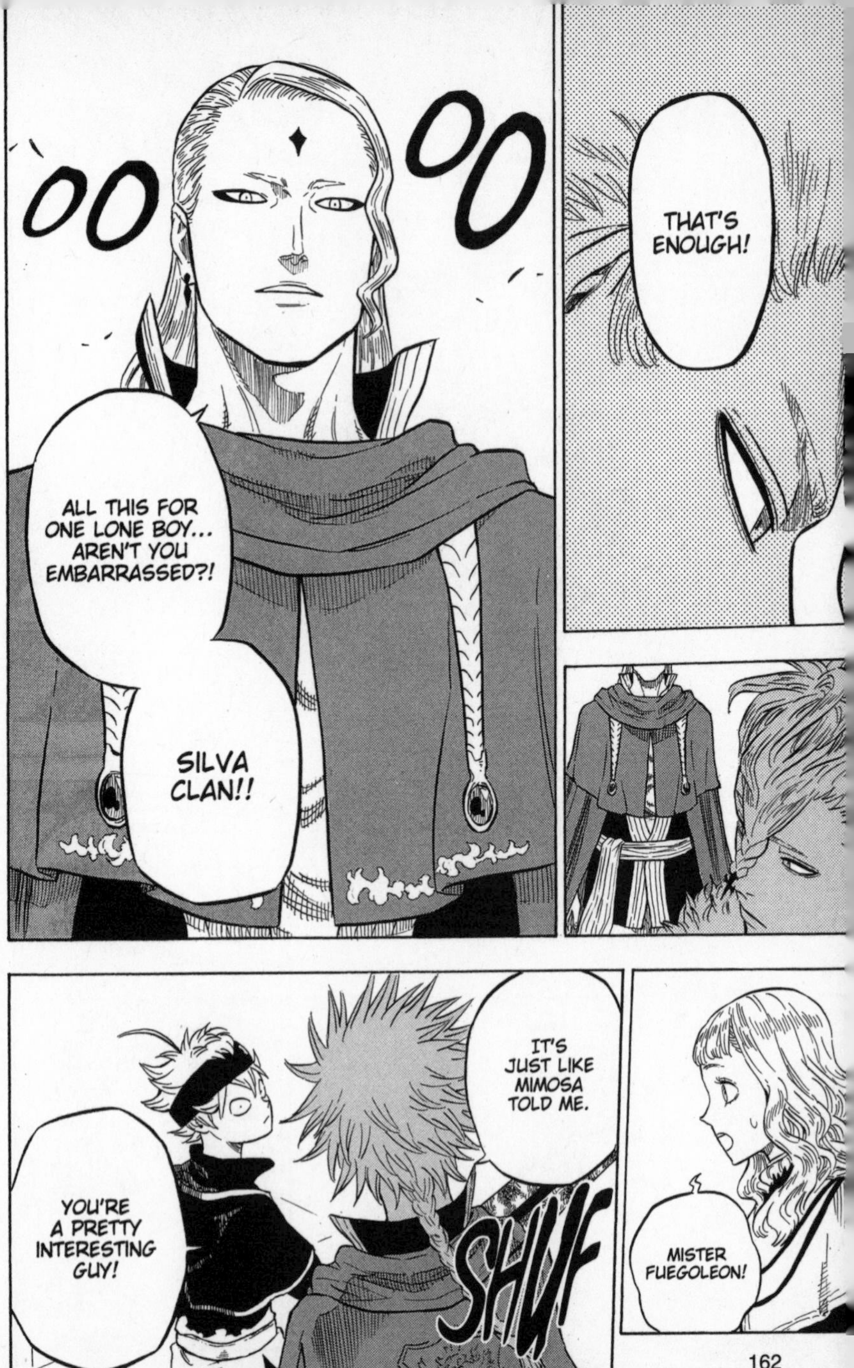
THAT'S ENOUGH!
OOOO
ALL THIS FOR ONE LONE BOY... AREN'T YOU EMBARRASSED?!
SILVA CLAN!!
MISTER FUEGOLEON!
IT'S JUST LIKE MIMOSA TOLD ME.
SHUF
YOU'RE A PRETTY INTERESTING GUY!

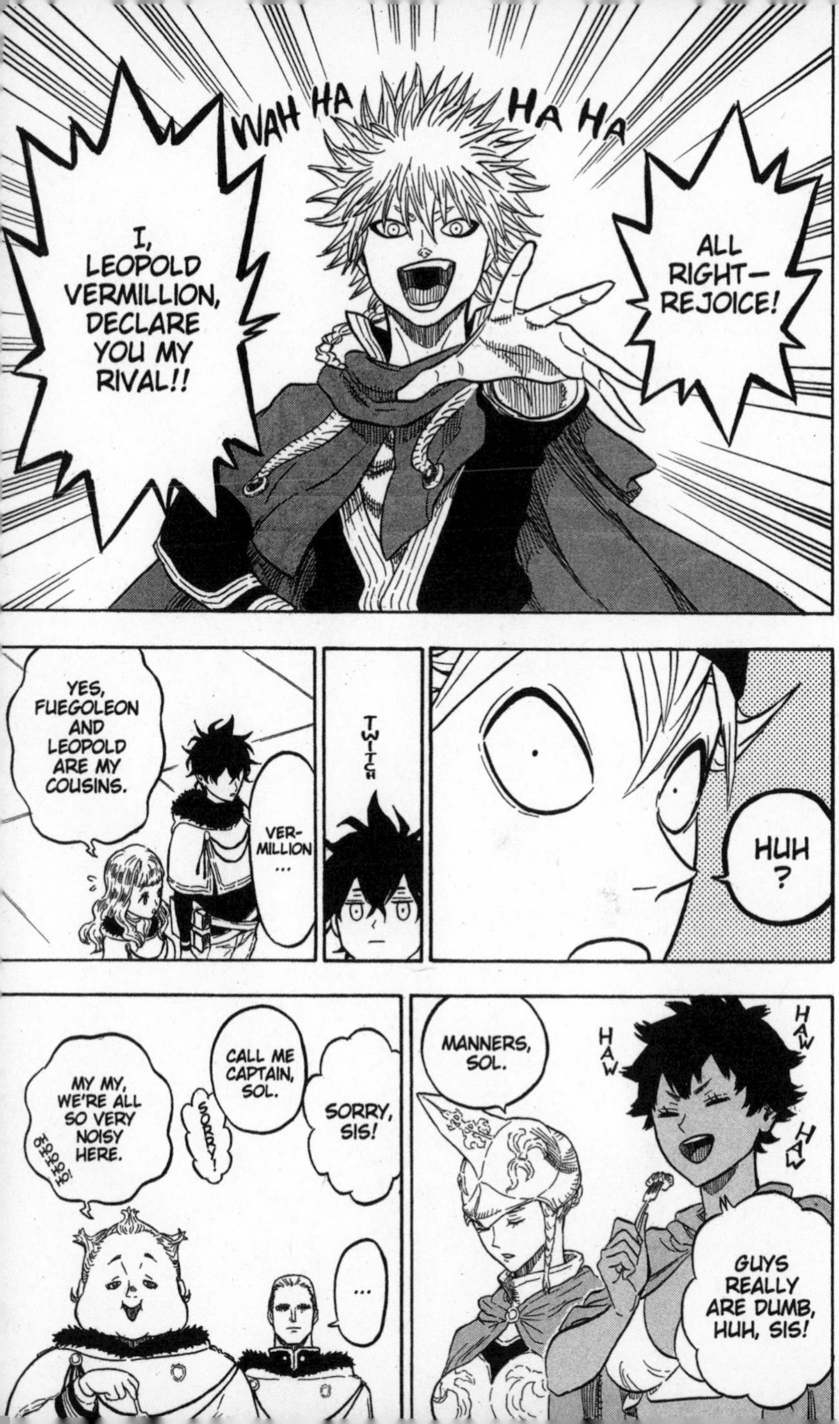
WAH HA HA HA
ALL RIGHT—REJOICE!
I, LEOPOLD VERMILLION, DECLARE YOU MY RIVAL!!
HUH?
TWITCH
VER-MILLION...
YES, FUEGOLEON AND LEOPOLD ARE MY COUSINS.
HAW HAW
HAW HAW
GUYS REALLY ARE DUMB, HUH, SIS!
MANNERS, SOL.
CALL ME CAPTAIN, SOL.
SORRY, SIS!
SORRY!
MY MY, WE'RE ALL SO VERY NOISY HERE.
OH HO HO HO HO!
...

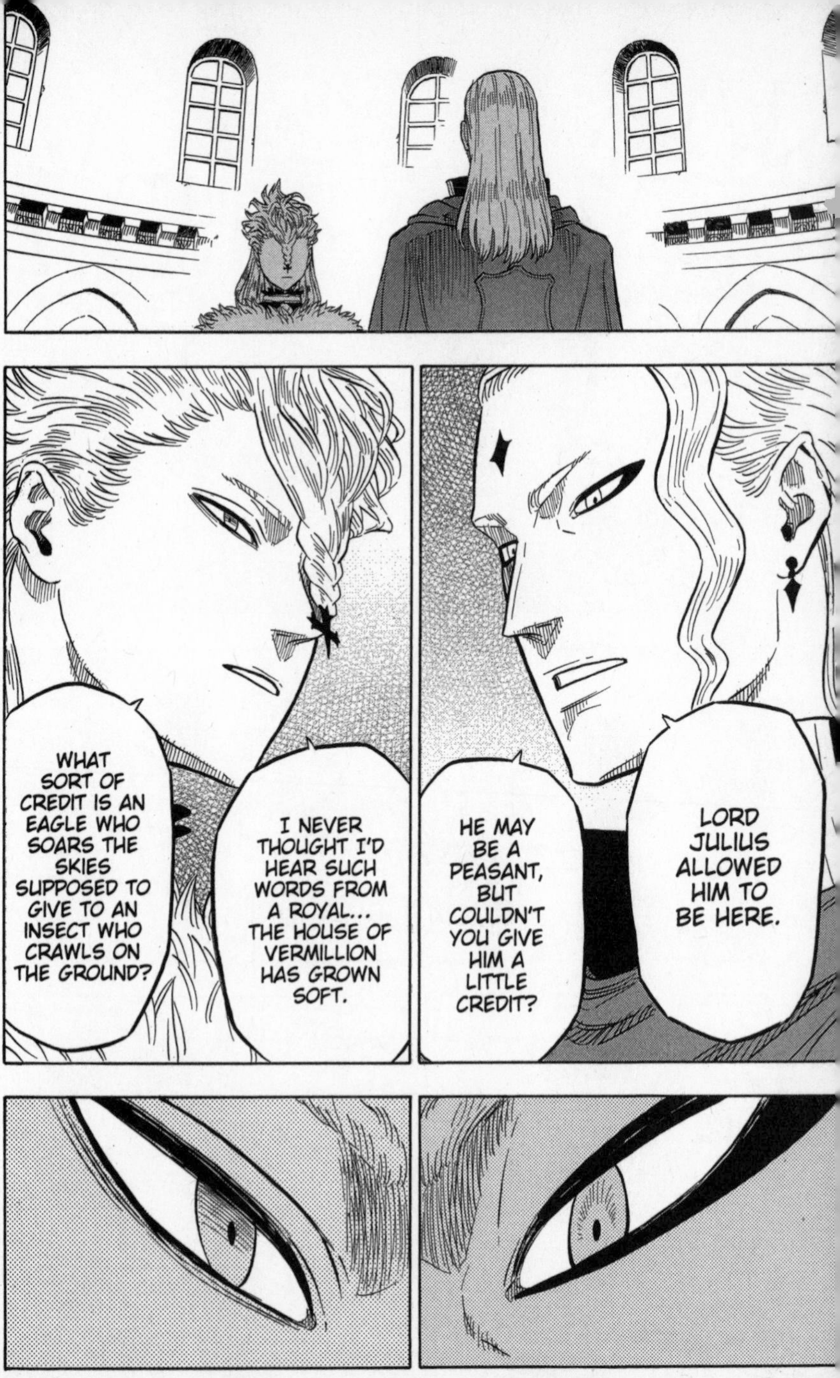
LORD JULIUS ALLOWED HIM TO BE HERE.
HE MAY BE A PEASANT, BUT COULDN'T YOU GIVE HIM A LITTLE CREDIT?
I NEVER THOUGHT I'D HEAR SUCH WORDS FROM A ROYAL... THE HOUSE OF VERMILLION HAS GROWN SOFT.
WHAT SORT OF CREDIT IS AN EAGLE WHO SOARS THE SKIES SUPPOSED TO GIVE TO AN INSECT WHO CRAWLS ON THE GROUND?

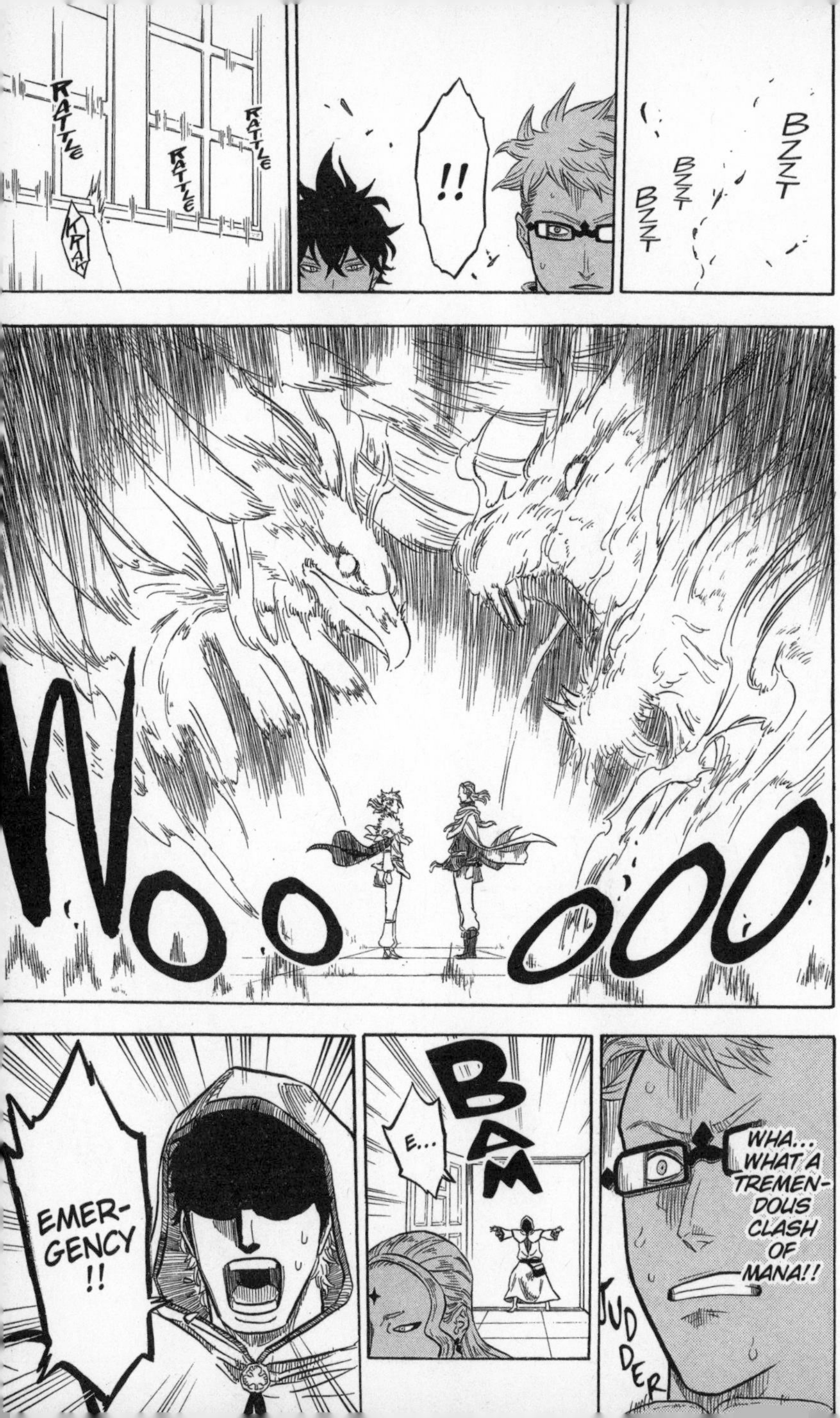
BZZT
BZZT
BZZT
!!
RATTLE
RATTLE
RATTLE
KRAK
WOOOOOO
WHA... WHAT A TREMENDOUS CLASH OF MANA!!
JUDDER
BAM
E...
EMERGENCY!!

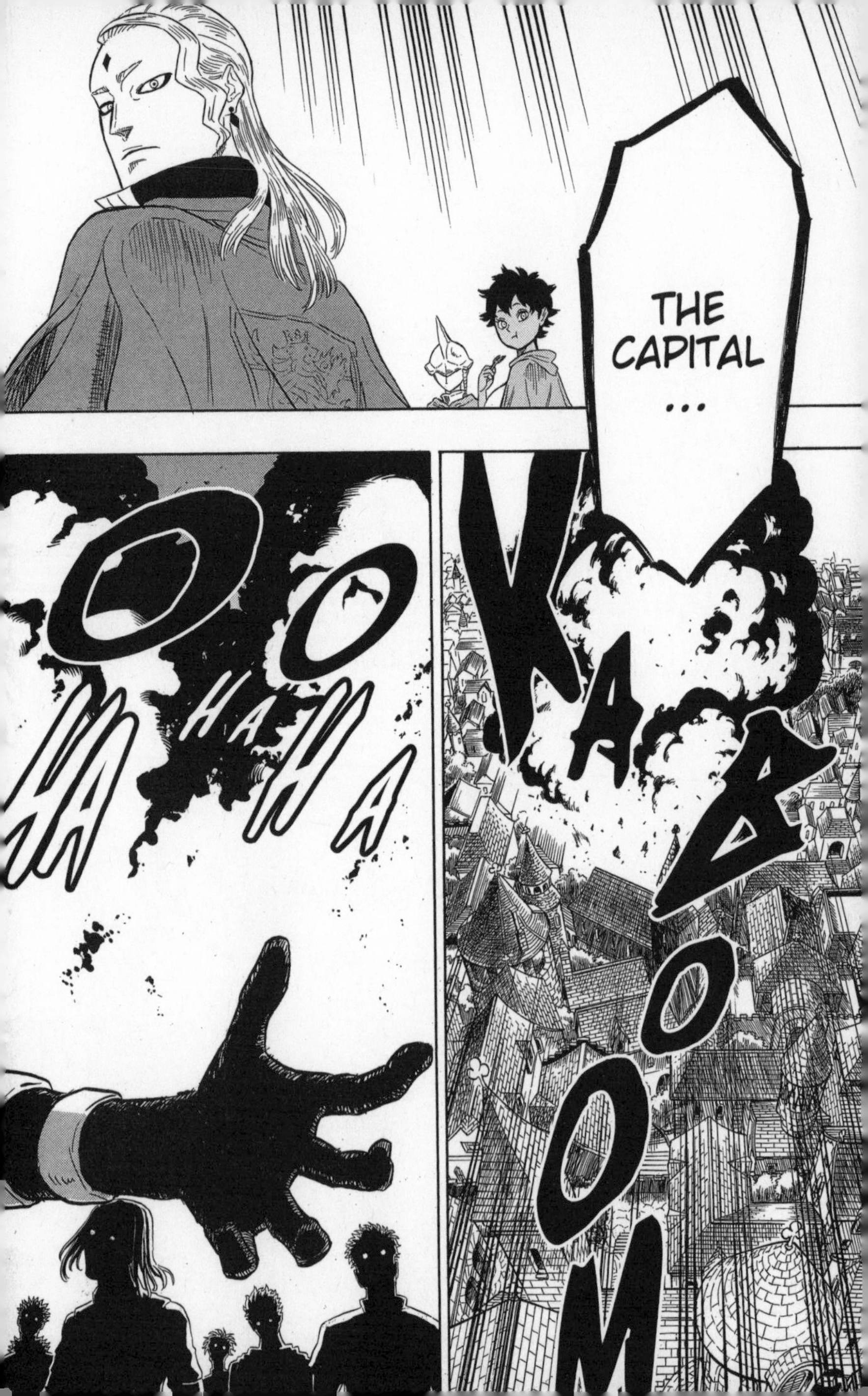
THE CAPITAL ...
VAAOOM
OOHAHAHA

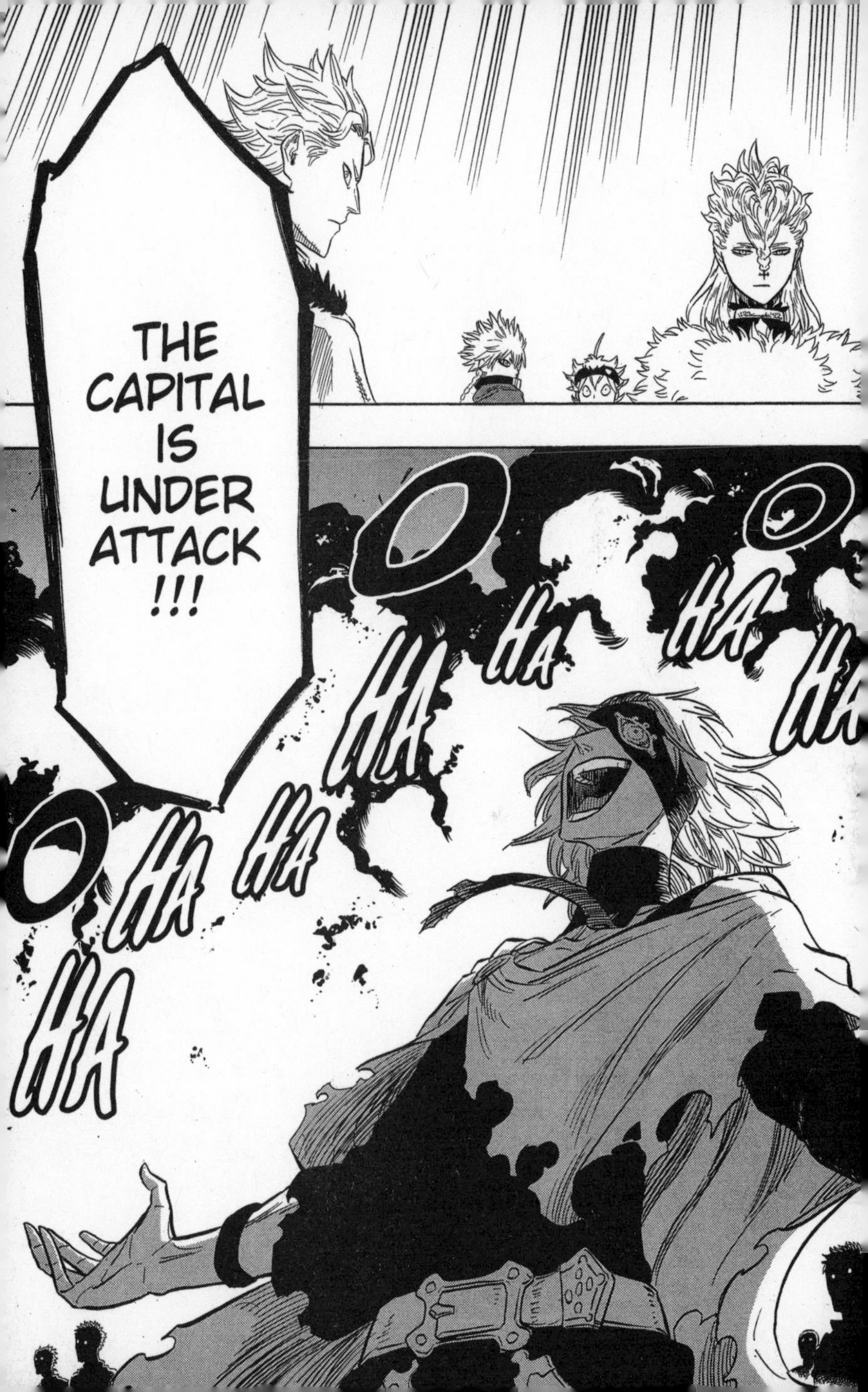
THE CAPITAL IS UNDER ATTACK!!!
O HA HA HA
O HA HA
O HA HA HA

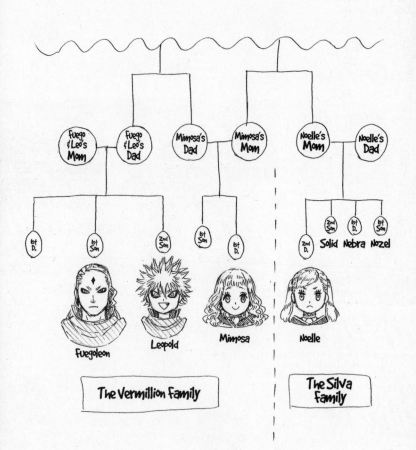

Fuego & Leo's Mom • Fuego & Leo's Dad • Mimosa's Dad • Mimosa's Mom • Noelle's Mom • Noelle's Dad

1st D. • 1st Son • 2nd Son • 1st Son • 1st D. • 2nd D. • 2nd Son Solid • 1st D. Nebra • 1st Son Nozel

Fuegoleon

Leopold

Mimosa

Noelle

The Vermillion Family

The Silva Family

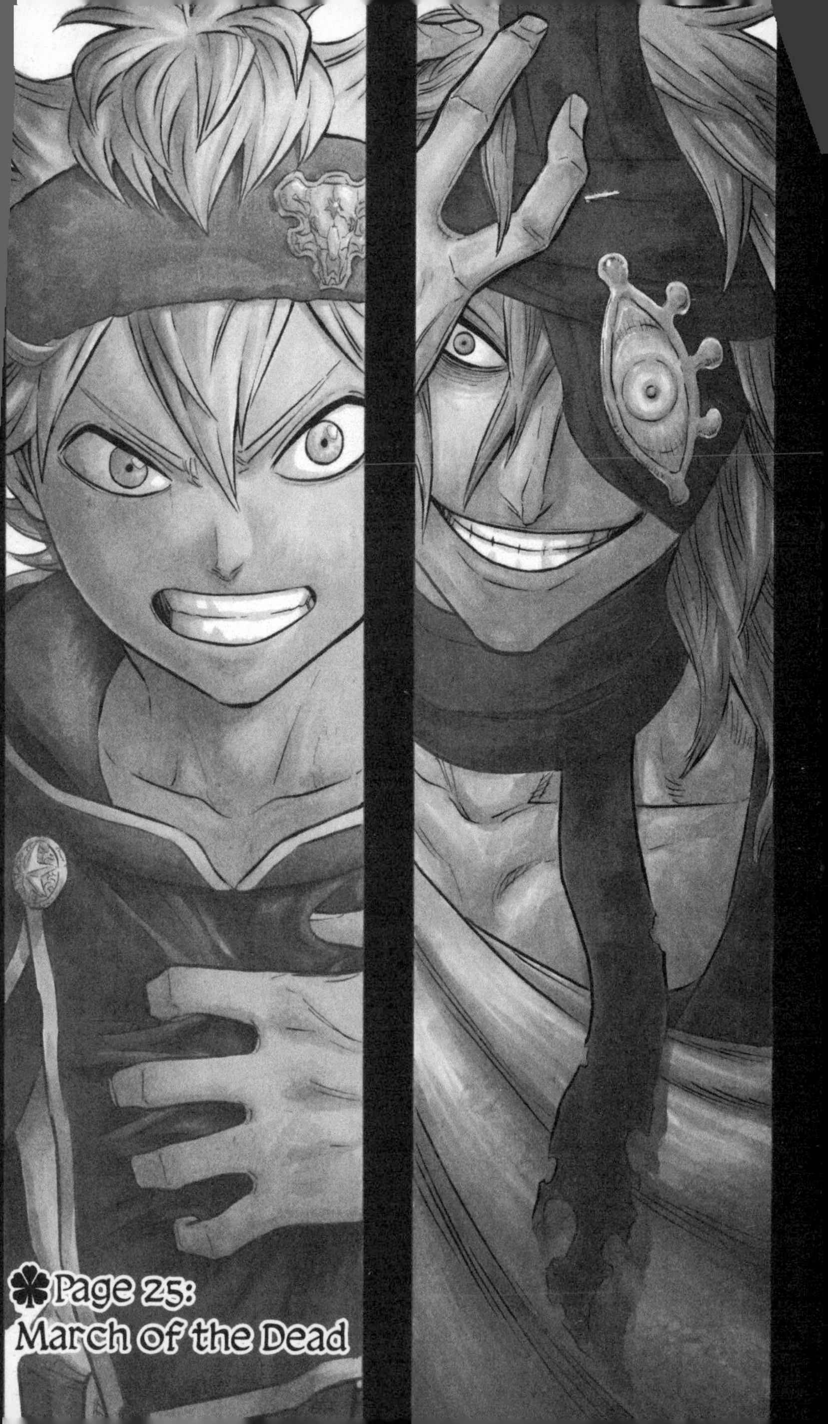
Page 25:
March of the Dead

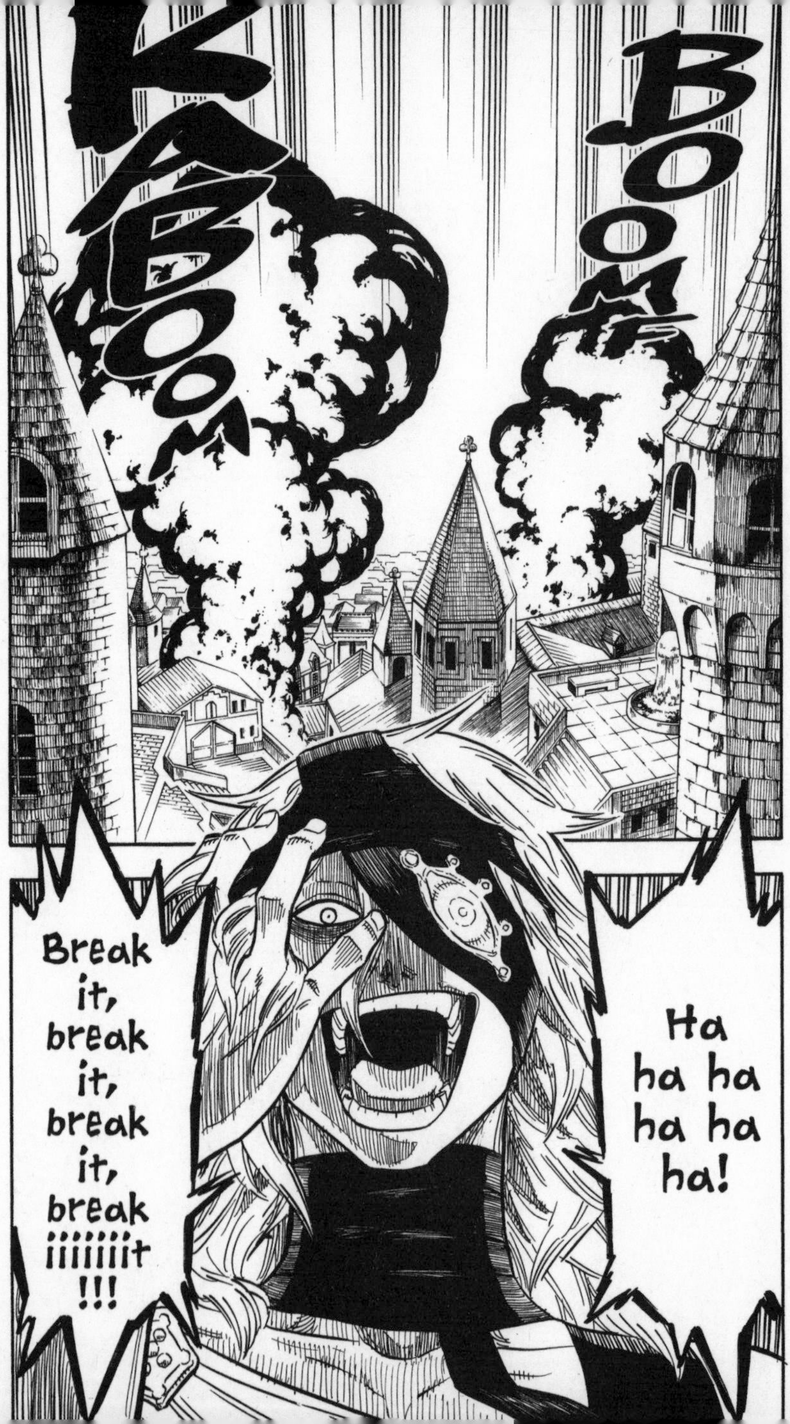
BOOM
KABOOM
Break it, break it, break it, break iiiiiiiit!!!
Ha ha ha ha ha ha!

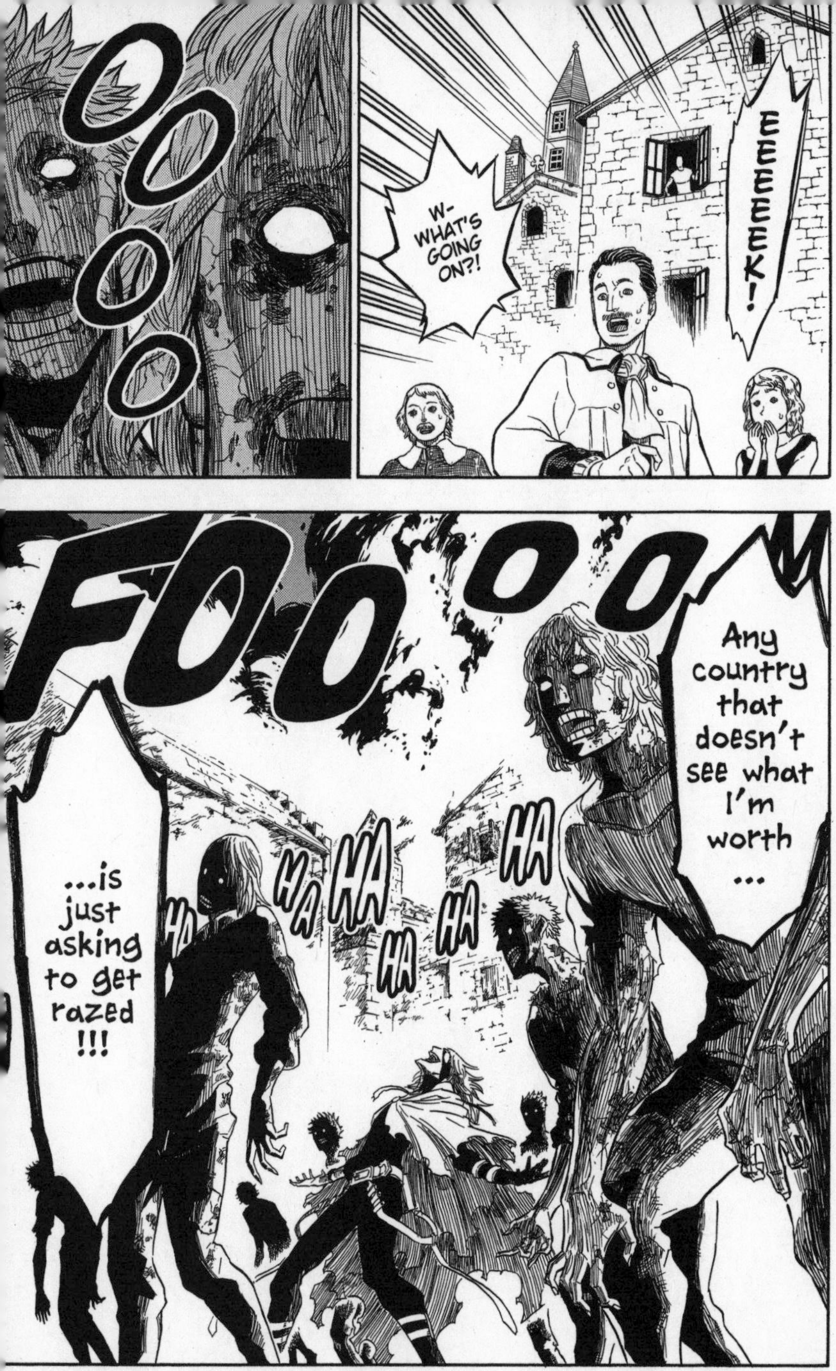
EEEEEEK!
W-WHAT'S GOING ON?!
OOOO
FOOOO
Any country that doesn't see what I'm worth ...
HA HA HA HA HA HA HA
...is just asking to get razed !!!

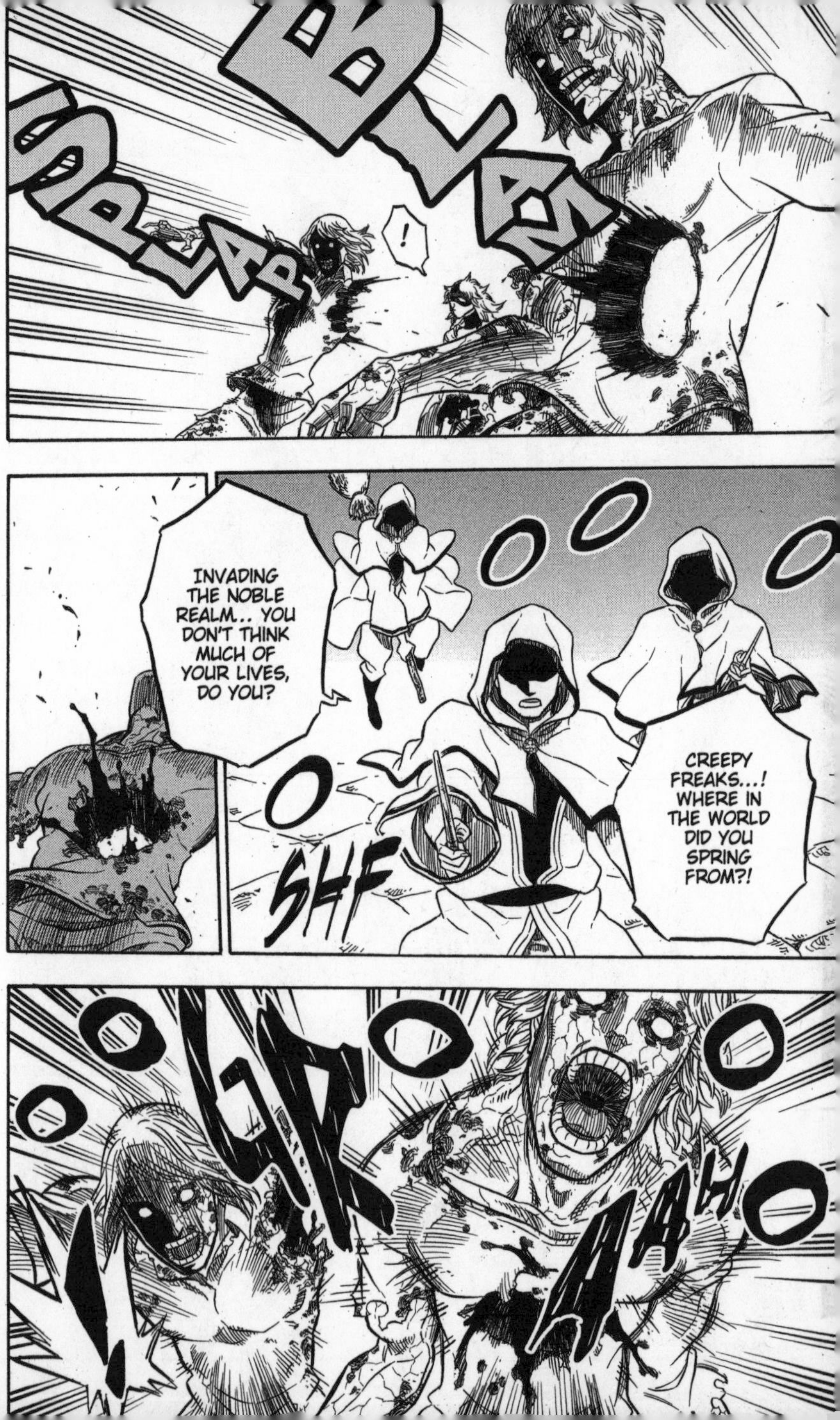
BLAM
SPLAP
!
SHF
CREEPY FREAKS...! WHERE IN THE WORLD DID YOU SPRING FROM?!
INVADING THE NOBLE REALM... YOU DON'T THINK MUCH OF YOUR LIVES, DO YOU?

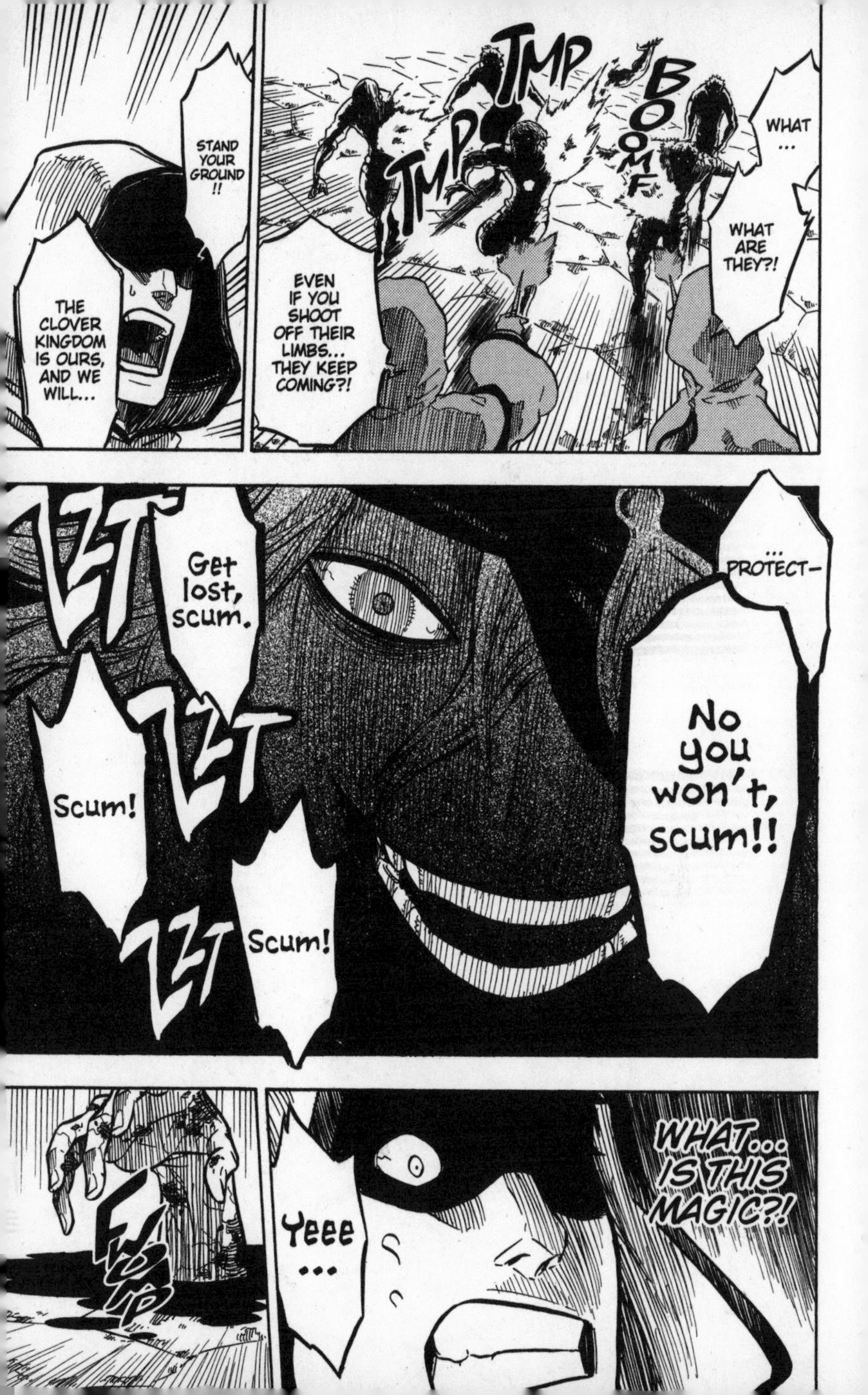
BOOMF
TMP TMP
WHAT...
WHAT ARE THEY?!
EVEN IF YOU SHOOT OFF THEIR LIMBS... THEY KEEP COMING?!
STAND YOUR GROUND!!
THE CLOVER KINGDOM IS OURS, AND WE WILL...
...PROTECT-
No you won't, scum!!
Get lost, scum.
ZZZT
Scum!
ZZZT
Scum!
ZZZT
WHAT... IS THIS MAGIC?!
Yeee...

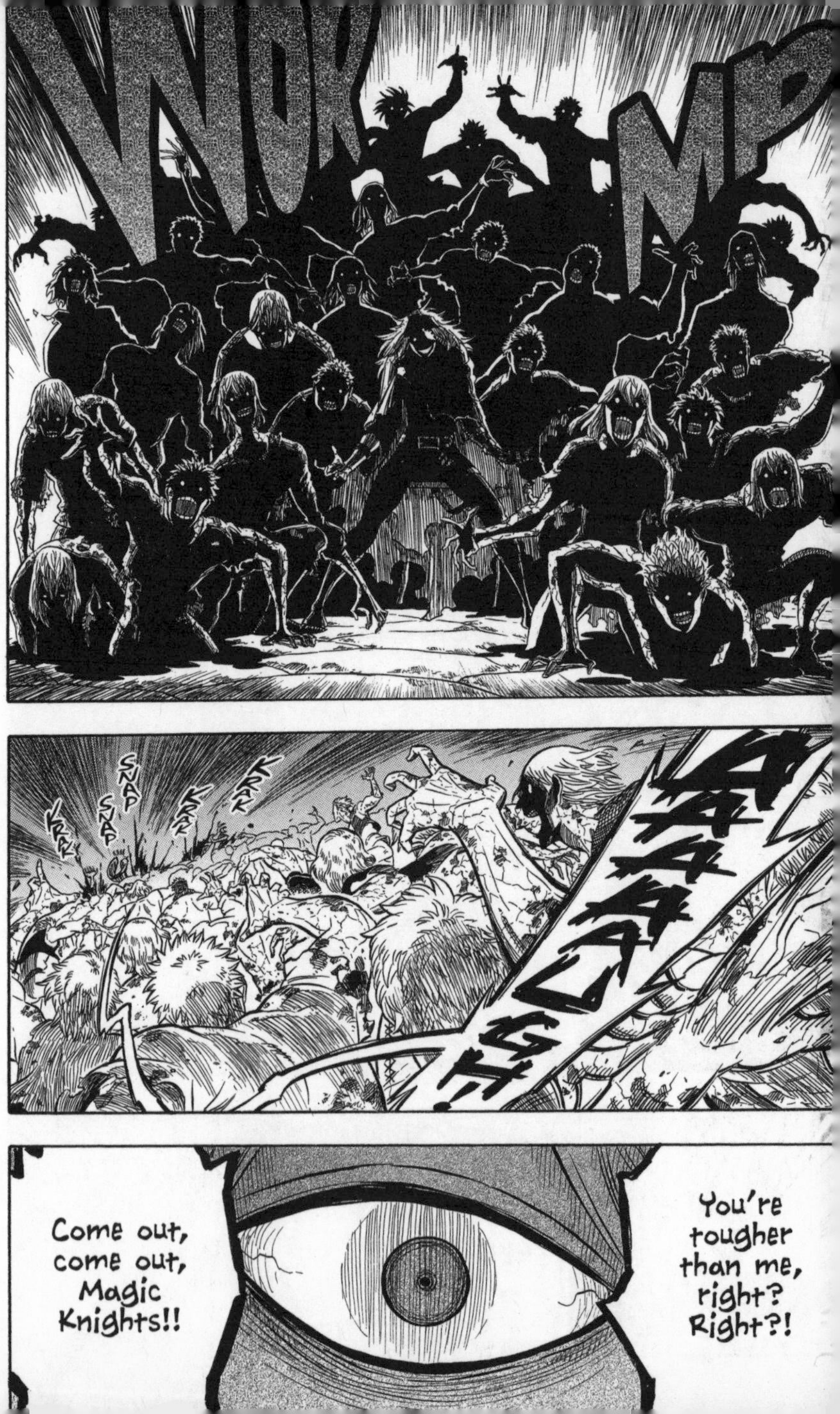
AAAAUGH!!
KRAK
KRAK
SNAP
SNAP
KRAK
You're tougher than me, right? Right?!
Come out, come out, Magic Knights!!

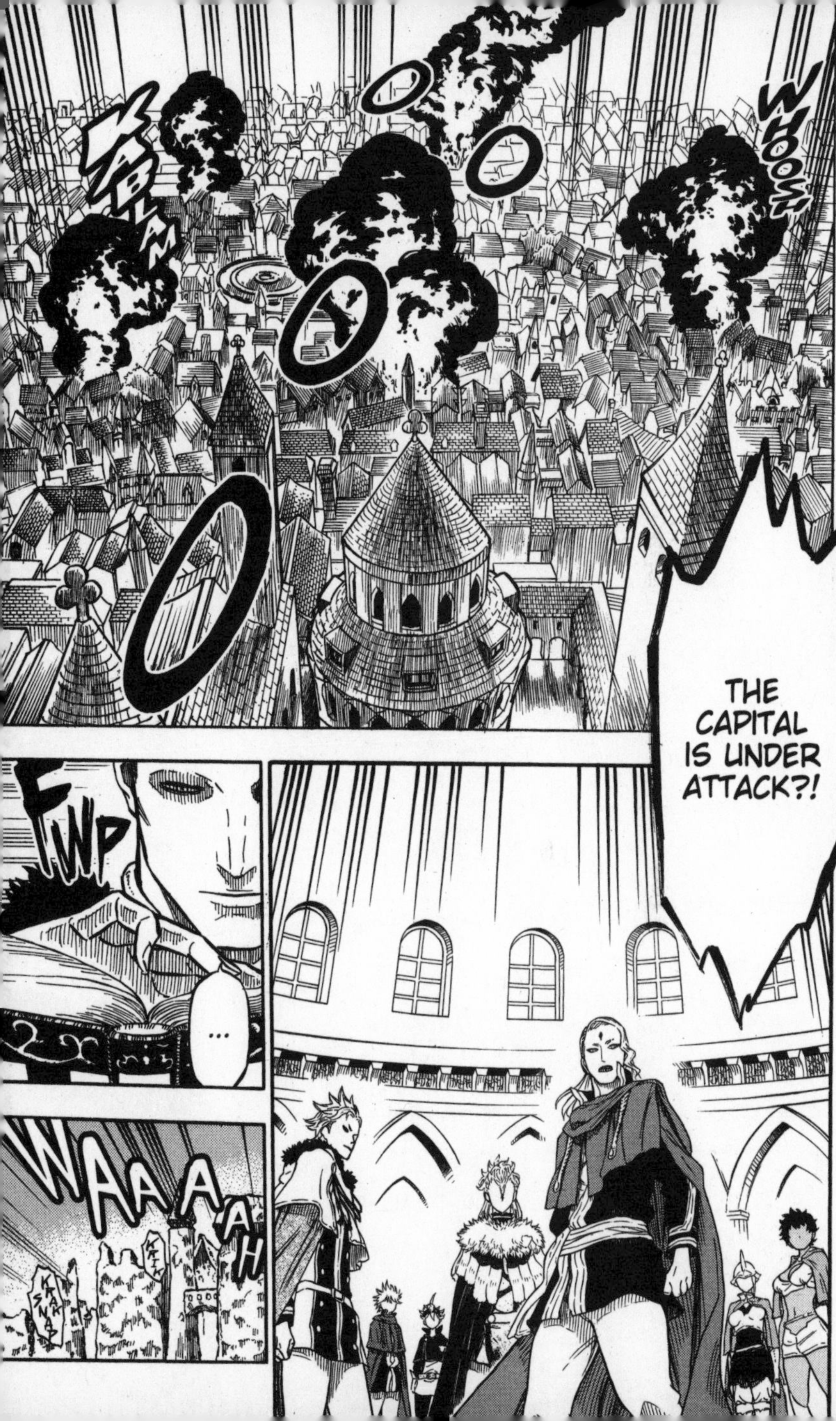
WHOOSH
KABLAM
THE CAPITAL IS UNDER ATTACK?!
FWP
...
WAAAAAH
KRIK

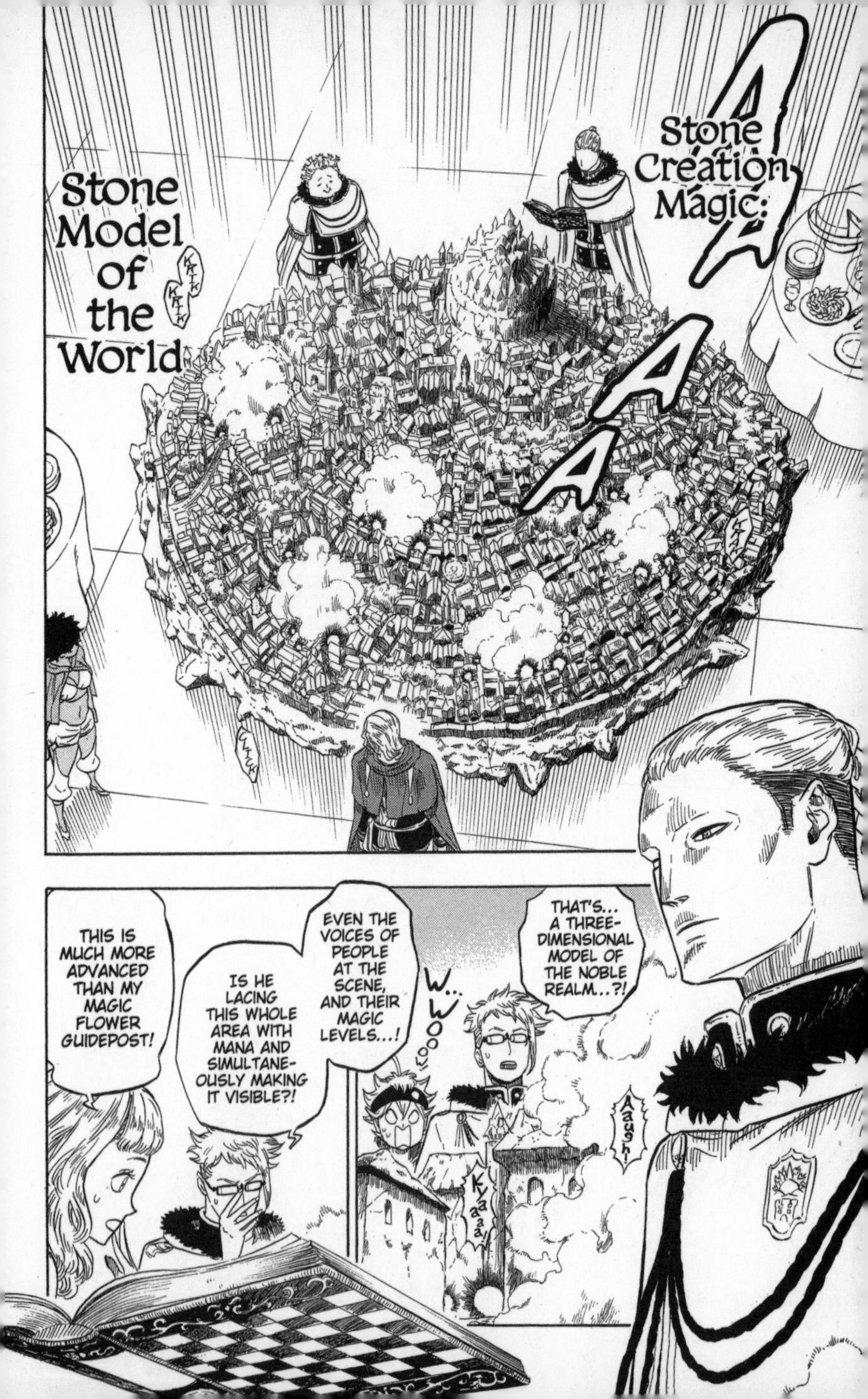

Stone Creation Magic:
Stone Model of the World
KRIK
KRIK
AAA
CLICK
THAT'S... A THREE-DIMENSIONAL MODEL OF THE NOBLE REALM..?!
W... WOOOW!
Aaugh!
Kyaaaa!
EVEN THE VOICES OF PEOPLE AT THE SCENE, AND THEIR MAGIC LEVELS...!
IS HE LACING THIS WHOLE AREA WITH MANA AND SIMULTANEOUSLY MAKING IT VISIBLE?!
THIS IS MUCH MORE ADVANCED THAN MY MAGIC FLOWER GUIDEPOST!

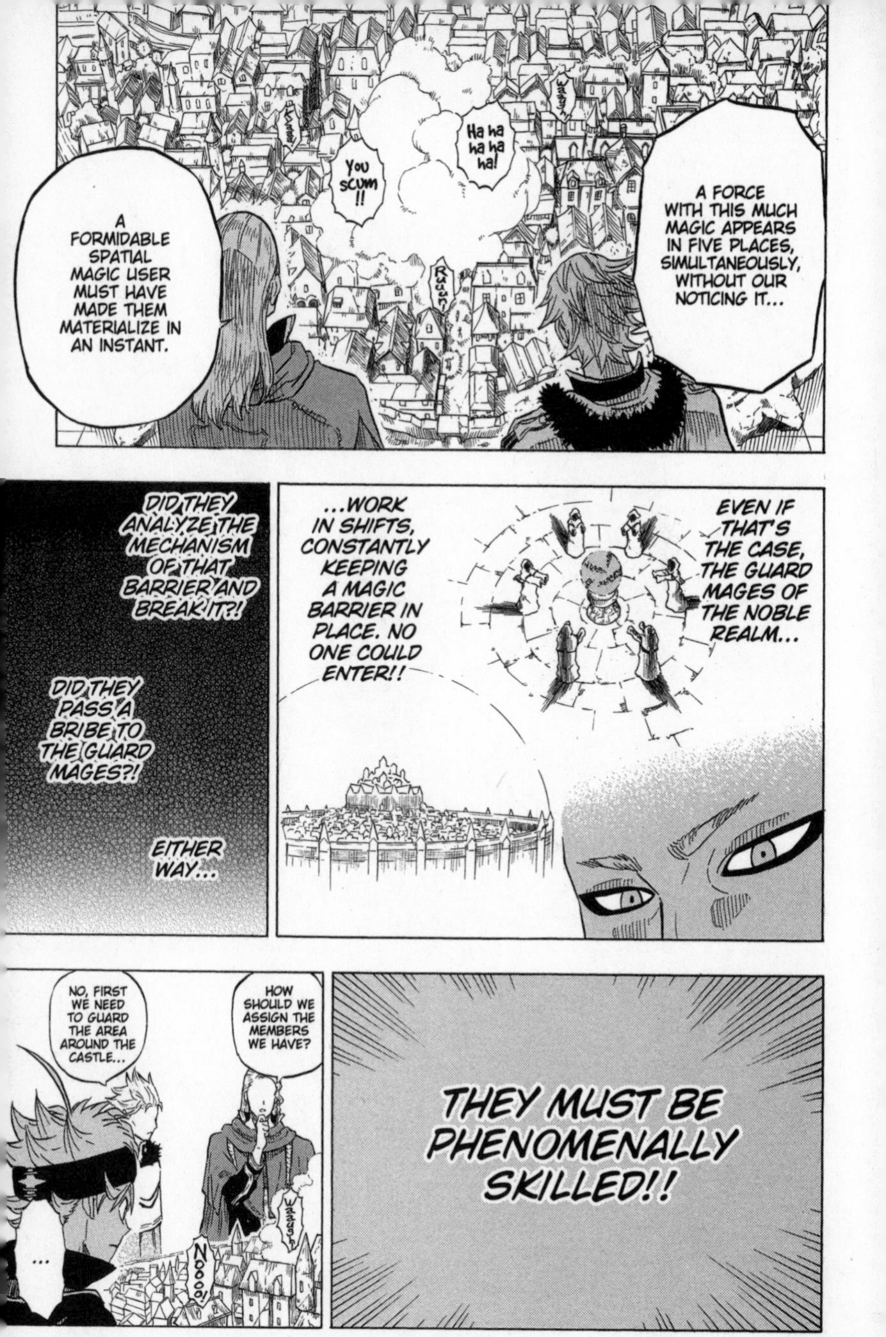
A FORCE WITH THIS MUCH MAGIC APPEARS IN FIVE PLACES, SIMULTANEOUSLY, WITHOUT OUR NOTICING IT...
Ha ha ha ha ha!
You scum!!
Ruuun!
A FORMIDABLE SPATIAL MAGIC USER MUST HAVE MADE THEM MATERIALIZE IN AN INSTANT.
EVEN IF THAT'S THE CASE, THE GUARD MAGES OF THE NOBLE REALM...
...WORK IN SHIFTS, CONSTANTLY KEEPING A MAGIC BARRIER IN PLACE. NO ONE COULD ENTER!!
DID THEY ANALYZE THE MECHANISM OF THAT BARRIER AND BREAK IT?!
DID THEY PASS A BRIBE TO THE GUARD MAGES?!
EITHER WAY...
THEY MUST BE PHENOMENALLY SKILLED!!
HOW SHOULD WE ASSIGN THE MEMBERS WE HAVE?
NO, FIRST WE NEED TO GUARD THE AREA AROUND THE CASTLE...
Noooo!
...

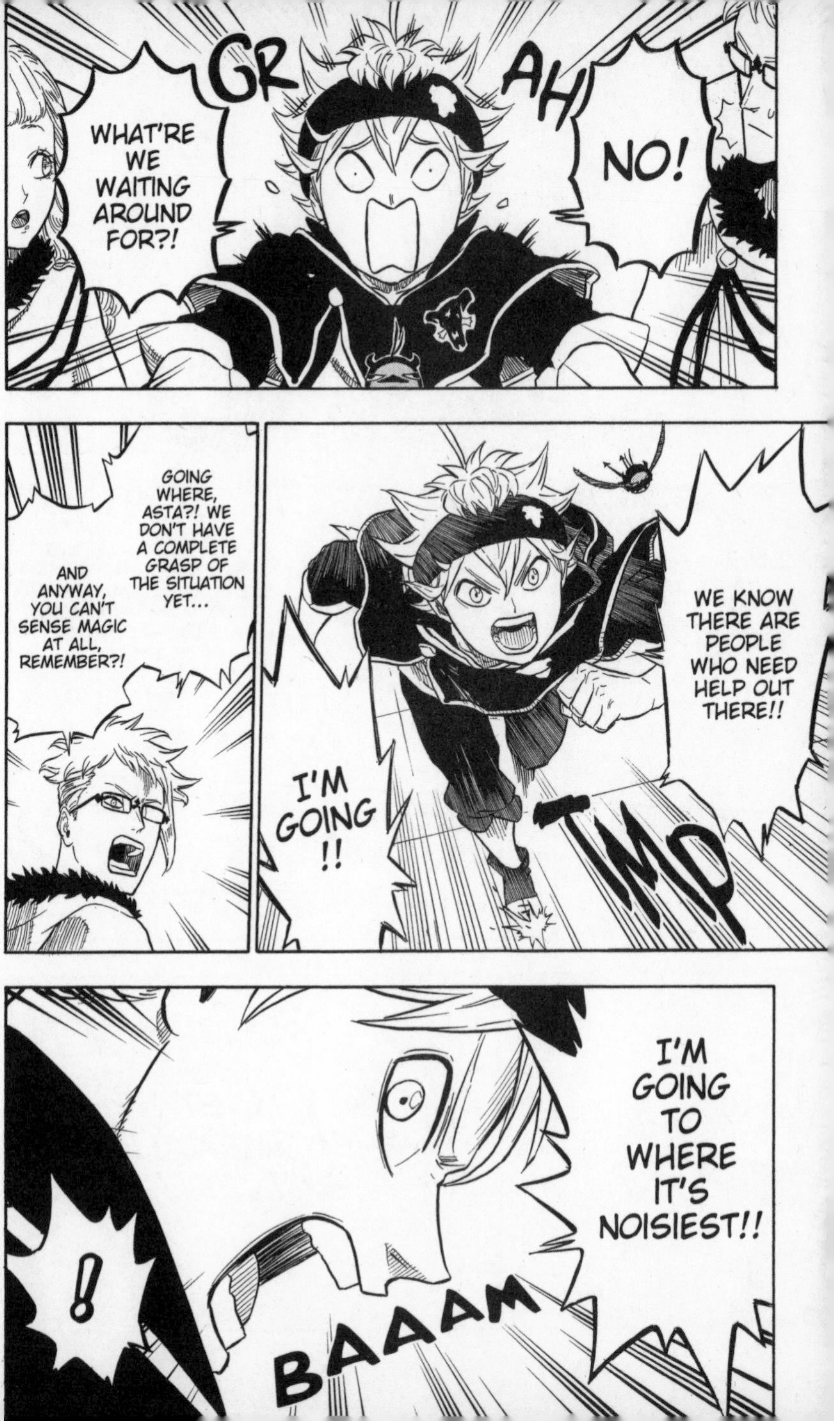
NO!
GRAH
WHAT'RE WE WAITING AROUND FOR?!
WE KNOW THERE ARE PEOPLE WHO NEED HELP OUT THERE!!
I'M GOING!!
TMP
GOING WHERE, ASTA?! WE DON'T HAVE A COMPLETE GRASP OF THE SITUATION YET...
AND ANYWAY, YOU CAN'T SENSE MAGIC AT ALL, REMEMBER?!
I'M GOING TO WHERE IT'S NOISIEST!!
BAAAM
!

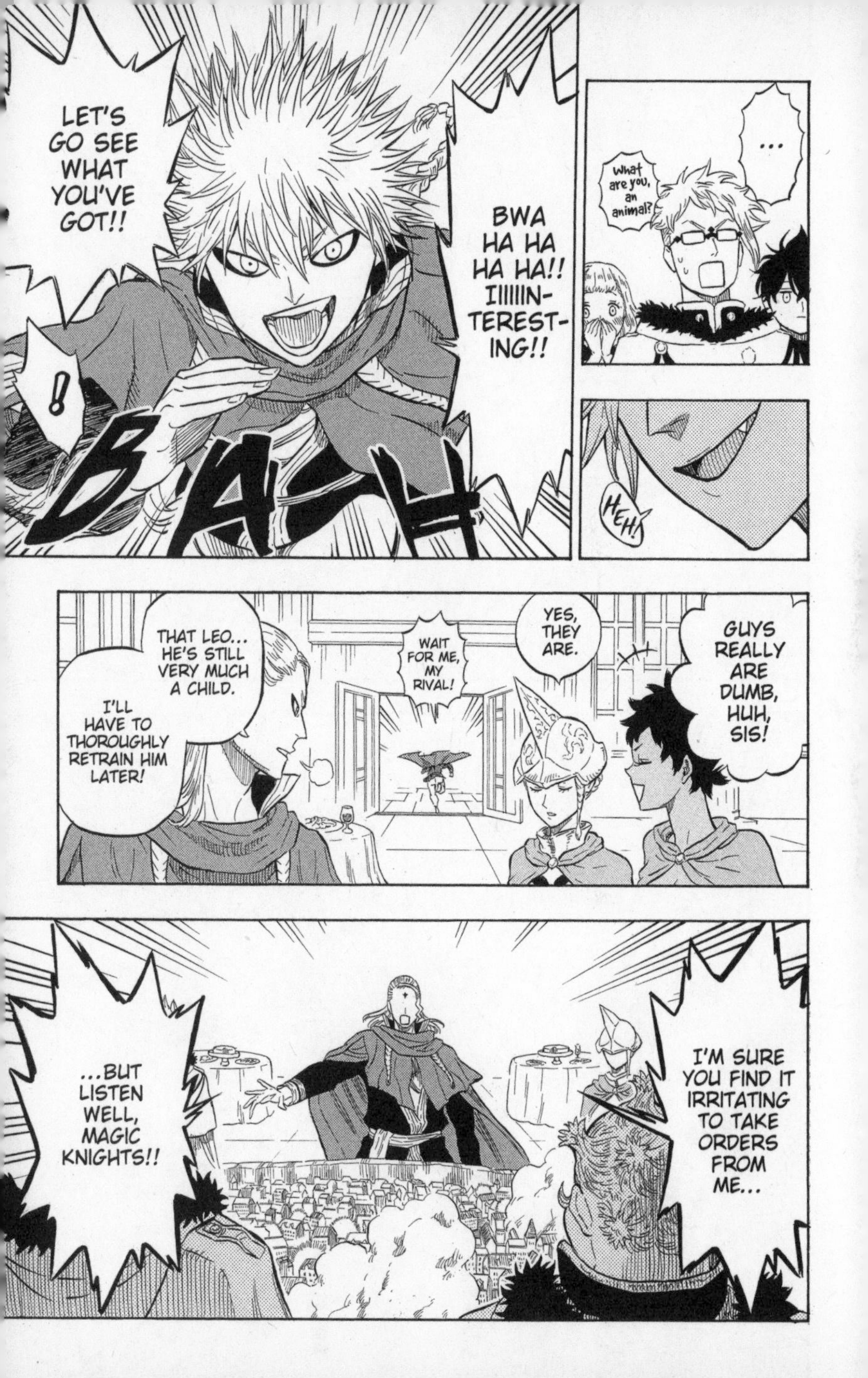
...
What are you, an animal?
HEH!
BWA HA HA HA HA!! IIIIIIN-TEREST-ING!!
LET'S GO SEE WHAT YOU'VE GOT!!
!
BASH
GUYS REALLY ARE DUMB, HUH, SIS!
YES, THEY ARE.
WAIT FOR ME, MY RIVAL!
THAT LEO... HE'S STILL VERY MUCH A CHILD.
I'LL HAVE TO THOROUGHLY RETRAIN HIM LATER!
I'M SURE YOU FIND IT IRRITATING TO TAKE ORDERS FROM ME...
...BUT LISTEN WELL, MAGIC KNIGHTS!!

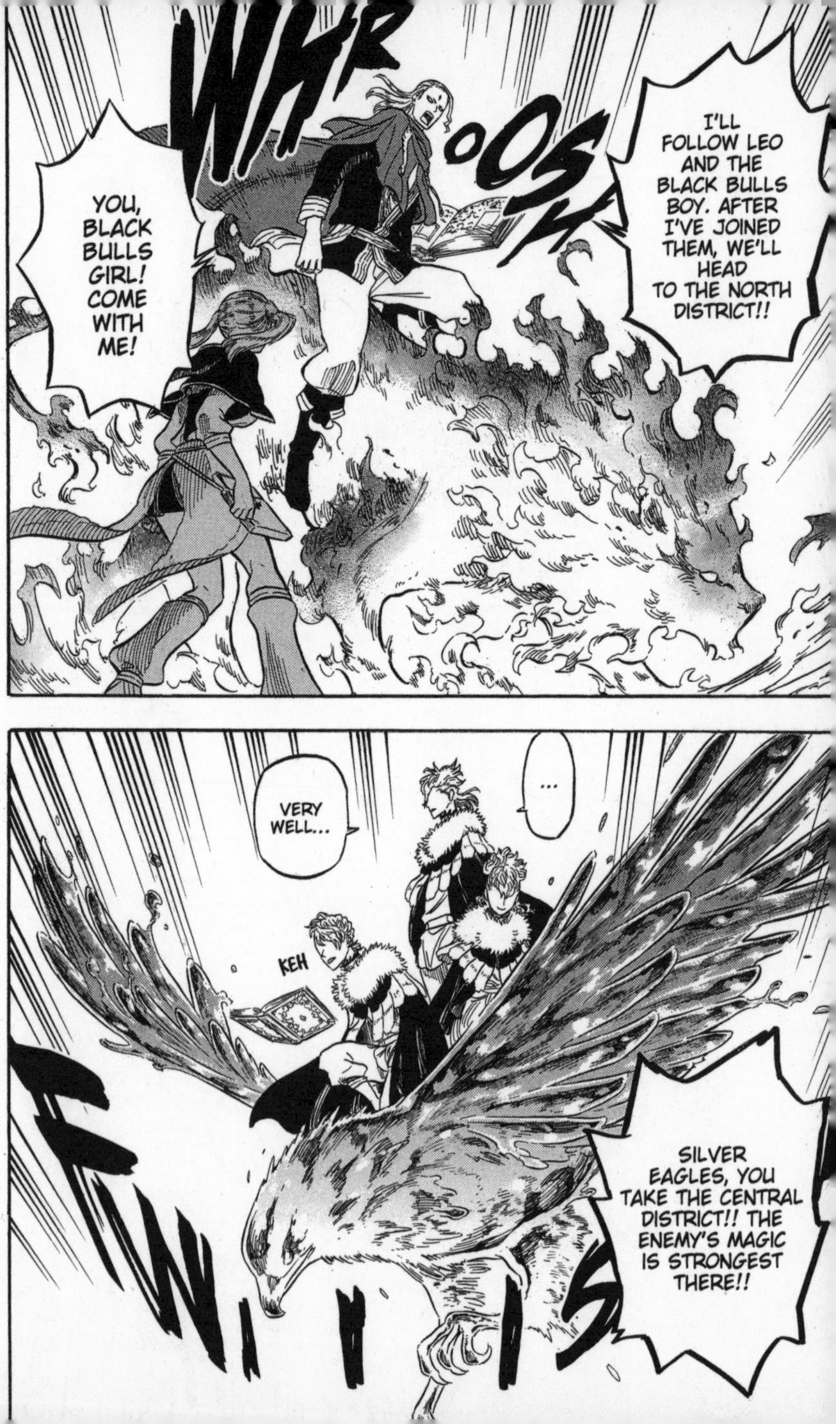
I'LL FOLLOW LEO AND THE BLACK BULLS BOY. AFTER I'VE JOINED THEM, WE'LL HEAD TO THE NORTH DISTRICT!!
WHROOSH
YOU, BLACK BULLS GIRL! COME WITH ME!
...
VERY WELL...
SILVER EAGLES, YOU TAKE THE CENTRAL DISTRICT!! THE ENEMY'S MAGIC IS STRONGEST THERE!!
KEH

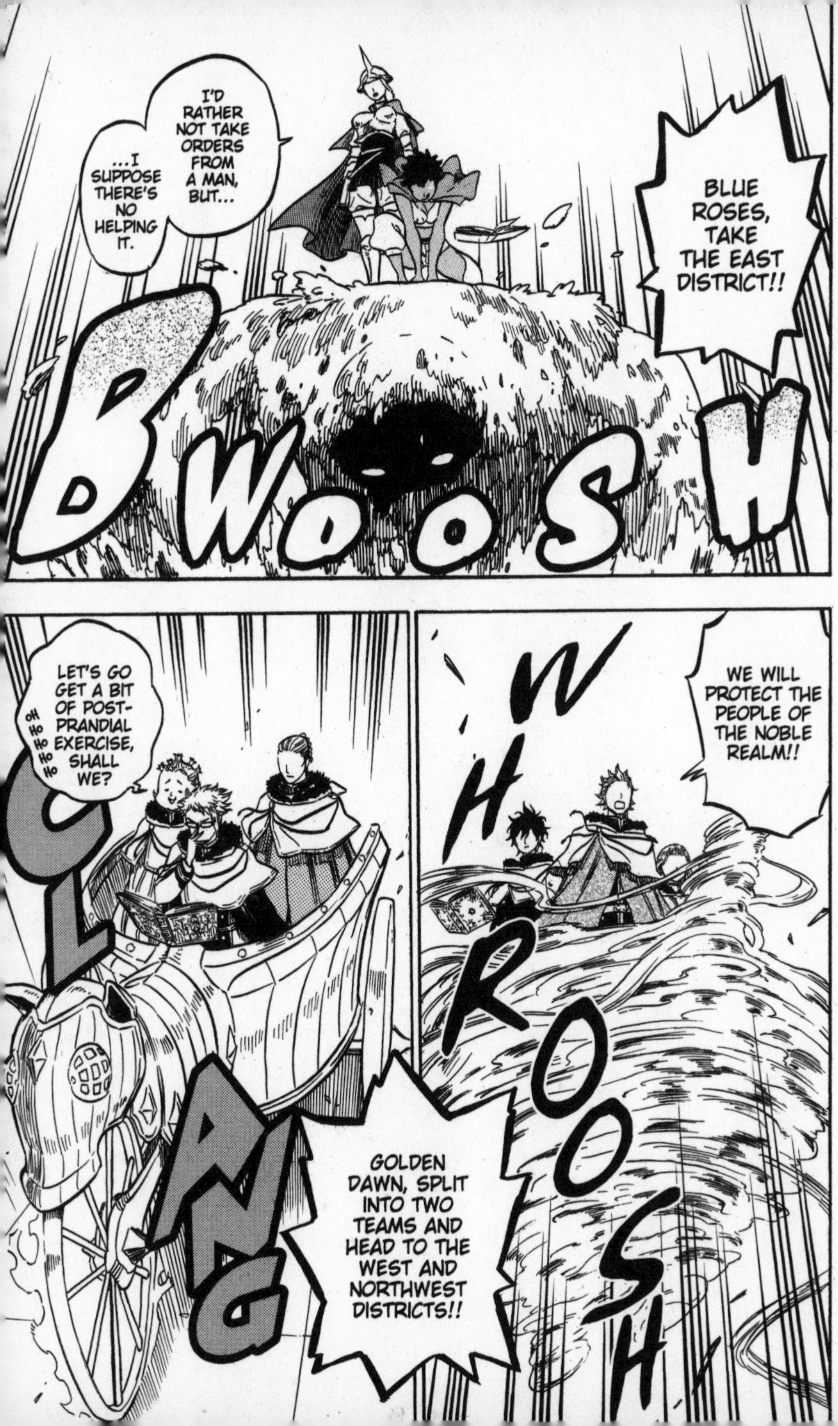
BLUE ROSES, TAKE THE EAST DISTRICT!!
I'D RATHER NOT TAKE ORDERS FROM A MAN, BUT...
...I SUPPOSE THERE'S NO HELPING IT.
BWOOSH
WE WILL PROTECT THE PEOPLE OF THE NOBLE REALM!!
WHROOOSH
LET'S GO GET A BIT OF POST-PRANDIAL EXERCISE, SHALL WE?
OH HO HO HO HO
GOLDEN DAWN, SPLIT INTO TWO TEAMS AND HEAD TO THE WEST AND NORTHWEST DISTRICTS!!
CLANG

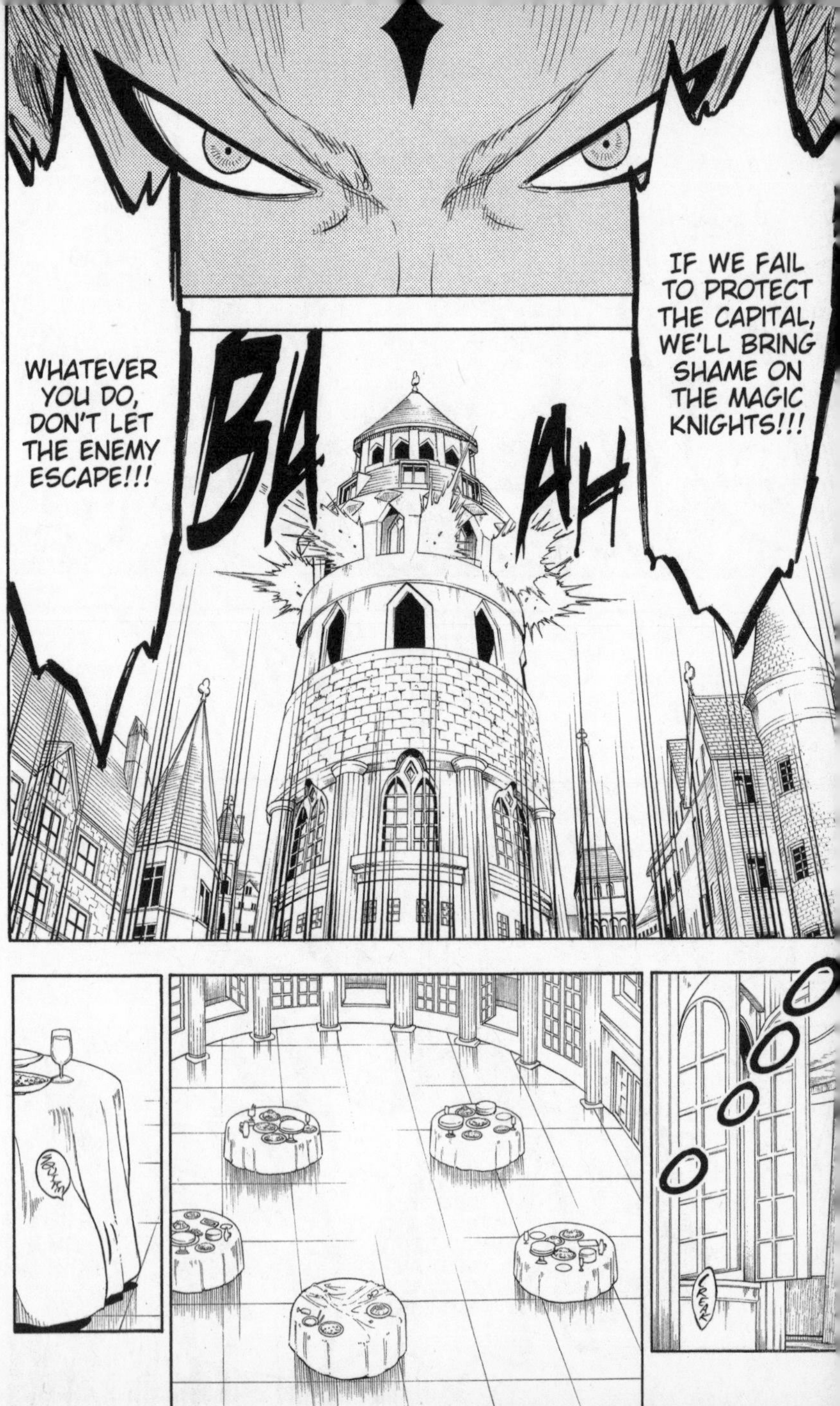
IF WE FAIL TO PROTECT THE CAPITAL, WE'LL BRING SHAME ON THE MAGIC KNIGHTS!!!
WHATEVER YOU DO, DON'T LET THE ENEMY ESCAPE!!!
BA
AH
CREAK

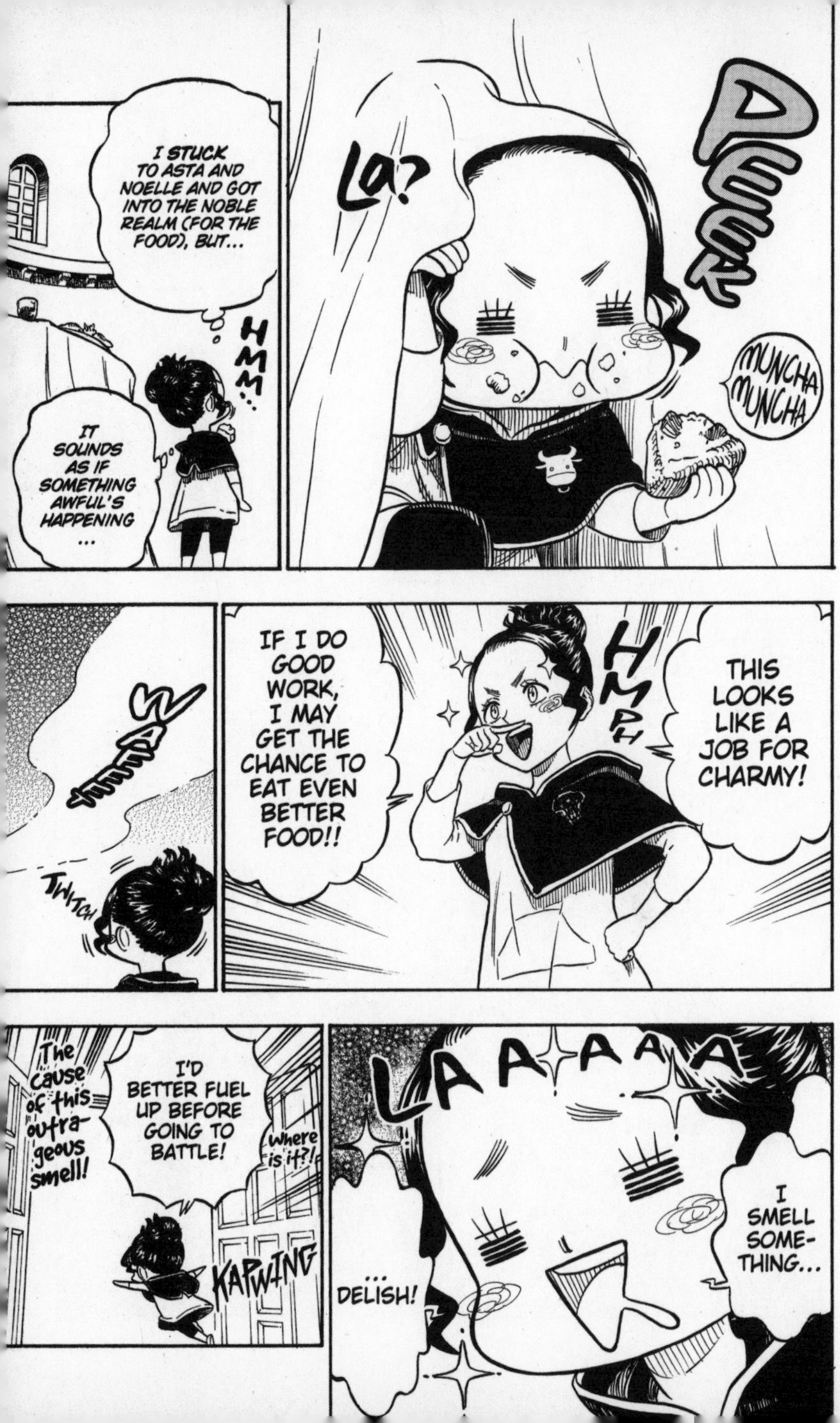
PEEER
MUNCHA MUNCHA
La?
I STUCK TO ASTA AND NOELLE AND GOT INTO THE NOBLE REALM (FOR THE FOOD), BUT...
HMM...
IT SOUNDS AS IF SOMETHING AWFUL'S HAPPENING...
THIS LOOKS LIKE A JOB FOR CHARMY!
HMPH
IF I DO GOOD WORK, I MAY GET THE CHANCE TO EAT EVEN BETTER FOOD!!
WAFT
TWITCH
LAAAAA
I SMELL SOMETHING...
...DELISH!
Where is it?!
I'D BETTER FUEL UP BEFORE GOING TO BATTLE!
The cause of this outrageous smell!
KAPWING

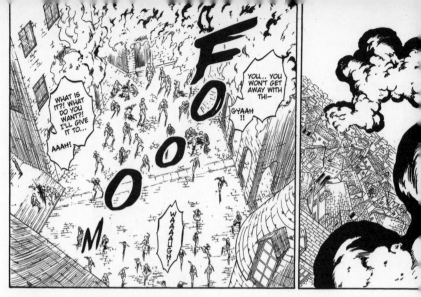

YOU... YOU WON'T GET AWAY WITH THI-
GYAAH!!
FOOOOM
WAAAAUGH!
WHAT IS IT?! WHAT DO YOU WANT?! I'LL GIVE IT TO...
AAAH!
...
HEY, LITTLE GIRL!
SHUF
DO YOU LIKE THE CLOVER KINGDOM?

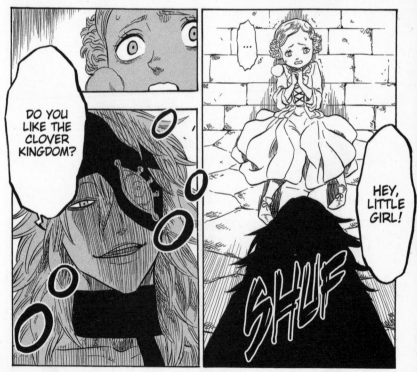

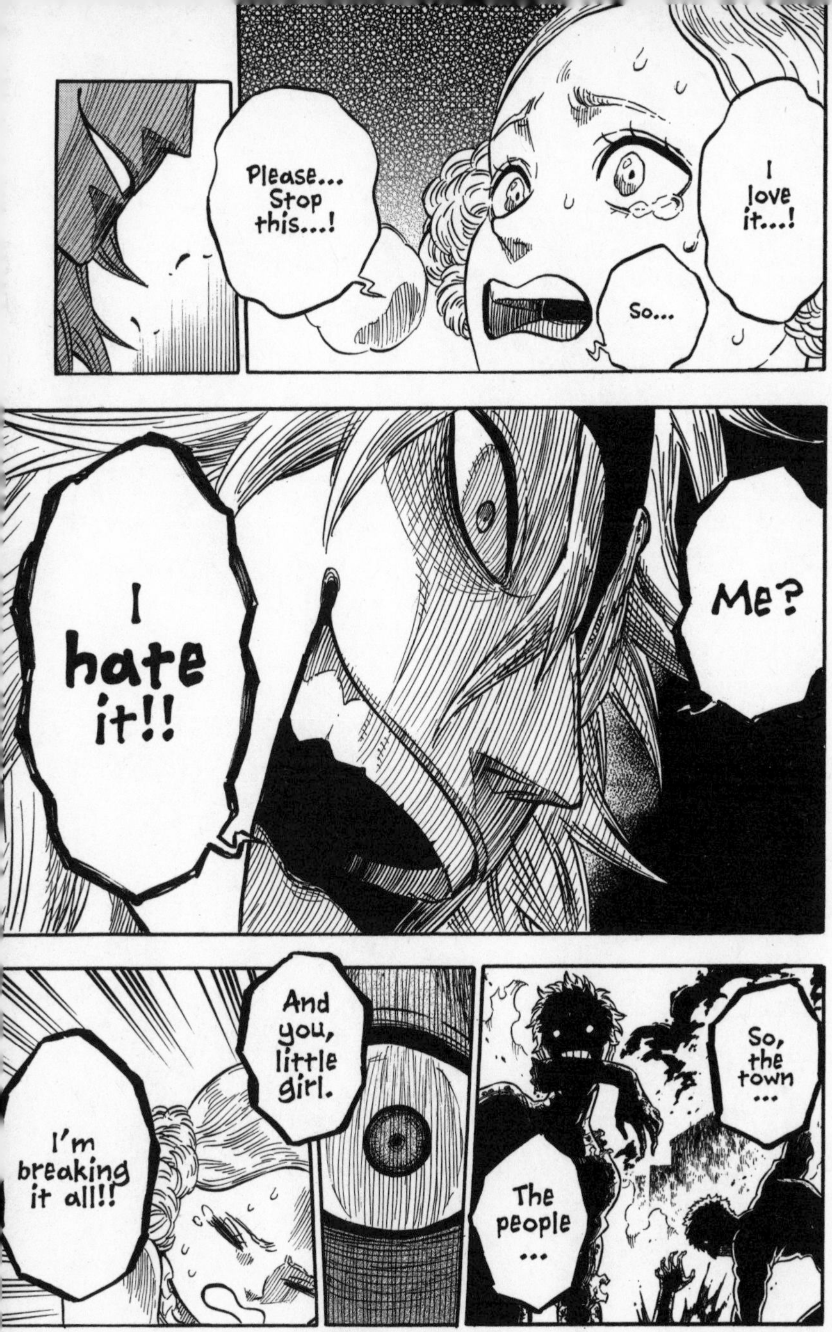
I love it...!
So...
Please... Stop this...!
Me?
I hate it!!
So, the town ...
The people ...
And you, little girl.
I'm breaking it all!!

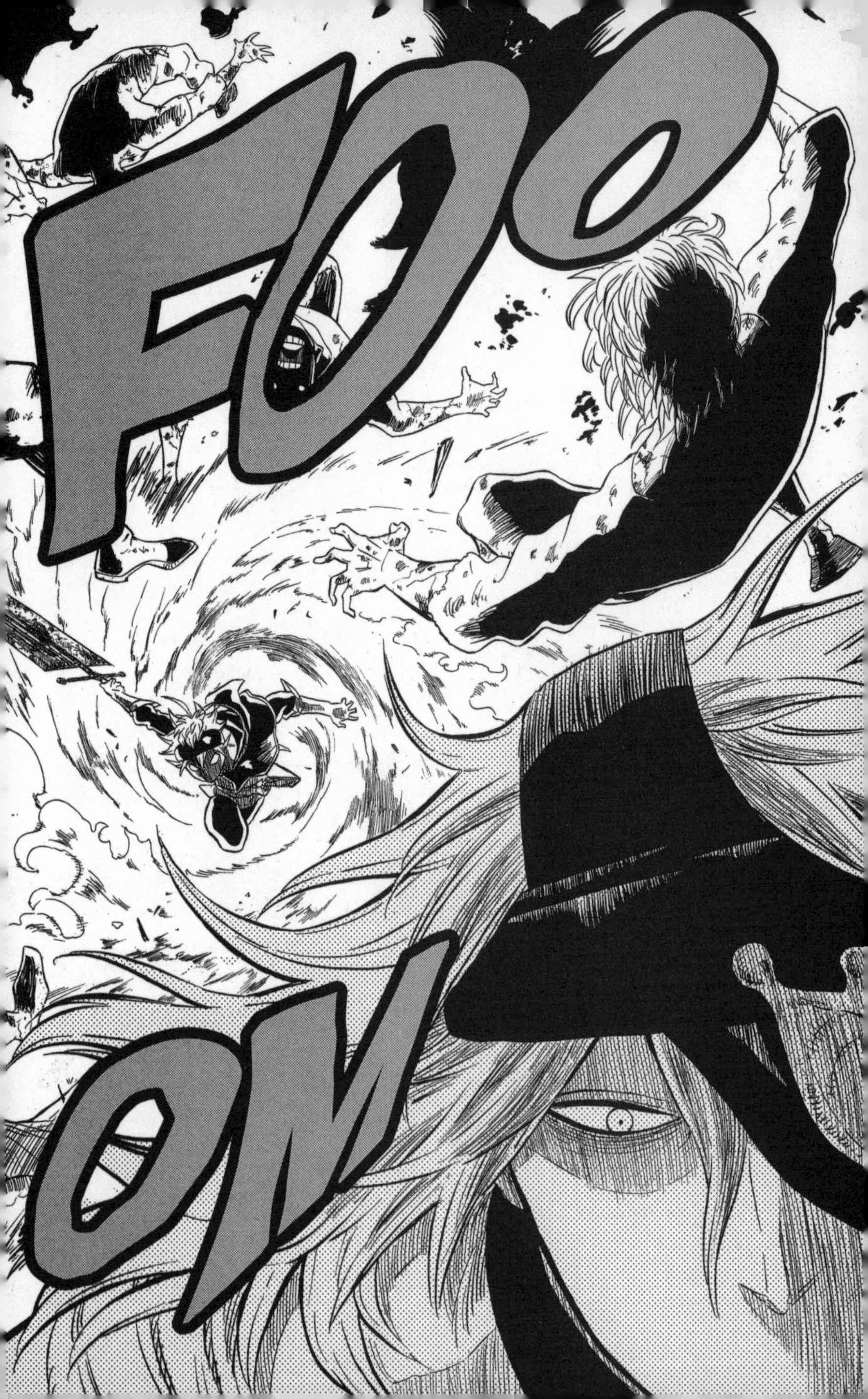
FOOOOM

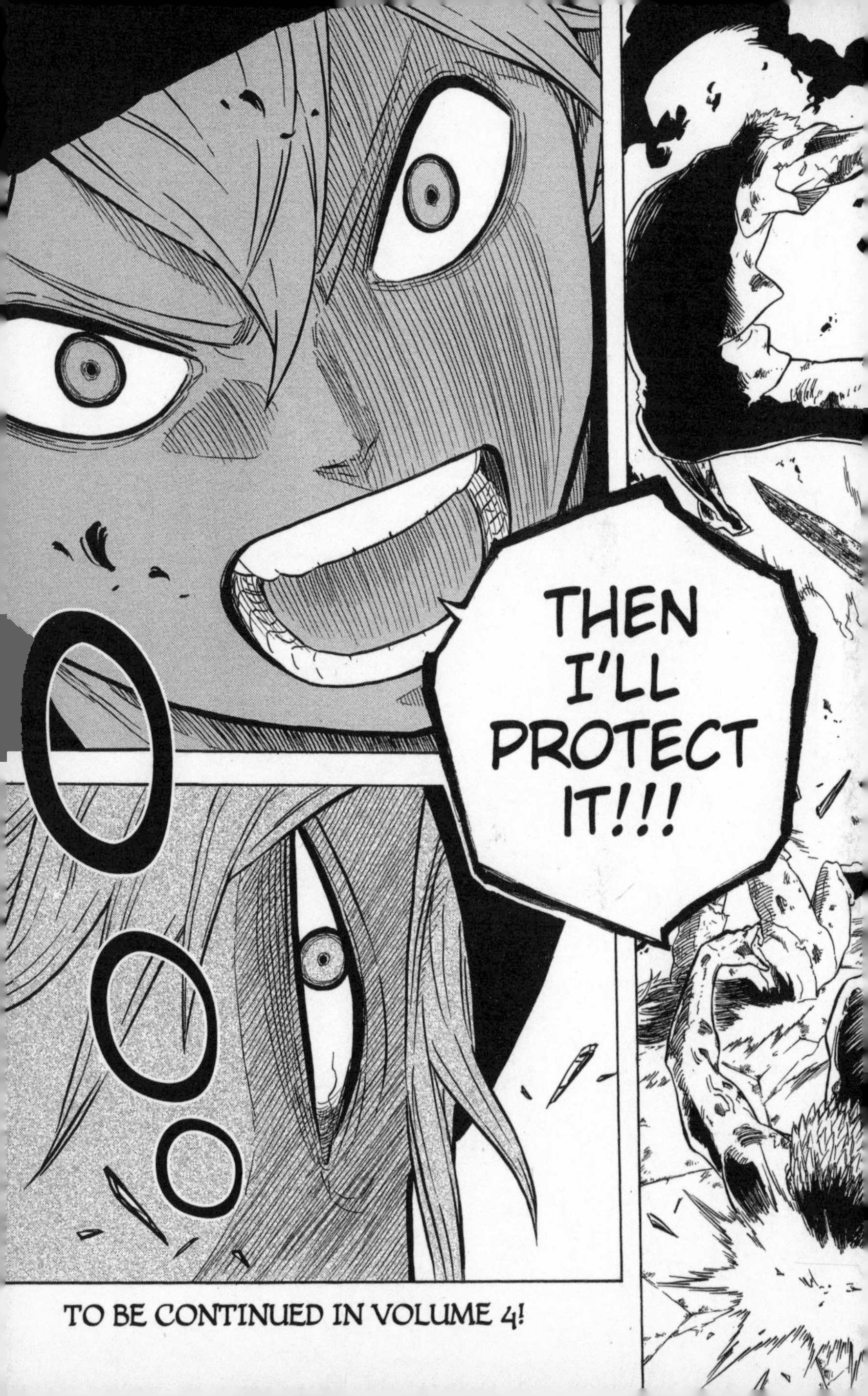
THEN I'LL PROTECT IT!!!

TO BE CONTINUED IN VOLUME 4!

Black Clover Side Story
How the Black Bulls Beat the Late Summer Heat

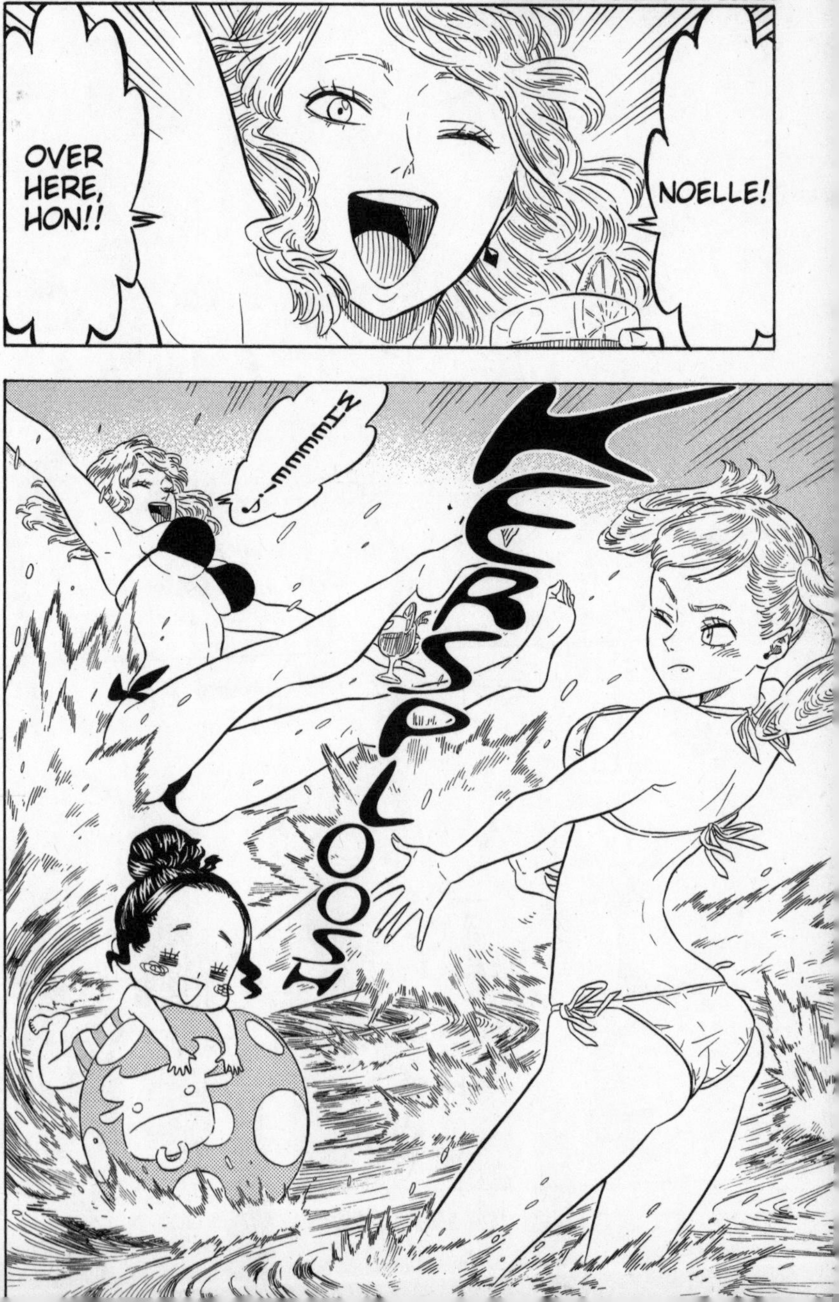
NOELLE!
OVER HERE, HON!!
WHEEEEEE—! ♪
KERSPLOOOSH

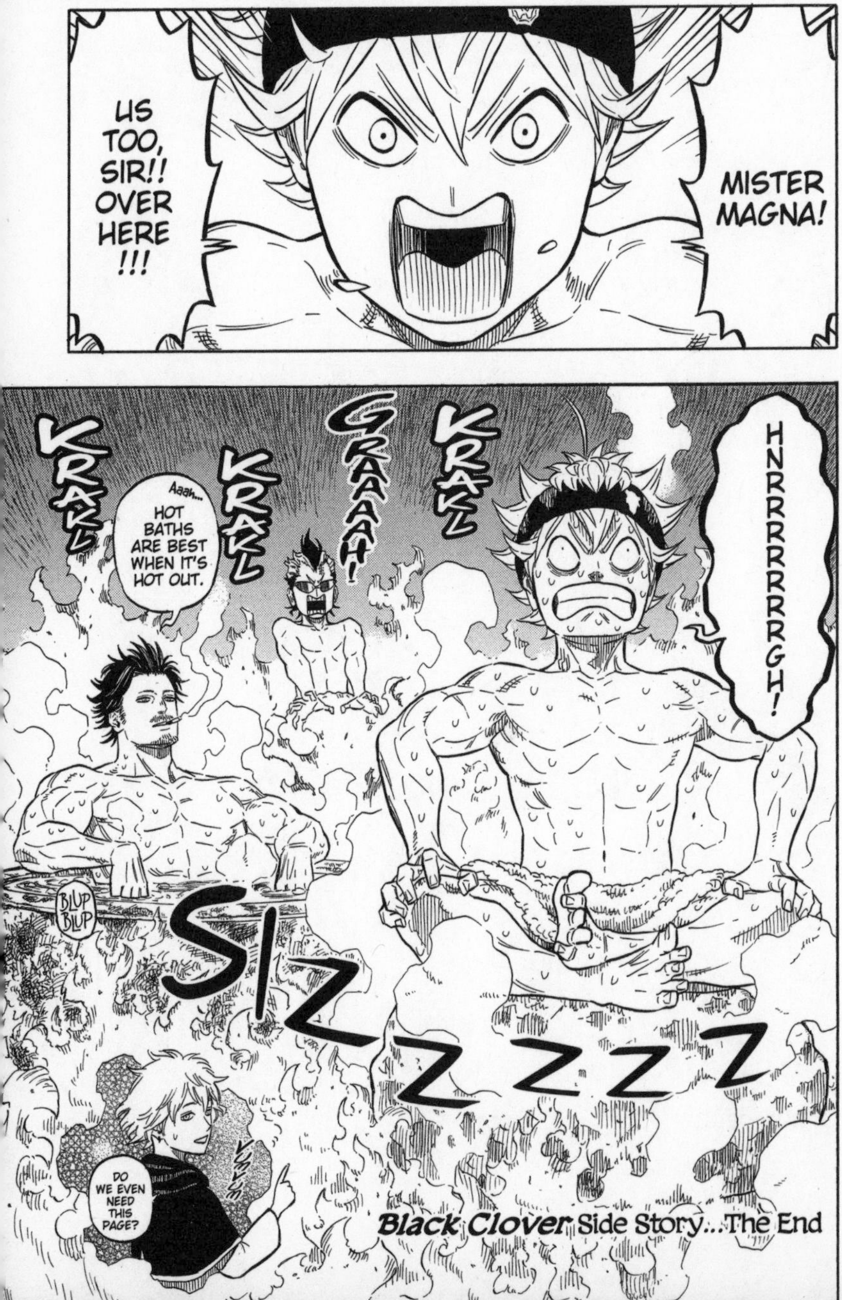
MISTER MAGNA!
US TOO, SIR!! OVER HERE!!!
HNRRRRRRRGH!
KRAKL
GRAAAAH!
KRAKL
Aaah... HOT BATHS ARE BEST WHEN IT'S HOT OUT.
KRAKL
BLUP BLUP
SIZZZZZZ
DO WE EVEN NEED THIS PAGE?

Black Clover Side Story... The End

The Blank Page Brigade

This volume's topic:
What are your nicknames?

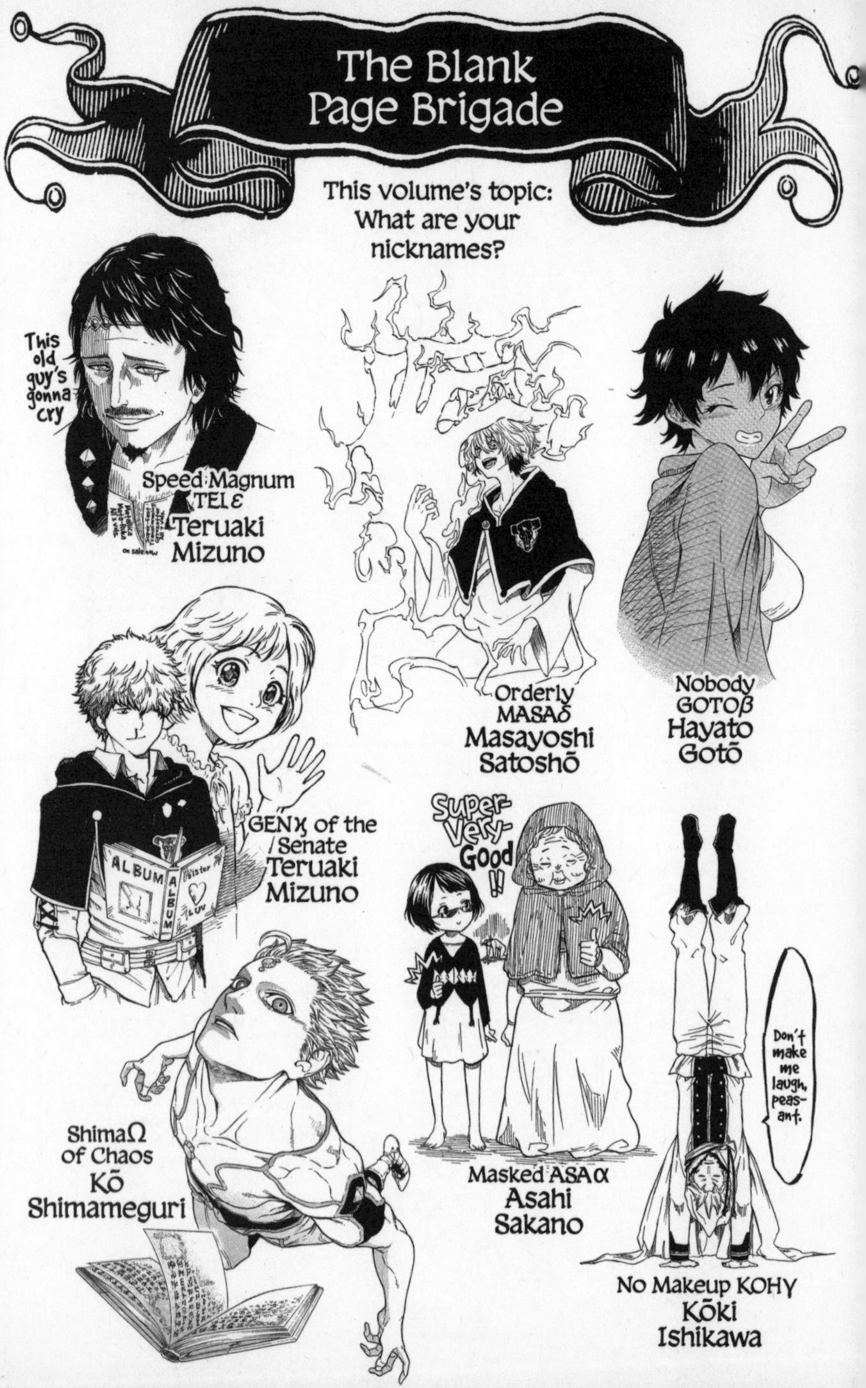

Nobody GOTOβ
Hayato Gotō
Orderly MASAδ
Masayoshi Satoshō
This old guy's gonna cry
Speed Magnum TELε
Teruaki Mizuno
Don't make me laugh, peasant.
No Makeup KOHY
Kōki Ishikawa
Super-Very-Good!!
Masked ASAα
Asahi Sakano
GENχ of the Senate
Teruaki Mizuno
ALBUM
Sister LUV
ShimaΩ of Chaos
Kō Shimameguri

The crazy captain, Falling-to-Pieces Tabata, who makes his wife ink solid areas and tone on the day of his deadlines.

HWOoOo

GRUNCH GRUNCH

Katayama, the editor who keeps getting stood up and has no faith in Tabata anymore.

My wife, being made to ink solid areas and tone on the day of my deadline. Surprise Crusher©.

AFTERWORD

❀

I wonder how long it will be before I put my regrets from the last volume to work...

Please support the next volume, which will probably be made through the desperate efforts of this foolish manga creator~ who never learns, gets more and more cornered, and is falling apart~and his merry friends!!

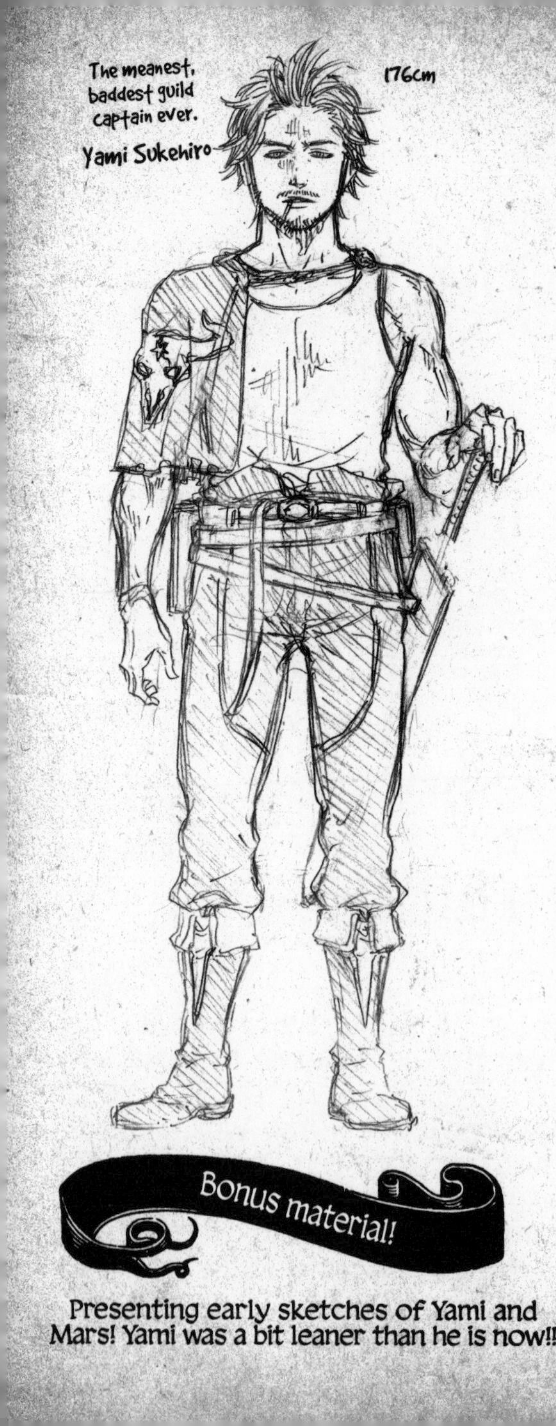
The meanest, baddest guild captain ever.
Yami Sukehiro
176cm

Bonus material!

Presenting early sketches of Yami and Mars! Yami was a bit leaner than he is now!!

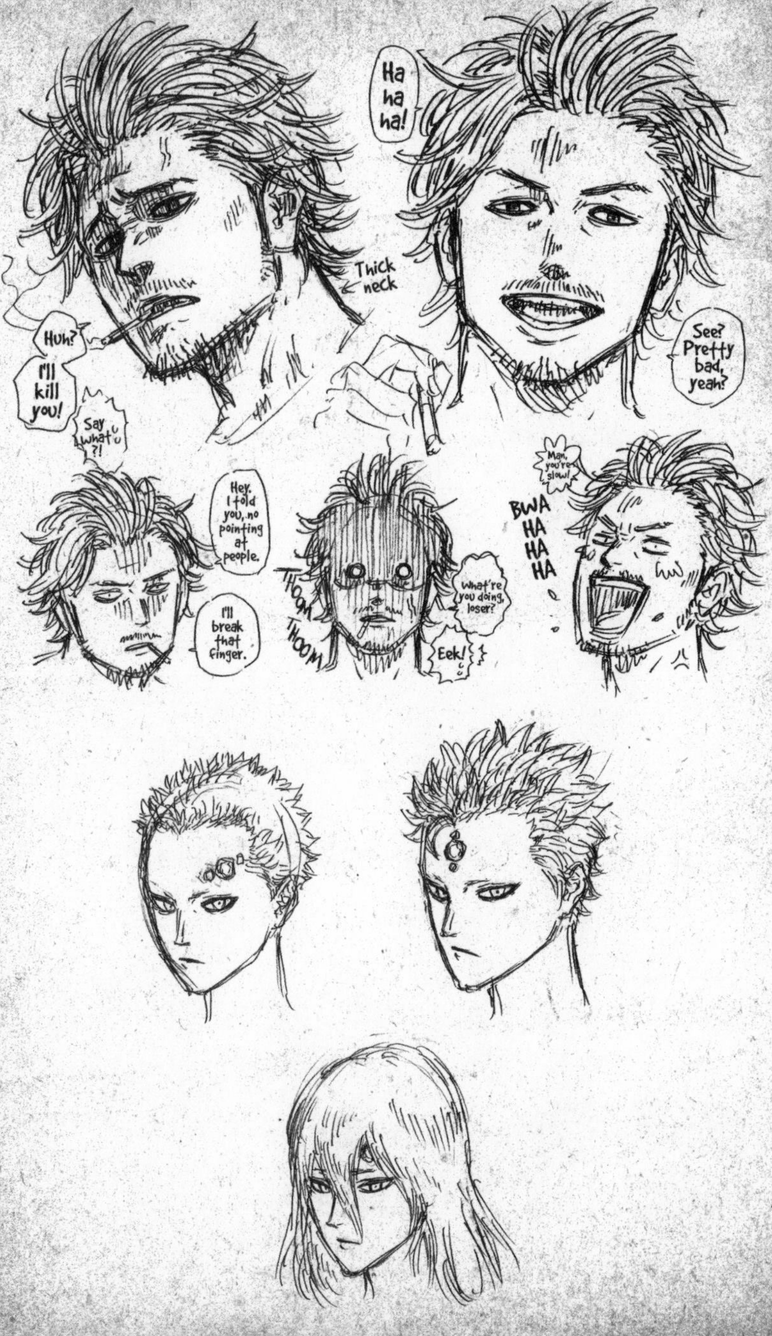
Ha ha ha!
See? Pretty bad, yeah?
Thick neck
Huh?
I'll kill you!
Say what?!
Man, you're slow!
BWA HA HA HA HA
What're you doing, loser?
Eek!
THOOM THOOM
Hey. I told you, no pointing at people.
I'll break that finger.

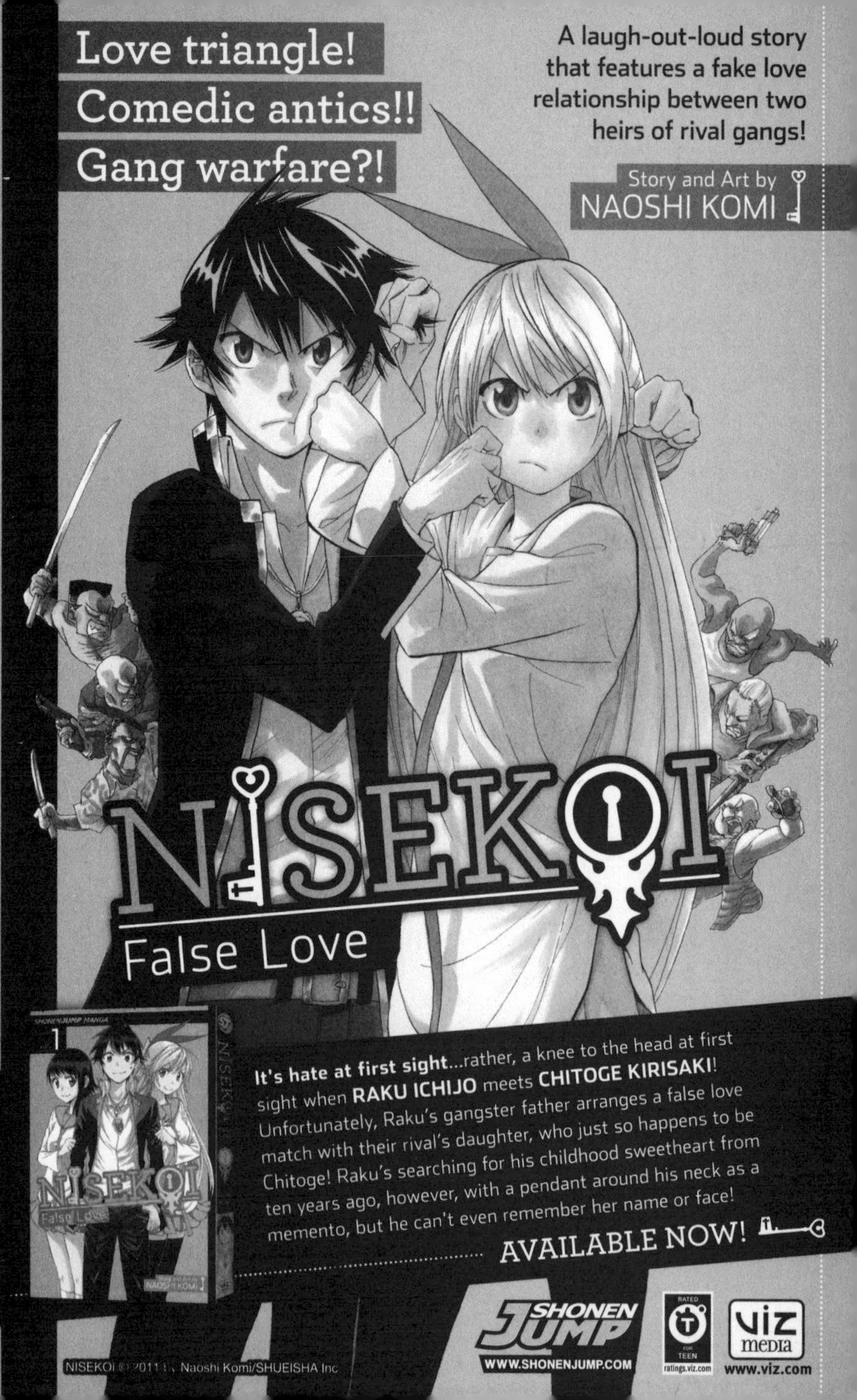
Love triangle!
Comedic antics!!
Gang warfare?!
A laugh-out-loud story that features a fake love relationship between two heirs of rival gangs!
Story and Art by
NAOSHI KOMI
NISEKOI
False Love
It's hate at first sight...rather, a knee to the head at first sight when RAKU ICHIJO meets CHITOGE KIRISAKI! Unfortunately, Raku's gangster father arranges a false love match with their rival's daughter, who just so happens to be Chitoge! Raku's searching for his childhood sweetheart from ten years ago, however, with a pendant around his neck as a memento, but he can't even remember her name or face!
AVAILABLE NOW!
SHONEN JUMP
WWW.SHONENJUMP.COM
RATED T FOR TEEN
ratings.viz.com
VIZ media
www.viz.com
NISEKOI © 2011 by Naoshi Komi/SHUEISHA Inc.

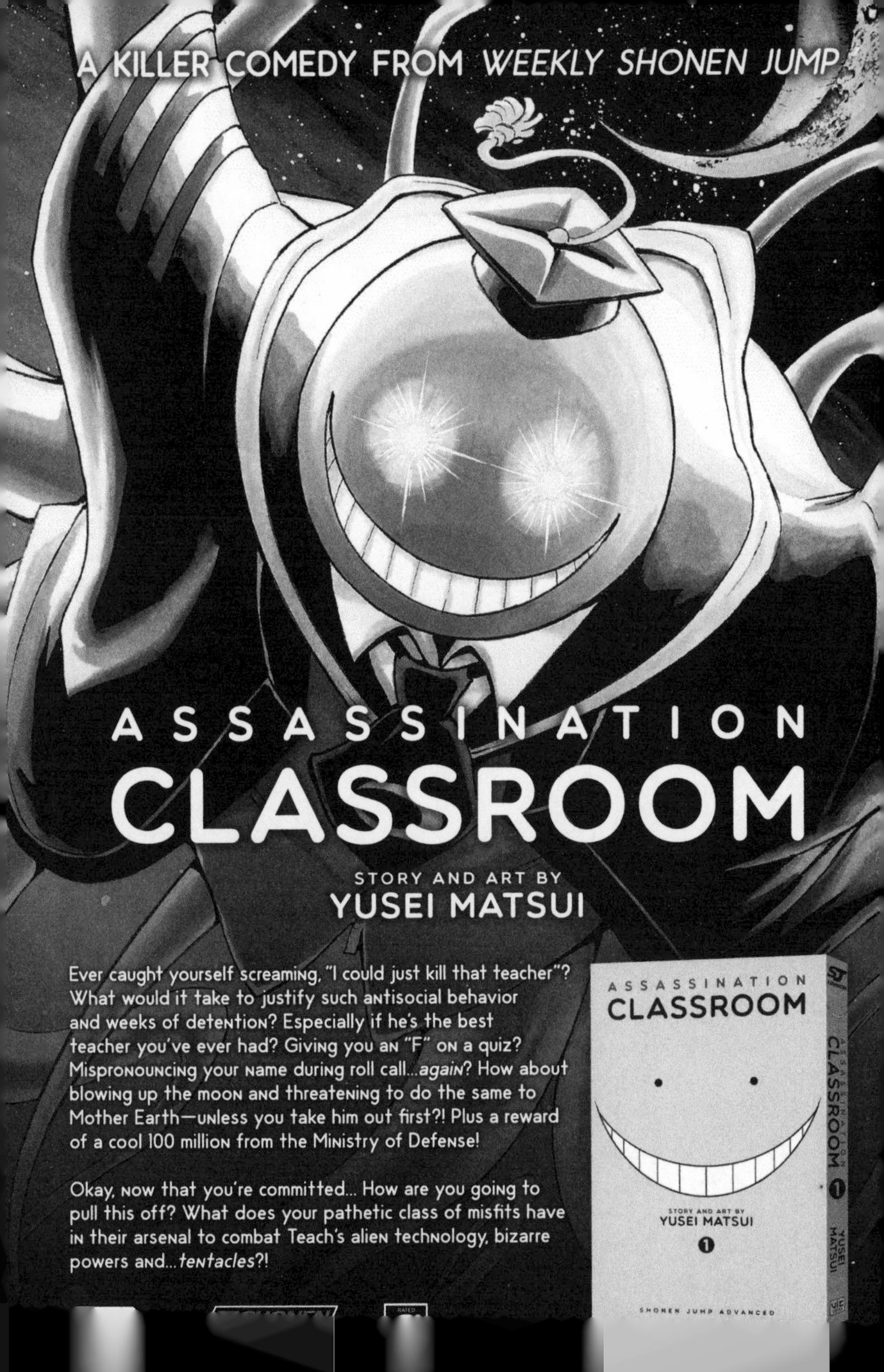
A KILLER COMEDY FROM *WEEKLY SHONEN JUMP*
ASSASSINATION
CLASSROOM
STORY AND ART BY
YUSEI MATSUI
Ever caught yourself screaming, "I could just kill that teacher"? What would it take to justify such antisocial behavior and weeks of detention? Especially if he's the best teacher you've ever had? Giving you an "F" on a quiz? Mispronouncing your name during roll call...*again*? How about blowing up the moon and threatening to do the same to Mother Earth—unless you take him out first?! Plus a reward of a cool 100 million from the Ministry of Defense!
Okay, now that you're committed... How are you going to pull this off? What does your pathetic class of misfits have in their arsenal to combat Teach's alien technology, bizarre powers and...*tentacles*?!
ASSASSINATION
CLASSROOM
STORY AND ART BY
YUSEI MATSUI
1
SHONEN JUMP ADVANCED

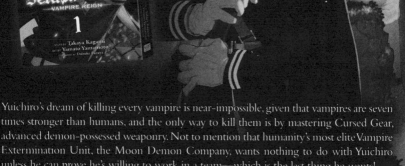

Stop

YOU'RE READING
THE WRONG WAY!

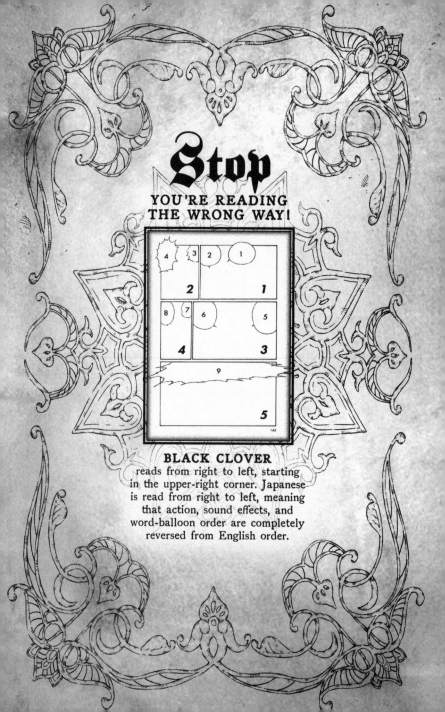

BLACK CLOVER
reads from right to left, starting
in the upper-right corner. Japanese
is read from right to left, meaning
that action, sound effects, and
word-balloon order are completely
reversed from English order.